THE CHINA TANGLE

The
China Tangle

The American Effort
in China
from Pearl Harbor
to the Marshall Mission

BY HERBERT FEIS

PRINCETON   NEW JERSEY
PRINCETON UNIVERSITY PRESS

1953

Grateful acknowledgment is made for permission to
quote from the following: *On Active Service in Peace
and War*, by Henry L. Stimson and McGeorge
Bundy, Harper & Brothers; *The Hinge of Fate* and
Closing the Ring, by Winston Churchill, Houghton
Mifflin Company; *The Stilwell Papers*, by Joseph
W. Stilwell, Arranged and Edited by Theodore H.
White, copyright 1948 by Winifred A. Stilwell, by
permission of William Sloane Associates, Inc.

Printed in the United States of America

FOREWORD

THIS is an attempt to tell what the American government tried to do in and with China during the war and the critical period of peace-making. The opening part is concerned with the grim effort to sustain Chinese resistance, marking the decisions and strains which influenced later events in ways not clearly foreseen. From this theater of war, the story broadens out in the determination of China's future place in the Pacific, the contest between the Chinese government and the Chinese Communists, and the worried American diplomatic exertions at Moscow, Cairo, Teheran, Yalta, Potsdam, and beyond to carry out the concept of the United Nations in the Pacific. This regrettably makes a tale of crumpled hopes and plans that went awry.

Before he starts, the reader may want to know the main sources from which the narrative is derived.

First, there are the published ones of growing amplitude, particularly:

The volume published by the American government in 1949, title: *United States Relations with China*, with Special Reference to the Period 1944-1949. This is popularly known as the China White Paper.

The volumes of documents and testimony resulting from the Hearings of the Senate Committee on Armed Services and the Committee on Foreign Relations on the *Military Situation in the Far East* (evoked by the recall of General MacArthur).

The volumes of documents and testimony resulting from the Hearings of the Subcommittee of the Senate Committee on the Judiciary on the *Institute of Pacific Relations*.

The volumes of documents and testimony resulting from the Hearings of the Subcommittee of the Senate Committee on Foreign Relations on *State Department Employee Loyalty Investigation*.

Winston Churchill's great history of his wartime experience.

I have besides been enabled to consult many other sources. Most important of these were:

The original records of the State Department.

Those records of our military action in the China-India-Burma Theater of war that were being used by the Office of the Chief of Military History, Department of the Army, in its task of writing the official history of that effort. The most instructive of these—in fact to me invaluable— were the first two (of three) volumes written by Charles F. Romanus and Riley Sunderland. They, as authorized, generously allowed me to read their studies in approved pre-publication form. These are cited in this book as the Sunderland-Romanus Manuscript, Volumes I and II. The first has since appeared in print entitled *Stilwell's Mission to China*, and the other is scheduled to appear in due course. Students of our recent Far Eastern military policy and action will surely wish to read them.

Extensive notes on the pertinent papers of Harry Hopkins, made before they were put in the custody of the Roosevelt Library at Hyde Park.

Comprehensive notes on the papers of the Honorable Patrick J. Hurley, former Special Representative of the President and Ambassador in China. These notes were made from the original papers by Sunderland and Romanus, and Ambassador Hurley most kindly allowed me to consult, use, and cite them freely.

The voluminous records, entitled: *Diaries*, kept by the former Secretary of the Treasury, Henry J. Morgenthau, Jr., which he with equal generosity allowed me to use.

Selected papers in the Roosevelt Library at Hyde Park, mainly those of a sort which could be accounted as part of the State Department files.

A variety of other documents, notes, or diaries kept by participants in this history which I was permitted to study for information and guidance.

This work was made possible only by the wish of the State Department to have this historical experience as fully explored and objectively told as it could be at this time while the meaning of so much of it is still hard to grasp. For this reason the former Secretary of State, Dean G. Acheson, encouraged the enterprise, and the competent Departmental Committee authorized me to consult the official files. From beginning to end many members of the Division of Historical Policy Research in the State Department aided me in locating the pertinent records and gave me the benefit of their own knowledge; for such help I am greatly indebted to Dr. G. Bernard Noble, the Chief of that Division, and to Dr. E. Taylor Parks, who most particularly supported my search for information in every direction and put me in touch with others who might help me, and Miss Marion L. Terrell for the same sort of enthusiastic interest; to Mr. Robert C. Hayes, Dr. Benjamin Bock, and Dr. G. M. Richardson Dougall for allowing me to consult papers they had prepared on some of the most important diplomatic activities. I am also as greatly indebted to Mr. Charles A. Patterson of the Division of Communications and Records for his constant and good-natured assistance in searching and using the records, without which I would have missed or mistaken much; and to Mrs. Mary Ellen Milar for similar guidance.

I owe thanks also to many individuals who helped me to carry out this study. To former President Harry S. Truman for his direct responses to queries asked of him about several important episodes; to the former Ambassador to the Soviet Union, W. Averell Harriman, and the former Ambassador to China, Clarence E. Gauss, for long and enjoyable talks about matters with which they were concerned; to Joseph C. Grew, former Under-Secretary of State, the Hon. Stanley K. Hornbeck, the first Director of the Office of Far Eastern Affairs in the State Department, and Joseph C. Ballantine, his successor in that post, for similarly patient search of their memories; to Ambassador Charles E. Bohlen, who was the American interpreter at most of the talks with Stalin and Molotov of which this book tells; to former Ambassador George Kennan and former Assistant Secretary of State Dean Rusk for thoughtful comment on various perplexing points; to John P. Davies for the loan of his notes on the Cairo Conference; to former Special Assistant to the Secretary of War Harvey Bundy and former Assistant Secretary of War John J. McCloy for enlightening information; to the Honorable T. V. Soong, who during much of the period of this narrative was Acting President of the Executive Yuan and Foreign Minister of China, for talking over various impressions with me; to Joseph Alsop for vivid and dramatic recollections of things seen, heard, and done while he was in China as an aide to General Claire L. Chennault and an intimate of T. V. Soong; to Herbert Elliston, Editor of the *Washington Post*, who has long been an intent and knowledgeable student of American policy in China; to former Secretary of State James F. Byrnes for his readiness to review his experience with China matters with me; to Captain Tracy B. Kittredge, and Dr. Rudolph A. Winnacker of the Department of Defense, Professor McGeorge Bundy of Harvard University, Mr. Arthur W. Page, Mr. Paul G. Hoffman and Mr. Richard M. Bissell, and Mr. Clayton Fritchey.

In connection with these acknowledgments it is essential to repeat a tatement made in the Foreword to *The Road to Pearl Harbor* that 'The help given me by many people in the government must not be taken as indicating any kind of official approval, sponsorship or responsibility. This book is the work of a private scholar."

Throughout I was assisted by Mrs. Arline Van Blarcom Pratt, who did much of the research in the records and checked the manuscript critically, by Mrs. H. Freeman Matthews, Jr., and Miss Alice Pusey,

who patiently carried on the typing of the manuscript through its many revisions, and by my wife, Ruth Stanley-Brown Feis, who gave me great editorial help and read the proofs.

Again I am grateful to the Institute for Advanced Study, Princeton, New Jersey, for appointing me to membership and for providing aid and favorable environment; and to the Ford Foundation for a grant which enabled me to write this book.

On learning of the task on which I was engaged, a friend sent me a quotation from Horace, writing to Pollio, who was then composing a history of the Civil Wars: "You are treating of the civil strife that began with Metellus' consulship, the cause of the war, its blunders and its phases and fortunes, fame, friendship of leaders (triumvirs) and weapons stained with blood as yet unexpiated—a task full of dangerous hazard—and you are walking, as it were, over fires hidden beneath treacherous ashes."

The fiery disputes ignited by the failure of our efforts in China are still burning bright. We remain suspended before the cineramic screen of this experience, unable to grasp its import with assurance. Thus I leave to the hour of more confident judgment the argument over what was done right and what was done wrong, who is to be praised and who is to be blamed. I have not sought in telling the story either to console or condemn. But now that it is written I greatly hope that by assisting just understanding of what occurred and why, it will reconcile us in the task ahead of redeeming our purposes in China.

CONTENTS

CONTENTS

PART THREE

From the Surrender of Japan to the Marshall Mission

PART ONE

From Pearl Harbor to the Cairo Conference

CHAPTER 1

December 1941: The Longed-for Combination

OUR full induction into this last World War followed our refusal to let China fend for itself. We had rejected all proposals which would have allowed Japan to remain in China and Manchuria. In November there had been a week of wavering—when a chance gleamed of getting time to make the Allies' position in the Pacific so strong that Japan would retreat. But then the American government had decided not to ease, even briefly or slightly, the way of the transgressor. This resolve was hardened by signs that the Chinese would regard even a short truce as desertion. Japan had struck—rather than accept frustration. The American people, in a war which they had not sought, had full right to feel that they had been not only true to their ideals but most faithful defenders of the people of China.

The Chinese for some time past had sustained themselves by the belief that the United States and other Allies would soon be on, if not at, their side. Then China would no longer be a neglected and almost isolated battleground. In prospect the Generalissimo, Chiang Kai-shek, saw American ships coming across the Pacific to reopen ports and land American troops. They would bring food, clothing, medicine; weapons and ammunition for the Chinese armies; trucks and oil to carry them into battle. American planes would fly in from India, the Philippines, Siberia. They would protect the Chinese cities and spread death among the Japanese soldiers in China. The forces of the British Commonwealth and of the Netherlands, after resisting the Japanese southern thrust, would come to the rescue of China. The soldiers of the Soviet Union would march down from the north to drive the Japanese out of Manchuria and North China. The tired Chinese armies which had for four years been battling alone would be merely one element in an overwhelming alliance. The inland refugee capital of Chungking would become a center of joint strategy and command.

This was the longed-for great combination, revolving about China. A composite plan for the conduct of the war expressive of this design was sketched out within days after we entered the war. It was swiftly found unusable and discarded. But, until the chances of realizing it grew faint, the American government remained partial to this basic conception of how the war in the Far East might be fought. Chiang

Kai-shek clung to it to the end, as a script of the role which China ought to be enabled to play in the war and in the world settlement to follow. His attitude was thereafter touched by the sense that his Allies had been recreant.

This narrative is the story of what the American and Chinese governments tried to do together and what they did; of how and why their effort waned and failed. It is the tale of the wearing out of a conception that was not well enough aligned with reality.

In December 1941 the United States was sending Lend-Lease weapons and supplies into China through Burma and India. It was trying hard to improve the transport system toward and within China. American airmen, recruited and supplied with combat aircraft by favor of the American government, were fighting in China (the American Volunteer Group, known as the Flying Tigers, under command of the skilled and determined General Chennault). An American military mission, headed by General John Magruder, was beginning its work. It had been sent out to advise and assist the Chinese in the use of our weapons and in the training of their forces.

But there was no agreement between the American and Chinese governments in regard to combined action should the United States come to war against Japan. Neither our Ambassador in China, Clarence E. Gauss, nor General Magruder had been told what to do to meet the effects of the extension of the war over the whole of the Pacific. Nor had China any understanding with the other opponents of the Axis in the Pacific—Great Britain, the Netherlands, Australia, New Zealand, and the Soviet Union. Nor, to tell the whole position, was there any joint or combined program for the defense of the Southwest Pacific. Despite much talk between military staffs, none was completed and ready for use.

Chiang Kai-shek was first to speak up for common decision and action. As soon as the news of Pearl Harbor was flashed to Chungking, he asked the American and British diplomatic and military representatives who were stationed there to come together and discuss what was to be done. In two conferences on December 8th (the day of the Pearl Harbor attack by Chungking time) he outlined his ideas for a great coalition to share with China the task of defending the Pacific.[1] All enemies of the

_____
[1] Chungking time is 12 hours in advance of Washington time. Thus in our histories the time of attack on Pearl Harbor is stated as about 2:00 p.m., December 7th; the

Axis, he thought, should participate in a military alliance and unify their operations under American leadership—China, Great Britain, Canada, New Zealand, Australia, the Netherlands, and the Soviet Union. They should at once establish a joint military war council to plan and to coordinate the strategy of the war in the Pacific. Further, he suggested, they should at once sign an agreement not to conclude a separate peace. These proposals are an index to the scope of Chiang Kai-shek's visions and hopes.

The first failure in response came quickly. On the next day, December 9th, the Soviet military representative in Chungking, General Chuikoff, gave the Generalissimo a note which read, "In regard to a Soviet declaration of war it is essential that we should make adequate preparations and work out comprehensive plans for war cooperation among the Soviet Union, China, the United States and Great Britain." Chiang Kai-shek, in a talk with Magruder, wishfully construed this to mean that the Soviet government would not enter the Pacific war until the democratic powers worked out a comprehensive plan for joint action. He asked Magruder again to urge Washington to take the lead in formulating and initiating such a plan, and not to wait for the Soviet Union to enter the war. The details, Chiang Kai-shek thought, could best be worked out in Chungking since the plan should cover both military operations and mutual aid.

The next day the Soviet Ambassador, Litvinoff, in Washington, called upon Secretary of State Hull. He had gone to see the President and Hopkins about Lend-Lease allocations. They had touched on the question of whether Russia was going to join in the war against Japan. Chiang Kai-shek had asked the President to inquire. The Soviet Ambassador told Hull that he had just heard that his government had decided that because of the strain of the struggle against Germany it could not at that time cooperate with us in the war against Japan. This he stated "rather positively." The Secretary of State did not argue, but he hinted that the Soviet Union might be making a wrong decision. He told Litvinoff that he knew that Japan had promised Germany to attack the Soviet Union whenever Hitler asked it to do so. He pointed out that if the United States could get air bases in the Maritime Provinces of Siberia its heavy bombers could strike at both the Japanese naval bases and cities. By allusions and illustration, Hull tried to convey the opinion that all opponents of the Axis would stand or fall together. Finally, to

---

calendar and clock in Chungking at the time when the attack occurred stood at 2:00 a.m., December 8th.

quote from the memo that the Secretary made of this long conversation, "I constantly came back to the point that if Russia should refrain from cooperation with us in the East while we continue to aid her, there will be a constant flow of criticism about why we are aiding Russia in a world movement involving all alike and Russia in turn is not cooperating with us in the Far East."

The President, the State Department, and War Department, all were meanwhile trying to see what could be done to give actuality to the proposals which Chiang Kai-shek had sent on. Hull told the Chinese Ambassador that he had discussed with both the President and Secretary of War Stimson the question of unifying and coordinating Allied forces in Asia, especially in the South Sea areas, and that the American government would soon have some proposals. He went over the same ground with the British Ambassador, Lord Halifax. The latter said that talks were going on with the Australian and Canadian Ministers of War.

On the 14th the President sent messages to Chiang Kai-shek and Stalin. He suggested to the Generalissimo that he call a joint military conference in Chungking not later than December 17th for the purposes (1) of exchanging information and considering what action, especially in East Asia, could best be used to beat the Japanese; (2) of trying to formulate a definite, though preliminary, plan for joint action by December 20th. He told Chiang Kai-shek that he was suggesting to the British that while this meeting in Chungking was going on, they should hold in Singapore an army-navy conference of British, Chinese, American, and Dutch officers to make operational plans for the southern zone. He also reported that he was letting Stalin know that he would be glad to learn his, Stalin's, views from the northern standpoint.

Roosevelt's message to Stalin, sent through Litvinoff, told of the moves which he was trying to initiate toward joint action. It concluded, "I venture to hope that the preliminary conferences I have outlined for this coming week may lead to the establishment of a more permanent organization to plan our efforts." The War Department supplemented the President's message by a telegram to Colonel Faymonville, our Military Attaché in Moscow, appointing him to represent the War Department at the Moscow conference. He was informed (in paraphrase) that "The reason for this preliminary conference is to give Stalin a chance to express his particular views rather than to set out and urge any special American viewpoint. For your own information, the War Department believes that the Japanese forces are greatly over-extended and they ought to be prevented from concentrating on a succession of single objectives. The United States has the fixed intention of maintaining our Far Eastern defenses and we are immediately reinforcing the Philippines with air and by air."

The President further extended his effort by sending a message to Wilhelmina, Queen of the Netherlands, who was then living in London. He explained the proposals that he had made for conferences at Chungking and Singapore, and expressed the hope that the Netherlands government would be represented in both meetings.

Chiang Kai-shek eagerly called the foreign representatives together again to formulate the plan wanted by the President. But the senior American and British officers who had been designated for these consultations (Generals Brett and Wavell) were delayed. Their deputies (Magruder and Dennys) were without instructions. The only Dutch official who could get to Chungking on time had no authority. The Soviet member was there only to listen and observe. This makeshift group was then asked to do in utmost haste what the American and British top military planners had failed to do in prolonged earlier attempts—that is, to produce a plan for concerted resistance to Japan in the Far East; and to do this while the Japanese were knocking the Allied forces about from point to point.

Chiang Kai-shek invited General Magruder to prepare the agenda—an awesome task. How awesome was made plain when Chiang Kai-shek outlined his ideas to Generals Magruder, Dennys, and Chuikoff informally at dinner on the 17th. The details, reread now, arouse wonder at the faith of what could be achieved among a group of countries, each of which was beset by worry as to what might happen to it at any moment. In sum, the Generalissimo thought that the conference should devise a comprehensive plan for war operations in the Pacific; this was to include plans for the joint defense of Singapore, the Philippines, Hong Kong, Burma, the Netherlands East Indies, as well as China; and be supplemented by operation plans for land, sea, and air forces and the distribution of Lend-Lease supplies. There ought to be, he thought, in Chungking a joint general staff, and in Washington a supreme war council of the countries fighting in the Pacific.[2]

Soviet participation sometime *in the future* was still anticipated. But the answer which Stalin sent to Chiang Kai-shek left the time vague—sometime could be any time, no time. In his message of the 12th Stalin

[2] Memo by MacMorland, December 17, 1941.

said again that he thought that the Soviet Union ought not to divert its strength to the Far East, and adjured Chiang Kai-shek not to keep asking that it declare war on Japan. The Generalissimo might have drawn some comfort from the last paragraph, "Soviet Russia must fight Japan, for Japan will surely unconditionally break the neutrality pact. We are preparing to meet that situation, but it takes time to prepare. Therefore, I again implore you not to take the lead in demanding that Soviet Russia at once declare war on Japan." The British government was not disposed to press the question. Eden, Secretary for Foreign Affairs, was in Moscow talking with Stalin. He informed the American Ambassador in London, Winant, that Stalin had said that to his regret he was not able to help us in the Far East. Eden added that he thought the Soviet attitude in the Far East was perfectly loyal; that Stalin was determined not to provoke Japan at that critical hour but that he would be in a position to help in the spring. Therefore, Eden said he thought it unwise to talk to Stalin at this time about allowing the United States to use air bases in Siberia.[3] The American government concluded that nothing would be won by doing so.

The planes bringing Brett and Wavell to Chungking arrived on the 22nd, and they joined in the talk at once. By then it ought to have been clear to all that the forces which Japan was sending on this southward advance were so strong, skilled, and mobile that the defenders must fight as one if any part of the area was to be saved. But the points which emerged during the following days of discussion showed how mistaken was the idea that an all-over strategic program could be defined in China. For the necessary power both to make and execute decisions was elsewhere, and very hard decisions they were. In order to have a systematic combined plan of defense there would have to be jointly accepted preferences and priorities. One or more countries would have to agree to allow its territories to be exposed in order that others could be more strongly defended. The same questions that had divided the American and English staff planners in earlier meetings emerged again, and in more complicated form. Should the available air and naval forces and Lend-Lease supplies be devoted first of all to the defense of the Philippines, or of Singapore, or of the Netherlands East Indies, or of Burma and the Burma Road; or should they be divided among these tasks, and in what portions? Could the operations of the separate national combat forces be coordinated without some unified top command, and who was to exercise that? Such questions, it became plain, and Wavell made it

[3] Telegram, December 19, 1941, from London.

doubly plain, could not be decided in Chungking. Chiang Kai-shek tried to have them answered in a vague way which would confer upon China and himself a central role. But his proposals were lost in the depths of the differences. All that the representatives at Chungking could really agree on was the need for mutual aid and long-range planning.

Even though these preliminary talks had shown that definite decisions could not be made, the Generalissimo on the next day called the joint military conference into formal session—its only formal session. The participants continued to find the assignment out of reach.[4] They spent a good deal of time upon the very definite problem which the Japanese were thrusting upon them as they talked—how, during the next critical month, to defend Singapore and Burma. They continued to make an earnest attempt to frame some plan of the kind which the President had asked. Chiang Kai-shek's original program was already impaired by the defection of the Soviet Union and cracked by the victories of the Japanese. Still, he continued to redeem what he could of the concept. He sought at least some endorsement of the basic principles of combined or joint strategy of the United States, the British Commonwealth, and China over the whole Pacific area; and more immediately of (1) concerted Chinese-British strategy for the defense of Burma and Malaya, and (2) cooperation between the air and land forces of the United States and China. The range of his hopes was still broad enough to lead him to suggest that the strategic council to be established in Chungking (and of which he would presumably be chairman) should include in the scope of its consideration even the Indian Ocean.

The expectation that the other Allies would center effective powers of decision over the vast Pacific area in Chungking was unreal, in view both of their states of mind and the condition of their military forces. It was out of proportion because it implied that Chiang Kai-shek should be given an active, and possibly superior, part in determining the use of armed forces and resources far stronger than those of China.

But these things having been said, a substantial measure of reasoned

---

[4] This formal meeting was a large one. The Chinese group, in addition to Chiang Kai-shek and Madame Chiang Kai-shek, included the Minister of War and five other Chinese generals. For the United States there were Brett and Magruder and some subordinates; for Great Britain, Wavell, Dennys, and some subordinates; for Australia, Sir Frederick Eggleston, the Australian Minister. After dinner these were joined by the British Ambassador, Clark-Kerr (afterwards Lord Inverchapel), General Chennault, and Owen Lattimore, then adviser to Chiang Kai-shek.

This account of the discussion, as of the other portions of the history of the Chungking conference, is derived mainly from (1) the papers of the Magruder mission, particularly the memos made by Colonel MacMorland, and (2) the Sunderland-Romanus manuscript, Vol. 1.

and reasonable purpose could be found in the Generalissimo's approach:

1. Up to then both the American and British governments had attached far more importance to the war in Europe than to the war in the Pacific. They had provided China with only a thin margin of support. If China were to be left on the edge of the struggle, even after the United States had come in, it was a gloomy and, he thought, unfair pros-pect. The Generalissimo hoped to have the balance made more even by the formulation of a global strategy plan which included China. His thought, as expressed in the records of the formal session, was that ". . . there should be reasons and facts to determine the handling of the various war fronts: if such facts should indicate that the Asia front is the most important then grand strategy would put the emphasis on priority for that war area."

2. Every other country in the Pacific hemisphere was concerned first of all with the safety of its own segment; the United States with the Philippines, the Netherlands with the East Indies, Britain with Malaysia, Australia and New Zealand for themselves. Each was seeking forces and equipment. In the battle of priorities, China was likely to fare no better than it had in the past, perhaps less well—unless there was a basic change in the recognition of its status.

3. Moreover, China was being called upon to aid in the defense of other countries. Chiang Kai-shek was being asked (and had offered) to send Chinese troops into Burma. He was being asked to allow a squadron of the American Volunteer Group, which had been recruited to protect China, to fight in Burma (and was agreeing to do so). He was being urged to give up Lend-Lease supplies designated for China which were on the docks at Rangoon. What guarantee did he have that other countries would give back what he was now called upon to give up, and in their turn contribute to the defense of China? A general plan which fairly defined the rights of each might be such a guarantee.

In sum, Chiang Kai-shek's ideas and plans were not merely vain or unbalanced. But time and events were all against him. It was hard to refute Wavell's contention that it was not practicable to plan beyond present resources and immediate actions. No government, except pos-sibly the Chinese, was ready to obligate itself in regard to the future direction of its war effort until it had further chance to measure the dan-gers it faced.

Despite these obstacles to both vision and decision, the conference at Chungking did compose and approve an answer to the President. This was called a plan, but it was only an unfinished outline of intent. Students of that most difficult task of arriving at combined military plans for a large group of nations, each in danger, and none knowing where danger may come hardest, would find its details of interest.[5] But this account will pass them by, noting merely the conclusion which General Dwight D. Eisenhower, then Deputy Chief of the War Plans Division for the Pacific and Far East, passed on to his colleagues after studying it that ". . . very little, in the way of concrete results" had been achieved. Soon thereafter, the President's first outline for the combined planning and direction of the war in the Far East, having shown itself impractical, was given up. The task was taken over by the American and British Chiefs of Staff, meeting as the newly-formed Combined Chiefs of Staff.

Roosevelt had been in so great a hurry because he was expecting Churchill in Washington to talk grand strategy. The Prime Minister found ". . . the extraordinary significance of China in American minds, even at the top, strangely out of proportion. I was conscious of a standard of values which accorded China almost an equal fighting power with the British Empire, and rated the Chinese armies as a factor to be mentioned in the same breath as the armies of Russia."[6] He made it clear that he thought this judgment foolish; in his later words, "I told the President how much I felt American opinion overestimated the contribution which China could make to the general war. . . . I said I would of course always be helpful and polite to the Chinese, whom I admired and liked as a race and pitied for their endless misgovernment, but that he must not expect me to adopt what I felt was a wholly unreal standard of values."[7]

It is not to be wondered that the President and Prime Minister failed

---

[5] It had six main points:

"1. As a first essential to secure against enemy attack Rangoon and Burma, both of which are vital for China's continued resistance and any extension of joint action from China. Meanwhile to take offensive air action against Japanese bases and installations to the greatest extent that resources permit.

"2. Maintain China's resistance by continued supplies of material to enable Chinese armies to prepare and train for ultimate offensive against Japan.

"3. Meantime the Chinese armies should continue to occupy the Japanese forces on their front by attacks or threats of attacks and by action against their vulnerable lines of communication.

"4. As soon as resources permit, to pass to an offensive against Japan with all forces available, Chinese, British and American.

"5. This joint military council sitting in Chungking will meet and submit information and proposals to enable the Allied Supreme War Council to work out strategy for East Asia.

"6. Hope is expressed that a permanent organization to be set up in the United States will soon materialize."

[6] *The Hinge of Fate*, Winston S. Churchill, 1950, page 133.

[7] *Ibid*.

—as the conference in Chungking had failed—to work out an agreed or joint strategy for the whole Pacific area. But they took what probably both thought was a first and essential step toward it: they agreed upon the organization of two combined commands—one for the Southwest Pacific and one for China.

The President went to pains to make sure that Chiang Kai-shek would feel that his ideas and wishes had been kept well in mind; and that China was counted on to have a real and inner part in the proposed arrangements—not a focal part or wholly equal one, such as the Generalissimo had sought, but still one which China could make important by its effort. He explained, by a message sent on December 31st, that he and Churchill had agreed to the appointment of a Supreme Commander of American, Dutch, Australian, and British forces in the Southwest Pacific Theater to coordinate the common effort.[8] There seemed to be, he observed, a similar need in China for a similar command arrangement. Therefore, he suggested that Chiang Kai-shek should undertake, by agreement, to exercise supreme command over all the forces of the united powers that would operate within the China Theater. That theater, as then conceived, was to include not only China but such parts of Thailand and Indo-China as might be occupied by the United Nations. In order to make the command effective, he advised Chiang Kaishek to organize at once a joint planning staff to which the American, British, and Chinese governments should appoint members. This joint staff was to function under the Generalissimo's direction.

Such an arrangement, the President said, would give the Generalissimo a chance to exercise his influence and advice in the formulation of general strategy for the conduct of the war in all theaters. But in a note which Harry Hopkins wrote about this plan, he acutely observed that all Chiang Kai-shek was getting that he did not have already was that American and British troops in China would fight under him. This

[8] ABDA COM for the Southwest Pacific was set up during this meeting of British-American authorities, known as the ARCADIA Conference, 24 December 1941 to 14 January 1942, and approved by the Australian, British, Dutch, and American governments, whose initials formed the name of the command. Designed to stem the tide of Japanese advance, it was composed of American, British, Dutch, and Australian forces, and included all the land and sea areas in the general region Burma-Malaya-Netherlands East Indies, and the Philippines. It did not include India. A British officer, General Sir Archibald Wavell, was selected as supreme commander. General Wavell arrived in Batavia on January 10, 1942 and actually assumed command on January 15, 1942. ABDA COM was short-lived. After the fall of Singapore, the Combined Chiefs of Staff dissolved it, and it ceased operations on February 25, 1942.

Burma was nominally included in ABDA. But in practice, as will appear in the following account of the campaign in that country, Chiang Kai-shek retained actual command of the Chinese forces that fought there.

judgment was justified in the sense that the American-British proposal did not schedule large actions in the China Theater in the near future; nor did it give assurance that American forces would be sent to fight alongside the Chinese; nor even that China would get any larger share of the total military production of the Allies. But it did give the General-issimo a recognized share of authority. It also left him a future chance to play a part in main strategic decisions if the Chinese, through their great numbers, could make their theater of war important.

On January 5, 1942, Chiang Kai-shek answered that the proposed arrangement was acceptable to him. He said that he would assume the post of Supreme Commander of the China Theater. He asked the President to appoint an American officer to be chief of the joint general staff which was to serve under him. The American government was already engaged in selecting that officer, preparing his orders, and worrying about what could be done to create through him a combined war program in China.

By then the Japanese forces had captured Hong Kong and were advancing on Manila. They were moving down the Malay peninsula to Singapore, and were entering Lower Burma across the Thailand frontier. As soon as they took one place, they moved troops and air forces with great swiftness to the next point of assault, giving the Allies no chance to collect enough strength anywhere to stop them.

CHAPTER 2

The Dispatch of the Stilwell Mission

ROOSEVELT and Churchill had agreed on the global strategy that was to govern the direction of the war against the Axis. The American and British military staffs had given their confirmation. It was to direct all needed means to defeat Germany first, and to use only such means as could be safely spared to push Japan back in the Pacific and out of China. The place of China is concisely located by Secretary of War Stimson: "In Anglo-American grand strategy the war against Germany came first. Second came the great 'triphibious' movement across the Pacific toward the Japanese island empire. The China-Burma-India Theater was a poor third. Yet in its strategic and political significance this part of the world was of enormous importance . . . it constantly offered the possibility of striking military and political success, at a remarkably low cost. . . . Strategically, the object of American policy in this area was to keep China in the war, and so to strengthen her that she might exact a constantly growing price from the Japanese invader."[1]

The Far Eastern segment of the "Anglo-American grand strategy" during the first months after Pearl Harbor visualized a cordon of defense against further Japanese expansion that would include China. One anchor of this cordon was to be in Australia, and the other in India and Burma. From the center there would be a growing air assault upon the Japanese in China; and later, with supplies that would be moved over the Burma Road, Chinese armies, working with the American air force, would begin to expel the Japanese. Meanwhile the combined naval forces, mainly British and Dutch, were to protect and keep open the ports of Australia, Burma, India, and Ceylon. The defense on land was to be made by a combination of British, Dutch, Australian, New Zealand, Indian, and Chinese forces with supporting American air power —the entire operation conducted through the ABDA Command. Such was the plan in mind when first it was decided to send a senior American military man to China to serve on Chiang Kai-shek's combined staff and to join the Chinese war effort to our own. But even as the officer selected, General Joseph W. Stilwell, started to work out with his colleagues in the Pentagon Building the features of his assignment, it was perceived

[1] *On Active Service in Peace and War*, Henry L. Stimson and McGeorge Bundy, 1947, page 528.

that by the time he got to China this vulnerable plan might have fallen apart.

The War Department did not find it easy to tell Stilwell what he should try to do, or to inform him what means he could count on. The swift advances of the Japanese made it hard to forecast whether there would be any other forces left besides the Chinese to fight in the Pacific. The loss of the main Allied naval units in the heroic battles of the Java Sea made it doubtful whether it was going to be possible to convey men and materials to China by sea or land. And, also, no one knew how long the wearied Chinese armies could continue to stand up in battle. Within and beyond these uncertainties, there was at this time a difference of opinion in the Pentagon as to how important the China Theater might be. Secretary of War Stimson, thinking in somewhat the same way as Chiang Kai-shek, believed it might presently be turned into a main theater of operations against Japan, both upon land and as a base for air attack. That would depend a great deal, he thought, on the abilities of the American officer in charge of our military effort in China. General Marshall, who had served in that country, regarded the possibilities of action in and through China as more limited. As time went on, Marshall's opinion came gradually to seem the more correct.

The War Department tried to make sure that the Generalissimo would confer on Stilwell enough authority to enable him to accomplish whatever circumstances might permit. T. V. Soong, in Washington as Chiang Kai-shek's special representative, acted as intermediary in the discussions about the mission and Stilwell's relations with the Chinese government. Marshall, after a talk with Soong on January 23rd, thought all questions were settled. He told Stilwell that he was to leave at once for the Far East; that he would become Chief of Staff to the Generalissimo and, as such, China's representative on an Allied staff still to be created. Soon, Marshall added, it was expected that he would proceed to Burma, where it was hoped he would take command of the Allied forces, end disputes and rivalries, and save Burma for the United Nations.[2] But he dryly added, "By the time you get there you may be in command in Australia."

The Secretary of War in a letter to Soong on January 29th wrote out

[2] Sunderland-Romanus manuscript, Vol. I. Substantially the same information was given the next day by Assistant Secretary of War McCloy to the State Department, but he also seems to have anticipated that Stilwell would be given authority as well over some Chinese forces other than those in Burma.

his understanding of the functions of the United States Army representative that we were about to send to China, as follows:

"To supervise and control all United States defense-aid affairs for China.

"Under the Generalissimo to command all United States forces in China and such Chinese forces as may be assigned to him.

"To represent the United States Government on any International War Council in China and act as the Chief of Staff for the Generalissimo.

"To improve, maintain, and control the Burma Road in China."[3]

Soong confirmed this statement in his answer. Before doing so he had assured the War Department that the Generalissimo understood the arrangement, welcomed it, and authorized him to enter into it. But later, when disputes occurred as to the nature and range of Stilwell's authority, the Chinese said that Soong had not given Chiang Kai-shek a clear and full explanation of what the Americans thought the agreement meant.

Stilwell was told to be guided by this exchange of letters. His mission was, his orders stated, to increase the effectiveness of United States aid to the Chinese government for the prosecution of the war and to improve the combat efficiency of the Chinese army. In so doing he was authorized, ". . . to accept any appropriate staff and/or command position that may be tendered you by the Generalissimo."[4]

Stilwell prepared to leave for China. Critical doubts were already rumbling in his mind about the determination and motives of the Chinese and British. He was asking himself, and with reason, "Will the Chinese play ball? Or will they sit back and let us do it? Will the Limeys cooperate? Will we arrive to find Rangoon gone?"[5]

His farewell call at the White House on February 9th went awry. The President, it would seem, did not think it wise or useful at the time to discuss thoroughly and systematically the problems that Stilwell would find in China and Burma. Quite possibly his reason was that at the time he did not know what support and aid he might be able to give China; but he knew enough to know that in the near future it would not be much. Stilwell's fragmentary notes of the talk record the

<hr />

[3] *United States Relations with China*, with Special Reference to the Period 1944-1949. Based on the files of the Department of State, United States Government Printing Office, 1949, page 469.
[4] Sunderland-Romanus manuscript, Vol. I, and message, Lauchlin Currie to the President, June 28, 1942.
[5] *The Stilwell Papers*, entry January 28, 1942.

President as predicting that the war situation would turn within a year; and as asking Stilwell to assure Chiang Kai-shek that he, the President, regarded all enemies as equally important; and that the United States would see it through, and fight until China regained all its lost territory. Stilwell found him ". . . very pleasant and very unimpressive. . . . Just a lot of wind. . . . He was cordial and pleasant . . . and frothy. . . ."[6] Harry Hopkins seems also to have allowed his thoughts to roam rather than to settle. Stilwell remembered that he said, "You are going to command troops, I believe. In fact, I shouldn't be surprised if Chiang Kai-shek offered you the command of the Chinese army."[7]

With such a slighting impression of the seriousness and grasp of his commander-in-chief, it is probable that Stilwell wondered whether he could count on thick and thin support from Washington. The amount of American help in sight for China was small. He asked the War Department for substantial amounts of equipment for the forces he expected to command, and for the construction of air bases and of roads in and to China. But urgent demands for the same resources were being made by American, British, and Russian commanders in every section of the war front. The issue of many of the other battles being fought or about to be fought was judged more vital than what happened in China. So Stilwell was promised only a small part of what he asked.

In accord with Marshall's view it was decided that in this phase of the war the main form of American power that could be supplied and well used in China was air power. Stilwell was told that we planned to increase the American squadrons operating in China as fast as planes could be had. Limited means would also be provided to protect the roads and air lines into and within China, and to maintain and improve the transport service and services of supply. In all, it was contemplated there would be about one thousand Americans in Stilwell's task force.

Early in February, just before Stilwell left for China, General Arnold, head of the Air Force, advised the President that it was essential to develop a new air transport route from India into China in view of the imminent loss of the chief port of Burma, Rangoon. He estimated that with planes which could be acquired from the American commercial air lines, the service could be started in a few days. The President grasped at the plan with enthusiasm. He hastened to tell Chiang Kai-shek on February 9th that this air line into China would be maintained whether or not Rangoon was lost, and whether or not the land route

[6] *Ibid.*, entry February 9, 1942, and Sunderland-Romanus manuscript, Vol. I.
[7] *The Stilwell Papers*, entry February 9, 1942.

from India to China via Burma was kept open. This air transport service, with its last five-hundred-mile lap between Assam (in India) and the Yunnan plateau over the towering "Hump" of the Himalaya Mountains, was to become the greatest effort of its kind in the war. It was hoped that the promised skyway—to be made larger as fast as facilities could be provided in China—would allay the Generalissimo's discontent over the small secondary support which was all that China was to get in the near future and his anxiety over the prospect that China might be wholly cut off from outside help. Chiang Kai-shek was afraid that if this happened the Chinese people might give up the struggle, that provincial commanders and officials might separate from the government and deal with the Japanese. Then China, in effect, would be out of the war.

Stilwell faced utmost complexity in regard to the chances of developing a plan for the defense of Burma and the Burma Road and of carrying it out effectively. Decisions required agreement among the British, Chinese, and American governments, and also had to take into account the problems and fears of the governments of India and Australia. Action had to wait on their willingness to devote men and materials to the China-India-Burma combat area. Each wanted the others to contribute more than it was ready to provide and risk.

Stilwell's command relationships were also, it so turned out, unsettled. He was to find himself in some degree and respects subject to the orders of three different higher authorities: the Generalissimo, under whom he was to serve as both chief of staff and field commander; the American government, in regard to the employment of United States forces and resources (including the distribution of Lend-Lease supplies for China); and the commanding British officer (Wavell, and after him, Alexander) about operations in Burma. With all three he would have difficulties. The situation in regard to command in the field in Burma was to prove no better. The exchange of letters between Stimson and Soong left up in the air the question as to what Chinese troops were to be placed under Stilwell's command in Burma or in China. The Generalissimo—it will appear—gave, took away, and gave again. Then the British Commander-in-Chief in India (Wavell) sought to maintain a presumptive right to exercise a coordinating field command over all forces in Burma, including the American air force and the Chinese ground forces.[8]

[8] The Combined Chiefs of Staff tried to define Stilwell's relations with the British.

These were the troubles which Stilwell was to find in wait for him. While he was on his way the American government carried through one main measure which, it was hoped, would make his task easier. The Chinese government felt the need of some plain proof that it had the support of the Allies, and some notable demonstration of their interest in the plight of the Chinese people. The Allied governments were saying they could not send men or guns, or trucks or shoes, or huge flights of planes. But they could at least put to China's account dollars and pounds—future power to procure these and other things. Such action would be an augury of later help, and would also sustain China's finances against the stresses of staying in the war.

Giving reasons of this kind, on December 30th Chiang Kai-shek had asked the American government for a loan of five hundred million dollars, and asked the British government for a similar sum. The request stated in general terms that the money would be used to support Chinese currency and ease the Chinese economic situation. But it did not explain in what ways this was to be done. Ambassador Gauss on January 8th said that he concurred with the Generalissimo's statement as to the need and effect of such a credit. But he thought the amount too great in relation to the needs of the situation. A small sum, he advised, could be well used to stimulate increased production, finance reforms in land ownership, and possibly to get some essential imports. But a loose lump sum credit would be poorly used, he thought, to support ". . . the retrogressive, self-seeking, and, I fear, fickle elements in and intimately associated with the [Chinese] Government. . . ."[9] Gauss was staying on his rocky New England hillside, not in the streets shouting with the rest about our friendship with the Chinese.

On January 9th, Finance Minister Kung explained in a letter to the Secretary of the Treasury that he thought the loan justified both on economic and military grounds, but added, "Frankly, however, my reason for approaching you is political above all; and the import of a loan of this nature is even more important than the Lend-Lease Bill's

His forces, he was told, were, as they entered Burma, to come under the ABDA command, which would ensure the necessary directives for his cooperation with the British. He would also be, it was visualized, the principal liaison agent between the ABDA command and the Generalissimo. But in practice these arrangements went awry in various ways and for various reasons—which the military historians will no doubt explore in detail. Thus to the end—despite transient accords—there was no firm understanding adjusting Stilwell's authority to the British authority. See *The Stilwell Papers* and General The Honorable Sir Harold R. L. G. Alexander, K.C.B., "Report on the Operations in Burma, 5th March, 1942 to May 20, 1942," Supplement to *London Gazette*, March 11, 1948.
   [9] Telegrams, Gauss to State Department, December 30, 1941, January 8, 1942, in *United States Relations with China*, pages 471-476.

import. The essence of such a move is timeliness, so as to demonstrate that China's confidence in the allied powers is matched by equal confidence in China of the allied powers, in the most crucial months of emergency immediately before us."[10]

All branches of the American government were inclined to respond. They were willing to provide the means of dealing with the problem as pointed up by Hornbeck, political adviser on Far Eastern affairs in the State Department, as that ". . . of giving Chiang Kai-shek and his close and loyal entourage a sufficient amount of support to enable them to overcome objections or defections . . . of certain opposition groups, not disaffected groups by any means, but the defeatists and the appeasers. . . ." All were ready to accept the conclusion stated by Hull in the letter which he wrote to Morgenthau on the 10th: ". . . I feel that, as an act of wartime policy and to prevent the impairment of China's military effort which would result from the loss of confidence in Chinese currency and the depreciation of its purchasing power, it is highly advisable that the United States extend financial assistance to the Government of China. . . . I feel that the greatest possible expedition in reaching a position where an announcement can be made is highly important."[11]

But still they were bothered by some aspects of the transaction. No one saw how China could use well in the near future so large a sum. The Chinese government had drawn only a small part of the large Lend-Lease allocation which had been made to it; but our delays in delivering the war materials asked by China was the main reason. Then there was also the risk that the proceeds would be misspent, used mainly for the benefit of persons or groups close to Chiang Kai-shek rather than in ways which would help the Chinese people and encourage their resistance.

The Secretary of the Treasury felt himself responsible for the good use of American funds. So he tried to probe further. Soong did not deny the relevant financial points which the Secretary raised. The essence of his answer was, "I have got to put it [the matter of the loan] in the language of the Generalissimo. He is a general. How can he say where he is going to use five hundred million troops? He has got to have them in reserve and then use them."[12]

The President had already told the Secretary of the Treasury that though China could give little security he was anxious to help "Chiang

[10] *Ibid.*, page 476. [11] *Ibid.*, page 477.
[12] Record of conference in office, Henry Morgenthau, Jr., with Treasury and State officials, January 13, 1942. Morgenthau Diary.

Kai-shek and his currency," and hoped that Morgenthau could invent a way of doing so.[13] The first scheme that was thought up—either in the White House or in the Treasury—was startling. The two governments, it was proposed, should work out a program under which the American government would directly compensate each of one million Chinese soldiers at the rate of ten American dollars a month, five for pay, and five for maintenance. This would be paid them not in the same American dollar used in the United States, but in another unit of currency which the American and Chinese governments would devise together. It might be named the DEMO, short for democracy. The vagrant notion recalled that once a special dollar, named the Trade Dollar, was used in China, and another silver coin called the Maria Theresa Dollar was used in Abyssinia. Churchill, who was at the time in Washington, shared the President's and Morgenthau's almost gay enthusiasm for the idea. Or so Morgenthau was led to believe by Churchill's statement to him, "I authorize you, Mr. Morgenthau, to go ahead and make any arrangements you want with Dr. Soong, and I will back you up one hundred per cent."[14]

The novelty of the suggestion and the historical association may be regarded as bright panoply over a real purpose. The thought was that only by providing this special dollar in this way could we be sure that the benefit went to the common soldiers and their families. It appealed also as a way of dramatizing American partnership with the Chinese.

The Secretary of the Treasury tried it on Soong. After explaining it he added, "Mr. Roosevelt likes it, Mr. Churchill likes it and I hope the Generalissimo will like it."[15] Soong seems to have repressed his thoughts about the suggestion. But Chiang Kai-shek a week later sent word that although he deeply appreciated Morgenthau's efforts which materialized in this proposal, he doubted whether it was practicable. He pointed out that if Chinese soldiers were paid in American currency there would be cleavage between the army and the general economic structure in China; and this might actually hasten the collapse of the Chinese currency. Some of the economists in the Treasury had thought the same. The Generalissimo reverted to his original request for a political loan of five hundred million dollars. He thought this loan should be regarded in the light of "an advance to an ally fighting against

[13] *Ibid.*, entry of January 9, 1942.
[14] Memo, talk Morgenthau-Soong, January 13, 1942, *ibid.*
[15] *Ibid.*

a common enemy, thus requiring no security or other prearranged terms as to its use and as regards means of repayment."[16]

After a further bout of talk it was worked out as Chiang Kai-shek wished. The President's compliance was due in part to the compulsion he felt to evade Chinese requests to share in the making of decisions about the distribution of weapons among the various Allies. General Marshall urged quick action, since he thought that the fall of Singapore and Rangoon might give great force to the Japanese appeal to the races of Asia to stand together. Stimson agreed, believing that we must at any price keep China in the war. On January 31st Hull again wrote to the President in favor of giving Chiang Kai-shek what he wanted. One sentence of this letter read, "The brilliant resistance to aggression which the Chinese have made and are making, and their contribution to the common cause, deserve the fullest support we can give."

Thus assured that the State and War Departments would share responsibility, the Secretary of the Treasury also began warmly to endorse it, though some of his advisers were still distressed at giving Chiang Kai-shek such large and loose means. Morgenthau thereupon tried to see whether the Soviet Union could not be induced to contribute. Perhaps with the knowledge of the President, he told the Soviet Ambassador in Washington of the loans which the American and British governments were about to give China. Litvinoff's comments were cool. He said it was doubtful whether the Japanese, then drunk with victory, would make peace with China. He thought that it was more probable that the Japanese would, if Singapore fell, synchronize their actions with the Germans, and attack the Soviet Union. That, Litvinoff said, his government expected. He felt that once the Soviet Union began to fight the Japanese, the Chinese ought to be greatly encouraged. Of the loan, he said not once but several times, "It is nothing but blackmail." And he suggested that negotiations be dragged out as long as possible.[17] Moscow, he told Morgenthau a few days later, had not replied to the report he had sent on the subject.[18] It was dropped.

The State, War, and Treasury Departments joined in an urgent and effective appeal to Congress to authorize the loan. The bill they sponsored left the Executive free to work out terms and conditions. The House of Representatives approved it by a joint resolution on the 4th

[16] Letter, Soong to Morgenthau, January 21, 1942. *United States Relations with China*, page 478.
[17] Memo, talk between Morgenthau and Litvinoff, January 29, 1942. Morgenthau Diary.
[18] Record, telephone conversation, Morgenthau and Litvinoff, February 2, 1942. *Ibid.*

of February by a voice vote without debate. On the next day the Senate passed it unanimously. The President's message (February 7th) to Chiang Kai-shek, notifying him of the action, construed it as a marked sign of faith in the common cause.

Morgenthau was left to do the best he could to keep some chance of examining the uses of the loan even if he could not control them. All he managed to secure was a letter from Soong which said that in connection with the loan agreement concluded that day, ". . . I wish to inform you that it is the intention of my Government, through the Minister of Finance, to keep you fully informed from time to time as to the use of the funds provided in the said Agreement."[19]

Later, when the memories of emergency grew dim and the feelings of friendship with the Generalissimo grew tired, there was regret that we had not been more stubborn. After the Burma Road was closed, it became even less possible than before to transport goods into China. Much of the proceeds were used up in measures conceived as brakes on the course of inflation in China and the decline of value of the Chinese currency.[20] These failed. The ways in which the operations were conducted caused widespread report that much of the funds had gone to enrich individuals in the Generalissimo's close circle. This charge figures in the brief of those who later argued that the United States should no longer rely on Chiang Kai-shek. The loan conceived in a rush of vivid sympathy and alliance turned later into a cause of fault-finding. Of this, more hereafter.

[19] Soong's letter of March 11, 1942 is printed on page 484 of the *United States Relations with China*. The loan agreement is printed on pages 510-512.

[20] On March 24, 1942, the Chinese Ministry of Finance announced an Allied victory loan of one hundred million dollars, to be backed by the new American credit at the rate of twenty Chinese dollars for one American dollar; and an equal issue of short-term certificates similarly supported. The amount of both bonds and certificates sold was small until July 1943. Then there was heavy rush buying. In the meanwhile the amount of currency issue had substantially increased; and the purchasing power of the Chinese dollar, both in terms of domestic goods and foreign currencies, had declined.

CHAPTER 3

China Is Isolated

WHILE these decisions were being made, Stilwell was on his way to China. He arrived at New Delhi on February 25th, and after a week of talk with the British hurried on to Chungking. By then the defenders of Burma were in a state of shocked retreat. A short review of what had happened there before he came will make it easier to understand what happened afterwards.

Chiang Kai-shek had, in his first rushed talks with the foreign military representatives, recognized the need for coordinated action to defend Burma. He had asked what Chinese forces might be needed. General Dennys' answer had been that one regiment would be wanted, and then perhaps a little later, two others—a division in all. The Chinese (Chiang Kai-shek and his Chief of Staff, General Ho Ying-chin) had said that they were ready to provide a much greater force, three divisions at once and three more shortly.[1] Dennys had not pursued this offer nor did he when it was repeated a week later, on the 15th. He had said that Britain could not promise to provide the food and other supplies for the larger force. He had indicated that he thought that the Chinese government could help most in the defense of Burma by starting an offensive within China, thereby deterring the transfer of Japanese troops from China to Burma.

There was another problem. Chiang Kai-shek was saying that he was willing to provide a large force, some eighty thousand men in all, if there was a comprehensive plan for their use. He did not want to "dribble" them in, or to have them scattered around Burma. He wished them to operate as an independent unit in a selected area, preferably to take over the front along the northeast borders of Burma. As summed up by him, if a plan was worked out and if China was given a definite area to defend he would supply enough troops and assume responsibility; otherwise he would not.[2]

Wavell, who was soon to be head of ABDA, was due in Chungking any day. Meanwhile nothing had been done about the Chinese proposal, even though the British had not disputed the Chinese forecast

---

[1] Chinese divisions are small. Their average size was about six or seven thousand men.
[2] Memo, conference, December 15, 1941, Chiang Kai-shek, Madame Chiang Kai-shek, General Ho Ying-chin, Chief of Staff, Generals Dennys and Magruder, and others. Magruder Mission, War Diary.

that the expected formations from India might be slow in coming. Then in his first talk with Chiang Kai-shek on the 23rd, Wavell had explained that circumstances—by which he meant the fast-moving Japanese advances—were defeating all attempts to produce the comprehensive plan which the Generalissimo desired. No one, he had continued with conviction, could tell what forces or equipment would be available for the fight in Burma or how strong the Japanese attacking forces might be. As for the proffered Chinese help, Wavell had said he was willing to receive in Burma at once the elements of one Chinese division; and he had asked that another be kept on the alert on the frontier pending further disposition. The rest of the Chinese forces, he thought, had better remain for the time being in reserve at Kunming (in the adjoining Chinese province of Yunnan) and not be moved to the frontier.[3]

Of the several reasons given for taking no more help, the most salient ones were the limited supply of rice and the difficult means of transport. But Wavell had also said that it would be hard to give Chinese forces their own separate sector and lines of communication. He was still counting upon the arrival in time of British and Indian divisions from India. They were then at sea and with these and the Chinese troops already promised he felt he could hold Burma without the further help offered by the Chinese. He asked Chiang Kai-shek for more time to see if his own troops arrived from India; if so the troops offered beyond the two divisions could be used to fight Japan in China and prevent them from moving more troops south.[4] Still other reasons may have affected his answer. He had thought, as he later recorded that, ". . . Obviously it was desirable that a country of the British Empire should be defended by the Imperial troops rather than foreign."[5] Also, if the impression of American observers was correct, he had a rather low opinion of the combat value of Chinese troops.

Churchill, writing of these early and brief strains in the softer afterlight, views them as a passing misunderstanding which ". . . though it did not affect the course of events, involved high politics."[6] But they did

[3] As recorded in the report he later made to Churchill in answer to the Prime Minister's request for an explanation, "I accepted both these divisions when I was at Chungking on December 23rd, and any delay in moving them down has been purely Chinese. These two divisions constitute Fifth Chinese Army, I understand, except for one other division of very doubtful quality. All I asked was that Sixth Army should not be moved to Burmese frontier, as it would be difficult to feed." *The Hinge of Fate*, Churchill, page 134.

[4] MacMorland memo of conference, December 23, 1941.

[5] Dispatch on operations in the Southwest Pacific, Jan. 15 to Feb. 25, 1942. Supplement to *London Gazette*, January 1948.

[6] *The Hinge of Fate*, page 133.

in fact have an effect upon the course of events, stretching all the way from the first campaign in Burma to the final discussions in 1945 about the closing strategy of the war. For they infected the attitudes between the Allies. Chiang Kai-shek had construed Wavell's answer as a refusal and resented it. It caused him thereafter to be more resistant to proposals for Chinese participation in other Burmese offensives, and more insistent upon knowing what the British would do before he risked Chinese armies. Stilwell, who had just been told that he was to be American military representative in China, had expressed his thought about the incident in his notes for January 24th: "The British have one brigade east of Rangoon and one more on the way. That's what they thought sufficient to hold Burma. And the Supreme Commander, Wavell, refused Chiang Kai-shek's offer of two corps. [He] didn't want the dirty Chinese in Burma."[7] The General had thereby illustrated his gift for rushing to the most harsh conclusions with the utmost speed. But more temperate minds in the War Department had shared his impression. General Marshall had let Wavell know clearly that he thought a mistake had been made. On the other hand, General Brett had thought Wavell's reasons for refusal logical. In his opinion it was most difficult to use large Chinese forces quickly, to transport them over poor roads the eight hundred and twenty miles from Kunming to Mandalay, and to provide the food, equipment, and motor vehicles that would be needed. This is one of the many questions which—the reader will find as he follows the narrative—I am compelled to leave to the judgment of more thoroughly informed military historians.

While these awkward differences were hindering Sino-British action in defense of Burma, Churchill's thoughts had turned to another possible source of support. Struck by the failure of British forces to cope with the Japanese advances down the Malay Peninsula, he had already begun to wonder whether the base at Singapore could be held; and whether it was wise to risk further losses that would be hard to bear for a naval base that would be of little use without a Far Eastern fleet. He had begun to incline to the judgment that it might be best to concentrate on the defense of Burma and on keeping open the Burma Road. On January 21st, he had quizzed the British Chiefs of Staff by memo, asking, "What is the value of Singapore [to the enemy] above the many harbours in the Southwest Pacific if all naval and military demolitions are thoroughly carried out?" "On the other hand," he had observed, "the loss of Burma

[7] *The Stilwell Papers*, entry, January 24, 1942.

would be very grievous. It would cut us off from the Chinese, whose troops have been the most successful of those yet engaged against the Japanese. We may, by muddling things and hesitating to take an ugly decision, lose both Singapore and the Burma Road." His idea had been to divert to Burma the British Commonwealth forces then at sea on their way to Singapore. A message from Curtin, the Prime Minister of Australia, had caused him to suspend this line of thought. On January 23rd, Churchill had heard from him that ". . . the evacuation of Singapore would be regarded here and elsewhere as an inexcusable betrayal. . . . Even in an emergency diversion of reinforcements should be to the Netherlands East Indies and not Burma. Anything else would be deeply resented, and might force the Netherlands East Indies to make a separate peace."[8] Before renewing the suggestion, Churchill had waited to see how the fighting went throughout the region.

It had gone badly both in Burma and around Singapore. In Burma Japanese soldiers marching east from Thailand had captured Moulmein, a port on the Bay of Bengal, east of Rangoon.[9] They had quickly spread over the lower coastal area, and had begun the heavy and demoralizing bombing of Rangoon. Chiang Kai-shek had gone down to India and Burma to resume the discussions about concerted defense. By then all the help that China could give was wanted. Churchill was impressing on Wavell the interest which the President attached to bringing Chinese troops down into Burma.[10]

Then, as the British strove to form a line to hold Rangoon, Singapore had fallen on February 15th. Wavell, with that base gone, had concluded that the chances of holding Java were small. Its loss, though a severe blow from every point of view, he thought, would not be fatal. Therefore he had advised against further efforts to reinforce Java, which might compromise the defense of Burma or Australia. To indicate how in this time of disaster blame moved on a chainsaw, on this same day (February 16th) the State Department had just received a message from the Governor-General of the East Indies deploring the fact that the Chinese had not brought relief to the English and Dutch defenders of Malaya and the Indies by starting a great offensive against the Japanese in China. He had charged that Chiang Kai-shek had the means of doing so, but was waiting until the end of the war "probably for political reasons."

[8] *The Hinge of Fate*, pages 56-58.
[9] Kipling's "Mandalay" comes inevitably to mind.
[10] Message, Churchill to Roosevelt, February 7, 1942.

Churchill had informed the President and the British Chiefs of Staff that he agreed with Wavell that it was more important to try to hold Burma than Java. Therefore he had resumed his effort to send to Burma the only experienced and well-equipped Commonwealth forces that could be gotten there quickly. "It seems to me," he had summed up for the President, "that the most vital point at the moment is Rangoon, alone assuring contact with China."[11] Thus on February 20th he had asked the Prime Minister of Australia to consent to the diversion to Rangoon of the Australian division then at sea south of Ceylon, on the way home from the Middle East. He asked it as the only way to save a vital war situation—as the only force that could reach Rangoon in time to save its loss and the severance of the land route into China. To Wavell on the same day he had sent word that he was concentrating everything on defending or regaining Burma and the Burma Road.

Roosevelt, at Churchill's earnest plea, had also appealed to Curtin. He sent word that the American government was determined to send twenty-seven thousand fully equipped men to Australia in addition to those who were already on their way and that the American navy had in view operations to protect the Australian coast. For the sake of the whole Far Eastern war effort he asked that this Australian division be ordered to land. Before the answer was in, the need for this help had grown more extreme, and the chance that it could save the situation more doubtful. The retreating British-Indian forces had met disaster at a river-crossing. As Churchill later wrote, this "seemed to settle the fate of Burma, where again the resources and arrangements of the Imperial Government were shown to be woefully inadequate."

Curtin had refused the combined appeals made by Churchill and Roosevelt. He had answered on February 22nd in substance that the Australian government had done all it could, and he thought it a great deal, to reinforce the ABDA area. The Japanese were advancing south to the Anzac area and all Australian forces might be needed to repel them. He had made the further points that since the Japanese seemed to have superior sea and air power it was doubtful whether the Australian division could be landed in Burma; and even if it were possible, it was doubtful whether it could save the situation; and in the event of failure it was even more doubtful whether it could ever be rescued from Burma. In sum, his answer had been that the action requested was not a reasonable hazard of war. Both the President and the Prime Minister had

---

[11] Message, not dated, probably February 17th, Churchill to Roosevelt. This and the other messages referred to in the following pages are in Chapters 8 and 9 of *The Hinge of Fate*.

repeated their appeals. Curtin had repeated his refusals, adding that the imminent fall of Java meant "Australia's outer defenses are now quickly vanishing and our vulnerability is completely exposed." Churchill and the President had concluded that there was no further use in trying to get Australia to go to the—perhaps foolhardy—relief of Burma.

Churchill, in telling the Governor of Burma of this final refusal, had told the British-Indian forces to "Fight on." But how long could they? General Alexander, who had been in command at Dunkerque at the last, had now taken over from Wavell the direction of field operations in Burma. Almost at once he decided that Rangoon had to be abandoned. It was cut off by sea and was rapidly being encircled by the Japanese, who blocked the railway north to Prome. There was a grave risk that if the British-Indian forces did not start north at once their last way out would be cut. Though badly hurt, most of them had gotten away in good order, with most of their transport and artillery. With Rangoon lost, the battle had to be sustained by the troops who were in Burma and those who might still be brought in from India and China. Their numbers were small; many were exhausted and down in spirit; and the natives were doing them harm. The Allied air force was almost gone. Chinese troops were by then moving in, both the Fifth and Sixth Armies; some were nearing the line of battle, which was four hundred miles south of the frontier of China.

This was the situation Stilwell found when he took up his mission. Under orders he flung himself into it. He found the Chinese leaders "courteous, friendly, and planless." No agreement had been reached on a general plan for operations, and the Chinese troops in Burma were waiting for orders. The Generalissimo, it was Stilwell's impression, was willing to fight, but ". . . fed up with the British retreat and lethargy. Also extremely suspicious of their motive and intentions."[12] After reading the message from Roosevelt which Stilwell bore with him, and listening to Stilwell's account of prospective American help, Chiang Kai-shek remarked, "I told those army commanders [in Burma] not to take orders from anybody but you and wait till you've come."

But Stilwell soon found the path criss-crossed. Within two days (March 8th) he was entering in his notes, "Got word from Shang Chen [director of the Foreign Affairs Bureau of the Chinese General Staff and liaison officer with Stilwell] he would be in with the staff setup. At 7:00 he came, with the expected abortion, making everyone equal and

[12] *The Stilwell Papers*, entry March 6, 1942.

with me the Chief of Staff for Allied forces alone." This was quite out of accord with what Stilwell and Marshall thought had been agreed on. Chiang Kai-shek became more indignant than ever about the British, accusing them of failing to tell the Chinese liaison officer before leaving Rangoon. He was convinced that the British really did not intend to fight and he was unwilling to have them command the Chinese forces.

Stilwell sought to do what he had been told to do: end this discord. As he tried, he himself began the argument with the Generalissimo that was to become standard during the next three years. He thought the Japanese were exposed and that a quick, determined movement could succeed and possibly even recapture Rangoon. Therefore he urged that all available forces start a counterattack at once. His plan was to have the British forces hold on to their positions along the Irrawaddy as long as they could, while the Chinese were brought into battle. But Chiang Kai-shek did not want his troops to rush into an offensive. His idea was to maintain semi-passive resistance, known as defense in depth, and then sometime later, perhaps, to try a cautious movement forward. Though Stilwell found him "a stubborn bugger," he did get consent to move at least one more division in line of battle with the British, instead of keeping it in reserve in Mandalay as a garrison two hundred miles to the rear. But Chiang Kai-shek specified that they would be expected to fight only as long as the British fought, and if the British retreated the Chinese were to do the same. He asked Stilwell to remember that because of lack of arms, equipment, and transport, it took three Chinese divisions to deal with one Japanese division.

Wavell, who as Supreme Commander-in-Chief in India was still concerned in the campaign in Burma, matched Chiang Kai-shek in pessimism. His report to Churchill on March 19th as Stilwell was winning provisional and wavering consent to take Chinese forces into battle, stated, "I do not think we can count on holding Upper Burma for long if Japanese put in a determined attack. Many troops [are] still short of equipment and shaken by experiences in lower Burma and remaining battalions of Burma Rifles of doubtful value. There is little artillery. Reinforcements in any strength impossible at present. Chinese cooperation not easy. They are distrustful of our fighting ability and inclined to hang back. Not certain that they will compete with Japanese jungle tactics any more successfully than we have." The British and Indian governments were beginning to worry about the security of India. Wavell was doubtful whether he could protect that country with the forces available to him. Ground and air detachments that had been assigned for Burma were therefore diverted to Ceylon, and the troops within India were kept there.

By the end of March Stilwell was forced to admit that it would not be possible to hold the existing line. But despite all deficiencies and hindrances he still thought that it could be made hard for the Japanese to get as far north as Mandalay. On March 25th, after several changes of mind, the Generalissimo authorized him to use still another division —three in all—to defend Mandalay from the south. In his notes for that date, Stilwell summarized the Generalissimo's message, "Use your judgment and give 'em hell." He added, in capital letters, "WHAT A RELIEF!"

But the military actions which Stilwell had in mind swiftly fell into disorder. The Japanese were bringing in substantial numbers of more troops and equipment by sea through Rangoon. The Chinese divisions did not move when and where expected. Stilwell attributed that to secret interference or cancellation of his orders. Rage and frustration speak in the entry that he made in his notes about this time, "Then the flood of letters begins [from Chiang Kai-shek]. To Tu. To Lin Wei. To me. All of them direct. I never see half of them. They direct all sorts of action and preparation with radical changes based on minor changes in the situation. The Chinese commanders are up and down. . . . They feel, of course, the urgent necessity of pleasing the Generalissimo, and if my suggestions or orders run counter to what they *think* he wants they offer endless objections. . . . I can't shoot them; I can't relieve them. . . . So the upshot of it is that I am the stooge who does the dirty work and takes the rap."[13]

It is not to be wondered that when Stilwell and Chiang Kai-shek next met the occasion was not pleasant. Stilwell threatened to ask for his relief. The Generalissimo, either because he felt regret, or simply because he wanted to avoid a crisis with the American government, promised that it should not happen again. He went further. He said that he would go down to Burma again and make it very plain that Stilwell was to command. He did so quickly, and in what Stilwell thought was a satisfactory way. Even more, after talking with both Alexander and Stilwell, the Generalissimo agreed, or so Stilwell took it, that the Chinese forces would stand where they were and fight, no matter what. "Chiang Kai-shek," Stilwell entered in his notes for April 7th, "has come around to my contention: i.e., it is necessary to fight where we are, to hold the oil and food, we *must* fight a decisive battle now." Plans for an attack

[13] *Ibid.*, undated entry, pages 76-77.

were made. But before they were completed, the British positions were lost; the Japanese drove them back again. Alexander asked Stilwell to come to his field quarters. There Stilwell found "Disaster and gloom. No fight left in British."[14]

On April 17th Churchill gave Harry Hopkins, who was in London, a copy of an appeal sent by the Generalissimo. It was an urgent and afflicted treatment of the situation. Chiang Kai-shek began by saying that he had just visited the Burma front, and there he found conditions which caused him to state, "In all my life of long military experience, I have seen nothing to compare with the deplorable unprepared state, confusion and degradation in the war area of Burma." He gave examples which did not reflect well on the British administration of the British-Indian forces or of the Burmese natives. All, he found, were thinking of nothing but their own safety. The Chinese—this bill of complaint continued—had been fighting in Burma for almost a month. But they had not yet received a single machine. When the Chinese expeditionary force was sent it had been thought that they would be given Allied air help and protection. But they had not gotten it. The Chinese were sticking it out. But unless something was done quickly the Chinese officers and men would get a very bad impression of their Allies —an impression which would be hard to remove. The Burma war area, the Generalissimo's outburst ended, ought not to be considered as a subsidiary field of operations, since it was basic to the conduct of the war in the whole Far East. If Burma was lost, nothing would remain in the way of a Japanese threat to India; the line of transport and communications to China would be cut; and the base for land operations against Japan would be lost.

Churchill's depressed view of the situation was reflected in the message which on the next day (April 18th) he sent to Roosevelt: he did not, he said, know of anything more that could be done for General Alexander.

Stilwell was rushing part of his Chinese reserve forces to the support of the British. While he was doing so the Japanese struck at the end of the line held by the Chinese, the eastern end, and broke through and scattered them. They began to fall back northwards toward Lashio, a central station on the road from India. Stilwell tried hard to achieve some kind of orderly retreat to positions in North Burma which could be held until the heavy rains came. But it turned into a disorganized rout. The Japanese moved on wheels and controlled the air. They had

14 *Ibid.*, entry, April 15, 1942.

captured by then the airfields in Burma from which the British and American planes had operated. The British air squadrons and the American Volunteer Group could carry on their hard fight no longer.

While Stilwell was struggling back with his Chinese troops the Japanese seized Lashio on April 29th. The Burma Road, the escape road to China, was cut. The Japanese forces had traveled three hundred miles in eighteen days, outracing the torrential rains which the Allied commanders had hoped would bog them down in sticky red mud and jungle floods. Stilwell and a small band began their trudge through the jungle and over the mountains from Burma to India "ahead of the Chinese horde." On arriving in New Delhi, three weeks later, the General said to the press, "I claim we got a hell of a beating. We got run out of Burma and it's humiliating as hell. I think we ought to find out what caused it, go back and retake it."

One night (May 10th) while up in the hills, Stilwell had hastily jotted down a list of the reasons to which he attributed the defeat. It was a long one: hostile population, no air service, Japanese initiative, inferior equipment, inadequate ammunition, inadequate transport, no supply setup, improvised medical service, stupid, gutless command, interference by Chiang Kai-shek, British mess on the railway, rotten communications, British defeatist attitude, vulnerable tactical situation.

Stilwell's critics—and an American, General Chennault, was among the most bitter of them—thought he should have taken these matters into account before he pulled the Chinese armies into the campaign. His answers, plainly suggested by his papers, would have been: first, that the battle could have been won despite them; and, second, that it was the only chance to keep China as an active participant in the war. To which perhaps he might have added another thought: after all, Japan had been compelled to use in Burma forces which otherwise might have been sent toward India, Australia, or elsewhere. This was the best way in which China could at the time contribute what it had—men—to the Allied cause.

CHAPTER 4

After the Defeat in Burma

WHAT a trail of harm this debacle left behind!

The last remnants of the ABDA plan and organization were smashed.

Much of the small supply of heavy weapons of the Chinese armies was lost. All usable land and sea routes over which men, weapons, and supplies could be brought into China were barred. The only way thereafter by which the Chinese could procure anything from outside was by air—from India over the high Himalayas. More and more planes, skilled airmen, material, and energy had to be devoted to it. Even so, this system of transport remained inadequate, and the limitations on supply long postponed the chance of so building up Chinese forces that they might push back the Japanese army in China. The defending people and government of free China were forced to get along without main producing areas of food, raw materials, and fabricated goods.

All idea that China could be turned into a main theater of ground warfare had to be put aside. But the hopes of using it as a land base for air measures against Japanese shipping and outposts, and later even against Japan itself, survived.

The Chinese government had to stay a refugee government, in its distant mountain capital, far away from the big cities and ports of the east. This made it easier for the Communist movement in the north to recruit throughout China.

In Chungking gloom deepened. Ever since the forced retreat to this inland town, the government had lived on the wishful belief that when the United States went to war with Japan all this would change; that it would be quickly succored. Now—five months later—it seemed worse off than ever, more confined and harassed, shaken by the loss of the armies and the closing of the Burma Road. It was hard to be cheerful there even when the news was fair; very hard when it was bad. Living conditions for foreigners as well as Chinese were wearing. It was hot and damp during the summer, and a fog stayed over the city and nearby hills through the chilling winter. Japanese bombing planes forced everyone into shelters for long hours of the day. Mud and dirt were everywhere; there was not enough clothing and food. Isolation from the foreign world was almost complete.

The Chinese government seemed able to do little to relieve the situation. Almost all foreign witnesses agreed that the Chinese government seemed even less able than before to organize its forces; to improve command in the army or the conduct of civil government; to expel fear and self-seeking, or cure the spirit of division. Chiang Kai-shek was issuing laws and decrees for the fuller use of the combat resources of China and the relief of the suffering. But these were without vitality. Few believed that they would be put into effect, or, if they were, that they would improve matters. The Chinese officials seemed more avid for foreign aid and support, and more convinced that they were entitled to it. Control over provincial commanders and regimes weakened, and the Generalissimo felt an increasing compulsion to avoid conflict with them.

It was not only general misery and weakness that spoke, however, during the months right after the rout in Burma. There was an active fear that Japan would soon strike harder than ever at China. During May the Japanese had begun to move up the Burma Road one hundred thousand strong with tanks, artillery, and air support. Their first object, it was judged probable, would be India. But they might also cross into China, drive on to Kunming, and from there bomb Chungking out of existence. At the same time the Japanese armies in the north might go on the offensive. Soong sketched out the dreaded possibilities in a letter written to Hopkins even before the end had come in Burma, telling him that "On April 16th a friend in Chungking in whose objective judgment I have great faith cabled me that the Japanese threaten to attack the most important strategic centers: 'The situation looks ominous. I personally believe that in May or June the Japanese will attack Changsha and Hengyang [in Hunan Province] and at the same time attack Sian [in Honan Province].' "[1] Even the more assured officials—American as well as Chinese—were greatly worried as to whether the available Chinese forces could deal with these dangers.[2] Some of the field commanders were not trusted. The troops in the south were of

[1] *Roosevelt and Hopkins, An Intimate History*, Robert E. Sherwood, 1948, pages 514-515. Sian is not in Honan but in Shensi Province.

[2] On May 8th Gauss reported that General Magruder had been talking to him about the possibility—if not the probability—that the American military mission in China would be forced to withdraw from Chungking and maybe from China itself. Gauss had cautioned against any action which would cause the Chinese to suspect that we lacked confidence in the Chinese government and army. The State Department discussed the matter with General Marshall, urging him to discourage any preparations for withdrawal. Marshall cabled the American representatives in Chungking that it remained the policy of the War Department to give maximum practicable aid to China; that in view of the reverses in Burma, it was more important than ever to maintain an attitude of "calm optimism" regarding the future of China; nothing should be done to imply that our military personnel would be evacuated.

poor quality and had little equipment; the people of Yunnan were of no help.

The British took the rout more calmly than the Americans or Chinese —perhaps because they had already suffered greater ones and were facing more dangerous risks elsewhere. Perhaps also the edge of defeat was dulled for them because India was not lost. There is evident satisfaction in the comment with which Churchill concludes his telling of Alexander's success in bringing the remnants of his forces safely back into India (to Imphal where they could protect the frontier), "The road to India was barred."[3]

The Chinese (by which is meant Chiang Kai-shek, his government, and his military commanders) found everyone and everything to blame except themselves. To three things in particular they attributed the disaster: that so little in the way of war equipment had been given to their forces, particularly no planes and no artillery; that the British commanders had mismanaged the fight, and the British-Indian forces had failed to do their part; that Stilwell had rashly risked the Chinese armies.

These opinions Chiang Kai-shek and his associates did not keep to themselves or forget quickly. But they refrained from criticism of the American government and managed to subdue the bitterness in their complaints. The defeat in Burma made them even more dependent on the United States than before. They retained their belief that whatever the American government did—or failed to do—was inspired by good will for China and the determination to have it emerge from its troubles. But their discontent found vent upon Stilwell. They began to mark him as the cause of their tribulations. He had overcome their fears and doubts about engaging so fully in the defense of Burma; he had disputed their view that the Japanese were too strong; and he had scorned their wish to stay on the defensive. His memos and comments exposed their inside deals and weaknesses, and blamed them for conditions and facts for which they preferred to blame others. He had won little for them in Washington to compensate for these trials. His appointment had failed to bring with it as quick or as much aid as they had hoped. In sum, most governing Chinese officials turned against Stilwell for every reason that ill fortune can summon.

As for Stilwell, his was the unrelaxing will to keep China active in the war. He saw in Burma the only chance to engage the large Chinese

[3] *The Hinge of Fate*, page 171.

[36]

armies, in concert with the Indian, against the Japanese until more combat resources became available from other theaters of war. But he found that many of the Chinese officials and officers, tired and self-sparing, longed to have the next round of battle fought out by men of other countries, with the great planes and guns which the Chinese did not have.

Stilwell's opinions of the Chinese government and military command are etched in abusive acid in his notebooks and messages to Washington. His state of mind is recorded in an entry in his notes made on June 19th just after he had come out of the Burma jungles and talked with Chiang Kai-shek. "The Chinese Government is a structure based on fear and favor, in the hands of an ignorant, arbitrary, stubborn man. . . . Only outside influence can do anything for China—either enemy action will smash her or some regenerative idea must be formed and put into effect at once."[4] They, he thought, looked at the war as a game of chess—a continuation or extension of self-seeking activity. For the ways in which the Chinese military organization had behaved during the Burma campaign Stilwell had nothing but condemnation. In his blazing memory, the Generalissimo had failed to keep his promise to allow him to command the Chinese army in Burma, and had confused the whole conduct of the campaign by his secret orders. Most of the Chinese generals he regarded as incompetent; and more often than not, he believed, officers ignored and oppressed the men under them. Only the soldiers had merit.

Stilwell's views, vigorously conveyed, influenced estimates—especially in the Pentagon Building—of what might be expected of China in the war, and what use the Chinese forces would make of combat weapons greatly needed elsewhere. They were noted in the White House—but with reserve. The President and Hopkins, and Hull in the State Department, all felt it essential to preserve a basically friendly attitude toward the Chinese government. They could not let it be too deeply scarred by hard feelings following one military defeat. Moreover, it may be surmised that the President was inclined to think that there was some justice in Chiang Kai-shek's claims for more help and for his view that the war in China should be carried on largely from the air.

For this view General Chennault was an aroused advocate. He shared the Generalissimo's grievances—early and later—over the lag in air action in China, and over promises that were not carried out. The

[4] *The Stilwell Papers*, entry, June 19, 1942.

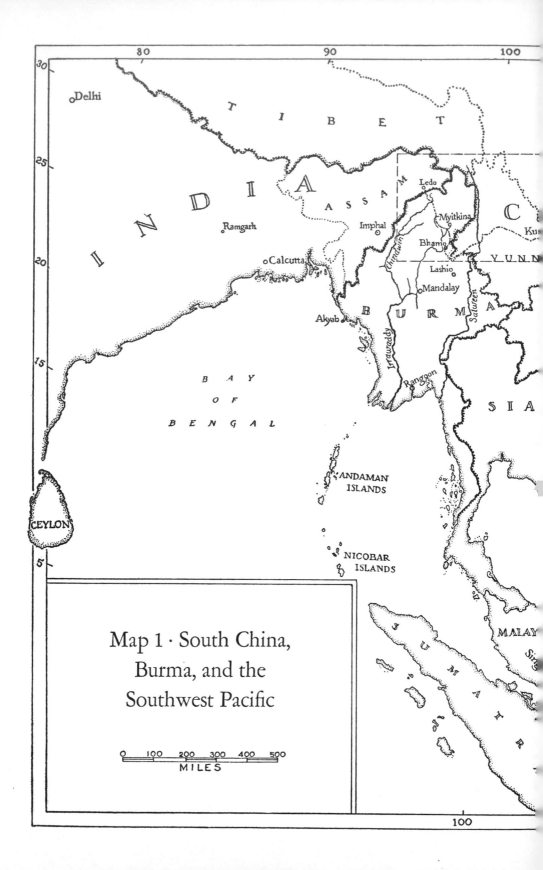

Map 1 · South China,
Burma, and the
Southwest Pacific

0 100 200 300 400 500
MILES

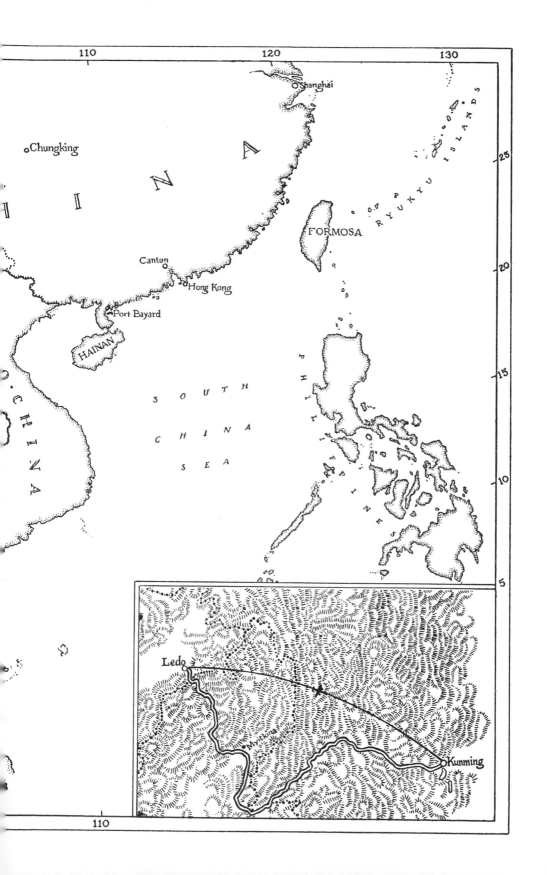

110　　　　　　　　120　　　　　　　　130

Chungking

CHINA

Shanghai

FORMOSA

RYUKYU ISLANDS

Canton

Hong Kong

Port Bayard

HAINAN

SOUTH

CHINA

SEA

PHILIPPINES

INDO CHINA

Ledo

Myitkyina

Kunming

25

20

15

10

5

110

American Volunteer Group had been fighting in China under a contract with the Chinese government that was due to expire in July. Chiang Kai-shek had agreed to dissolve this unit in return for a promise of a complete U.S. fighter group and other types of planes. Those members who wished were to be absorbed in the Tenth Air Force, which was then based in India and was under Stilwell's command. Chennault was named head of the China Air Task Force, a segment of the Tenth Air Force. But the means which he had reason to expect did not arrive on time, and his orders were delayed. Stilwell himself was trying his angry best to get better results from the Tenth Air Force. But in the words of two well-informed students of these military matters, these disappointments ". . . embarrassed Stilwell in his relations with the Generalissimo and Chennault, who mistakenly believed that Stilwell was indifferent to the possibilities of China-based air power."[5]

Beyond such causes of grudge against Stilwell, Chennault thought Stilwell's military judgment and plans bad. His ideas of how the fight in China ought to be conducted appealed to the Chiang Kai-shek circle, with whom he was on terms of admiring intimacy. Upheld by them, and sometimes speaking for them, he contested Stilwell's strategy and programs, and became an active rival for American support. As time went on, he did all he could to have his ideas known in Washington. It may be said—looking forward—that American relations with China during the next two years went along on two divided lanes: one, the lane or communication between Chiang Kai-shek and the White House was kept smoothly paved; the other, the lane of military communication which ran through Stilwell, was rough and cracked with tension.

It was the State Department that amid these agitations seemed to plead China's case for sympathy and help most warmly. Perhaps this was easier for it to do because it did not have to face the direct responsibility if battles elsewhere were lost as a result of quickening help for China. The views it put forth are well indicated in a memo of May 20th written by Stanley Hornbeck, then adviser on Far Eastern Political Relations:

"Reports from our own sources in China, sent from or through Chungking, have breathed a sense of frustration and defeatism. The feeling of our officials and officers reflects in some measure the feeling of the Chinese circles in which they move. The Chinese have seen the United States and Great Britain sustain military defeats. They have seen the Japanese gaining victories elsewhere and closing in on China;

---

[5] Sunderland-Romanus manuscript, Vol. I.

they have seen the failure of the Cripps mission in India and they have sensed the ineptitude of British military and political operations in the Far Eastern theatre and the Indian Ocean area; they have heard and have rejoiced in American promises that we would get goods into China and they have seen that the goods do not arrive; they are now hearing that the goods do not arrive because we cannot send them and that we cannot send them because (a) high mountains are an obstacle and (b) we and the British need for other fronts (British and Russian) all planes available and therefore cannot spare more than a couple dozen (three dozen at the outside) transport planes for traffic into and out of Chungking. . . .

"China has no air force, is woefully lacking in artillery and anti-aircraft, is short on machine guns and has no large reserves of small arms and ammunition. Chinese morale has been preserved for many months past by expectation of aid from the United States and Great Britain and assurances that she shall have aid by the United States. So long as the Chinese remain confident that such aid is going to reach them, there is a fair chance of their morale holding up and their resistance continuing. But let once the point be reached, at which they reach a conclusion that aid cannot or will not reach them, that their hope and confidence will evaporate, at and from that point there will be no reason for them not to say to themselves that the chance of the United Nations defeating Hitler and Japan is certainly not better than 50/50 and the sensible course for them to follow is to make with Japan the best compromise possible. . . .

"From now on there is only one way by which we can make sure of maintaining China's confidence; we must deliver goods. Deliveries can be made and an artery of communication between China and us can be maintained if we will put into the job of creating and maintaining an air transport service such courage, such ingenuity and such effort as we have been and are putting into a variety of operations in other places and other contexts. . . . The number of planes needed for doing this job is ridiculously small in comparison with the relatively huge numbers that we are sending to other fronts. Is there not something wrong about a strategy . . . which in theory or in practice would call for investing everything in several scattered theaters and investing absolutely nothing in a theater which, if occupied by the enemy, would mean the loss of a useful ally and the acquisition by the enemy of that prize which has been the major objective of political and military operations on his part for a period of nearly 50 years."

The State Department entered its observations in the contest for American assistance. But it was not bold, and it did not at this time have much influence in top councils. It could flutter about strategy but could not make it. Even so its sympathetic temper, exemplified by Hull, helped to soften differences and sustain friendship.

In short, the will of the American government to keep China in the war remained firm and its ultimate purpose friendly and faithful. But rather than imperil vital military situations elsewhere in order to hasten its rescue, we left China well toward the end of the line of our effort.

During June, Chiang Kai-shek asked for the third time that China be given a place on the Munitions Assignment Board which allocated military equipment among the Allies. This request was again politely parried. But plans were approved to satisfy the Generalissimo's prime wish for greater air support. The United States Tenth Air Force would, he was again told, get more bombers and fighters. The main bases of operations were to be moved to China, the fighters and medium bombers at once, the heavy bombers later. More and better planes were also to be assigned to the air transport route over the Hump. Due to many causes, the tonnage being brought into China was pitiably small: only eighty tons in May, one hundred and six in June, seventy-three in July.[6]

But once again, necessity crowded against wish and intention. In Egypt, Tobruk was lost (on June 21st) with frightening shock, and the British were in full retreat with their backs against the Suez Canal. As the Middle East went, so would India go, the British military thought.[7] The Russians were maintaining a desperate defense, and ways were being sought to hinder the German eastward drive.[8] The American military authorities thought these crises much more acute and decisive than anything that could happen in China. Thus they canceled part of the programs underway for enlarging the air activity in and for China. They did it because they felt they had to, knowing well that once again the Chinese government would think itself hurt and badly treated.[9] The Americans had already begun to repossess the stock-piles

---

[6] Sunderland-Romanus manuscript, Vol. I.

[7] *The Army Air Forces in World War II*, Vol. II, Europe, Torch to Pointblank, page 15.

[8] *Ibid.*, page 9.

[9] The Chinese government was smarting at the time over the fact that on signing (on May 26th) a twenty-year Treaty of Alliance between Great Britain and the Soviet Union, the Secretary of State for Foreign Affairs, Anthony Eden, had remarked that the destiny of the world thereupon lay in the hands of Great Britain, the United States, and the Soviet Union.

of Lend-Lease supplies and equipment which had been accumulated in the United States and India for China, but could not be moved into China after the Burma Road was closed. They were needed elsewhere at once. The Chinese government reluctantly consented to the transfer.[10]

On June 24th Stilwell received instructions from Washington: "Brereton [Commander Tenth Air Force] will come at once to the Middle East with available heavy bombers with mission to assist Auchinleck."[11] The bombers were wanted to smash up the Axis supply route from Italy to Africa. Simultaneously another squadron of light bombers en route to China was detained in Egypt. And a number of transport aircraft already in service on the Assam-China air line with needed personnel were also ordered out to the Near East. These orders, decided at a White House conference, were issued without prior notice to the Generalissimo.

On being told of them, Stilwell wrote in his diary, "Now what can I say to the G-mo? We fail in *all* our commitments, and blithely tell him to just carry on, old top."[12] Chiang Kai-shek had been brooding and fretting over his failure to receive the help he thought due China. His response to this latest news that China's needs again would have to yield to others is shown by the entry which Stilwell made in his notes the next day: "In any case, I was to radio and ask for Yes or No on the question 'Is the U.S. interested in maintaining the China Theatre?' "[13] Madame Chiang Kai-shek, who was present, underscored the query by remarking that the Generalissimo in the speech he was to give to mark the end of the fifth year of the war against Japan, July 7th, would have to tell the truth. "[He] wants a yes or no answer to whether the Allies consider this theatre necessary and will support it."[14] Stilwell trans-

---

[10] Letter, Soong to Assistant Secretary of War McCloy, May 21, 1942.

[11] The Brereton Diaries, entry, June 24, 1942.

[12] *The Stilwell Papers*, entry, June 25, 1942.

[13] *Ibid.*, entry, June 26, 1942.

[14] From American minutes of this talk. According to the Chinese minutes, at one point the Generalissimo blamed Stilwell: he said that since President Roosevelt in his telegram promised to supply China with planes and war materials she needs ". . . what is being done amounts to disobedience of his orders. . . . Less than ten per cent of what he had agreed to give China has been supplied. I do not entertain any doubt that the President is sincere. What has been done is perhaps without his consent or knowledge. As Chief of Staff to me, you are responsible for seeing to it that the promised material is forthcoming." Sunderland and Romanus note in this connection references made by Chiang Kai-shek and Madame Chiang Kai-shek to current messages from Soong—of which Stilwell was ignorant; these apparently were the basis of the impression expressed by the Generalissimo and the suspicion that the measures reducing support for China were being made on Stilwell's orders or suggestions.

mitted the question to Washington. Roosevelt's first response (June 27th) Stilwell found "quiet and dignified and promised nothing."[15]

Then, on the 29th, Chiang Kai-shek put down in writing his ideas of the minimum help to which China was entitled.[16] He gave Stilwell a note for transmission to Washington, stating "Three minimum requirements essential for the maintenance of the Chinese Theatre of War." They were:

1. Three American divisions to arrive in India between August and September to cooperate with Chinese forces in establishing communications through Burma.

2. Beginning in August, the Air Force should have five hundred planes in continuous combat operations and maintain that strength.

3. From August on, monthly transport deliveries over the Hump to be at least five thousand tons.

This was fifty times the volume then coming by air into China, and about ten times the volume that Stilwell reckoned could be brought in by a hundred planes—more than the Chinese airfields could then accommodate.

The policy makers in Washington recognized that the trouble with the Generalissimo was serious, perhaps critical. Soong, the Foreign Minister, had previously urged Harry Hopkins to accept the Generalissimo's invitation to visit him. At the end of June, Chiang Kai-shek himself asked the President to send Hopkins, or some other similarly situated person, to confer with him. Hopkins could not be spared and was not in fit shape to take the trip. When Chiang Kai-shek's protests came in, the President instead sent Lauchlin Currie, one of his administrative assistants. During late July and early August he had twelve long talks with Chiang Kai-shek and was able to report fully on the state of mind and state of defense of Free China. He found the Chinese-American attachment coming loose. He thought the Generalissimo and the Chinese very wearied, but nowhere did he detect "the slightest sign of defeatism or desire to give up the struggle." He concluded that Stilwell ought to be relieved, and so advised the President. His visit was helpful both in soothing feelings and in stimulating the flow of help to China.

[15] *The Stilwell Papers*, entry July 1, 1942.
[16] *Ibid.*, and Sunderland-Romanus manuscript, Vol. 1.

CHAPTER 5

Ardors and Refusals: During the Rest of 1942

BUT the actual military aid given during the rest of 1942 was small. Except for the portion that could be wrested from more urgent needs, satisfaction of the demands made by the Generalissimo was deferred. For, grave as the wants of China were, the energies of the American government centered elsewhere. Other situations and plans were to the fore: the crucial battles in the Eastern Mediterranean and on the eastern front in Europe, the projected invasion of North Africa, the protection of Australia, and the first counteractions in the southwest and central Pacific.

While waiting for Washington to decide, in the face of these competing requirements, what means it could provide for the war in China, Stilwell devoted himself to the two tasks which the War Department most wanted done: (1) to plan for, and get started as soon as it could be managed, a campaign to recapture Burma; (2) to improve the combat efficiency of the Chinese army.

The operation which he proposed to the Generalissimo looked not only toward the recapture of North Burma and the reopening of the Burma Road, but also to reentry into the port of Rangoon.[1] No other measures, he thought, in the China-Burma-India theater might achieve as much at so little cost. But he was aware that neither the Chinese nor the British would eagerly consent to engage upon it. There was method in his mind. He thought to gain his way by first extracting from the War Department a promise to provide necessary minimum means for this plan; then, using this conditional promise of help as a lure, to join with the War Department to get the Chinese and British to go ahead.

At the same time Stilwell did his utmost to impel the Chinese government into a reorganization of its army. That army was a coalition army rather than a unified national force. Most of the divisions were bands of lightly armed and poorly trained men, but tough and often courageous, with allegiance to their commanders. Their pay was extremely small and they were sometimes cheated of part of it. The supply of food for many divisions was irregular. Conscription was

[1] Stilwell memo, July 10, 1942, Subject: What is the Future of the China War Theatre? and Plan for Retaking Burma; and memo to Generalissimo Chiang Kai-shek, July 18, Subject: Suggested Letter from the Generalissimo to the President. Sunderland-Romanus manuscript.

rough. There were many desertions and much sickness. Both the system of command and the use of the forces were weakened in order to conform to the intricate pattern of influence within the government. Various area commanders were also provincial governors. The forces were widely dispersed for a variety of reasons, some poor. Divisions were kept in locations where they were of little combat use because local commanders would not agree to their departure; or just to maintain the influence of the Central Government; or because Chiang Kai-shek feared they might defect if moved. The National Military Council was supposed to coordinate action in threatened areas but was not effective. It acted more like the national committee of an American political party than a military organization.

All this Stilwell tried to get changed, and quickly. Out of the three hundred odd divisions of which some thirty were directly under the Central Government, he wanted to form a much smaller force of the best, retrain, reequip, and feed them. Then he wanted to use them where they could do the most good in the war against the Japanese. An entry in his notes, made after he had spent some months trying to achieve this, gives the run of his impressions:

"Troubles of a Peanut dictator. At first the Peanut thought that military and political functions could not be separated, so he combined the authority under the military commanders. *Now* he finds that it makes the boys too powerful, and he's been trying for a year to shake them loose, without success in Hupeh . . . . Hunan . . . . Honan . . . . Kansu . . . . Shansi . . . . Chekiang . . . . Yunnan.

"The way it works is by threat. The Peanut wants to shake Hsueh Yueh [Governor and Commander-in-Chief in Hunan] loose. If he [Chiang Kai-shek] pulls out troops Hsueh squawks, 'I cannot be responsible for the security of my area,' and he might even arrange for a Jap reaction. The under-strappers are told to pressurize, and a flood of protest reaches various officials of the Central Government. They then tell the Peanut opposition is very strong, and the forcing the issue might cause dirty work. So the Peanut lays off and waits. The plain fact is that he doesn't *dare* to take vigorous action—they are sure to be sulky and they may gang up. His best cards are the air force, the artillery, and the ten armies whose training is under the Central Government.

"Why doesn't the little dummy realize that his only hope is the 30-division plan, and the creation of a separate, efficient, well-equipped, and well-trained force?"[2]

[2] *The Stilwell Papers*, entry, October 5, 1942.

As Stilwell found how many reasons the Chinese officials had for taking their time or keeping on with their old ways, what was left of his patience was sorely tried.

Chiang Kai-shek was willing to discuss all the matters that any and all branches of the American government insisted were important to win China's battle: the reorganization of the army, the assignment of command, the allocation of troops for a Burma operation, more effective measures of economic and financial control, and social justice. But on all these he had his own problems and designs, his own pace, and his own self-assurances.

The Generalissimo thought Stilwell and the War Department were demanding too much of China too soon, while offering too little. But he did not stand on the three minimum demands which he had presented in June. He agreed to go along with Stilwell's plan to retake Burma provided (1) as much as one American combat division was sent, and (2) the American combat air force and air transport service were substantially increased, and (3) when the land campaign started the British navy and air force attacked the Andaman Islands (which were in the Bay of Bengal about one hundred and twenty miles south of Rangoon) and made a landing at Rangoon. He wanted to take no chances that the Japanese could reinforce through that port. In sum, he insisted that the assault on Burma must be not only by land from China and India, but by sea from the south.[3] For such a campaign China would provide the divisions whose training at Ramgarh in India was beginning (known as the Ledo Force) and other troops presently to be assembled in the province of Yunnan, near the frontier of Burma (known as the Yoke Force).

The American and British Combined Chiefs of Staff pondered over the possibilities, in touch with Soong in Washington. The main elements and phases of the decisions that followed are sufficiently indicated by entries in Stilwell's notes:

September 21, 1942. "Dinner at Chiang Kai-shek's. . . . Everything [of India training plan] approved. Reinforcements for Ramgarh OK. We can pick our man, too. That's the way it goes—you worry yourself sick for weeks and struggle around, and then suddenly it all crystallizes in a moment. . . . We are doing our damnedest to help him, and he makes his approval look like a tremendous concession."

September 27, 1942. "At last. Answer [from Washington] to Three-

---

[3] Letter, General Shang Chen to Stilwell, August 1, 1942.

Demands scaled down. 265 combat planes, 100 transports. No ground troops. Tonnage would be built up to 5,000 if, as, and when. 'Appreciate your cooperation.' 'Will assist at Ramgarh.' It amounts to doing *nothing* more than at present. I suppose I am to kid them into reorganizing the Army. [Forces for the] Burma [offensive] will be the Ramgarh Detachment, the Tenth Air Force, the Yunnan mob, and a 'limited British detachment.' In other words, what we've got. How *very* generous. . . ."

October 2, 1942. "———arrived with mail and news. Washington is just what we've thought, one big mess. This theater kaput. No help coming. General impression, pessimistic. Major strategic effort not in the Pacific. Henry [Stimson] sympathetic, but no offer of help. Chief of Staff says no ground troops. McCloy noncommittal."

Stilwell presented to Chiang Kai-shek on the 13th of October the President's formal answer to the modified three demands. It gave more and demanded less than had been expected. No American combat troops were to be sent to Burma. But the President offered (1) about five hundred aircraft for a larger United States air force in the China Theater, and one hundred transport planes to be operated in the Hump Route by early 1943. (2) Lend-Lease help to reorganize and equip the Chinese divisions in India. (3) Such Lend-Lease equipment as could be brought over the Hump for the Chinese divisions in China.

The Chinese government took this answer in good part. But its idea of what was needed before engaging in a Burma campaign had not changed; the same requirements which Chiang Kai-shek had defined before were written into the plan which he now authorized Stilwell to discuss with the Americans and British. Even so, Stilwell was briefly pleased enough to enter in his notes on October 14th that the Chinese plan looked good; and that the Generalissimo was encouraging him to hurry with the training of the Chinese troops in India—" 'Giving you full authority in India. Be sure and keep strict discipline.' "[4]

Having also received further guidance from Washington, Stilwell flew down to New Delhi to get the British views. At first (October 17-19) he found Wavell reserved, and cool even to the Ramgarh training project—his reasons being the inadequacy of all forms of transport, the insufficient supply of both food and water, and fear that the demands of the Chinese forces would hinder the development of the Indian armies.[5] Wavell had in mind only a limited action, short of the capture

---

[4] *The Stilwell Papers*, entry, October 14, 1942.
[5] Quite possibly Wavell was merely putting forward objections held by the govern-

of Rangoon. But for reasons not identified—probably new word from London—Wavell's answers abruptly changed. As recorded in an undated entry in Stilwell's diary [but somewhere between October 18th and 24th, New Delhi] "Remarkable change. . . . They will give us a sector at Ledo. They will supply us . . . they can move the Chinese up [to the North Burma front] in time to go in. Everything is lovely again, so obviously George [Marshall] has turned on the heat. Wavell's plan fits in fairly well with mine." After this talk the British authorities in India zealously began to plan for an offensive in Burma, and to take care of the needs of the Chinese divisions at Ramgarh. But in actual fact they still were not willing to agree to a campaign as large as the one Stillwell wished, nor to contribute as much as the Chinese wanted.

At this juncture Stilwell found a supporter in Soong, who was back in China. This was unexpected, for Stilwell thought, and not without some reason, that the earlier reports and advice which Soong had sent from Washington depreciated, and in some instances, distorted his ideas. Marshall and Stimson, it is now known, had before Soong's departure reviewed with him Stilwell's problems, and the reasons why he had had to be troublesome—"a fighting military leader, not just a smooth diplomatic type." The great issue, they explained to him, in their view was Burma, not merely a harmonious group at Chungking; that meant a properly trained force at Ramgarh, an improved and selected Chinese force in Yunnan, and a practical basis of cooperation with the British in such an operation—in other words—Stilwell.[6]

Stilwell, back in Chungking, told the Generalissimo of Wavell's plan for a limited offensive, making clear that Wavell had not promised that the British would make an amphibious attack on Rangoon. The Generalissimo said by February 1943 he would be ready to use some twenty divisions in the operations. But once again he said that this was only on condition that the Allied sea and air forces were present in strength to control the Bay of Bengal and prevent Japan from using the port of

---

ment of India. General Marshall discussed the problem with Marshal Sir John Dill, of the Joint Staff Mission to Washington. Dill explained that the government of India was not enthusiastic about the Ramgarh plan because it thought Chiang Kai-shek had been too close to Indian nationalist opinion, and feared that if there should be domestic trouble within India the Chinese might side with the Congress Party; and also because it did not relish the idea of the contrast between a Chinese army equipped by Lend-Lease supplies and Indian forces. Letters, Dill to Marshall, October 13th and 19th, Sunderland-Romanus manuscript, Vol. 1.

[6] As recounted later by Marshall in memo to the President, November 5, 1942, in Sunderland-Romanus manuscript, Vol. 1.

Rangoon. As recorded in Stilwell's notes for November 3rd, " 'Naval and air domination must be assured,' or he wouldn't move."

Stilwell's enthusiasm rose. It must be surmised that he felt the difference could somehow or other be resolved. A fortnight later, November 19th, after talking with the Chinese Board of Military Operation he was writing in his diary, "We're rolling. We have now gotten both the Limeys and the Chinese committed, and working at it. If we can keep a fire lit under Wavell and horn in on command and training on this side, the job is in a fair way to get done, bejesus. And since everybody said it was impossible, naturally I'm pulling for it hard."

Thus Stilwell came to believe—or came near believing—that he was going to be able to launch an extensive combined offensive in Burma in the spring of 1943. If in full scope, the object of that operation would be to recapture Rangoon and expel the Japanese from all of Burma. That is what Stilwell most wanted—an adequate port of entry through which enough supplies could be brought into China to restore it as a main theater of war. But if that was not possible, in partial scope the campaign would at least reopen a land route from India into China.

But Stilwell's ardent will was working against facts and attitudes which made the project unrealizable, if not unreal.

The Chinese were promising to go into full action only if the British gathered large naval forces in the Bay of Bengal and made an amphibious landing in the south of Burma. The British government still was not disposed to send out to this part of the world the three or four battleships, the six or eight aircraft carriers, and the troop landing vessels that would be needed. Its liking for a major effort to retake Burma in early 1943 was in reality as wan as before.

There was another unfaced difficulty. The only way to bring in oil, weapons, and ammunition for the fifteen Chinese divisions in Yunnan that were to move into Burma was by air transport over the Hump. If cargo space were used for that purpose, Chennault's air force would be compelled to restrict their operations. The Chinese did not want that to happen.

The American government was measuring strictly the means it was able or willing to provide for the Burma campaign. These would not be much. Stilwell, on November 24th, was brought up to date, and entered his opinion in his notebook. "From George Marshall: For our 'war,' we are graciously allotted (1) the Lend-Lease stuff we already have, (2) the personnel for training, (3) some engineer equipment, how much not known, (4) the 'increasing effectiveness of the ferry line.' My God. So that's the support we get to put on a campaign. I wonder what they gave them in Africa. Am I to comfort the Chinese with this prospect? . . ." With the grim humor which hard times evoked, he wrote home, "Peanut and I are on a raft, with one sandwich between us, and the rescue ship is heading away from the scene. They are too busy elsewhere for small fry like us, so we can go right ahead developing our characters and working on that shoestring I had presented to me."[7]

He told the War Department in blunt terms (in the answer which he sent back on the 28th) what he thought about this offer—ending in the statement that he was content if nothing could be done for him, but he would be greatly obliged if the War Department would not go on telling him of its intention of backing him to the limit.[8] The Chiefs of Staff and the Munitions Assignment Board had another quick look at its schedules, and thereupon expanded its offering of supplies, air support, and service forces. Marshall was ready to divert cargo vessels to bring Stilwell road building and other equipment, engineering and signal troops, and medical personnel. Six thousand American Army service troops were to be rushed out to the China-Burma-India Theater. On December 8th the President approved both the provisional plan for the Burma operation and the allocated modest means, giving them a high priority.

But the British still had their doubts, and the Chinese still maintained their demands. Wavell listed for the War Cabinet in London all the supply, transport, and medical problems which he faced, and questioned whether the Allies ought even to try to recapture North Burma in the coming spring. On December 17th he told Stilwell definitely that he did not see how he could maintain a campaign in Burma during the coming monsoon and that no amphibious landing against Rangoon would be possible before the next autumn. His mind was set on a far smaller and more restricted operation, which in fact he had already begun. He was skeptical of the value of the Yoke force.

The Generalissimo's anxiety about risking his troops also re-emerged in full vigor. He was not satisfied with the American participation. He was on notice that the British naval and amphibious operations would not be undertaken in the spring. He was becoming more attentive to the view advanced by General Chennault that a strenuous and costly land campaign in Burma was unneeded; that Japanese forces in China

[7] *The Stilwell Papers*, entry for November 26th and letter to Mrs. Stilwell, page 171.
[8] Sunderland-Romanus manuscript, Vol. I, citing message Stilwell to Timberman, November 28, 1942.

could first be weakened by attack from the air, and then crushed by converging assaults. Chennault's view of how Japan was to be beaten was like an easily opened fan: to drive the Japanese air force north of the Yangtze valley, then let the bombers cut Japanese sea routes to the south, and strike Japan proper as its aerial defense weakened; by these measures the Japanese forces in China and the Southwest Pacific would be cut off. Then the Chinese army, the American navy, and MacArthur's troops could defeat them at small cost.[9] All this Chennault thought could be done—or very well begun—with a relatively small force of fighters and bombers.[10] Thus he argued, and Chiang Kai-shek heard him gladly, that American and Chinese efforts should be concentrated on building up the American combat air force operation in China, and on expanding the transport route over the Hump, rather than on a land campaign to recapture Burma. This argument was to recur with increasing intensity, in a variety of military forms and forums during the coming months.[11]

On December 28th Chiang Kai-shek drew the issue firmly. He informed the President that while the Chinese forces would be ready in March to advance into Burma they would not do so unless the British threw themselves into the operations on sea as well as land. The President tried to keep the Generalissimo committed to some spring campaign in Burma if only a limited one. In his answer of January 2, 1943 he argued that it was more important for China that the Burma Road be opened than that the whole of Burma be reoccupied, and therefore Chinese efforts should not be delayed. He promised to discuss the situation at once with the highest Allied authorities. He did; the British answer remained the same: they did not have the necessary forces to undertake large fleet operations in the Bay of Bengal or any substantial amphibious attack either at the Andaman Islands or at Rangoon; and they would not be forced prematurely into these actions by Chiang Kai-shek.

The American government had no new inducement or assurance to offer the Generalissimo in the recommended venture. Chiang Kai-shek was not to be swayed; he refused to go ahead. He summarized his rea-

[9] As explained in a letter for the President which Chennault gave Wendell Willkie, October 8, 1942.

[10] As specified in the Willkie letter, one hundred and five fighters, thirty medium bombers, and twelve heavy bombers kept up to full strength. Later on, Chennault increased his estimates of force needed and supply requirements.

[11] When Stilwell had first presented his plan in July, Gauss had predicted that it could not be realized at that time, and had expressed the opinion that the most substantial contribution we could make to China then and there would be to increase the combat air force and air transport supply service.

sons in another message to the President (January 8th): that the Japanese were now well fortified in Burma and would fight obstinately; that the Chinese supply lines were not good enough; that the forces which the British intended to use were inadequate; that in order to be reasonably assured of success a combined land and sea-borne operation was essential; and that he could not risk defeat since another failure in Burma would be disastrous. Instead, he suggested a large early air offensive.

Stilwell's diary entry for that day, January 8th, is headed "Black Friday" and under it he wrote, "What a break for the Limeys. Just what they wanted. Now they will quit, and the Chinese will quit, and the god-dam Americans can go ahead and fight. Chennault's blatting has put us in a spot; he's talked so much about what he can do that now they are going to let him do it."

Again on January 9th the President urged Chiang Kai-shek to stay his final decision until he talked with Churchill, whom he was soon to meet [at Casablanca]. Chiang Kai-shek paused. He allowed Stilwell to work with what he had to improve the forces at Ramgarh and to struggle with the Yoke forces in Yunnan; and he waited until, as he had expressed it in his message to the President of January 8th, ". . . our Allies are ready."

The flaw in that attitude, it may be remarked, was that the Chinese were doing too little of what they could do for themselves. This failure, which prolonged itself, meant that the Chinese government later lacked the strength to play an important part in the defeat of Japan, and to take control of China after Japan was beaten. Stilwell's effort to arouse the Chinese government to realize what must be done, and why, is well set forth in one of the memos which he presented as Chief of Staff to the Generalissimo:

"This is our opportunity to equip and train a force that will make China strong and safe. The opportunity must be seized while the supply of weapons is available. If the first 30-Division Plan is carried out and the force used offensively, I will have a basis for demanding the equipment for another thirty divisions. . . .

"I recommend that the program for the Y-Force be pushed; that the concentration of the troops be expedited; that General Ch'en Ch'eng be relieved of all other duties at once; that any necessary changes in Armies for the Y-Force be made at once; that financial arrangements be authorized; and that the training program be approved. Also that the units of the second 30-Division Plan be designated; that their reorganization and re-equipping be started at an early date; and that a plan of training similar to that proposed for the first thirty divisions be adopted.

"If these things are done now, by next fall the first thirty divisions should be an efficient field force, and the second thirty divisions should be well advanced in tactical training. With a supply line open, both groups could be equipped promptly with their weapons, and from then on China would have nothing to fear from the Japanese. Without such a definite plan, there will be difficulty in continuing the present flow of supplies from the United States, let alone increasing it materially; as I am trying to do at present."[12]

The conferences at Casablanca were confirming the view that the Chinese government ought to understand the importance of making a singleminded, utmost effort to retrieve the situation in Burma, with what limited help could be given it right away.

[12] Memo, Stilwell for Generalissimo, 28 Jan. 1943. Stilwell Document, OCMH. This was prepared after discussions with Soong and General Chen, and in accord with Stilwell's communications with Marshall.

CHAPTER 6

How Best to Keep China in the War: The Dark
Winter of 1942-1943

Roosevelt and Churchill, their spirits high, shared the sunshine of Casablanca (January 14th-23rd) with their invading forces. Stalin had been asked to join them, but he had said he could not come because of the battle situation on the Eastern Front. Chiang Kai-shek had not been asked, and again he felt slighted. Stilwell had been trying to find a way of meeting his wish to share in main strategic decisions affecting China. He had suggested to Marshall that the Combined Chiefs of Staff form a subcommittee for Pacific operations, on which China would have a place. But it was judged that this would create more problems than it solved.

The American and British military staffs at Casablanca made a thorough survey of the whole war, theater by theater. In that totality the operations in China and Burma again fell into the distant ground. It was decided to give first call on Allied resources to the four connected segments of the fight against Germany: the air offensive, the Mediterranean campaign, support for Soviet forces, and assembly of a force for later invasion of Europe from the West. The essential means were to be provided with equal priority for a two-way advance across the Central Pacific and up from the Southwest toward the Philippines.[1]

Not much, compared with these other purposes, was assigned to the China-Burma-India Theater, but more than before; and the Chinese and British-Indian authorities were also called on to provide more. About the best strategy for that area, American military opinion was divided. The senior advisers disagreed as to whether or not to sanction during 1943 the large Burma campaign into which Stilwell had been seeking to shove the Allies. All accepted the fact that the means would not be available to start this action during the coming spring. Stilwell's schedule, already rejected by Chiang Kai-shek, was discarded. The new debated proposal looked toward action after the summer rains ended.

Marshall was strongly for the Burma campaign, so strongly that in one of the meetings of the Combined Chiefs of Staff (January 17th) he went so far as to say ". . . unless Operation Anakim [the Burma campaign] could be undertaken, he felt that a situation might arise in

[1] *The Army Air Forces in World War II*, Vol. IV, pages 131-134. Churchill in *The Hinge of Fate*, pages 692-693, gives a lucid summary of the main decisions.

the Pacific at any time that would necessitate the United States regretfully withdrawing from the commitments in the European Theater."[2] Admiral King was as ardent an advocate, being willing even to release precious landing and other naval craft from the South Pacific for the operations in the Bay of Bengal wanted by Chiang Kai-shek. But the airmen seemed to share Chennault's opinion that this arduous land campaign was unwise and unnecessary. Thus General Arnold, even after the Combined Chiefs had again approved the plans for the Burma campaign, told Hopkins that in his opinion ". . . the only intelligent move immediately is to strengthen Chennault's Air Force and get at the bombing of Japan as soon as possible."[3] Hopkins' judgment was of the same inclination.

In the upshot, the Combined Chiefs decided that this land battle to reopen a land route into China was essential. Roosevelt was satisfied; Churchill was blithely consenting. The plans which were approved visualized the full campaign—from two or three directions on land and from the sea in the south—target date the 15th of November. But the final decision as to whether actually to carry it through was deferred to the summer, not later than July. In the meanwhile the British were to go on with the small operations they were conducting in South Burma; and the air transport service over the Hump was to be expanded.

At the end of the conference cables were sent to Stalin and Chiang Kai-shek, telling them of these decisions. For the dual purposes of explaining the governing reasons to the Generalissimo, and of getting his assent to the plans for Burma and China, a special mission was hustled out to the East. General Henry H. Arnold, head of the Army Air Forces, accompanied by General Brehon B. Somervell, head of the Army Service Forces, and Marshal Sir John Dill of the British Joint Staff Mission, flew off for India and China. Arnold was carrying promises that we would quickly build up both the China Air Task Force and the air transport service over the Hump. Somervell was a firm believer in the necessity of reopening the Burma Road.

At New Delhi this mission talked with Wavell and Stilwell. The provisional Casablanca plans for action in Burma were, with slight revision, endorsed by all. The unsettled question was taken to be: would the Generalissimo authorize full Chinese participation? Arnold and Dill went up to Chungking to get him to do so. They found him far from

---

[2] Sunderland-Romanus manuscript, Vol. I.
[3] Hopkins' memo of talk with General Arnold January 19th, *Roosevelt and Hopkins*, Sherwood, page 681.

easy of mind. While willing to consider the projected Burma offensive, his real desire was to get more help for China right away. He asked that three things in particular be done at once. These were:

1. That the American air force in China should be made independent under Chennault.

2. That the air lift over the Hump be increased to ten thousand tons per month. Arnold patiently explained why this was not as easy as ordering a meal: there was a great shortage of transport planes in all theaters of war; the bases in both India and China were wholly inadequate; and the effort needed to provide the fuel and other supplies for such an air lift was very great. Such matters, Arnold found, "The Generalissimo and Chennault glossed over . . . with a wave of their hands. They could not, or would not, be bothered with logistics."[4]

3. That the American air force should have five hundred operative combat aircraft in China by November of that year. The Chinese air force could no longer be counted on even to defend Chungking against the Japanese attacks that would begin again in the fair spring weather; and the Americans would have to take on that job—another claim on Hump tonnage.

Having explained with real regret why these wishes could not be fully met at the time set, Arnold and Dill reaffirmed how much more the United States planned to do than it had been doing. The Generalissimo did not pretend to be satisfied. But he said he would join in with the Burma operation planned for the next November. At the end of the letter he sent off to Roosevelt on February 7th he wrote, "Finally I wish to assure you that in the combined plan of operation for the Burma Campaign . . . the Chinese army will be in readiness to perform its assigned task at the specified time without fail." Stilwell snorted to himself. He had been unable to get answers to his most recent urgent recommendations as to what must be done to get the Chinese armies in good combat shape.

Arnold and Dill stopped off at Calcutta on their way home for further talk with Soong and Wavell. At the end of their conferences, Wavell was enough pleased to sum up by saying, ". . . that all were in agreement, and it remained only for all to press on with the greatest possible energy their preparations to start the battle immediately after the monsoon."

Now the President, with the Arnold-Dill-Somervell report and Chiang

[4] *The Global Mission*, General Henry H. Arnold, 1949, page 419.

Kai-shek's letter of February 7th before him, was confronted more flatly by the clash of opinion among his advisers over the issues presented. He listened to Marshall and Stimson, and to Stilwell through them, and to Arnold, and to Harry Hopkins, and to Chennault directly and through Hopkins and Alsop, and to Madame Chiang Kai-shek.

Madame Chiang Kai-shek was making a tour of the eastern United States. During her long stay in Washington she talked to the President, Hopkins, Admiral Leahy, the American press, and both houses of Congress.[5] She allowed a hint of reproach to show itself in her public words, and of grudge in her private words. In the speech which she made to the Senate on the 18th, her point was brought out by a parable.

"One day we [the Generalissimo and herself] went into the Heng-Yang Mountains, where there are traces of a famous pavilion called 'Rub-the-Mirror' Pavilion. . . .

"Two thousand years ago near that spot was an old Buddhist temple. One of the young monks was there, and all day long he sat cross-legged with his hands clasped before him in an attitude of prayer, and murmured 'Amita-Buddha! Amita-Buddha! Amita-Buddha!' He murmured and chanted day after day, because he hoped that he would acquire grace.

"The Father Prior of that temple took a piece of brick and rubbed it against a stone hour after hour, day after day, and week after week. This little acolyte, being very young, sometimes cast his eyes around to see what the old Father Prior was doing. The old Father Prior just kept on his work of rubbing the brick against the stone. So one day the young acolyte said to him, 'Father Prior, what are you doing day after day rubbing this brick on the stone?'

"The Father Prior replied, 'I am trying to make a mirror out of this brick.' The young acolyte said, 'But it is impossible to make a mirror out of a brick, Father Prior.' 'Yes,' said the Father Prior, 'It is just as impossible for you to acquire grace by doing nothing except "Amita-Buddha" all day long, day in and day out.'

". . . And so to you, gentlemen of the Senate, and to you ladies and gentlemen in the galleries, I say that without the active help of all of us our leaders cannot implement these ideals. It is up to you and to me to take to heart the lesson of the 'Rub-the-Mirror pavilion.'"

The President gave Madame Chiang Kai-shek every chance to explain her thoughts and feelings. To Hopkins, whom she knew to be sympathetic, she stressed the wish for planes and made blunt references to

---

[5] During her visit, she and Soong did not work closely together, and she avoided joint talks and occasions.

various past unfulfilled promises. She also urged that China be included in the talks regarding the settlements after the war. Hopkins received the impression that, despite the gush of public acclaim and the applause in Congress, Madame Chiang Kai-shek was not altogether happy about her visit, not overimpressed by the promises she received, "tired and a little dispirited."[6]

Dissenting as he rarely did from the recommendations of his Chief of Staff, Roosevelt acceded to Chiang Kai-shek's pleading. He engaged the American government to make a much greater effort in the air for and in China—as rapidly as the greater number of planes could be handled there. At the same time, however, he reaffirmed the opinions of the War Department: that air transport and air combat alone would not be enough to strike a vital blow at Japanese forces in China or Japan, and that it was essential to reopen a land route through Burma. He asked the Generalissimo to regard this as the most necessary task before them and to do all he could to carry through the campaign which had been put on the calendar at Casablanca. The United States would, this message continued, soon send to India ten thousand service troops and twenty-five thousand tons of equipment to augment the forces building the road through Burma. The first section of the road—from Ledo, in the Indian province of Assam, into North Burma—had already been begun, and it was planned to carry it along toward the frontier of China just as fast as the Japanese could be driven back.

The President wrote a letter to Marshall explaining his course. In this he questioned whether the War Department was giving enough weight to the damage that could be done to Japan by an increased air effort in China; and he clearly hinted that he felt Stilwell was acting unwisely in his dealings with Chiang Kai-shek. Marshall's defensive answer holds interest in the light of future events. He said that he would impress upon Stilwell that he must give all the help he could to Chennault and all practical latitude in operations. He then proceeded to expound again the views of the War Department as to what tasks should be put first in China. He observed that the problem of providing by air transport enough supplies to allow Chennault greatly to expand operations would be tremendous; and the risk of expanding them until the Chinese army was strong enough to protect the bases would be great. In his words, ". . . the problem which we will face later in continuous air operations is ground protection for the China airdromes we use,

---

[6] *Roosevelt and Hopkins*, Sherwood, page 706.

as well as for the air freight route. We must build for that now. *Here is the most serious consideration*: [Marshall's italics] as soon as our air effort hurts the Japs, they will move in on us, not only in the air but also on the ground. The air situation Chennault can take care of with his fighters, but the ground effort against our bases must be met by men on the ground. . . . Ground protection for our airdromes in China and the terminals of the air transport route must come from the Chinese army."

These were the reasons, Marshall continued, why it was essential for any large sustained and protected air effort in China, (1) to have dependable and well-trained units in the Chinese army and (2) to reopen the land supply route through Burma, for which also qualified army units would be needed. And, he continued, these were the main factors in Stilwell's strategy and activity. In his efforts to induce the Chinese government to create a force that could be depended on for these two essential tasks, he had met obstruction, delay, and a disposition on the part of the Chinese leaders to let others do their fighting. His sense of urgency about these essentials, along with his knowledge of the present low combat value of the Chinese army, have driven him to talk very plainly to the Generalissimo. He was tough, but only such a man, Marshall thought, would have survived the Burma campaign, battered down the British-Indian sluggish resistance to all our plans, and made some headway with the reorganization of the Chinese forces.[7]

A message from Stilwell (which Marshall passed on to the President), reporting on a visit to Kunming, underscored these points. The Chungking government, Stilwell found, could not or would not enforce its orders in Yunnan. The impression that had been created in the United States about the Chinese military effort, he noted, was entirely false. The Chinese army in reality was ". . . in desperate condition, underfed, unpaid, untrained, neglected, and rotten with corruption. . . . If we can train and equip the Yunnan force we can save the situation, but I may have to call for backing in case a showdown is necessary. You may think a year of this has had its effect on me. My opinion of the Chinese people and the Chinese soldier is unchanged. It is the gang of army 'leaders' that is the cause of all our grief."[8]

As a military problem the question of how best to help China at this

[7] Memo, Marshall for President, March 16, 1943. Sunderland-Romanus manuscript, Vol. I.

[8] Message, Stilwell to Marshall, March 15, 1943. Sunderland-Romanus manuscript, Vol. I.

stage was most complex. It required judgment of facts hard to determine, and an estimate of risks and advantages that were conjectural; the further exposition of these must be left to those who have studied them more fully. Bearing more and more demandingly on the decision was fear of the collapse of the Chinese government and of the Chinese will to fight on. Whatever aspect of the China situation incoming reports from both the Embassy and the Chinese representatives in Washington dealt with, they described it as miserable and growing worse. As Hornbeck remarked in a memo that he wrote on April 3rd, "The Chinese are thinking with their eyes, their hands, their feet, their tired bodies, and their empty pocketbooks rather than with their ears." The news from China seemed clearly to mean that victories and benefits which would require more waiting and struggle were at a discount; and if the American government wanted Chinese resistance to continue, it had better favor such measures as might bring quick relief.

The State Department during this period did what little it could to secure more regard for China's claims for military help. The staff concerned with Far Eastern Affairs tried by word and memo to keep whomever they could reach reminded of the needs of China and its grounds for complaint. So Maxwell Hamilton, head of the Far Eastern Division, in one of the memos he sent forward during February, warned that ". . . The Chinese are becoming increasingly disappointed and resentful at the lack of military aid; some Chinese spokesmen are beginning to talk of the possibility of China ceasing to be an active belligerent; and question whether China will, unless helped, continue to resist Japan."

In this mood during this winter of 1942-1943, the State Department intoned gloom. It gave the impression of dull didacticism. It was crowded out, and it vaguely knew it. Secretary Hull had limited knowledge of, and less share in, the decisions about Far Eastern military matters. These decisions were being made by the military departments, in close touch with the President and his circle, particularly Hopkins, Leahy, and Currie. Whether restrained by pride from seeking a more active part, or whether just as well satisfied not to be involved in these sharp decisions, the Secretary of State made no complaint. His daily mood was darkened by the cold shadow that had come between him and the Under-Secretary, Sumner Welles. His spirit seemed attracted more and more toward general ideas about how to make the world better after the war; and to retreat from the crude contests over the conduct of the war.

But in the traditional diplomatic sphere Hull carried through one notable action. The United States, along with other countries, had preserved some special extraterritorial rights in China. These—particularly the maintenance of International Settlements at Shanghai and Amoy and the administration and control of the Diplomatic Quarters at Peiping—had long been resented by the Chinese as a mark of imposed inferiority. Hull decided that there was no better way within his power of showing our recognition of full Chinese freedom and equality than by arranging to give up these privileges. The British government—which had a greater historic part than we in the development of this system of special rights—was brought to agree. Then with skill and patience Hull negotiated a treaty with the Republic of China, giving them up. This treaty was signed on January 11, 1943.[9] The Senate approved it unanimously.[10] Some of the rights voluntarily yielded we had held for almost a century. The American government hoped that this act would be convincing proof that we were ready not only to accord China full sovereignty but help her to maintain it; and that it would remove the last vestige of the accusation that the United States was pursuing in China selfish or imperialist ends.

The action was duly noted and hailed in China and outside. Chiang Kai-shek, on the occasion of signing the treaty, issued a statement to China's armed forces and people, which read, "Today marks a new epoch in Chinese history and by their action our Allies have declared their Pacific War aim to sustain the rule of human decency and human right—and prove their high ideals and lofty purposes. . . . With abolition of the unequal treaties, an independent China on equal footing with Great Britain and the United States has become a real friend of those two nations. . . . Henceforth if we are weak, if we lack self-confidence, the fault will be ours." The Chinese press acclaimed the treaty as the end of one hundred years of humiliation, and as realization of the aim of the national revolution.

But it was no cure for the woes which were besetting the Chinese people. Diplomacy could not manage that, only force of arms.

[9] The British and Chinese governments signed a similar treaty on the same day.

[10] The text of the treaty and accompanying notes are printed in the *United States Relations with China*, pages 514-519.

CHAPTER 7

For the Relief of the Siege of China:
The Argument Prolonged

THE Generalissimo had asked Roosevelt to call Chennault back to Washington, so that he might hear for himself the prospects for air action in China. The President did so, asking Stilwell to return at the same time to discuss Anakim. He was awaiting the arrival of Churchill and the British Chiefs of Staff to settle, among other matters, how far and fast to go with the plans for Burma and China which had been formulated at Casablanca.

Stilwell and Chennault arrived in Washington at the end of April. The President and the Joint Chiefs of Staff listened to their views and arguments. They were reading at the same time the keyed-up messages which the Generalissimo kept sending through Soong and Madame Chiang Kai-shek. His pleas were a clatter that could not be ignored. Stilwell presented his case with what some witnesses took to be stiff reserve, others a sullen rudeness. Even Stimson had the feeling that he was showing the effects of his experience in Burma, and that, while he was incisive as always, he needed a good rest. Chennault pressed his claims for the air program with a faith that had not been cooled by previous disappointments. He stressed two somewhat new points in his talks: (1) that the route of the proposed new Burma road was much harder than the old; at both ends it would have to be built across high mountains, while the older one had·turned south and west through the valleys to Rangoon; (2) that the Japanese would not be able to capture Kunming by land attack from Indo-China; to do so they would have to cross mountains, and his air force would repel them. The Japanese, he said, needing the rivers and the railways, had never been able to advance more than one hundred miles against land obstacles.

The President, with one ear turned to Chungking, bent further in the direction in which he had been leaning, but not as far as the Generalissimo was now asking him to bend—as marked in the note which Soong delivered to the President on April 29th. That began, "I am instructed by the Generalissimo that after careful consideration he has concluded all resources must be concentrated in the immediate future on launching an air offensive in China. Specifically, after weighing the various claims, he now desires that the entire air transport tonnage during the months of May, June and July be devoted to carrying into China gasoline and aviation supplies, in order to build up the required reserves for decisive offensive action. . . ."

Any such measure, Stilwell had been arguing, would mean decisive delay in equipping the troops in Yunnan that were, in accordance with the plan agreed on during the Arnold-Dill visit, to take the offensive in Burma in the coming November. Chiang Kai-shek in his note denied the objection. "Such a concentration of present resources on the air effort need not," he wrote, "interfere with the program of ground action. . . . The capacity of the air transport line into China is planned to expand very rapidly; and as this expansion occurs, all needed ground supplies may also be carried into China in ample time to be on hand when called for. . . ."

The strands of argument are the more twisted because it was Chennault who at this time was most alert to the danger of an imminent Japanese advance against the American air bases. As far back as the 22nd of February he had warned Stilwell that he thought that the Japanese would soon start a major offensive in China, which might even go on to the main American airfields in East China; and had then stated his belief that ". . . the Japanese cannot obtain their military objectives if opposed by an effective air force. It is assumed that the Chinese Ground Armies will offer resistance similar to that offered in previous years and that, given support of an effective air force, they will be able to block the Japanese advances in the directions indicated."[1] Chiang Kai-shek now in substance reaffirmed this opinion. "The Generalissimo wishes me [Soong] to transmit to you his personal assurance that in the event the enemy attempts to interrupt the air offensive by a ground advance on the air bases, the advance can be halted by the existing Chinese forces."

On May 3rd Roosevelt decided that General Chennault should be authorized to go ahead with his program without delay. When he told Marshall of his intention, the Chief of Staff again warned him of the danger that if a premature attempt was made from China to bomb Japan or her important shipping lines, the Japanese would wipe out our bases. But the President accepted the risk, telling Marshall that he felt that "politically he must support Chiang Kai-shek and that in the state of Chinese morale the air program was therefore of great importance."[2] Roosevelt did not mean to give up the idea of starting operations in

[1] Letter, Chennault to Stilwell, February 22, 1943. Sunderland-Romanus manuscript, Vol. I.
[2] Memo, Marshall for Stilwell, May 3, 1943. *Ibid.*

Burma in the autumn. He thought he could get the Generalissimo to agree that enough of the tonnage coming over the Hump should be allocated to the Yunnan force, so that it might continue preparations for that campaign.

Roosevelt did not tell Chiang Kai-shek of these decisions at once. He waited to consult with the British leaders who were on their way to Washington for the conferences called in the war glossary, Trident. He wanted them also to have the chance to hear both Stilwell and Chennault. Our Allies were still seeing the Chinese area of combat only out of the corner of their eyes.

Stalin was at this juncture most bluntly urging that the Americans and British establish a second front in Europe before the summer was out. He was taking every chance to tell them that he thought they were called on to disregard all else. His aggrieved impatience showed in every message that he sent to Roosevelt and Churchill. Thus, on February 16th he had as much as told the President that he did not think American efforts to end the campaign in Tunis were adequate, and complained that as a result of the continuation of that campaign the second front would not be opened until August or September. ". . . It is very important, in my opinion, that the blow from the west should not be postponed until the second half of the year, but that it should be delivered this spring or at the beginning of the summer." Roosevelt had answered, denying that there had been any suspension of the campaign in Tunisia. Stalin had brushed aside the denial, asserting that the American and British failure to do more was allowing the transfer of thirty-six German divisions against the Soviet army. He had found Roosevelt's statements vague and said that Churchill's message in regard to the opening of the second front in France "provokes alarm which I cannot suppress."

In short, the American and British governments during this spring of 1943, when measuring what combat aid or resources they might devote to China, had to weigh the chance that Russian resistance might falter. Simultaneous demands from within the American military organization were hardly less obstinate than those of Stalin. General MacArthur's headquarters in the South Pacific wanted to make and take its chance to begin to push the Japanese out of the Southwestern Pacific. The navy and air force commanders were all eager to extend operations in the Southern and Central Pacific. Each American branch of action fought for all it could get from the Joint Chiefs of Staff and the Munitions Assignment Board, in the spirit recalled by General Kenney: ". . . representatives of both the Southern and Central Pacific areas were watching the situation very closely to see that, if anything was passed out, they would get their share of it before MacArthur's crowd from the Southwestern Pacific grabbed it off."[3]

The British, it became plainer than ever at Trident, did not want to devote to the campaigns in China and Burma effort and resources for which there was great need elsewhere. They were not greatly worried over a possible breakdown of the war effort there or its political consequences. Churchill has given a lively account of his reflections on these subjects while at sea on his way to Washington.[4] In flattened summary they were: at Casablanca a provisional date, November 1943, had been fixed for an assault in Burma, subject to review of forces available in July; but two of the preparatory measures that had been attempted— particularly the advance on Akyab—had come to little; thus it seemed to him clear beyond argument that the full Anakim operation could not be attempted in the winter of 1943-1944. The Americans, he foresaw, would be disappointed since "The President and his circle still cherished exaggerated ideas of the military power which China could exert if given sufficient arms and equipment . . . [and] feared unduly the imminence of a Chinese collapse. . . . I disliked," his thought continued, "thoroughly the idea of reconquering Burma by an advance along the miserable communications in Assam. I hated jungles—which go to the winner anyway —and thought in terms of air-power, sea-power, amphibious operations, and key points. It was however an essential to all our great business that our friends should not feel we had been slack in trying to fulfill the Casablanca plans and be convinced that we were ready to make the utmost exertions to meet their wishes."[5] But his thought was roving away from action in Burma or along the Burma coast. He and his military advisers wished to use elsewhere the large forces standing in India and such British naval and amphibious resources as they might be able to send to the East. They thought more could be done and more safely by starting operations against the tip of Sumatra and the waist of Malaya at Penang.[6]

[3] General Kenney Reports, pages 211-213.

[4] The Hinge of Fate, Book 2, Chapter 20.

[5] In a long paper which Churchill prepared on the same voyage he developed his feeling about fighting in jungles, "Going into swampy jungles to fight the Japanese is like going into the water to fight a shark. It is better to entice him into a trap or catch him on a hook and then demolish with axes after hauling him out onto dry land. How then to deceive and entrap the shark?" Ibid., pages 785-786.

[6] This was the trend of the statement that Churchill made in opening the discussions of the Trident Conference in Washington before the Combined Chiefs of Staff on May 12th.

The American Chiefs of Staff—especially Marshall and King—once again upheld the position that the campaign to recapture Burma was essential, and that the means for it could and should be provided.[7] The consequent argument was marked by a rampageous rift in regard to the best way to use the tonnage flown in over the Hump. Stilwell and Chennault appeared before the Combined Chiefs of Staff. Once again in this debate Stilwell was short of temper.[8] Chennault, in contrast, was quietly assured.[9]

On the 17th, Soong told the Combined Chiefs of Staff that China would make a separate peace with Japan unless adequate measures were taken to relieve it and carry out the promises made after Casablanca. He stressed the point that since the Generalissimo was in supreme command in the China Theater his wishes should prevail.[10] On the next day, without waiting for the conference to formulate its final decisions, the President told Soong that Chiang Kai-shek's most urgent requests would be met: Chennault's air force would be given a substantial guaranteed minimum tonnage over the Hump; and urgent measures would be taken to see that the total tonnage over that route was brought to ten thousand tons a month or more by September. It had been of recent months far below this figure, which Roosevelt had previously accepted as a target, and had actually tumbled from about thirty-two hundred tons in February to about twenty-five hundred in April.

The program resolved on by the Combined Chiefs of Staff on May 20th gave high priority to the increase of air transport into China. Chennault was to have the bulk of the freight for his extended air operations.[11] But Stilwell's Burma offensive was kept on the schedule for the end of the monsoon in the fall, with coordinated amphibious operations

---

[7] Admiral King was as confirmed and stubborn an advocate of Stilwell's strategy and believer in his qualities as Marshall. He too was impressed by the potential part that vast Chinese manpower, if equipped and well led, could play in the defeat of Japan. His arguments with Churchill and others at this Trident Conference are recounted in *Fleet Admiral King, A Naval Record*, page 436.

[8] At a later plenary session he seems to have thought that he did not get an adequate chance to speak his piece. *The Stilwell Papers*, undated entry, page 205.

[9] As expressed in *The Army Air Force in World War II*, Vol. IV, page 442, "He had no fear that the Japanese might capture American bases in China, and he looked forward to a successful aerial offensive preparing the way for an Allied landing on the China Coast."

[10] Summary minutes meeting, Combined Chiefs of Staff, May 17, 1943. Sunderland-Romanus manuscript, Vol. I.

[11] Rough division of the tonnage during the months ahead assigned to Chennault priority of the first forty-seven hundred and fifty tons of transport space across the Hump; the next twenty-two hundred and fifty tons were assigned to Stilwell for equipping the Chinese ground forces and other purposes. All in excess, if there was an excess, was to be divided.

now limited to two small coastal actions. The execution of this dual program was dependent on achieving the large and fast increase of transport capacity over the Hump which Roosevelt had promised. Even if the planes and men could be found for this effort, the desired result would not be obtained unless much greater effort was made in India. Stimson went into that element of the problem thoroughly with Churchill, who said that he was not satisfied with the actions of his commanders in India and Burma, and that he was going to change them and see that punch was put into the effort.

In the messages which Roosevelt and Churchill sent Chiang Kai-shek, telling him of their decisions, they assured him that "No limits, except those imposed by time and circumstance, will be placed on the above operations which have for their object the relief of the siege of China." That Chiang Kai-shek was not persuaded by these promises to engage himself definitely to the Trident program was shown by his response on May 29th to the message sent by Roosevelt and Churchill. It was a list of queries. He asked whether the British had promised to engage its navy in support of joint action in the Andaman Sea. Would the United States give naval support also, and how many divisions would it provide? Were the British determined to take Rangoon? He again voiced his fear that unless the attack in North Burma was synchronized with amphibious operations in the south, it would be exposed to defeat.[12]

The President was quick to see the new cracks in the plaster that had been set at Trident. He tried to find a personal adhesive. Late in June he suggested to the Generalissimo that they should get together soon, "at some place midway between our two capitals" during the autumn.[13] The Generalissimo answered that he would welcome such a meeting as early as August or September.

Admiral Leahy, Generals Marshall and Somervell were called to the White House to discuss whether the whole direction of our operations in China should not be changed. The President told them that he was greatly dissatisfied with the way in which the show was going. He was displeased by Stilwell's obvious hate of the Generalissimo and of other Chinese leaders, and the Generalissimo's kindred feeling for Stilwell.

---

[12] The American government was aware that it was not yet clear whether needed landing craft and British naval vessels for the Indian Ocean would be available by November in view of operations in Europe at the time being discussed with the British.

[13] *Roosevelt and Hopkins*, Sherwood, page 739.

He was on the verge of ordering his recall. Marshall's and Stimson's defense dissuaded him.

Stilwell was chafing under the adverse treatment of his views at Trident. He had confided to his notes, "At the same time they decided on Saucy [the new code name for the modified Burma operation] they made it practically impossible for me to prepare the Y force, and then ordered it used in an offensive."[14] But he went on with the effort, still visualizing an advance into Burma from three directions, with a promise of some naval strength in the Bay of Bengal and American and British commando participation. His determination to prepare the men and preserve the means for these operations led again to a tussle with Chiang Kai-shek. A Japanese force was then advancing up the Yangtze. The Generalissimo and his military advisers were afraid it might continue to Chungking. They ordered that troops, weapons, and ammunition assigned for the Yoke force be diverted. Stilwell's disgust is recorded in his notes (June 28th). ". . . Words fail on this one; not only does he [the Minister of War] fail in his own duty but beyond that he obstructs all my efforts to build them up, and crowns it by trying to take away what we have so painfully accumulated."[15]

Chennault was enjoying his new freedom and scope of action. By arrangement from this time on he kept in touch with the White House through letters to the President and Hopkins. His first reports after his return to China on the first phases of his operation were as buoyant as ever. The Japanese advance, which the Generalissimo had feared, had been halted. Chennault shared in the widely diffused version that the Chinese armies had gained an important victory by sturdy fighting. He wrote to the President on June 18th, "I believe that this campaign bears out my statement that the Japanese are unable to supply an offensive effort capable of penetrating more than one hundred miles into the interior of China in any area where they are unable to bring up supplies and reinforcements by water."[16]

But during the following weeks the air offensive did not progress or succeed as well as he had forecast. The 14th Air Force did not get either the planes or equipment as fast as promised in May. For this and other reasons, operations could not be expanded as fast as planned. The air force did not win undisputed control of the air in China, nor did it destroy great amounts of Japanese shipping. Both Chennault and Chiang Kai-shek were ready to think Stilwell was at fault.

[14] *The Stilwell Papers*, pages 204-205. [15] *The Stilwell Papers*, entry, June 28, 1943.
[16] Letter, Chennault to the President, June 18, 1943.

Despite these strains, the program that had been approved at Trident went forward—slowly and unevenly, but still forward. On July 12th Chiang Kai-shek at last notified the President that he consented to it. In doing so he again expressed the hope that the United States would send strong ground units to join in the operations from the India side; and he also indicated that he was counting on British land and naval forces to secure command of the Bay of Bengal and to get control of the Burma coast. Stilwell headed his notes for that day, "Red Letter Day," and then wrote, "The answer came from Peanut to the Combined Chiefs of Staff Saucy proposals. In *writing*. And *signed*. After a year of constant struggle, we have finally nailed him down."[17]

But in reality the plan as drawn at Trident and approved by Chiang Kai-shek was still conditional, loose, and easily fractured. It was conditional in several ways: on the attainment after many failures of the needed air transport capacity over the Hump; upon the course of the war elsewhere in the world; on the capabilities of the Chinese armies. It was loose in the sense that execution of each part was connected with the rest. Thus each of the participants could wait on the others to play their part before it played its own. It was easily fractured because the several planned actions were in competition for resources not readily available in amounts sufficient for all.[18] In sum, there *still* was not a solidly supported, coordinated plan of operations to break the siege of China.

[17] *The Stilwell Papers*, entry, July 12, 1943.
[18] Rival claims compounded themselves as the summer and autumn went on. If adequate road and railroad capacity, construction and engineering forces, and raw materials were used to make the needed air bases in Assam, it appeared that there would not be enough to carry the Ledo Road forward. If needed transport, rail, and air capacity were used to bring in supplies and stocks for the Yunnan and other Chinese ground forces, it became likely that the 14th Air Force would have to defer its offensive. If the Burma campaign were given the required air support, the combat air action in China and against Japanese shipping would, it transpired, have to be curtailed. The task of more fully exploring and explaining this overload of plans as compared with firmly allocated and ready resources is deeded to the military historians.

CHAPTER 8

Further Plans and Discords: The Later Months of 1943

THE need for coordinated strategy became clear when Roosevelt and Churchill met again in the middle of August at Quebec. By then the Italian government had surrendered, yielding open mastery of the Mediterranean to the Allies. The Soviet armies were pounding the Germans back. The outlook seemed so promising that the military planners began to take into account the possibility that Germany would be defeated before the end of 1944. The conference (known as Quadrant) determined that the main effort should still be kept centered on that decisive aim; May 1944 was confirmed as the target date for the invasion of France. While the Allies were waiting for the final victory in Europe—which would allow great transfers of forces to the Pacific—it was agreed that bolder attacks should be made against the line of islands held by the Japanese in the central and southwestern Pacific.

On all this the Americans and the British agreed with ease. But as before, when they turned to consider what next should be done in China and South Asia, they found themselves somewhat at odds. Churchill's ideas, always in evolution, seemed to give even less heed than before to the reasons for an all-out Burma campaign. He and his military colleagues thought the landings and incursions along the coast of Burma and into South Burma demanded by Chiang Kai-shek were only ". . . the future right to toil through the swamps and jungles of Burma. . ." In a minute which he sent on August 20th to the British Chiefs of Staff, he reminded them of his position: "I remain absolutely where I was at the last Conference, and where we all were, that a campaign through Rangoon up the Irrawaddy to Mandalay and beyond would be most detrimental and disadvantageous to us."[1] Further, by then he felt free to express his belief, kept in restraint by his wish to work with us, that the recapture of Burma was not necessary to defeat Japan. The best way to do that, he contended, would be by sea power and air power from the sea.

This view of how best to use Allied power in the war against Japan was shared in greater or less degree by some American military commanders. But it would have left China isolated for an indefinite time.

[1] Winston Churchill, *Closing the Ring*, page 88.

Meanwhile the Chinese armies would remain on the defensive, and the British-Indian forces would be idle unless used to land in Sumatra, as Churchill urged. The President, in accord with the Joint Chiefs of Staff, once again maintained sturdily that more had to be done right away in and for China; and that it was essential quickly to secure both a land route into China via India and Burma, and a sea entry into Burma for China. He argued also that air bases in China, if not essential to bring about the ultimate defeat of Japan, would at least be most valuable.[2]

Again the American views were accorded formal deference. The conference resolved on a group of connected actions including (1) operations for the capture of Upper Burma—the target date now put off to mid-February, 1944; (2) preparation for smallish amphibious actions in the spring of 1944; (3) enlargement of the air route into China and air supplies for China and the development of air facilities in India and China.

Roosevelt and Churchill notified Chiang Kai-shek directly of the gist of their conclusions. Soong had been invited to Quebec, but had not been in on the formal discussions. He had a chance to talk at intervals with Hull and Eden and to learn what he could about the military decisions. At the end of the conference he was told of the main points and principles of the Final Report, particularly of the planned operations in the region of China.[3] But he was put on notice by Sir Alan Brooke, liaison for the British Chiefs of Staff, that the date of the Burma operation was not yet fixed and that the size of the British air forces was also not settled. Soong asked him what amphibious operations were to be carried out. Brooke's answer left the British much leeway: "It was to take place from India and would have a direct bearing on operations in Burma and Western China." Marshall and Leahy emphasized that the colossal effort ahead was dependent on the trustful cooperation of the Chinese force, and on unity of action by India, Britain, and China, with no one holding back.

The meeting at Quebec also approved an important change in the command arrangement for Southeast Asia. A new command was estab-

[2] General Arnold had submitted a plan for the reduction of Japan by bombardment to be conducted from bases in East China and increasing in scale until ultimately using all the heavy bombers of the United Nations.

[3] The main sections of the Final Report of the Combined Chiefs approved by the President and Prime Minister on August 23rd are printed in Appendix A, *Report to the Combined Chiefs of Staff*, by the Supreme Allied Commander South East Asia 1943-1945, Vice-Admiral the Earl Mountbatten of Burma, His Majesty's Stationery Office, 1951, London. This source will hereafter be cited as Mountbatten, *Report*.

lished, the Southeast Asia Command (SEAC). This, as conceived, was to exercise control over all Allied forces in Burma, Malaya, Sumatra, Ceylon. India was not included, but its command was directed to give all the help it could to the planned operations in the other areas. China was left as a separate theater with the Generalissimo as Supreme Commander, and the United States Joint Chiefs of Staff in charge of Allied strategy.

Lord Louis Mountbatten was named Supreme Allied Commander of the SEAC. Stilwell was appointed his Deputy Chief Commander, while remaining in direct charge of the Chinese troops in Burma and of the American ground and air forces in Southeast Asia. This designation made Stilwell's lines of engagement more involved than ever. His comment in his notes was unusually relaxed, "The East Asia Command is set up . . . Mountbatten at the top. I am deputy and have to kid the Peanut into using the boys. But George [Marshall] is leaving me in command of all U.S. troops, air and ground. The command setup is a Chinese puzzle, with Wavell [elevated to Viceroy of India], Auk [Auchinleck, Commander-in-Chief in India], Mountbatten, Peanut [Chiang Kai shek], Alexander and me interwoven and mixed beyond recognition."[4]

The Generalissimo was told of the new arrangement. He made no objection except on one point: he wished Indo-China and Siam to remain within his own command. It was agreed that both he and SEAC would have the right to operate in these countries.

Once again the Americans, British, and Chinese seemed to have agreed on an extended plan of action for and in China. A prospect seemed confirmed that before long China's troubles would be relieved and its fighting chances restored. The following months were given over to a harried attempt to provide the required means to bring them into place. During this period American forces—aviation, construction, engineering and supply—were rushed to India. There they worked hard to reduce physical obstacles and human lethargy so that there might be enough transport capacity for the projected movements. The American combat air force in China and the American air transport force took on bigger, more tiring, and more dangerous tasks.

Stilwell kept up his agitation to get the Chinese forces in shape. He was by then wholly convinced that the only way to deal with the Chinese government was to bargain toughly; to provide it with aid only on terms that would assure that it did what was wanted of it. The Gen-

[4] *The Stilwell Papers*, page 218.

eralissimo gave assent to many of his proposals in regard to the formation and schooling of the army. But often the results that followed were small. The wish to get rid of Stilwell became more lively. The Chinese around Chiang Kai-shek were hurt by his blunt way of dismissing their ideas, of treating as trivial matters that meant much to them. They felt reduced in standing and in face by his directness, and wounded by his epithets. Moreover, they regarded his opposition as the dam which was holding back American aid.

The friction was given a fresh rub when on September 6th, in connection with a diversionary attack in the north which he wanted the Generalissimo to make in order to prevent the Japanese from starting a new campaign in the Yangtze valley, Stilwell suggested that the 18th Group Army (Communist) be used along with the National forces. Such a combined movement under the direction of the Generalissimo would, he advised, reduce the danger to Chungking and the American air bases. His letter to Chiang Kai-shek on the subject concluded "I recommend that this plan be adopted, that the troops in the Northwest be given sufficient supplies to put it into effect. . . . At the worst it costs nothing in troops and little in supplies, it makes use of units that are otherwise idle, and it will make plain the degree of reliability of the forces in the Northwest [Communists]. If we do not move, the Japs will."[5] This proposal was at the time quickly passed over, but remembered in later days of anger.[6]

The strain between Stilwell and many of the Chinese leaders was becoming distinctly personal. But the basic subject and cause of their mutual dissatisfaction was not personal. Purposes were focused differently in Washington and Chungking. American intent was centered on the wish to win the war as quickly as possible. To this end the American government sought to apply all the human effort and resources of the United States and expected China to do the same. But the reckonings of the Chinese government were diffused. The worldwide war against the Axis had to be won. But while it was being won the Chiang Kai-shek regime wanted to be sure that it would survive in power. It was convinced that the maintenance of its position was essential for an orderly and unified China after the war. Hence it was afraid to take military chances; the loss of the capital, Chungking, might mean the end

[5] Stilwell memo to Chiang Kai-shek, September 6, 1943. Sunderland-Romanus manuscript, Vol. I.

[6] According to the entry in the Stilwell diary for October 5, 1943, Madame Chiang Kai-shek told Stilwell he "was in Dutch over the Northwest proposal." Sunderland-Romanus manuscript, Vol. I.

of the government, no matter what victories might be won elsewhere. It was afraid of making demands which might cause local military commanders and politicians to desert; and afraid of offending elements within the Kuomintang by radical measures of reform. Never out of mind was the knowledge that up north the Communists were waiting their chance to extend themselves and gain power; the government was determined they should not get it.

Stilwell and measuring minds in the War and State Departments were disturbed by the way in which these anxieties deflected and reduced the effort that China might be making in the war. Not only that, by giving in to these fears the Generalissimo was making mistakes, they thought, which, if not corrected, would bring about the very overturn he feared. In their view, the eventual political influence and power both of the Generalissimo's regime and of China would be only as firm, and no firmer, than the military force they commanded; and Chiang Kai-shek was failing to use our help to create an adequate force. Stilwell marked that point clearly at the end of a memo which he gave to the General-issimo on September 29th: "The manifesto of the Central Executive Committee of the Kuomintang states that 'It is China's responsibility to undertake the major operations on the East Asiatic continent.' This will be impossible without a thorough reorganization. With it, China will be able to do her part and refute her critics, and will emerge at the end of the war with the means of assuring her stability."[7]

Stilwell for the first time had turned to the American Embassy in Chungking for aid. Ambassador Gauss was still in the United States. General Hearn, Stilwell's Chief of Staff, called on George Atcheson, who was in charge of the Embassy. He explained the many reasons why he and Stilwell were disturbed. Hearn had asked the Embassy to inter-cede, not on Stilwell's personal behalf, but to help him get done what he thought had to be done. Hearn suggested also that the President and Churchill might send messages to Chiang Kai-shek to embolden him, by assuring him that they were determined to fight through by China's side.

Atcheson had agreed with this sense of the situation. He transmitted approvingly to Washington the idea that special messages be sent to the Generalissimo. He went on to talk with many high officials. Of these H. H. Kung, then President of the Executive Yuan, threw the most light on what the Chinese government was really thinking. As

[7] Sunderland-Romanus manuscript, Vol. 1.

reported to the State Department on September 17th: ". . . He [Kung] made no forthright statement in regard to the apparent lack of interest in some military circles in prosecuting the war with Japan, but went on at some length about the Kuomintang-Communist difficulties. . . . He . . . indicated his opinion substantially as follows: the Burma campaign was not a comparatively minor matter and offered great difficulties . . . that even if Burma should be recaptured, it would be a long time before the road could be opened and even then the difficulties of transport would not make the reopening of the road of any considerable value to China; and now that Italy had surrendered, British and American naval forces could come into the Indian Ocean in force and in the immediate future; and that the thing to do would be to recapture Singapore and Haiphong as stepping stones to a direct attack upon Japan." Most of the other Chinese officials, according to Atcheson, held similar views.

Whether or not due to the activity of the Embassy, the Executive Committee of the Kuomintang, which was then in session, issued a manifesto affirming that China must increase its efforts to win. But the significant result of this exercise of our diplomatic influence was preventive: the Executive Committee was prevailed on to discard a resolution favoring direct military action against the Communists in the north. Of the way in which Chiang Kai-shek curbed this impulse of his party—which would have hurt the prospects for the Burma campaign—more will soon be told.

The State Department approved Atcheson's efforts to liven up the Chinese war effort. Ambassador Gauss was told to carry on with these efforts upon his return. He did so. His report of what he thought he might have achieved, sent to Washington on October 18th, read "In conclusion, I would say that while we have perhaps succeeded in impressing on some officials the need for increased and more effective war effort on the part of China, and while also there may result some minor improvement in some aspects of the situation, we cannot safely count under present conditions (which involve of course the question of equipment for the Chinese forces) on effecting any significant psychological change in the Chinese attitude which will impel Chinese leaders and soldiers to put forth materially greater effort in the war against Japan. The Chinese have persuaded themselves that the war in Europe will shortly end and that the United States, possibly with help from Great Britain, will defeat Japan; that the Chinese are too tired and too worn out and too ill-equipped to make the greater effort, especially when such effort may not be necessary; and that the Chinese can sit back holding what they have against the Japanese and concentrate their planning upon China's post-war political and economic problems."[8]

By this time, it will be perceived, the crossing beams of attitude between the Chinese and American governments were becoming rigidly fixed. While the Americans in China were finding the Chinese effort short of what they could and ought to be making, the Chinese government was bewailing the failure of the American government to keep its engagements. Chennault had not received promised planes, parts, and other supplies. For example, in May, assurances had been given that he would get two more fighter squadrons and two more medium bomber squadrons by July 15th. Of these, only one fighter squadron had reached China by the end of September. The results of his operations were far below what he and the Chinese believed could and should be accomplished by attack from the air.

The reasons why promised equipment did not reach China in time were various; and their complexities so great that a careful study of vast military records would be required to explain them adequately. This has not yet been made. New causes of trouble seemed to arise whenever old ones were corrected. Some of the fault was American, sometimes British, sometimes Chinese.

The Generalissimo's reproofs were polite but decided. The President wearily admitted they had much reason. On the 27th of September he told Marshall that he was most disturbed over the lag in the expansion of the Hump route and of Chennault's force, and asked the Chief of Staff to push the agreed plans with vigor. No doubt Marshall did. But on October 15th the President was writing to him again: "I am still pretty thoroughly disgusted with the India-China matter. The last straw was the report from Arnold that he could not get the B-29s operating out of China until March or April next year. Everything seems to go wrong. But the worst thing is that we are falling down on our promises every single time." He asked Churchill to see to it himself that the air facilities in Assam in India were developed faster.

This situation gave further impetus to the personal animosity between Stilwell and the Chinese authorities. Soong, when in Washington in September, conveyed to the President the wish that Stilwell be taken out of China. The President let him know that if the Generalissimo directly

[8] Gauss dispatch to State Department, sent October 18th, received November 6th.

asked this he would accede.[9] So when General Somervell came to Chung-king along with Admiral Mountbatten to discuss the new command structure (SEAC) and the preparations for the Burma campaign, Chiang Kai-shek presented his request. Somervell soothed the feelings of the Generalissimo, quieted his suspicion, and cleared up misunderstanding. Mountbatten, at this juncture, despite Soong's warnings against accept-ing Stilwell as his deputy supreme commander in SEAC, also spoke in his behalf. He told Chiang Kai-shek that he would not want to go on with plans for using Chinese forces if the man who had commanded them was to be removed just as operations were about to begin.[10]

But it seems to have been the animated opposition of his wife and her sister, Madame Kung, that drove the Generalissimo to cancel at the last moment the message he had asked Somervell to send to Washing-ton asking for Stilwell's recall. Joseph Alsop, who was then an aide to Chennault and in close company with Soong, has given an account of this quarrel that vividly described the episode. ". . . A tremendous family fight which went on for about two days in the Generalissimo's villa up on the hill. I can recall Dr. Soong coming back from these sessions in a state of complete exhaustion. Madame Kung and Madame Chiang . . . maintained . . . that American aid for China depended on General Stilwell. . . . The ladies said 'If you throw the American hero out of command in China, you will become very unpopular with the United States and you won't get any airplanes or any guns, or

[9] Soong so stated to General Somervell when he met him at New Delhi while en route from Washington to Chungking. Sunderland-Romanus manuscript, Vol. 1.

Joseph Alsop also corroborates this. Testimony Subcommittee of the Senate Judiciary Committee, Eighty-second Congress. *Hearings: Institute of Pacific Relations*, page 1416.

Earlier in the year, Soong had been acting as friendly supporter of Stilwell in the Generalissimo's circle. He tried to find terms on which Stilwell and the Generalissimo could get along. He had proposed that on the one hand Stilwell should be more com-pliant to the expansion of American air effort in China as advocated by Chennault and desired by the Generalissimo; and that in return Stilwell's authority over Chinese mili-tary policy and operations should be strengthened. Stilwell had been indifferent to or wary of Soong's good offices.

Then when Soong proceeded to Washington he made known that he thought Stilwell was unsuitable for his post, and was doing injury to relations in military matters. In contrast Soong thought Chennault had shown himself to be not only an outstanding military man, but one able to win the good will of all his Chinese colleagues. The nature of his opinions is illustrated by what he said to Hornbeck on September 28th, as recorded in a memo of their talk: ". . . Probably there was some fault on the Chinese side, but that fault or no fault, and regardless on which side the greater fault lies, the simple fact is that in the relations between his Chinese contacts and Stilwell there is not mutually and reciprocally the harmony, the cooperativeness and the effectiveness which should exist in such a relationship. Under those circumstances, no matter what may be the 'oughts' of the situation, there cannot be achieved the unity of purpose and of effort which, for the good of China, of the United States, and of the Allied cause, should prevail. . . ."

[10] Mountbatten, *Report*, Section A, Paragraph 10.

anything else.' "[11] Whether that was the reason, or whether only for the sake of domestic peace, the Generalissimo relented, with the understanding that Stilwell would acknowledge afresh his authority.

Stilwell was induced to call upon Chiang Kai-shek and to tell him that any mistakes of his were due to misunderstanding and not intention and that he was then as always willing to cooperate. The occasion is noted in his diary: "Went over and put on the act, the Peanut doing his best to appear conciliatory. He made two points: (1) that I understand the duties of the commander-in-chief and the chief of staff, (2) that I avoid any superiority complex. This was all balderdash, but I listened politely and Peanut said that under those conditions we could go on working harmoniously again."[12]

Marshall was of the opinion that Stilwell would not, after this dispute, have a fair chance of making good, and was disposed to relieve him. But Stimson believed that Soong was at the bottom of the trouble and that Stilwell should be allowed to go on trying; the President gave in. One result of the family quarrel was that Soong, who had lost his temper in talking with the Generalissimo, was deprived for some months of all authority and chance to take part in public affairs. He was ordered to remain about his house in Chungking; and he was still there when in December Chiang Kai-shek went off to Cairo for his first meeting with Roosevelt and Churchill. Soong had been on the whole a spokesman for American liberal ideas of reform within the Chinese government and economic system. American military purposes at this juncture crisscrossed with our political aims and inclinations.

After this crisis the contest of wills and ways between the American military officials in China and the Chinese leaders briefly eased. Preparatory measures to break the siege of China went ahead better—so much better that in early November Stilwell, always quick to hope when on the scent for action, informed Marshall that it was beginning to look as though the hindrances to the Burma campaign and the training program might at last be cleared away.

But around the bend all the problems which had from the start

[11] Alsop testimony, *Hearings: Institute of Pacific Relations*, page 1415.

[12] *The Stilwell Papers*, entry, October 17, 1943. In the series of entries which Stilwell made on this day he entered into conjecture as to the causes of Chiang Kai-shek's capitulation, ending with the comment that "at any rate, this fuss is over. The next may be just around the corner. . . . Both Ella [Madame Kung] and May [Madame Chiang Kai-shek] reiterated that they had put the family jewels on me, and would continue to back me up. All through this mess I have felt free as air—no regrets and no self-blame. A grand and glorious feeling."

bedeviled the Burma project still lurked. Command arrangements were in another snarl. So were the operational plans. The British aim to defer any large amphibious action off or on the coast of southern Burma—a primary wish of the Chinese—was still firm. The combined needs of the several approved military actions in mind exceeded the means that would be at hand, particularly the capacity of the land routes of transport within India and of the air transport lines over the Hump. General Stilwell regarded the several planned concurrent actions in Burma and China not as alternates but a "conjunction of compatibles." But were they really so? I must leave this question to the military historians.

Besides, the whole Burmese project and the results remained subject to events outside the area. Men, guns, planes, ships were all on strict ration which might be reduced. The battle in Italy was stalled; the effort to bring into Britain troops and everything needed for the invasion of France was growing more intense; the requirements for General MacArthur's campaign in the Southwest Pacific were stretching. Treatment of the Far East was still subject to the commanding principle of sending what there was where it might serve best to win the war most quickly and at the least cost of life.

Also, the Japanese were very likely to try to prevent or defeat the planned operations by counteraction. They, it was correctly guessed, would strike energetically.

The Generalissimo was soon going off to Cairo to meet the President and the Prime Minister. He looked forward to talking with them not only about his military needs and the campaign in Burma but also about China's future plans and prospects. He brought Stilwell and the Minister of War together to work out with him in advance the military proposals to put forward. Then he asked his strong-willed American Chief of Staff to go with him to Cairo.

But before we follow Chiang Kai-shek on that journey, it is needful to tell of related matters which had been taking the attention of the State Department during this long season of discord over military matters: first of what had been happening between the Chinese government and the Chinese Communists; and, second, of the steps which the American government had been taking to have China accepted as one of the future four main powers of the world.

CHAPTER 9

To Keep Peace Within China

DURING this period of which I have just been telling—the autumn of 1943—fears arose that the long dispute between the Chinese government and the Chinese Communists might flare into civil war.

The story of earlier relations between the National Government and the Communist forces has been fully told by others.[1] But as a reminder of the perspective along which American officials concerned with China viewed the internal struggle, some of its main earlier phases may be very briefly recalled.

The Chinese Communist Party had once been part of the Kuomintang. It had become so in 1923, when that party was a revolutionary party appealing for support to the peasants and workers. A united front had been formed in order the better to subdue foreign influence, to put down war lords in the north, and to erase certain vested interests and established ways. During this phase, agents of the International Communist movement (both of the Soviet government and of the Communist International) had been active and influential in the party—though there was an accepted working premise that China was not yet ready for full conversion to communism or sovietism.

Then in 1927 there had been a deep split between one section of the Kuomintang, established at Nanking, and another section of more determined revolutionists, established at Hankow. The main group had wanted to get the support and use the cooperation of the middle classes —especially of the commercial and banking groups in Shanghai. The left wing had opposed this; it had wanted to carry forward a thorough social revolution through peasant and worker armies. Chiang Kai-shek had turned on his opponents and by July 1927 defeated them. The Kuomintang expelled all Communist elements and exterminated many. Thousands of the defeated, perhaps several hundred thousand, were put to death.[2] Shortly after this rout of the Communists, the Kuomin-

[1] *China in Revolution*, by Harley F. MacNair, Chicago, 1931, is a clear and calm narrative of these relations up to 1931. A summary of later events is given in *United States Relations with China*. A more complete and analytical record of both the actions and statements of the Communists is to be found in a special report on the Chinese Communist movement, prepared by the Military Intelligence Division of the War Department, published as Part VII A of *Hearings: Institute of Pacific Relations*. The report is dated July 5, 1945.

[2] *United States Relations with China*, page 44.

tang Party had been reorganized under the leadership of Chiang Kai-shek. It had gradually secured official control of the whole country, reducing the power of the war lords. The Communist survivors had gone into open rebellion against the National Government, and built up regular and guerrilla forces of their own. Expelled from the cities, they had lost their worker and industrial base. They had concentrated at first in a small area in south Kiangsi (the remnant of a much larger South China peasant base). Since the economy of this area was wholly agrarian, they had changed their tactics. They organized the peasants and introduced a new and improved system of relations on the farm. Their practical program of correction and production proved to have vitality and appeal.

From 1930 to 1935 the National Government had made open attempts to try to wipe out the Communist nucleus. Though using large forces in several expeditions, it never wholly succeeded. But it drove the Communists from their bases in southern China, and forced them to flee to the northwest in what became known as the "Long March" of 1934-1935. An incidental effect of these anti-Communist campaigns was that the National Government consolidated its control over many of the provinces. The new Communist base—with headquarters at Yenan, in the province of Shensi, about four hundred and fifty miles southwest of Peiping—was less accessible than the old. The country was rough and badly cut up, the roads were poor, and it was four or more days of hardest travel by car from Sian, the capital of Shensi province. The new location—a fact that later was to become important—was closer to the Soviet frontier.

Despite the mutual mistrust and hatred, the Japanese invasion of North China had brought the Communists and the Kuomintang together again in 1936-1937 in a wartime understanding. This compact had grown out of an offer made by the Communists in August 1936 to form "a strong revolutionary united front with you as was the case during . . . the great Chinese Revolution of 1925-1927." This proposal was probably stimulated by the Soviet government, which wanted all China to resist the expansion of Japan. While it was being discussed, Chiang Kai-shek had gone north to meet with some of the local military commanders at Sian. His real purpose, it has been said by some historians of the episode, was to induce them to attack the Communists. Whether or not this was so, some of these commanders instead had turned against him, accused him of not going on with the revolution, and arrested him with the probable thought of killing him. But he was released, perhaps

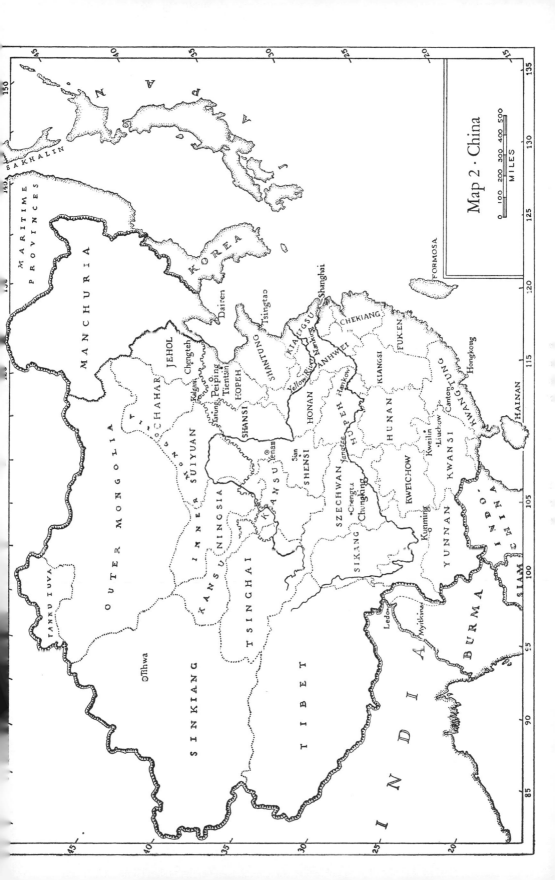

Map 2 · China

MILES
0 100 200 300 400 500

SAKHALIN

MARITIME PROVINCES

MANCHURIA

KOREA

JEHOL

CHAHAR

Chengteh

Kalgan

Peiping

Tientsin

Tatung

HOPEH

SHANSI

SHANTUNG

Tsingtao

Dairen

KIANGSU

ANHWEI

Shanghai

CHEKIANG

Nanking

Yellow River

Hankow

HUPEH

HONAN

SHENSI

Yangtze

KIANGSI

FUKEN

Hongkong

HUNAN

KWANGTUNG

Canton

Liuchow

Kweilin

KWANGSI

KWEICHOW

Kunming

YUNNAN

Chungking

Chengtu

SZECHWAN

SIKANG

KANSU

Sian

Yenan

NINGSIA

SUIYUAN

INNER MONGOLIA

TSINGHAI

TIBET

INDO-CHINA

BURMA

SIAM

Myitkyina

Ledo

INDIA

HAINAN

FORMOSA

OUTER MONGOLIA

SINKIANG

TIHWA

TANNU TUVA

as a result of promises he gave while under arrest. A Kuomintang-Communist understanding, or the semblance of one, was reached.

This understanding was never formalized in any single signed document. It was contained in a series of parallel statements issued by the two parties—in which the Kuomintang announced the change in the Chinese government's policy from one of an attempt to suppress Communism by force to one of seeking a political settlement; and in which the Communist Party proclaimed that it was giving up forceful insurrection and sovietization in favor of cooperation with the government against Japanese aggression.

As a feature of this agreement, during the next few years the Communist army had been reorganized into the 8th Route Army (later the 18th Group Army). It remained under Communist generals and was designated as the garrison for the border region of the three provinces, Shensi-Kansu-Ninghsia (in the north-central interior of China south of the Great Wall). Local governments organized and dominated by the Communists in near-by areas received formal recognition. The National Government had briefly given a small monetary subsidy and a small allotment of ammunition to these Communist governments.

The one year, 1937-1938, had witnessed some real compromises and cooperation. There was almost a truce, a peaceable living side by side—but no coalition or unification of either civil authority or armies. Then, late in 1938, after the National Government had been forced by the advancing Japanese to take refuge in Chungking, new quarrels had started. The National Government had sought to assume control of the Communist area and to bring the rebel Communist army under its command. The Communists had resisted.

During the next five years the accord of 1937 had gradually fallen apart. Hard words were spoken again and border clashes and disputes had grown serious. The area of Communist influence had spread. Young and rebellious minds from many parts of China were attracted to it. The Communist armed forces had also expanded. The government had established a rigid military blockade south and west of the main Communist base. The primary purpose was to prevent Communist infiltration into Nationalist China. But it served two other purposes as well. The concentration of government troops in the Northwest, particularly those in the area south of the Yellow River Bend, guarded the vital Tung Kuan (Pass) against a possible Japanese offensive toward Sian. And it closed off overland travel between the Communist areas and the distant province of Sinkiang in the west, and beyond that, to the Soviet Union;

the other main route to the Soviet Union, northward toward Inner Mongolia, was controlled by the Japanese. The maintenance of this sheath against explosive contact with the northern neighbor became one of the avowed purposes of the blockade, as the Chinese government became more alarmed by signs of Soviet animosity.

By 1943 each side had its own black book of suppression and betrayal by the other. Many of the leaders on both sides of the great break within the Kuomintang Party in 1927 had remained alive, and were in comparable positions sixteen years later. Their memory of past dealings with one another expressed itself in distrust. Words and formulas had been worn down. Nerves were on edge and spirits hardened. Authority in both camps was moving into the hands of the stubborn opponents of compromise and continued truce. The National Government was counting on American victory to secure the ultimate defeat of the Communists. The Communists were counting on the Soviet Union to assure their survival, and in good time their victory.

Yet in June 1943 the Kuomintang and the Communists had renewed their discussions. Each had evidently still preferred to test its own skill and the other's position by diplomacy rather than by battle. The Chinese—as the discussions about a truce in Korea during 1952-53 well illustrated—are gifted in the use of talk to bemuse. Chiang Kai-Shek had offered, as often before, to grant legal status to the Communist Party and to go forward toward constitutional government provided that: (1) the Communists gave up their government at Yenan; and (2) the Communist armies were placed under the command of the Central Government. The Communist spokesmen in Chungking, as often before, had refused. They had said that they were afraid this would mean absorption, if not extermination.

Atcheson, reporting on July 6th about these negotiations, had added that Chiang Kai-shek was asking for a conclusive answer from Yenan by the end of August. He predicted that it was not likely that the government's terms would be acceptable. Two days later, Chou En-lai, who had been in Chungking for these talks and returned to Yenan, had sent word to Atcheson that the Central Government had transferred seven more divisions to the Kuomintang-Communist frontier. He asserted this was being done as a threat to try to force a settlement on Kuomintang terms. The Embassy told the State Department that it was unable to gauge, because of conflicting reports and interpretations, whether or not the government was really increasing its forces near

Communist areas, and if it was, whether the purpose was protective or aggressive.[3]

Whatever the case, the State Department had become afraid that this revival of tension would upset the plans for the campaigns which were being evolved. At this very time (July) Chiang Kai-shek, as just told, was urging the American government to devote much greater resources to the air transport service over the Hump for the Chinese armies and American combat air forces, and greatly to enlarge our air operations in China. He was also committing himself against his real wish to the Burma battle, a few months off. The American government had felt that it could not allow this whole program to be imperiled by civil war.

Not only that, but the American government was fearful lest internal dissension within China would also cause trouble with our other Allies. Rumors that the government was about to attack the Communists had reached London and Moscow as well as Washington. The British Foreign Office had mentioned them to the American Embassy in London. Then on July 14th, the Counselor of the Soviet Embassy in Chungking had called upon Atcheson. He went so far as to say that the Chinese government troops had fired upon the Communist outposts and positions. The Soviet official accused the government of seeking to coerce the Communists to accept its terms—the same allegation which a few days before Chou En-lai had made. The Chinese government was aware, he had gone on to say, that it was not desirable to attack the Communists at this time because of the effect on international relations; but he was afraid that local commanders might, being under tension, take some action on their own that would start a war. Other signs of Soviet interest had followed. On August 11th the Soviet military attaché had also called at the Embassy to express concern over the Kuomintang-Communist relations. He had persistently tried to find out what the attitude of the United States would be, especially in regard to supplying aid to China, if the government and the Communists fought.

The State Department had informed the American Embassy in Moscow of these Russian approaches in Chungking. On August 18th Ambassador Standley informed the Secretary of State that he found it meaningful that in recent press statements the Soviet government was for the first time openly championing the cause of the Chinese Communists, and playing up their part in the Chinese struggle for inde-

[3] Various reports and interpretations were sent by the Embassy on July 9th, 13th, and 17th, and October 16, 1943.

pendence.[4] While not openly slurring Chiang Kai-shek, the Soviet press was accusing elements among his supporters of being traitors, and warning against "the renewed dangers" of civil war. In the same stories the Communist war effort was lauded. This guarded press campaign, it may be hazarded, had a dual purpose: to avert civil war in China since that would make it easier for Japan, and to protect the Chinese Communists.

The State Department concluded it had better take heed of the danger. The Quadrant Conference was starting at Quebec. Roosevelt and Churchill and the Combined Chiefs were reviewing plans for action in China and Burma. Secretary Hull was about to engage himself in talks with Eden and Churchill, to mark the path toward the future United Nations Organization in which both China and the Soviet Union were to be formative participants.

On August 19th, Hornbeck, as instructed, indicated to Soong (the Foreign Minister), just before he left for Quebec, our official interest in the intentions of the Chinese government. Hornbeck used a polite touch. He said that the State Department was recently informed from Chungking "that an official agent of another power" had told an American officer that the United States and Great Britain were urging the Chinese government to take action against the Communists; that he wanted to assure Soong that this was not so; that we hoped trouble would be avoided; but that "we have scrupulously refrained from urg-

---

[4] Telegrams of August 18, 1943. The change in the expressed attitude of the Soviet government was reviewed at length in various telegrams and dispatches from the American Embassy in Moscow.

Similar articles—some of them based on, or reprints of, articles in the Soviet press—began to appear in the United States. Louis Budenz, the ex-Communist who was at that time connected with the *Daily Worker*, testified before a Senate subcommittee that during the summer of 1943 word was received that the line to be taken in regard to Chiang Kai-shek was to be changed to one of attack; that the Politburo of the American Communist Party cabled to Moscow for instructions, and received back an article which had been published in the Soviet trade union journal, *War and the Working Class*, by Vladimir Rogov, former Tass representative in China, which signaled the change in policy. An English translation was cabled from Moscow by the United Press and Intercontinent News and reprinted in the *Daily Worker* of August 12, 1943, and *Amerasia* of September 1943. *State Department Employee Loyalty Investigation*, Hearings before a Subcommittee of the Committee on Foreign Relations, United States Senate, Eighty-First Congress, United States Government Printing Office, 1950, page 492. This will hereafter be cited as *State Department Employee Loyalty Investigation: Hearings*.

This had been preceded in fact by a variety of articles in the American press exposing various unsatisfactory aspects of the situation in China and attributing them to the faults of the Kuomintang government. The one which received the most attention and disturbed Kuomintang officials most was that written by T. A. Bisson which appeared in the *Far Eastern Survey* of July 14, 1943.

ing on the Chinese Government any particular course of action in regard to matters of China's internal politics." Soong said that he understood; that he wondered whether the false story of government plans to attack the Communists did not come from Russian sources. He said also that he could assure the State Department that the National Government had no present intention of forcing the issue with the Communists. He, Soong, felt no present uneasiness on that score; and he, Soong, appreciated the Department's calm and correct attitude on the subject.

But new reports from Chungking followed to the effect that an important element in the Kuomintang was continuing to urge action against the Communists on the ground that if the government did not make them yield while the Soviet Union was fully engaged, they would later with Soviet help take over all North China and Manchuria. This group, the reports stated, was bent on passing a resolution during the meeting of the Central Executive Committee of the party which was then in session that would be virtually a declaration of war, or at all events, an ultimatum.[5] This was a few days after Stilwell had proposed to Chiang Kai-shek that Communist forces be asked to take part in a joint diversionary attack against the Japanese.

Chiang Kai-shek had rebuffed that suggestion, but he stepped in to moderate the impulse of the executive committee of his party to force a showdown with the Communists. He advised them that "After hearing the Secretariat's report on the question of the Chinese Communist Party and the views expressed by various members of the Central Executive Committee, *I am of the opinion that first of all we should clearly recognize that the Chinese Communist problem is a purely political problem and should be solved by political means.* [Italics mine] Such ought to be the guiding principle for the Plenary Session in its effort to settle this matter. If you share my views you should maintain the policy of leniency and forbearance which we have consistently pursued in dealing with our domestic affairs with the expectation that the Chinese Communist Party will be moved by our sincerity and magnanimity no matter in what way they may slander us nor in what manner they may try to create trouble."[6]

This statement took effect. The conference refrained from issuing an ultimatum to the Communists. Instead, it passed resolutions which disclaimed intent to use force, and urged increased resistance by all

[5] Atcheson telegrams September 9 and 11, 1943.

[6] This important statement of September 13, 1943, is printed in *United States Relations with China*, pages 530-531.

Chinese against the Japanese. Atcheson thought that his talks with government officials and Soong's messages from Washington had caused them to swerve from their first intention.[7] Knowledge of the alert Soviet interest may also have been a factor, as well as the fact that local military leaders in the province of Szechwan had not accepted an invitation to attend the conference, and their forces controlled the routes between government and Communist areas. Or maybe—and the thought is not to be dismissed—the intention had not been as serious as reported to the Embassy, and as passed on by the Embassy to the State Department.

Chiang Kai-shek's statement of September 13, 1943 may have been regarded by the debating elements in the Kuomintang as little more than a tactical move. But the policy which the Generalissimo then avowed, and even the phrases used, were gravely marked by the American officials concerned with China. They came to regard this statement as a governing and lasting pledge by the Chinese government. More than that, it was construed as recognition that force could not solve the Communist problem and that the effort to solve it in other ways—by peaceful means—had therefore to be continued, no matter how hard the task. In sum, the American government came to believe more thoroughly in the soundness of the avowal than many members of the Chinese government.

This affirmation of peaceful intent did not bring any genuine easing of the internal struggle. The Embassy in Chungking took a gloomy view of the prospect. Its summary comment, after a further review of the situation, was that "All these factors point to but one conclusion, to the continued struggle between the two rival parties—civil war at some undetermined future date."[8] But it thought that a chance remained to avert that event in either one of two ways. The first was some kind of compromise between the Kuomintang and its opponents under the pretext of democracy. Towards this kind of settlement the Embassy said it found two different attitudes among non-Communist political groups and leaders: most of the present influential figures in the Kuomintang thought there would be chaos in China without a strong central government, but "liberals" inside and outside the party thought it would work well, that the Kuomintang, forced to work with other interests, would remain the most influential force within the government. Or—

[7] Telegram, September 17th from Chungking, and Dispatch, October 9.
[8] Dispatch of October 14th, from Chungking.

this was the second possible way of averting civil war which the Embassy outlined—the Kuomintang might still by thoroughgoing democratic reforms deprive the Communist Party of popular support. To do so, the Embassy observed, these reforms would have to be many-sided: the Kuomintang would have to mend its own ways; it would have to carry out thorough social and economic changes—especially those which would improve the conditions and treatment of the peasants and workers; it would have to give more place and heed to many elements in Chinese life that had no influence in the government as then formed.

From this time on, these themes become innate features of the advice which the American authorities pressed on the Chinese government. They become the guiding and standard elements in our policy towards China. Therefore it may be well to sum them up again briefly.

1. Civil war in China should be averted. The internal struggle should be settled by peaceful political means.

2. This might be managed temporarily by some kind of political combination in which all Chinese parties would have a share; and more permanently by creating in China a democratic, constitutional form of government within which all parties would operate equally under the laws.

3. The Kuomintang must qualify itself to keep power and popular support by self-improvement and social and economic reforms.

All of this was a quick working-day response to Chinese conditions. The trajectory was figured by familiar currents of Western experience, not by winds of doctrine that Americans had not deeply explored. Neither those in Chungking who wrote the dispatches nor those in Washington who read them kept on their desks the articles and speeches of Marx, Lenin, and Stalin. They did not study closely the past resolutions of the congresses of the Soviets and the Comintern. Nor is it likely that it would have made much difference if they had. For most of them, almost all of them, thought of the Chinese as sobrietists, not extremists. They tended to discount the inner fury of the Communist revolution in China—which its leaders kept banked up though not hidden.

The State Department and its representatives in China were calmer and softer-tongued than Stilwell. But in their own way they tried just as persistently as he to induce or compel the Chinese government to follow our trail of advice. To them the reforms which they wanted the Chinese government to make were preservative: essential to avert civil war and save China from either Fascism or Communism. They also were moved by a longing that since China was their cause, and it *was* their cause, it should be a worthy cause. They did not think or write solely as American officials who wanted to win a war, indifferent to the plight of the people of China. They wanted China to become a well-governed and well-cared-for country as well as a strong ally.

The government, despite the alarms that were heard now and again during the months that followed, did not send its troops into areas occupied by the Communists. The Communists avoided conflicts with large, organized government forces. But both sides extended their forays against the other. The Communists made material out of every sort of hardship which the war brought to China. They filled every open funnel of publicity with blame of the National Government, for corruption and neglect of the people's welfare, for cruel conscription and mistreatment of the army. Even the most capable government would have been on the defensive—hard-tried to convince a weary people that their troubles were due not to its faults but to the hard facts of war.

The Communist forces were growing fast. By the end of 1943 their regular military units alone, our military reporters thought, would have half a million men, and perhaps as many more in lightly armed guerrilla forces, and as many more still banded together in villages for local defense.[9] "As a composite military force," the American Military Attaché in Chungking thought, "the Chinese Communists are not capable of much, if any offensive action. . . . [But] . . . it cannot be denied that they do possess a remarkable defensive capability. This, of course, reaches its zenith in guerrilla activity."[10] The Communist leaders—particularly Mao Tze Tung (Chairman of the Central Executive Committee of the party) and General Chu Teh (the Commander-in-Chief of the Communist army)—he thought had shown that they had exceptional capacity for leadership and organization. The Chinese government kept some twenty or more divisions of Chinese troops (two to three hundreds of

[9] Estimates of the size of various types of Communist armed organizations are even more diverse than those of the forces which were nominally counted to be government forces. The American government did not have at this time any permanently stationed representatives in the Communist regions or in direct contact with the Communist armed forces. In making a numerical estimate of the Communist military strength, there was always the difficulty of deciding what forces should be included. Almost every male and many of the females in Communist territory were in one way or another part of some organization which might or could take part in fighting. Some were full-time soldiers, others were only part-time. Some were organized in armies that were freely moved about; others were in units used only locally; and still others remained in their own village for defense and nearby guerrilla activities.

[10] Report, Colonel M. B. Depass, Jr., November 16, 1943, transmitted by the Embassy, November 20th.

thousands of men), including some of China's best, stationed in the northwest.[11]

This state of affairs within China bothered the American government most directly because it was reducing the power of the Chinese government to stand the strain of war and making it vulnerable in the event of further defeat. But the anxieties felt went beyond this immediate concern; it was feared that the division in China might bring about trouble between the Soviet Union and the West. It was becoming clear that the Soviet Union would emerge strong from the war. Its time of mortal peril was passing; already it was beginning to regain its freedom of action. Who was to know how that would be used—whether the suffering of the war would leave behind a wish to keep on good terms with the West, or whether it would arouse new as well as old Russian ambitions and Communist agitations? The Soviet Union might begin to give secret or open help to the Chinese Communists, and thus make it harder or impossible for the government to defeat them. The Soviet Union might do this in order that North China and Manchuria should become detached from the rest of China and form a Communist state in close relations with itself. Or it might, acting more independently, seek to secure direct control of Manchuria.

Foresight had caused the American government to begin to try to guard against these chances. It had made what seemed a promising start at reaching accords with its war allies, Britain and the Soviet Union, which might protect the future of China and avert disputes over it. Of this also an account should be given before we join Chiang Kai-shek at Cairo.

[11] The estimate of the size of the Chinese forces in the northwest is based on a talk between Atcheson and General Wu Teh-chen, the Secretary General of CEC, reported by Atcheson on September 17th. Numerous reports, originated by the American consuls in Sian and Lanchow, were sent in to Washington regarding the troop movements in the northwest. The most comprehensive review of this subject available to me is the report by Colonel Depass, just cited.

PART TWO

From the Cairo Conference to the Surrender of Japan

CHAPTER 10

To Make China a Great Power

THE Chinese government had made no issue of the Soviet refusal to join the war against Japan, or of the studied neutrality maintained since. It had used the chance to sever the many lines of Soviet influence in the vast and distant Chinese border province of Sinkiang. The Soviet government had allowed Chungking to resume its authority over the province with coldness but without open resistance.[1] For a short time the Chinese government had felt relieved, thinking that Soviet assent might be a sign of a wish for quiet and friendly relations. But its anxieties were revived by the critical articles that were beginning to appear in the Soviet press. They were read as storm warnings. Fear lest after the war the Chinese Communists would have Soviet support was reviving the repressed wish to fight out the issue with them at once. It was retarding both the conduct of the war and the making of reforms.

Some corrective for the fears weighing on Chungking was, the American government concluded, much needed. The reassuring words we were speaking were not enough. There seemed little or no chance of bringing the Chinese and Soviet governments together in a direct accord of lasting value while the future situation of both was so obscure. Hence, anxious minds in the State Department cast about for some intermediate measure. They resorted to a more enveloping diplomatic prescription— to have China written in among the great powers that were to guide the world after the war. The President and Secretary of State carried this purpose into a series of conferences at Moscow, Cairo, and Teheran.

They set about to secure promises that after the defeat of Japan China would (1) be restored as sovereign over the territories it had lost and (2) be granted a high place among the nations. Thus elevated and reassured, China, it was hoped, would fight more vigorously, and after the war be a competent partner of the West in maintaining peaceful

---

[1] Most of the people living in this province were of different stock from the rest of the Chinese and did not speak Chinese. The Chinese government had allowed its control of both the government and affairs of the province to become lax. Trade with Soviet territory had grown because of its nearness to Soviet trading centers and its great distance from Chinese centers. Joint Soviet-Sinkiang enterprises were established in oil production and refining, and other industries and mills. Soviet technicians were employed in health, agricultural, educational, and transport work. At the end of 1942 Chungking had set to reasserting its authority, replacing local officials friendly to the Soviet Union by others. After various local clashes and quarrels, the Soviet interests had given in. They closed up their enterprises and withdrew the military units they kept in the provinces, took away the airplanes and gave up control of the airfields they had been using.

[95]

and stable order in the Pacific. Steps to bring this about had in fact been started before Hull went to the first of these conferences at Moscow.

On August 18th, just as the discussions were starting at Quebec among Roosevelt, Churchill, and their advisers, Soong had made an earnest plea to Hull to the effect that the unity of the four great powers should be made a reality by including China in the conferences. The letter which Soong left with the Secretary of State recalled previous refusals of similar requests. It remarked that the Chinese government had not even been asked to present opinions and plans in regard to matters of utmost concern to China; and that even when given a hearing by the Combined Chiefs of Staff, Chinese spokesmen had not been allowed to share in the arguments and the making of decisions. If they had been, it was hazarded, there would have been fewer later misunderstandings. The Chinese government had been definite in its requests. It wanted to be included on a footing of equality in all existing joint and combined agencies, such as the Munitions Assignment Board. It asked that new inter-Allied machinery be created with equal Chinese representation in order to assure coordinated effort to carry the joint decisions into effect.

Hull had been gently reserved. He had said that the American government thought that China had great potential strength, politically and economically, and that "therefore we were showing China every consideration at all practicable." Soong commented that this might be true but that some other countries such as Great Britain did not seem to like the idea.[2]

The conferences at Quebec had decided that the Chinese request could not be granted. The reasons were several and real. The American and British governments were finding it hard to agree among themselves, and still harder to keep in working gear with the Soviet Union. If China were included as an equal in these councils, it would have been almost impossible to refuse a similar place to the Soviet Union. The

[2] The British government had up to then given passive assent to American wishes to strengthen China and give it rank and recognition as a great power. But its inner doubts remained. As Eden stated to the President the previous March, he was in a good deal of doubt about this, since he doubted very much whether China could stabilize itself and it might have to go through a revolution after the war. Besides, he said he "did not like the idea of the Chinese running up and down the Pacific" (*Roosevelt and Hopkins*, Sherwood, page 716). When in late July Soong had visited London, Eden had assured him that Britain wanted a strong and unified China, and had repeated the statement in a public speech. But Soong was evidently not convinced.

The Australian government was particularly doubtful as to whether China was qualified for such responsibility. Memo of talk between Hull and H. V. Evatt, Australian Minister for External Affairs, April 15th.

process of decision would then become unmanageable, and the more surely so since the Soviet Union was not at war with Japan. Then, too, various countries of Western Europe were accepting American-British decisions. But they did not want China to be able to decide their fate. Finally, the Allies did not dare trust the ability of the Chinese government to guard the essential secrecy of their plans and operations. These reasons in total had dictated the conclusion that to grant the Chinese request would seriously endanger the whole conduct of the war. The decision was the only possible one.

But Soong had been invited to be about at Quebec, and was told all that it was thought prudent to tell him. And, as recounted, a most qualified group of senior Allied military leaders had been sent out to Chungking to go over with Chiang Kai-shek the whole program of action in China and Burma. And further, as also told, the President had promised the Generalissimo the kind of help he most wanted. But these measures had not satisfied Chiang Kai-shek. On September 15th he had petitioned again for full admission into the Combined Chiefs of Staff and Munitions Assignment Board.

China thus had been refused an equal place and share in the conduct of the war. But at the same time a way had been seen to make redress. The State Department had been seeking a method of doing so. Eager devotees were composing a statement of principles to be endorsed by the Allies as rules to govern their acts and relations during and after the war. This, the authors hoped, would provide a propitious approach toward the troubling problems of the Pacific. China was to be one of the four originating great powers, the Soviet Union another. The two might, through the act of pledging themselves to the same principles of behavior, become more trustful of one another. Another related thought might have been in Hull's mind: unless the Soviet Union were pledged to pursue the same basic lines of conduct after the war as the United States and Britain, we might later regret the great support we were giving it; while if it took the proper vows, then we could continue our aid with assurance.[3]

[3] The American military establishment was already looking forward to the time when the Soviet Union would join the Pacific war. Hopkins had carried with him to Quebec a document prepared by the military which read, "Finally, the most important factor the United States has to consider in relation to Russia is the prosecution of the war in the Pacific. With Russia as an ally in the war against Japan, the war can be terminated in less time and at less expense in life and resources than if the reverse were the case. Should the war in the Pacific have to be carried on with an unfriendly or a negative attitude on

Hull had taken with him to Quebec a draft that might serve as a joint declaration. The President had discussed it with Churchill and Eden. They had liked it. Its principles were approved as a basis of common conduct for enduring international cooperation. Hull and his staff had gone forward eagerly with this, their first big chance since Pearl Harbor to make policy. Soong had been informed by Hull on September 2nd of what was in mind. A provisional text was sent to the Soviet government. This prospectus of future cooperation fitted in with the advice that the American government was giving in Chungking—not to resort to force against the Chinese Communists. Then days later (September 13th), it will be recalled, Chiang Kai-shek made the telling affirmation to his party that the Communist problem was a purely political one, to be solved by political means.

The first Soviet reaction to the proposed joint statement disappointed Hull, mainly because of the objection made to the inclusion of China. But he got set to carry his purpose through at the meeting of foreign ministers soon to be held in Moscow. He was worried as to whether he could stand the hard trip. But his body and spirit were reanimated by the ideal purpose of the task before him. The Chinese showed how great their interest was in his undertaking by their repeated inquiries as to what he proposed to do at Moscow. They followed the news of his visit (October 18th-30th) intently and learned the results with pleased surprise.

The three Foreign Secretaries (Hull, Eden, and Molotov) agreed upon a statement of the principles which their governments were willing to pronounce. Its text was submitted to Chiang Kai-shek, who hurriedly approved it. Thus China appeared as one of its original signers. This was a proof that a place was being assigned to it among the governing powers of the world, since this declaration was of worldwide scope.

The main passages of the Moscow Declaration were:

The Governments of the United States of America, the United Kingdom, the Soviet Union and China: . . .

Jointly declare:

1—That their united action, pledged for the prosecution of the war against their respective enemies, will be continued for the organization and maintenance of peace and security.

---

the part of Russia, the difficulties will be immeasurably increased and operations might become abortive." Sherwood, *Roosevelt and Hopkins*, pages 748-749.

2—That those of them at war with a common enemy will act together in all matters relating to the surrender and disarmament of that enemy. . . .

4—That they recognize the necessity of establishing at the earliest practicable date a general international organization, based on the principle of the sovereign equality of all peace-loving states, and open to membership by all such states, large and small, for the maintenance of international peace and security.

5—That for the purpose of maintaining international peace and security pending the reestablishment of law and order and the inauguration of a system of general security, they will consult with one another and as occasion requires with other members of the United Nations with a view to joint action on behalf of the community of nations.

6—That after the termination of hostilities they will not employ their military forces within the territories of other states except for the purposes envisaged in this declaration and after joint consultation.[4]

Paragraph 6 was read with particular satisfaction in Chungking.

This broad declaration had an easy birth. In fact, the only contested point was the inclusion of China as one of the original signatories. Eden stood by Hull. But it took quite a tussle, a flexing of the muscles, to get the Soviet Union to acquiesce. Molotov objected on the ground that China had no admissible interest in European matters. Hull has given an account of the hint which, privately spoken to Molotov, brought him around. He said to the Soviet Foreign Minister, "The American Government is doing everything and has done everything possible with respect to the Chinese situation. In my judgment it would be impossible to omit China from the Four-Nation Declaration. My Government believes that China has been in the world picture as one of the Big Four for the prosecution of the war. For her now to be dumped out on her face by Russia, Great Britain and the United States in connection with the Declaration would create in all probability the most terrific repercussions, both political and military, in the Pacific area. This might call for all sorts of readjustments by my Government to keep the political and military situation in the Pacific properly stabilized. . . . Furthermore, public opinion in my country would be hopelessly rent by the news that my Government had joined with the Soviet Government to throw China out of the war picture, as the public would probably interpret her exclusion from the [Four-Nation] Declaration."[5]

In his memo of this talk Hull comments that Molotov seemed to recognize the "reasonableness" of his remarks. At this time any sub-

[4] Signed in Moscow October 30, 1943.
[5] *The Memoirs of Cordell Hull*, Cordell Hull, Vol. II (1948), page 1282.

stantial readjustment of the distribution of weapons and shipping as between the European and Pacific combat areas might well have had a decisive effect on the course of the struggle on the Eastern Front. A few days later, Molotov said that the Soviet government would drop its objection if it could be arranged that China sign the declaration before the conference ended. This was managed. China's name was there on the same level with the powerful. The face of the Chinese government at the window showed pleasure at this distinction. On receiving the final report on the conference, the Generalissimo told Gauss on October 31st that he was much pleased with the declaration and most obliged to Hull.

To Hull this declaration was both reward for his mission and basis of hope for the future. The principles endorsed were to him the living and essential rules of attitude and conduct for a decent world.[6] But in reality the language left each country free to go far along its own way and still argue that it was being faithful to its principles. The intent which the American government poured into the document did not govern the later actions of the powers. China was not able to fill the part or carry out the assignment first set for her at Moscow, then confirmed at Cairo, and San Francisco. The demanding will of the revolutionary elements, led by Moscow, was too strong and ruthless to be contained by formalities and generalities. But here I am stealing conclusions from later pages and anticipating later tales.

Just before the Secretary of State left Moscow for home, Stalin made a short statement of dramatic consequence. Stalin asked him to tell the President the Soviet Union would enter the Pacific war and help defeat the enemy in the Far East as soon as the Germans were beaten. This promise was unasked and unqualified. Or, as Hull later commented, ". . . he asked nothing in return."[7] The Secretary was surprised and

---

[6] Two extracts from the address on the Moscow Conference which he gave to a joint meeting of the Senate and House of Representatives on November 18th indicate the range of his hopes. Apropos of Paragraph 6, which he called a "self-denying ordinance," he said, "Through this declaration, the Soviet Union, Great Britain, the United States, and China have laid the foundation for cooperative effort in the post-war world toward enabling all peace-loving nations, large and small, to live in peace and security, to preserve the liberties and rights of civilized existence, and to enjoy expanded opportunities and facilities for economic, social, and spiritual progress." And apropos of the whole declaration he observed that "As the provisions of the four-nation declaration are carried into effect, there will no longer be need for spheres of influence, for alliances, for balance of power, or any other of the special arrangements through which, in the unhappy past, the nations strove to safeguard their security or to promote their interests."

[7] *Memoirs of Cordell Hull*, Vol. II, page 1310.

delighted.[8] To the President he cabled at once, "A message has been given me from the person in highest authority to be delivered to you personally. The message promises to get in and help defeat the enemy in the Far East after the German defeat."

It is easy to understand why this statement gave such satisfaction to Hull and his colleagues. With the huge Russian forces bearing down on the Japanese armies in the mainland of Asia, they thought the war would be won sooner, and with much smaller loss of American lives and less strain upon American resources. Despite the cheering headway of our advances in the Pacific, the struggle ahead still looked long and terrible. The Japanese were fighting with the utmost determination and bravery. Each small Allied victory needed great preparation and took a sad toll. The invasion of Western Europe was ahead; we might win or lose, and no one knew how many Americans would give their lives to it. Stalin's promise meant certainly that the ultimate struggle in the Pacific would not be as maiming as we had feared. The satisfaction was not marred by any suggestion that the Soviet Union would set a price for its participation. It was not foreseen that by the time the Soviet Union was ready to act on its promise the help would not be greatly needed.

In any case, the Secretary of State regarded the outcome of the conference with uplifted spirits. His main impression was expressed in a passage in a memo referring to his talks with Stalin ". . . All the signs indicate that Mr. Stalin and his government are opposed to isolation and are whole-heartedly in favor of the movement of international cooperation launched by this conference, with Russia as a full partner with the United States, Great Britain and China."[9]

At the closing session on October 30th, Molotov spoke with warm appreciation of the unfailing cooperation he had received from Hull and Eden. Hull responded by saying that he had never seen a better example of skill and cooperation than Molotov had displayed. Eden went them both one better, proposing that at any future meetings of the three foreign secretaries, Molotov be chosen as permanent chairman. The last sentence of the American minutes of the conference read, "The Conference ended on this note."

[8] When General Hurley, then Ambassador to New Zealand, had passed through Moscow in November 1942 he had talked with Stalin; and he had informed Washington that he detected in his talk with Stalin an intention on the part of Russia in due course to enter the war with Japan. But he had added that Stalin's remarks to this effect were so modified by some of his other remarks that the American government should not regard it as a promise.

[9] *Memoirs of Cordell Hull*, Vol. II, pages 1310, 1312-1313.

How common enemies and common perils endear us to one another! How easily we fall apart when the enemies are defeated and the perils pass! What a contrast to the concluding sentence in the American minutes of the first conference after the war which brought together the foreign ministers of the same three countries at London in October 1945! It reads, "Over this question of procedure the conference broke up."[10]

Stalin's unsolicited statement was of even greater potential importance to China than to the United States. It meant almost certain liberation of China not too many years away. With the friendship of the Allies, suggested in the Four-Power Declaration, the defeat of Japan would open the way to the requisition of all the areas which China had been forced to yield to it. But it also made some disturbing possibilities more positive. The Soviet armies would be marching down through Manchuria, and perhaps into China. They might enter Sinkiang. They might join with or make some arrangement with the Chinese Communists.

Stalin's statement was not repeated to the Chinese government. It was kept in the utmost secrecy with which it had been made—lest Tokyo hear of it. Thus on November 1st, when the Chinese Ambassador in Moscow, after thanking Hull for what had been done for China, asked whether the Russians had said anything about Japan, Hull evaded the inquiry. The Ambassador tried to break the barrier of silence by remarking that he had been authorized by Chiang Kai-shek to say to Stalin that if and when Russia should decide to enter the war against Japan, China would be ready to make any kind of alliance with the Soviet Union. The Secretary nodded his head.

But the prospect of Soviet entry into the Pacific war gave further impetus to the wish to settle the future of China and straighten out Sino-Soviet relations. It gave greater scope to the discussions which Roosevelt and Churchill were about to have with Chiang Kai-shek at Cairo, and with Stalin at Teheran.

---

[10] Behind the difference over procedure, there was an issue of substance: what part was China to play in the decisions of the Council of Foreign Ministers?

CHAPTER 1 1

Cairo and Teheran Conferences: Political Plans

THE meetings at Cairo and Teheran were arranged directly and secretly by the White House. Though the Secretary of State knew that they were being planned, he did not actively share in the determination of American aims and decisions.[1]

One reason was that so many of the main matters in mind were military, connected with the conduct of the war. Another may well have been Hull's growing tendency to waver and his immersion in basic principles and plans of international organization. Still another may have been that the President had been led to think that the State Department did not appreciate the need for boldness, and would not keep secrets. At this time the working connections between the White House and the Secretary of State and his corps of assistants were flickering. The President had taken to conducting large foreign affairs himself, in close consultation with his military advisers, Harry Hopkins, and a few special representatives abroad whom he had chosen, such as Harriman and Hurley. The staff of the State Department consoled itself by writing memos, but it is doubtful whether the men who went to Cairo and Teheran read them.[2]

It was not easy in the midst of a worldwide war that was changing all power relations for Roosevelt, Churchill, Stalin, and Chiang Kai-shek to arrange to meet. Even though united in the war cause, each remained aware of real differences in aims and wishes. Place, time, circumstance— all were studied to find out whose advantage they might best serve. The President wanted to talk with both Chiang Kai-shek and Stalin.

[1] Hull's later comment on this is curious: "I learned from other sources than the President what had occurred at the Casablanca, Cairo, and Teheran Conferences. I had no special occasion to interrogate Mr. Roosevelt on developments at these conferences, but, if I asked him questions relating to his discussions, he was prompt, with few exceptions, to inform me frankly on the most secret matters." *Memoirs of Cordell Hull*, Vol. II, page 1110.

[2] One of the most interesting of these was written by Maxwell Hamilton, then Chief of the Far Eastern Division on November 15th. Its thoughts and recommendations foreshadowed in many ways the policy pursued by the American delegation at the Cairo and Teheran conferences and thereafter. It foresaw clearly the range of future Soviet territorial and other demands in the Far East and advised that we make it clear to the Soviet government that we favored the return to China of all its former territories. As regards Sino-Soviet relations, it advised that the American government should use its influence simultaneously (a) to bring together the Chinese government and the Chinese Communists within a liberalized government, and (b) to get the Soviet government to make clear that it had no connection with the Chinese Communists and would not interfere in Chinese internal affairs.

But they could not be brought together. Chiang Kai-shek was hesitant about meeting Stalin face to face; he was doubtful whether he could talk with the Marshal on the terms of amity becoming such an encounter.[3] Stalin wanted to avoid the personal meeting also, fearing that Japan might show its anger by closing the port of Vladivostok. Yet some of the most important of the subjects to be discussed concerned both China and the Soviet Union, and the assent of both would be required for useful decision. Which of the two conferences should take place first— that with the Generalissimo or that with Stalin? How could the order of business be arranged so as to respect the need for separation and yet reach essential decisions for which the approval of both was needed or wanted?

It will be recalled that back in June—when doubts emerged as to whether the Chinese government could or would continue active resistance to Japan—the President had told Chiang Kai-shek that he wanted to talk with him. The Generalissimo had suggested a meeting in Alaska in August or September. But other business had intervened. Quite possibly also the President thought it better to wait until he was in a position to promise greater military aid for China. While the meeting with Chiang Kai-shek remained in suspense, a rough and nasty exchange in August with Stalin over the business of an armistice with Italy had shown the need for closer touch. Mutual faith was essential for the great war movements that were in prospect. Stalin agreed; and in September it was settled between them that he, the President, and Churchill should get together soon after the foreign ministers of their three countries met in Moscow. This appointment was confirmed when that conference indicated that the heads of state would agree rather than quarrel.

The President sent word to the Generalissimo that he would like to see him soon, that he was planning to talk with Stalin either before or after he did so. Chiang Kai-shek answered that he would be glad to meet the President before the President conferred with Stalin; but if this could not be arranged he would rather put off his meeting with the President. It was contrived that he should have his chance to enjoy the first say. Roosevelt and Churchill set off for Cairo, and while on their way let Stalin know that as soon as the talks with the Generalissimo ended, they would go on from there to Teheran and join him.

Churchill and Eden were also concerned over the sequence in which

---

[3] Letter, Hurley to President from Cairo, November 20, 1943, after visit to India and China.

the consultations were to take place. The Prime Minister was afraid that Roosevelt, with what he thought an excessive notion of the part China could play in the war and peace, might enter into unwarranted engagements with Chiang Kai-shek; that he might give promises that would upset their plans for Europe. He also felt that as much of conference time and attention as possible should be spent on the many questions regarding the conduct and ending of the war in Europe, as little as possible on what he regarded as postponable issues in the Pacific. Thus he and his military colleagues wanted to have prefatory talks with the Americans. But the President was afraid that if the Americans and British met first, the Chinese and Russians might think that a combination was being formed against them. He was setting out to win them both over, and did not want to risk suspicion that he was pledged to British ideas. He wanted to be free in his dealings with all.

Thus Roosevelt went straight on to Cairo. There he immersed himself in talks with Chiang Kai-shek.[4] Churchill's annoyance lasted in his memory when later he wrote about the conference. "The talks of the British and American Staffs were sadly distracted by the Chinese story, which was lengthy, complicated and minor. Moreover . . . the President, who took an exaggerated view of the Indian-Chinese sphere, was soon closeted in long conferences with the Generalissimo. All hope of persuading Chiang and his wife to go and see the Pyramids and enjoy themselves until we returned from Teheran fell to the ground, with the result that Chinese business occupied first instead of last place at Cairo."[5]

As the President and Chiang Kai-shek talked at Mena House, looking out at the ancient Pyramids, passing events in China and the Pacific bore upon their attitudes.[6] The Chinese Communists were continuing their defiance. The Japanese were resuming their efforts to seduce a shaken government to make peace.[7] The first small actions in the Burma campaign were starting; British and Chinese forces had crossed the India-Burma frontier. Our naval task and amphibious forces were proving that they could drive the Japanese out of the islands in the Pacific, and the means for a major thrust across the Pacific were coming into sight.

[4] It is regrettable that no American notes or minutes of these talks have so far been found. Madame Chiang Kai-shek acted as interpreter.

[5] *Closing the Ring*, page 328.

[6] A wit in the American delegation suggested that a suitable code name for the conference might be Menapause.

[7] Secretary Hull so informed the President on November 29th, adding that the Chinese government was again rebuffing the Japanese.

The destructive power of the new long-range bombers (B-29s) was impressing planning staffs. Some elements in the Pentagon were advising that American strategy in China—based on the renovation and use of large Chinese ground armies—should be reconsidered.[8] In sum, the need or value of China in the winning of the war was on the wane; while in contrast the need for taking measures to secure its future unity and position was growing graver.

At Cairo the heads of state resolved that China should have every chance to be a great power. Simultaneously they gave form to a military program that would test whether it had the inner strength to become one.

The political affirmations of the conference about China were expressed in a statement known as the Cairo Declaration. Its main points had been talked about before.[9] Still, compared to the pangs and pains which were usual in historical operations of the sort, this one was remarkably easy. Chiang Kai-shek asked the return to China of all its territories lost to Japan. The President and Churchill granted the wish at once. They did not dispute the claim or try to impose a price upon it.

On November 24th, after his first stretch of talk with Chiang Kai-shek, the President told the assembled conference that there was no doubt that China had wide aspirations. But the actual text of the statement in which China's wishes were defined does not seem to have been discussed either in the full conference or in the sessions of the American Chiefs of Staff or the Combined Chiefs of Staff. Nor did the President give Hull, in Washington, or the State Department, a chance to pass upon it.[10] Its final composition was hurried in order that it might be finished before Chiang Kai-shek left for home and Roosevelt left for Teheran.

The Generalissimo had secured first attention for China's affairs and he thought it best not to wait about for Soviet assent. It was agreed that

[8] Sunderland-Romanus manuscript, Vol. II.

[9] At a meeting at the White House as early as March 27th, 1943, with Eden, the British Secretary of State for Foreign Affairs, Strang, Assistant Under-Secretary, and Lord Halifax, the British Ambassador, the President had told them that he favored the return of Manchuria and Formosa to China and an international trusteeship for Korea. No British dissent, then or later, is on record. Then on October 5th, just before Hull left for Moscow, the President repeated these ideas. He also said that he thought that Indo-China and the Japanese-mandated islands might be placed under international trustees, along with security points in other parts of the world (naming many). But he thought that the Kurile Islands should really go to Russia. *Memoirs of Cordell Hull*, Vol. II, pages 1595-1596.

[10] *Ibid.*, Vol. II, page 1584.

Stalin would be told at once of the statement and that it would be publicly issued as soon as possible thereafter.

The President made his promise good. In his first talk with Stalin at Teheran, before the conference went into formal session, he reviewed his conversations with Chiang Kai-shek, and his plans and projects for China and the Pacific. Stalin remarked only that he thought China had fought very badly because of poor leadership. Almost at once thereafter Molotov sent a note for the President which said that Stalin had acquainted himself with the statement to be issued concerning the Cairo Conference and had "no observations at all to make in regard to it." At luncheon on the 30th Churchill asked Stalin whether he had read it. Stalin answered that "although he could make no commitments he thoroughly approved the communique and all its contents. It was right that Korea should be independent and that Manchuria, Formosa, and the Pescadores should be returned to China. But," he went on to say that "the Chinese must be made to fight, which they had not thus far done." The President and the Prime Minister agreed.

Stalin reaffirmed what he had said to Hull a few weeks before—that the Soviet Union planned to join in the Pacific war against Japan. He repeated his regret that the Soviet Union had been up to then unable to do so. The forces which it had in Siberia were, he explained, about enough for defensive purposes but would have to be trebled before they could take the offensive. But, he went on freely, once Germany was defeated, the Soviet Union could transfer necessary forces to Siberia and "then we shall be able by our common front to beat Japan."

The President and Prime Minister, as well as their military staffs, were all made glad by these Soviet affirmations; though, as there is reason to believe, they perceived that Soviet entry into the war would be followed by Soviet demands to share in the rewards of victory, they welcomed this help in the hard, closing struggle against Japan. All wanted as short a war as possible, a victory won with the least possible shock and exhaustion to the peoples of the Western World. Both wanted to avoid a repetition of the attrition of the First World War and its damaging aftermath.

The President gave Stalin two memos which showed how eager the American military organization was to move into joint operations with the Soviet Union in the Far East. They included:

1. The establishment of American air bases in the Maritime Provinces of the Soviet Union.

2. Advance planning for the initiation of air operations against Japan immediately after Soviet entry in the Pacific war.

3. Preliminary planning for naval operations against Japan.

Stalin evaded these requests, which would have ranged the Soviet Union at once and conclusively against Japan. He said they would have to be studied further and that he would discuss them later with Ambassador Harriman.

The Cairo Statement was issued on December 1st, shortly before the President and Churchill returned to Cairo. It expressed the resolve of the three Allies, the United States, China and Great Britain, to bring unrelenting pressure against Japan, until they had obtained "unconditional surrender." It condensed in one paragraph the great determination that all the outside lands which Japan had acquired were to be taken away from her; and that all territories that had once been Chinese would be returned to that country. This read:

"The Three Great Allies are fighting this war to restrain and punish the aggression of Japan. They covet no gain for themselves and have no thought of territorial expansion. It is their purpose that Japan shall be stripped of all the islands in the Pacific which she has seized or occupied since the beginning of the first World War in 1914, and that all the territories Japan has stolen from the Chinese, such as Manchuria, Formosa, and the Pescadores, shall be restored to the Republic of China. Japan will also be expelled from all other territories which she has taken by violence and greed. The aforesaid three great powers, mindful of the enslavement of the people of Korea, are determined that in due course Korea shall become free and independent."[11]

These provisions and promises were thought by their authors to be good in themselves, as well as just retribution upon Japan. They were all at this time of the same mind that in the future Japan should be so greatly reduced in strength that it could not resume its expansive ventures. In the allocation of the lands from which it was to be separated, China would get most, but there would be something for each of the others as well. The Soviet Union could look forward to acquisitions near its maritime provinces; the United States to other island bases in the faraway Western Pacific; the British Commonwealth to relief from Japanese push and penetration.

[11] Statement on Conference of President Roosevelt, Generalissimo Chiang Kai-shek, and Prime Minister Churchill, Cairo, December 1, 1943. Department of State Bulletin, December 4, 1943. The statement makes no reference to the Soviet Union or to the fact that the government of the Soviet Union had been consulted before it was issued.

The promises to China were made in a spirit of historic justice. But there was, it may be surmised, purpose in conferring and announcing them at this time. A vision of the future was being used to redress the weakness of the present. All three governments, the American govern-ernment most, wanted to keep China in the war. But none wanted to provide much greater military resources for that purpose, leaving so much less for the struggle in Europe or the thrust over the Pacific. If China could be rallied by the reward of a great future, then it would engage its tired self longer and harder in the war. The promises were made, in any case, with good heart. The President was enthusiastic about them, Churchill doubtful but indulgent, Stalin matter of fact. Chiang Kai-shek was calmly pleased at getting what he thought was no less than China's due.

The President and the Generalissimo had parted with mutual senti-ments of friendship. Chiang Kai-shek left behind him a note of farewell dated November 26th, written in hand by Madame Chiang Kai-shek, "My dear Mr. President: You will, I hope, forgive me for this uncertain handwriting, for I am still Cyclops, and the letters all run together very un-neatly. But the Generalissimo wishes me to tell you again how much he appreciates what you have done and are doing for China. When he said goodby to you this afternoon, he could not find words adequately expressive to convey his emotions and feelings, nor to thank you suffi-ciently for your friendship. He felt, too, wistfulness at saying a fare-well, although he feels that only a short time will lapse before his next meeting with you. Meanwhile he hopes that you will consider him as a friend whom you can trust. . . ."

When the Cairo Declaration was published the Generalissimo hurried back another note to the President on December 5th. In this, he wrote, "Since our home-coming the Cairo Declaration has been published. Its effect of uplifting the morale of our army and our people has been electric. In fact the whole nation is articulate to a degree that has never been known before in unanimously hailing the Cairo Declaration as a sure sign-post leading the Far East toward post-war peace. . . ."[12]

When the President on Christmas Eve spoke to the nation about the conferences at Cairo and Teheran, he did not go into details about Far Eastern matters. After a tribute to Chiang Kai-shek, "I met in the Gen-eralissimo a man of great vision, great courage, and a remarkably keen

---

[12] This letter is also signed by Madame Chiang Kai-shek. It had a handwritten post-script, "I do hope 'Uncle Joe' came up to expectations, did he? MSC."

understanding of the problems of today and tomorrow. We discussed all the manifold military plans for striking at Japan with decisive force from many directions, and I believe I can say that he returned to Chungking with the positive assurance of total victory over our common enemy." He went on, "Today we and the Republic of China are closer together than ever before in deep friendship and in unity of purpose." The American people were glad to think so. In their eyes China and its place among the nations glowed as brightly as ever, though conditions affecting China's power to live up to that ideal were growing poorer. Could wish and reality be joined—in a democratic China, unified under Chiang Kai-shek and attached to us in trustful friendship?

If the President had doubts—and he probably did have—as to whether China would be capable of playing the part assigned to it, he put them behind him. If he had doubts whether the Chiang Kai-shek regime would prove qualified to realize on the chance—and again it is probable that he did have—he thought that the task would be taken over by others.

The task was not nearly as smooth or easy as a quick reading of the Cairo Statement led most Americans to think. Even before the invasion of Manchuria by Japan in 1931, the control of the Central Government over various parts of China had been incomplete and shaky. Now it was being challenged by vigorous enemies lodged in North China and seeking to enter all other sections. The Chinese armies were in poor condition, not in shape or in state of mind for hard, effective action. The Chinese people were tired and suffering. Within all of China there were not enough doctors and hospitals to care properly for a single province, hardly enough professionally trained civil servants to administer a few large cities, and only a scattered handful of experienced engineers and industrial organizers. To come into its inheritance, the Chinese government would have to defeat or make terms with its internal enemies, refresh the loyalty of the great peasant population, prove capable of governing such great cities as Shanghai and Tientsin and of providing new governors for Formosa, Manchuria, and other territories which had developed under Japanese control.

In short, those who knew the state of China in December 1943 had much reason to wonder whether the Chinese government and people could manage their affairs well enough to justify that concept of greatness with which the Cairo Declaration is imbued.

Other political matters, beside those specifically dealt with in the Cairo Declaration, were discussed at Cairo and Teheran. Two closely connected ones were of prime importance. One was in regard to the place to be assigned to China in the organization to be formed after the war for the maintenance of peace. The other concerned prospective Soviet claims for territory and privileges in the Pacific.

The main story of the talks on the first subject is left for others to tell. In brief, the President stubbornly urged that China should be one of the small directing group (then called the Four Policemen) which was to have the first responsibility in dealing with any emergency threat to peace. This was consistent with the Moscow Declaration and the territorial dispositions written into the Cairo Statement. Japan was to lose its empire, and henceforth be disarmed and confined. China was to regain great and rich territories, which would enable it to be strong, and to act as the dominating oriental power.

Stalin was opposed to granting China so leading a part and place in the settlement of the world's political affairs. He said that he thought the small powers of Europe would resent having China act against them. He also said he was doubtful whether China would be strong enough after the war to carry its assigned part. But he appeared to regard the matter rather indifferently and did not make an issue of it. His interest was centered elsewhere. Roosevelt left Teheran with the justified impression that the Soviet Union would agree that China should have a place in the future United Nations organization equal to that of any other state—another badge for the Generalissimo for which he and his country would have to qualify.

Talk about the territory to be returned to China extended itself to talk about the aims of the Soviet Union in the Far East. The Cairo Declaration, just approved, provided that Japan was to be made to give up all its external territories. Some—Manchuria, Formosa, and the Pescadores—were awarded to China. But the rest—the islands north and south of Japan, including the Kuriles and Sakhalin—would fall to someone else. Would the Soviet claim these, and what more besides?

Such records as I have seen suggest that Churchill and Roosevelt invited discussion in this field. It may be surmised that they thought it a good time to find out what the Soviet Union would be wanting. Current circumstances must have seemed to them conducive to reasonable discussion, and conditions might not always be so auspicious. Soviet armies were still engaged against enormous German forces on the eastern front. The United States was providing the vital means for the Soviet cause; it was agreeing to send about five and a half million tons of shipping around the Cape of Good Hope, over the Caspian Sea, and across the

Pacific for the Soviet armies and people. The date of the start of the great invasion of the western front was being definitely set, and the plans for synchronizing this with the offensive action of the Russian forces were being completed. In short, this was the time of closest military cooperation—and the suitable time to strive for similarly full political cooperation.

On November 30th, after Stalin spoke favorably of the Cairo Declaration, Churchill said that he was interested to know the views of the Soviet government on the Far East. He added that he recognized that such a large land mass as the Soviet Union deserved access to warmwater ports; and that although Britain had opposed this in the past, it no longer did so. Stalin answered that of course the Russians had their views on these matters but that it would perhaps be better to await the time when the Soviet Union was taking an active part in the Far Eastern war. However, he continued, the Soviet had no port in the Far East that was not closed off, since Vladivostok was only partly ice-free and was in addition exposed to the Japanese control of the straits. At this point the President mentioned Dairen as a possibility. Stalin said that he did not think that the Chinese would like the idea. The President went on to say that he thought they might in the form of a *free port under international guarantee*. Stalin said that would not be bad.[13] The President had discussed this matter with Chiang Kai-shek at Cairo, and the Generalissimo had indicated he would not object to this, provided the Soviet Union cooperated with China and that Chinese sovereignty was not impaired.[14]

Other elements of Soviet aims and wishes in the Far East were explored in the same provisional way; almost the whole realm of Soviet claims that were later adjusted in the Yalta accord were touched upon. But by wish of the Soviet government, decision in regard to them was deferred. It would be surprising if Stalin did not foresee that Soviet

[13] Sherwood, *Roosevelt and Hopkins*, pages 791-792, gives an interesting account of the main passages in this talk.

[14] Chiang Kai-shek told Vice President Wallace of this talk with the President when Wallace went to Chungking the following June. *United States Relations with China*, page 558. It was roughly confirmed by Hollington H. Tong, Director of the Office of Information of the Chinese government, when he was questioned by the press in regard to a statement to this effect in an article based on the papers of Hopkins in *Collier's*, August 28, 1948. Tong put the matter this way, "The reply of President Chiang was that he might give consideration to such a proposal when the time came provided there was no impairment of the sovereignty of China." He implied that this information came from Madame Chiang Kai-shek, who had been the interpreter during the talk between the President and Chiang Kai-shek on this subject.

demands would get closer attention when German defeat was assured and the Soviet armies were getting ready to march into Manchuria.

Roosevelt, not long after his return to Washington, summed up for the Pacific War Council the main points on which he had found understanding at Cairo and Teheran, as follows:

That Japan should be stripped of all its island possessions; that control of the islands north of the Equator should be taken over by the United Nations; and that the policing of the Western Pacific, and therefore the necessary air and naval bases in that region, should be taken over by those powers who were capable of exercising effective military control;

That Stalin specifically agreed that Manchuria, Formosa, and the Pescadores should be returned to China; and that Korea was to be under a forty-year tutelage;

That Russia, having no ice-free port, wanted one; and that Stalin looked with favor on making Dairen a free port for all the world, with the idea that Siberian exports and imports could be sent through the port of Dairen and carried to Siberian territory over the Manchurian railway in bond. Stalin, the President added, also agreed that the Manchurian railway should become the property of the Chinese government;

That Stalin wanted all of Sakhalin to be returned to Russia, and to have the Kurile Islands turned over to Russia in order that Russia might control the straits leading to Siberia.

After conveying this information, the President stated that it was gratifying to him to find that Marshal Stalin and the Generalissimo saw eye to eye with him on all the major problems of the Pacific. Therefore he felt it would not be hard to reach arrangements about the control of the Pacific after the defeat of Japan.

The Pacific War Council was made up of representatives of those of the United Nations who were fighting in the Pacific. Roosevelt was the chairman. China was represented by its Ambassador, Dr. Wei Tao-ming. Thus unless he was not present at this meeting or unless he failed to transmit this information to Chungking, which is unlikely, it would seem that the Generalissimo had at this early date an almost complete preview of Soviet desires in the Far East. The information does not seem to have dimmed his wish for an agreement with the Soviet government or, as will be seen, his disposition to send representatives to Moscow to arrange a settlement.

Roosevelt, Churchill, and Stalin parted at Teheran, genuinely taken by the belief that their three countries could and would continue to act in unison. As expressed in a note written by one member of the American group, after hearing the toasts at Churchill's birthday dinner on November 30th, "Back of all was the feeling that basic friendships had been established which there was every reason to believe would endure." Or, as spoken by Roosevelt on that same occasion in response to Stalin's cordial appreciation of the President's leadership, "We have proved here in Teheran that the varying ideals of our nations can come together in a harmonious whole. . . ."

Roosevelt and Churchill hurried back to Cairo for further discussion of the military steps that had been discussed at the first session there and at Teheran, and that were designed to win the way for the political dispositions in the Far East of which this chapter has told.

CHAPTER 12

Cairo and Teheran Conferences: Military Plans

AT CAIRO, while the heads of state sought solutions for the political problems of Europe and the Pacific, impressive military staffs were applying themselves to plans for the offensive which was to break the Japanese encirclement of China. The arguments were brisk. Americans and British alike were loath to divert to that purpose resources that could be used to carry forward actions elsewhere. But the ruling American participants were still convinced that the surest course would be to regain entryway into China through Burma, and thereafter use the vast Chinese manpower in concert with American air and naval forces. They thought that this was the only way in which a strong Chinese military force could be constituted; and they counted on this force to enable China to assume that primary place which was being marked out for it.

But in Sherwood's words, "Churchill viewed the proposals for large operations in Burma with scant enthusiasm." He and the British Chiefs of Staff were willing to let China get along as best it could for the time being with its own means and efforts. They would rather have used such resources as could be spared for the Far East to protect India and to try to gain a re-entry into Malaya and the Dutch Indies. However, they were ready to follow through with the American program, first approved at Casablanca, if not too much was asked of them. In contrast, Mountbatten and his staff in the SEAC were eager for the Burma campaign, and had prepared a plan of seven related operations, land, sea, air, and amphibious (this last against the Andaman Islands—Operation Buccaneer).

Chiang Kai-shek's reckonings and conditions were the same as those so often before expounded by him. He wanted greatly to have a land route of supply through Burma, but he was afraid of entering then on a campaign which he feared as hard and dangerous. "Burma," he explained to the Combined Chiefs of Staff at Cairo, was in his opinion ". . . the key to the whole campaign in Asia. . . . [Its] loss would be a very serious matter to the Japanese and they would fight stubbornly and tenaciously to retain their hold on the country."[1] Thus he was willing to bide his time rather than to risk the defeat and loss of valuable Chinese government forces. He did not want the air effort in China— under Chennault—to be reduced for an indefinite period. He was ready

[1] *Roosevelt and Hopkins*, Sherwood, page 772.

to wait until the Americans and British could provide great enough air and naval forces for converging assaults that would prevent the Japanese from sending more troops into Burma, and thus make success sure.

Here there is place only for notes on some phases of the discussion and decisions, particularly those about Burma and China, which caused lasting difficulty.[2]

The Generalissimo, sometimes through his Chinese military staff, sometimes through Stilwell, sometimes directly, proposed plans, and made reservations with quick changes of mind.[3] He was discontented with the size of the operations which (under SEAC plans) the British proposed to take on themselves. He was insistent in his wish for concurrent naval operations, and in his view that no matter what was done in Burma, tonnage over the Hump should not be less than 10,000 per month. But after the first three days of talk the American and British delegations thought that the Generalissimo had been persuaded to accept their proposals and terms. Then the Generalissimo again reversed himself. Admiral Mountbatten persuaded Churchill to make a last try, which he did on the 26th. In his war diary that evening, Mountbatten wrote ". . . At 4:15 the President, Prime Minister, Generalissimo and Mme. Chiang Kai-shek met. Unfortunately they had no secretaries present. And no comments or conclusions were taken down. But I was told by the Prime Minister that the Generalissimo had agreed once more to all the points he had rejected the day before. When I attended the Chiang Kai-shek's tea party, Madame told me I should be a very happy man, as the Plenary Meeting had agreed to everything I wanted."

[2] The chief points and subjects of difficulty are told in Mountbatten's *Report*, Churchill's *Closing the Ring*, and Sherwood's *Roosevelt and Hopkins*. Admiral Leahy in *I Was There* also tells something of the discussion. *The Stilwell Papers* spotlight the actions of the Chinese delegation and General Stilwell's own thoughts and position. Sunderland-Romanus manuscript, Vol. II, gives the most full and systematic account of the various plans prepared by SEAC, the War Department, and Stilwell.

[3] The Generalissimo again repeated his request for regular representation on the Combined Chiefs of Staff. This is told in *Fleet Admiral King: A Naval Record*, page 509: "In the first meeting of the Combined Chiefs of Staff at Çairo on 22 November, Marshall reported that Chiang Kai-shek would like to have a Chinese military representative on the Combined Chiefs, and suggested the possibility that it might facilitate the development of good faith and mutual understanding if the Soviet Union and China were each invited to have a permanent military representative. King pointed out, however, that the question involved a basic principle that might lead to the permanent expansion of the Combined Chiefs of Staff into a four-power body. Clearly the Chinese and Soviet representatives could not sit at the same table, since they were not engaging the same enemies. The Chinese could not discuss the war against Germany, nor could the Soviet representatives attend the deliberations of the Combined Chiefs of Staff dealing with the war against Japan."

Roosevelt and Churchill left for Teheran. Chiang Kai-shek got ready to go to the airfield to start back to Chungking. Before he went out of the door on the morning of the 27th, he told Stilwell that after all he was going to reject the Combined Chiefs' proposals, and asked Stilwell "to stay and protest." The General began his diary entry for that day with the query "So where are we?"

This abrupt, unsystematic termination of the talks left some main points open. The Chinese departed without having minutes of the meeting. The greatest unsettled question was whether or not there need be a concurrent amphibious operation near and/or along the South Burma coast. Chiang Kai-shek left Cairo without yielding in his view that it was essential. The President and the American military authorities had favored it. As later recounted by Churchill, "The President, in spite of my arguments, gave the Chinese the promise of a considerable amphibious operation across the Bay of Bengal within the next few months. This would have cramped 'Overlord' for landing and tank-landing craft, which had now become the bottleneck, far more than any of my Turkey and Aegean projects. It would also have hampered grievously the immense operations we were carrying out in Italy."[4] The British considered themselves unobligated and made that view of record. Such was the state of decision about the combined military campaign in Burma when the Cairo Declaration was issued.

At Teheran the President explained to Stalin the plans for operations in the Pacific and in Burma. Stalin had not much to say about them. He spoke against the scattering of forces among too numerous undertakings; he was all for Overlord. Churchill tried to impress Stalin with the advantages to be won by operations in Italy, the Adriatic, and Eastern Mediterranean.[5] The converging currents of purpose swirled around the snags, one of the most definite being the limited number of landing craft. Churchill tried to convince Stalin that if ventures in the Bay of Bengal were canceled there would be enough landing craft both for action in the Mediterranean and a punctual Overlord. At the same time

[4] *Closing the Ring*, page 328.

[5] The various possibilities that attracted Churchill at one time or another during the conferences at Cairo and Teheran were (a) to push the advance in Italy as far as the Po Valley by amphibious operations to the north, (b) an amphibious attack in the northeast Adriatic aimed at the Danube Valley, (c) to capture Rhodes or the Dodecanese Islands in connection with the effort to induce Turkey to enter the war, (d) operation in and from Turkey if it entered the war and (e) later, landings in southern France in connection with Overlord. The appearance and disappearance in his presentations of these projects can be followed in his own book *Closing the Ring*, and *The Strange Alliance*, by John R. Deane, New York, 1947, page 41 et seq.

he intently sought to persuade the President to ask relief from the promise given to Chiang Kai-shek. Roosevelt held out against him.

With the issue unresolved, the two returned to Cairo. And there Churchill renewed his pleas. Buccaneer, he continued to argue, should be postponed until after the end of the monsoon—the autumn of 1944. He gave two new reasons which had not been so evident during the first stages of discussion. One was that Stalin, in the interval between the first meeting at Cairo and this one, had confirmed his promise that the Soviet Union would enter the war as soon as Germany was defeated. Churchill took this to mean that the Allies would have better bases (in Siberia) for bombing Japan than they would ever get within China. Thus he thought that the whole plan of operations within the SEAC had lost some value. His second new reason was that the latest estimation of the force which would be required for the amphibious action was much higher than expected.

The argument grew in force as it went on. Marshall and King gravely warned that if Buccaneer were canceled the Generalissimo might not allow Chinese forces to take part in the Burma campaign. In that event they said they feared that there would be no campaign in Upper Burma; the Japanese would be able to resist our advances in the Pacific the more strongly; and there would be a revulsion of feeling in China. The President emphasized that the Generalissimo had left Cairo quite clearly under the impression that there would be a concurrent amphibious operation. Moreover, he added, he was a little dubious about putting all his eggs in one basket. What if Stalin was unable to be as good as his word? Then we and the British would have forfeited Chinese support without getting equivalent help. The British no less gravely maintained that Buccaneer was an unjustified diversion from the landing operations in France on which the Americans and Russians had so severely insisted. Further, Churchill denied that the cancellation of that enterprise would affect the Chinese will to continue to fight the Japanese.

The disagreement lasted almost until the hour of separation. Then on the afternoon of December 5th, Roosevelt sent Churchill a laconic private message: "Buccaneer is off." Churchill, on relaying this news over the telephone to General Ismay, quoted, "He is a better man that ruleth his spirit than he that taketh a city."[6] To run a bit ahead of the story, Mountbatten was notified that most of his landing craft might

[6] *Closing the Ring*, pages 411-412.

be ordered elsewhere soon and was asked to suggest an alternative operation smaller than Buccaneer. Within a few weeks, he was instructed by the Chiefs of Staff to send back to Europe almost all of his amphibious resources.[7] That made any operation against the Andaman Islands impossible.

The President, in conceding to the Prime Minister, had to surmount the doubts of some of his military advisers.[8] He may have been in part influenced to change his mind by the difficulties of finding the cargo ships that would have been needed for Buccaneer.[9] He was risking reproach by the Generalissimo that the American government had broken its promise and even a possible rejection of the whole Burma campaign. But evidently he had come to conclude that the opponents of Buccaneer were correct in thinking that the means needed for that operation could be more effectively used elsewhere during the spring of 1944.

The decision was recorded in the final report of the Combined Chiefs of Staff as presented to Roosevelt and Churchill and approved by them on December 6th. The section in regard to Burma was inconclusive. In essence it stated:

1. That major amphibious operations in the Bay of Bengal were to be postponed until the autumn of 1944 and the landing craft previously assigned to Buccaneer should be sent to Europe.

2. Alternative plans were to be prepared for either

a. the North Burma ground operation, with assisting air and naval actions but without any large amphibious operations, or

b. postponement of the North Burma ground operations, meanwhile increasing the air lift over the Hump to the utmost with the planes

[7] The remnants of the Overseas Assault Forces (Force G) which had been scattered after the invasion of Sicily had been detached to Southeast Asia. Most of this force was recalled to the Mediterranean in December. The remainder, with a few ships which had always been in Southeast Asia, became Force F, but this was also recalled to the European Theater. Mountbatten, *Report*, Section A, paragraph 69, and Section B, paragraphs 21-22 and 25.

[8] *Roosevelt and Hopkins*, Sherwood, pages 800-802. In *Closing the Ring*, pages 411-412, Churchill states that the President told him of this decision on the afternoon of December 5th. Admiral Ernest J. King in his book *Fleet Admiral King: A Naval Record*, page 525, relates a discussion on the morning of the 6th in which the President asked opinions as to the effect of changing the agreement with the Chinese; he writes that Leahy and Arnold had come to concur with Churchill, that Marshall also came to agree, but that he, King, remained obdurate; and that late that afternoon Roosevelt told the Joint Chiefs of his reluctant decision to abandon the Andaman Islands operation. If King is correct in dating this discussion on the 6th, the President made up his mind before this final consultation with the Joint Chiefs.

[9] *Roosevelt and Hopkins*, Sherwood, page 800.

available, and also taking measures to conduct long-range bombing raids against Japan (Operation Matterhorn.)[10]

Roosevelt and Churchill gave Chiang Kai-shek the choice between these two courses of action. The message which they hustled off to him explained that the discussion with Stalin at Teheran had involved the United States and Great Britain in vast combined operations in Europe in the late spring of 1944. This expressed the fact that from then on they were irrevocably obligated to carry through the Overlord plan for the invasion of France. As a consequence it was explained that it would not be possible to devote enough landing craft at that time to an amphibious operation in the Bay of Bengal. Chiang Kai-shek was asked whether, such being the case, he wanted to go ahead with the North Burma campaign (Tarzan) as planned, including a promise to maintain naval control of the Bay of Bengal and concurrent commando amphibious raiding operations. Or, would he prefer to postpone the North Burma campaign also until November, when a heavy amphibious operation could be carried out? If he chose the latter course, the United States would concentrate in the meanwhile on the expansion of the air transport route to carry supplies for the air and ground forces in China.

The President called in Stilwell—who as requested by Chiang Kai-shek had stayed on in Cairo—to tell him of this change in the program. Stilwell had a double interest in it. He was the most passionate advocate of the spring campaign in North Burma, and when he got back to Chungking he would have the unpleasant job of mollifying Chiang Kai-shek. But the talk between the President and Stilwell bobbled about without touching bottom.[11] The President, looking grim, told how stubbornly he had fought in favor of the amphibious operation. He had given in finally, he explained, only because he had not wanted the conference with Churchill to break on this issue. He dwelt on the other forms of support that would be given China.

Stilwell himself had not thought Buccaneer essential, and perhaps he did not even think it justified. Immediately after his talk with the President he radioed his headquarters in Chungking to urge the Generalissimo to go ahead with his part of the Burma campaign anyhow.

[10] Further information about Matterhorn, which was backed hard by Roosevelt and General Arnold, will be found in the next chapter.

The Combined Chiefs of Staff at Cairo also approved "the seizure of Guam and the Marianas," tentatively setting the date for October 1, 1944, with the primary purpose of using the Marianas as a base for bombing operations against Japan.

[11] The passages of the talk as remembered by Stilwell are given in dialogue form in *The Stilwell Papers*, pages 251-254.

Chiang Kai-shek seemed to take the news hard but with restraint. Mountbatten learned that he regarded the change as releasing him from his promise to have the Chinese Expeditionary Force advance from Yunnan into Burma. In his first answering message to the President on December 8th, the Generalissimo expressed fear of the effect of what he termed a "radical change of policy and strategy" upon the Chinese army and people and upon their ability to hold out. But, he continued, in recognition that a rapid defeat of Germany would be to the advantage of China as well as to that of the other United Nations, he was inclined not to make a fuss.

As between the two alternative courses suggested to him by the President, he would decide, he said, after Stilwell returned. In the meanwhile, in order to reassure the Chinese people, he asked for: (1) a billion-dollar loan to enable them to meet their dire needs, (2) an increase in support for the American and Chinese air forces in China, (3) a rapid expansion of the air lift over the Hump to twenty thousand tons per month. The message concluded by expressing fear that the Japanese, believing that the United States would be occupied in Europe during the coming year, would try an all-out offensive to end Chinese resistance. As events were to show, this fear was exaggerated but not foolish.

When Stilwell got back to Chungking, he found Chiang Kai-shek hesitant, estimating Japanese strength in Burma high and afraid of defeat.[12] The Generalissimo informed the President of his decision on December 17th. He tried to keep the advantages of both plans: that is, to prepare for an offensive in the spring, and then start it at such time as enough naval forces and transports could be assembled to make a large-scale landing on the flank of the Japanese.[13] He was willing to have the Ledo force go into action at once, with Stilwell in full command. But otherwise he wanted to remain watchfully on the defensive until time was more favorable for victory.

[12] Account of his talk with Chiang Kai-shek is given in *The Stilwell Papers*, entry, December 16, 1943, pages 264-265.
They differed as to the size of the Japanese forces in Burma. Stilwell in December thought there were only five divisions. The Generalissimo asserted there were eight. See *The Stilwell Papers*, entry for December 16, 1943. The estimate of Japanese strength later given by Admiral Mountbatten seems in agreement with that of the Generalissimo rather than that of Stilwell. In his Report he wrote (Paragraph B 66), "By January, Japanese army forces in Burma had been increased from one army of five divisions (a total of about 135,000 men) when the South-East Asia Command was formed, to two armies of eight divisions and one independent mixed brigade (a total of some 200,000 men)." The increase, it is probable, was partly in preparation for the planned attempt to invade India.
[13] Message Chiang Kai-shek to Roosevelt, December 17, 1943. *The Stilwell Papers*, entry, December 16.

Stilwell rushed to Burma to get the action going, it is safe to surmise, with the intention of somehow or other extending the operation as he went along. He was bent on bringing the Yoke force, the Chinese army in Yunnan, into battle in one way or another. But before telling of his tenacious efforts in that cause, we should make a brief note of other requests which had been made by Chiang Kai-shek at or shortly after Cairo. For they become fixed in the Generalissimo's vista of the future.

The American government was already trying to supply and train thirty Chinese ground divisions. And it had promised that it would, when it could, continue the same process for thirty more. Chiang Kai-shek had asked at Cairo that an American army corps be sent to fight in Burma. The President had told him that could not be done. But—wanting the Generalissimo to return to Chungking with a full baggage train—Roosevelt had agreed that the United States should provide means for a third thirty divisions—up to a total of ninety in all. Such chance records as are available indicate that Roosevelt had meant that this would be done eventually, but that he gave no promise as to when it was to be done.[14]

There was also the matter of the loan which the Generalissimo had asked as balm for breach of promise after Cairo. This request, as just told, was first made of the President on December 8th. Two weeks later Chiang Kai-shek asked Gauss to call upon him. He reviewed how bad conditions were becoming in this war-time China, and how crucial the need of supporting the value of the currency if he was to keep an army and government together. After the Generalissimo left the room, Madame Chiang Kai-shek spoke bitterly of how much it was costing China to maintain the American air effort. Gauss was unmoved. His opinion was that the economic situation in China would not be helped by an American dollar loan at this time, but only by successful military operations which would reopen land transport into China.[15]

The Treasury was of the same opinion. A loan of the kind asked might retard the decline in the value of the Chinese dollar and thus

[14] Marshall informed the Joint Chiefs of Staff on November 25, 1943, that Chiang Kai-shek had made the request; that the President had postponed any definite commitment but made it clear that the United States did plan eventually to equip ninety divisions. In September 1945 Secretary of State Byrnes, after consulting Hopkins, who had been at Cairo, concluded, and so advised President Truman (September 3, 1945) that a commitment of some sort in regard to equipping ninety divisions had been made by Roosevelt at Cairo, but that it was vague and loose. See Chapter 32.

[15] Telegram, December 23, 1943, Gauss to State Department.

slow up inflation, but not much or for long. Food, clothing, machines, trucks, oil, weapons—these were what the Chinese people needed; they could not get them until a broader road—over land or sea—was opened into China; and for that they were called on to fight soon and hard. For these reasons, Morgenthau told the President that the loan would be unnecessary and undesirable. He suggested instead some lesser measures of aid which might reduce the volume of Chinese currency.[16] Hull advised that the refusal should be a soft one, so as not to cause Chiang Kai-shek to feel unhelped and helpless. He proposed that the Treasury send a mission to China to study what could be done. The President was willing to do this. But he was becoming impatient over the Generalissimo's resistance to his pleadings for an all-out attempt to reopen the Burma Road the coming spring. Chiang Kai-shek's pauses and demands —of which more will shortly be told—seemed to add up to a wish to be taken care of by the United States while his regime remained safe. Thus on January 5th the President ordered that Morgenthau's memo stating the reasons why the loan was not justified be sent to Chiang Kai-shek. Hull told Gauss to explain when he delivered it that although this message on its face might seem unresponsive to the Generalissimo's wishes, it was in fact evidence of our confidence in our relations with him.[17]

This disposed of the matter of a loan. But during the following months disputes over other financial matters ran on. The rub of war costs is apt to infect even healthy coalitions. Others will tell elsewhere of the details of the prolonged argument (1) as to which of the outlays in China the United States should bear (2) and at what rates American dollars ought to be given for Chinese.[18] Differences over these matters touched off tempers already high-strung, and produced hints of separation. The impression prevailed that Chiang Kai-shek was placing this

[16] The Treasury views were stated in a memo to the President, December 18, 1943. *United States Relations with China*, pages 488-489.

[17] Entries, Morgenthau Diaries, January 1, and January 5, 1944.

[18] On the first point, the chief subject was argument in regard to the great cost of construction and maintenance of the bomber base at Chengtu. Mme. Chiang Kai-shek maintained that Roosevelt had promised to meet the full cost. On the second point— the rate of exchange which the American government should pay for Chinese dollars— the Chinese were unreasonable. The American forces in China needed Chinese dollars for troop pay, housing and subsistence, the airfield construction. The Chinese government was insisting that these Chinese dollars should be bought at the officially maintained rate of twenty to one, an unreal rate by any standard. At that rate the American outlay in China might have reached one hundred million dollars a month. The Chinese dollar was selling in the black market at about a hundred and thirty to one, and that was the rate which the War Department thought fair, though it was willing to compromise. The Chinese government took the position that to grant any such rate would ruin the currency.

price upon allowing the Yunnan force to take part in the Burma campaign. The War Department was at moments almost ready to reduce its air and training operations in China.[19] Chiang Kai-shek was justifying his financial proposals by comparing the small American outlay in China to the "astronomical" expenditures made for Britain and the Soviet Union. Kung, the Finance Minister, said to Gauss that unless the Treasury could find ways of easing China's financial burdens, which he described as unbearable, the American army in China would have to finance itself after March 1st, to arrange to buy the supplies, labor, and construction materials it needed—presumably at the twenty-to-one rate.[20]

The Treasury was willing to give in if there were military or political reasons why it should. But the War Department felt imposed upon. As stated by General Somervell to Morgenthau, ". . . he had taken up the matter with General Marshall and Secretary Stimson. He said they [the Army] had decided they were going to be tough with the Chinese Government. They were very dissatisfied with the cooperation they were getting in China and with the small amount of actual combat fighting which the Chinese armies were carrying on."[21]

Gauss favored the same strong line as the War Department. But the State Department warned against steps that might cause Chiang Kai-shek to lose control of the government.[22] It acted as conciliator and nervously sought to keep the argument within safe bounds. Secretary Hull advised the President not to risk a complete rupture in working relations at this critical time, and the President took heed of his caution. The military had second and softer thoughts. A temporary working compromise on war costs and the exchange rate was effected.[23] But it did little to ease

[19] Memo, conference January 19, 1944, Morgenthau, Bell, Somervell, and White. Morgenthau Diary.

[20] Telegrams, Gauss to State Department, January 16, 1944. *United States Relations with China*, pages 493-495; and February 4, 1944.

[21] Memo of conference, January 19, 1944, Morgenthau, Bell, Somervell, and White. Morgenthau Diary.

[22] Memo of conference, Under-Secretary of the Treasury Bell, General Lucius Clay, Hiss, Collado, Stanton, and McGuire of the State Department, February 14, 1944. Morgenthau Diary.

[23] A history of the discussions on exchange rate and war expenditures is found in the memo Stimson sent to the President on May 26, 1944. *United States Relations with China*, pages 496 et seq. The Finance Minister, H. H. Kung on April 19th reviewed the presentation of China's case for more favorable financial consideration. Extract of letter, April 19, 1944, H. H. Kung (Exec. Yuan) to White House (President):

"It is not generally realized and we do not wish it to be known that China has had to conduct her war effort with less aid in the form of materials and supplies than any other major member of the United Nations, and this in spite of the fact that she is confronted with difficulties such as beset the path of no other belligerent country. The powers of endurance of the Chinese people have proven themselves under the tremendous

the tension during the spring of 1944—while the second campaign in Burma was being fought.

---

strain of the seven long years of war. Since, according to this year's budget, nearly 50 per cent of the expenditure is already covered by taxation the National Government is extremely anxious to avoid these sacrificial powers beyond endurance. We had all been hoping for removal of the blockade of China sometime in 1944. Now that appears to be a remote contingency. If the present economic and financial difficulty continues and if we take steps that would drastically depreciate our currency, thus bringing about further inflation, the consequences may be grim indeed."

CHAPTER 13

Trouble in Burma Once More: Spring of 1944

STILWELL, in the pleased words of one of his staff, had "hung his battered musette bag in North Burma, donned his old campaign hat . . . and started a ten-month campaign in which the Chinese not only learned they could fight but learned to like it." Before he left on December 19th Chiang Kai-shek had given him full command of the Chinese divisions trained in India, with the caution that they were not to be sacrificed to British interests.[1] He had told him again that he would wait to see how the action went before engaging other Chinese forces.

While the troops struggled forward through the close and hostile jungles, the top command continued to argue about their mission. Although Roosevelt had put two choices up to Chiang Kai-shek—one of which was to wait until the means for a large amphibious move could be provided in November—Stilwell and the American military high command were set on the other. They were convinced that if the action underway was vigorously pursued, there was a good chance that it could be developed into a major combined effort to clear a road into China before the next rains (due in late May) began. They wanted to force the situation, not wait for it to force them. Roosevelt was moved by their eagerness. Thus in a series of messages during January and February he tried to persuade Chiang Kai-shek to commit the Yunnan force to the North Burma campaign despite the fact that there was not to be any large concurrent amphibious action in the south. He paraded the military reasons in somewhat new formation.[2] He increased all his previous

---

[1] *The Stilwell Papers*, entry, December 19, 1943.

[2] Military historians will tell more adequately of these reasons than I can. One new point made by the President was that long-range bombing operations from China against Japan could be started earlier than expected, as soon as the airfields could be made ready. He had in mind Operation Matterhorn, approved by the Combined Chiefs of Staff at Cairo. This was to use B-29s based in India and staged for their attack upon Japan at Chengtu (in the province of Szechwan). For this it was necessary to construct six large new airfields in India and five in China. The American government provided technical and engineering supervisors. But China was called on to supply labor and materials. It seems to have been supposed at first that these B-29s would be self-supporting, that is, they would carry into China what they needed for the maintenance and bombing operations. But, in fact, Operation Matterhorn used more freight tonnage over the Hump than was allocated to the Chinese armies in 1944. Its needs of air transport space became one element in the harsh dispute over the distribution of Hump tonnage. Chennault protested, thinking that the 14th Air Force could use this tonnage better. But the President and the Joint Chiefs insisted that the operation be maintained. It began in June 1944 and continued until January 1945, when the base of operations was shifted to the Marianas (Saipan).

offers of help, promising that the United States would soon provide many
new transport planes for the Hump and would do its utmost to bring its
capacity to twelve thousand tons per month. This was inducement for
action. To make his advocacy more telling, the President broadly hinted
that if the Yunnan force was not to be used soon, it would get no more
equipment or instruction.[3] His message of January 14th concluded "If
the Yunnan forces cannot be employed it would appear that we should
avoid for the present the movement of critical materials to them over the
limited lines of communication and curtail the continuing build-up of
stock-piles in India beyond that which will be brought to bear against
the enemy."

But the Generalissimo stood out against both the inducement and the
threatened penalty. He reiterated his fear of courting disaster for China
unless large forces were landed in South Burma concurrently with the
advance in North Burma. Perhaps, he went so far as to say, if and when
the Ledo force captured Mandalay or Lashio, he might change his mind.

Nor did Churchill in the weeks after Cairo come to think better
of the Burma operations. His lucid mind magnetized particles of argument against it: "I disliked intensely the prospect of a large scale campaign in Northern Burma. One could not choose a worse place for fighting the Japanese. Making a road from Ledo to China was also an immense, laborious task, unlikely to be finished until the need for it had
passed. Even if it were done in time to replenish the Chinese armies
while they were still engaged, it would make little difference to their
fighting capacity. The need to strengthen the American air bases in
China would also, in our view, diminish as Allied advances in the Pacific
and from Australia gained us airfields closer to Japan. . . . We of course
wanted to recapture Burma, but we did not want to have to do it by land
advances from slender communications and across the most forbidding
fighting country imaginable. The south of Burma, with its port of Rangoon, was far more valuable than the north. But all of it was remote
from Japan, and for our forces to become sidetracked and entangled
there would deny us our rightful share in a Far Eastern victory. I
wished, on the contrary, to contain the Japanese in Burma, and break
into or through the great arc of islands forming the outer fringe of the
Dutch East Indies."[4]

[3] Mountbatten was also becoming impatient at the Generalissimo's stubbornness, though
being equally stubborn in resistance to the Generalissimo's proposals. He favored the use
of pressure, remarking to the British Chiefs of Staff, "I do not see why we should continue to supply him with munitions if they are to be used solely for internal political
purposes." Radio, Mountbatten, December 24, Sunderland-Romanus manuscript, Vol. II.
[4] *Closing the Ring*, pages 560-561.

Mountbatten faithfully went forward with his limited assignments. But he was forming the view that if the Yunnan operation was canceled —and Chiang Kai-shek was then saying it was—it would not be possible to extend the Ledo Road into China during 1944; in that case he thought it likely that a sea route into China would be opened before the Burma Road was in service. In short, as he expressed it, "The Ledo Road strategy was likely to become stale before the road had been secured. . . ." Therefore he recommended that unless China devoted enough force to gain command of the Burma Road in the spring of 1944, it would be best to confine the operations in North Burma to those needed to protect the Hump transport line, and to use all other resources elsewhere in the Pacific.[5] General Auchinleck agreed with Mountbatten. Stilwell was caustic about this change of position.[6] He denounced it in a memo which his staff passed on to the Generalissimo.

As the argument involving Stilwell, Mountbatten, and Chiang Kai-shek flared high, it was transferred to Washington and London. There, planning conferences reviewed again everything that could be said for and against. Two missions were hurried to Washington from the East to plead for the views of their chiefs. Mountbatten arranged to send the senior American officer in his command, General Wedemeyer. Mountbatten regarded him as one of the originators of the "sea" as opposed to the "road" strategy.[7] This mission was given the code name of Axiom. Stilwell, hearing that it was going, hastened to send his own spokesmen— Generals Boatner and Ferris. One of the State Department officers serving on his staff, John Davies, went along.

The tide of contention flowed out of conference rooms of the Pentagon. Churchill and the British military found that they could not change the opinions or bend the wills of the Americans. Roosevelt tried to induce Churchill at least to allow Mountbatten to use what means he had for fighting in Burma. His reasoning was closely fitted together. Recent successes in the Pacific, he said, were creating a real chance for American forces to penetrate the Formosa-China coast-Luzon area before the summer of 1945; to obtain firm control of this area, maximum air sup-

[5] This summary of his train of thought is based on his memorandum to the British Chiefs of Staff, January 8, 1944, the substance of which is given in his *Report*, B Paragraph 28. A more general statement of the strategy toward which Mountbatten's thoughts were turning, akin to Churchill's, is given in *Closing the Ring*, page 573.

[6] His view was entrusted to his diary. "Louis [Mountbatten] welches on entire program [for Burma offensive]. G-mo's fault of course. Limey program: (1) Stop road at Ledo. (2) Do not attack Burma. (3) Go to Sumatra. (4) Include Hongkong in SEAC!" *The Stilwell Papers*, entry, January 8, 1944.

[7] Mountbatten, *Report*, B Paragraph 31.

port would be essential; and this necessitated the development of China as a base for this support; therefore every effort should be made to increase the flow of supplies into China—by increasing the air tonnage *or* opening a road through Burma. If the key point of Myitkyina in North Burma could be captured, the President's exposition continued, the air transport route into China would be made shorter and more secure against attack; thus its tonnage could be quickly increased.[8] Stilwell, the President went on, was confident that he could achieve this by the end of the dry season with the Chinese-American force under his command, provided Mountbatten's forces would do their utmost. More would be gained thereby than by actions against Sumatra and Malaya. These actions in any case would not be carried out until after the end of the war in Europe. Accordingly the President urged Churchill to back to the maximum a vigorous and immediate campaign in Upper Burma.[9]

The British authorities seemed to have been at the point—or possibly past the point—of giving in, when the Japanese (late February, early March) settled the question by turning against the central British-Indian front which was defending the eastern provinces of India. Thereupon the British joined with the Americans in urging Chiang Kai-shek to send more Chinese troops for the Ledo force, already in the battle, and to engage the Yunnan force.[10]

During this January-February clash of judgment just recounted, Stilwell was plunging deeper into Burma. He was leading his divisions with the bold, headstrong conviction that he could prove in action what he could not prove in words. His idea was to show how well the Chinese troops could fight, and thus make clear that the Japanese could be beaten in Burma. The War Department cheered him on.

The fighting in Burma went along on three separate fronts. Chinese forces proved their courage and endurance. American air-borne troops,

[8] If Myitkyina was captured, the transport aircraft could fly a route of lower altitude over the Hump and over a broader corridor, thus permitting more planes to travel the route at the same time. Also, if the pipeline from India could be carried to Myitkyina, the transports could take off from India with less oil and more cargo of other kinds, and refuel at Myitkyina.

[9] The President's arguments were based on the recommendations of the Joint Chiefs of Staff. They were most fully put before Churchill in a message sent on February 25th which is printed in *Closing the Ring*, Churchill, pages 561-562, and 574. There was at this time, as explained in *Fleet Admiral King*, page 537, a difference between Army and Navy thinking concerning the ultimate attack upon the Japanese homeland ". . . for while in the Navy view all operations were aimed at a drive through the Pacific, probably via Formosa to China, thus by-passing the Philippines, MacArthur was both opposed to the Central Pacific route and determined to recapture the Philippine Islands."

[10] Sunderland-Romanus manuscript, Vol. II.

known as Merrill's Marauders, and British air-borne troops, known as the Chindit Brigade under General Orde Wingate, justly won fame. The Eastern Air Command, formed by combining the Tenth Air Force with the RAF Bengal Command, made decisive contributions. It smashed so hard at Japanese supply reserves and stocks that some units literally starved. It gave Stilwell's and Mountbatten's forces mobility, combat resources, and close support in battle. The Fourteenth Air Force (Chennault's) greatly hindered Japanese sea transport to the south, and made the port of Rangoon of little use to Japan.

Chiang Kai-shek was pleased at the way in which the Ledo force fought its way into North Burma. But he continued to resist pleas and pressures to risk the Yunnan force. Stilwell continued to keep after him by memo and by courier. He was threatening to suspend the delivery of Lend-Lease supplies to the Yunnan force and the War Department was coming round to his way of thinking.[11]

By the middle of March, Stilwell found that he could not push his forces farther without great risk. On the 17th, he told the War Department that if ever he needed help, it was then and there. Mountbatten sent supporting messages, asking that the President and Prime Minister make a personal appeal to Chiang Kai-shek "with great urgency." The President responded at once. He told the Generalissimo on March 17th that it seemed to him that China now had the chance to inflict a decisive defeat on the Japanese, but if China did not seize the opportunity, the Japanese might recover and resume the offensive. The Generalissimo explained his continuing caution by reference to threatening dangers within China. The Japanese, he feared, were about to begin a serious new offensive and were moving troops from Manchuria for the purpose; the Communist elements in the north were preparing to

[11] Messages, General Stilwell (Burma) to General Hearn (Chungking) March 7, and General Dorn (Kunming) to General Hearn (Chungking) March 13th and 16th.

Not long afterwards, on March 31st, Stilwell, reforming his staff arrangements, proceeded to transfer the main U.S. Army Headquarters for the CBI Theater from Chungking to New Delhi. When Gauss complained to Washington about the possible political consequences, General Hearn explained that he had informed Madame Chiang Kai-shek in advance and that she had made no objections; also, that this administrative order would not have any actual effect, that in fact General Ferris was being transferred to Chungking to strengthen that advance headquarters. The State Department called the episode to the attention of the War Department as an example of Stilwell's indifference to political consequences. The War Department thereupon instructed Stilwell to take steps to assure an improvement in the liaison between his headquarters and the Embassy. Thereafter there was more contact, maintained however by Stilwell's military staff (Hearn and Ferris) and civilian advisers (Service and Davies) rather than himself, for he was absent so much from Chungking. Telegrams, April 2 and 3, 1944, American Embassy, Chungking, to State Department; Hornbeck memo, April 3rd; and telegram, April 4th, State Department to American Embassy, Chungking.

revolt and march against Sian, the base of government operations in the Yellow River Valley; the Soviet Union was taking threatening action in Sinkiang.[12] The burden of Chiang Kai-shek's answers was that seven years of war had so taxed Chinese military and economic strength that to insist on her doing something beyond her power would be to court disaster. For these reasons, the Generalissimo's answer concluded, it was not possible for the Chinese forces in Yunnan to advance. But he said that he would send to India by air as many of his troops in Yunnan as could be spared, in order to sustain the Ledo force in Burma.[13] Within a short while he authorized the dispatch of two more divisions, bringing the total to five.

Stilwell's reports on the battle situation on the Indian as well as the Burma fronts grew still more somber. The Joint Chiefs of Staff and the President evidently decided that a more blunt plea was necessary. In his next message (April 3rd) the President tried to dispel fears by assuring Chiang Kai-shek that if the Yunnan force with its American equipment struck out against the depleted Japanese, it would surely win. He edged his appeal by repeating that the United States had been equipping and training the Yunnan force just for such a chance as was at hand; and that if it was not to be used, our effort would not have been justified. "I do hope," the plea ended, "you can act."[14]

The Generalissimo gave in. On or about April 15th, he agreed that the Yunnan force should at the end of April join the action.[14a] The Americans, pleased at the news, said at once that this force would get back its share of the tonnage over the Hump. The task that faced it across the Salween River was, after clearing the Japanese out of western Yunnan, to link up with the Ledo force and establish the land

[12] Message, Chiang Kai-shek to Roosevelt, March 17, 1944. Sunderland-Romanus manuscript, Vol. II. This message crossed in transmission Roosevelt's of the same date.

[13] Message, Chiang Kai-shek to Roosevelt, March 27, 1944. *Ibid.*

[14] Roosevelt to Chiang Kai-shek, April 3-4, 1944. *Ibid.*
General Hearn got the impression that this message had been reworded in the Generalissimo's headquarters before it was given to him. He so told Marshall, who told Roosevelt. The President thereupon gave orders that all messages from him to the Generalissimo were to be taken personally by the senior U.S. Army officer in Chungking. Stilwell's later rigid observance of this order figured in his recall, as told in Chapter 19.

[14a] General Hearn, as authorized by Marshall and Stilwell, had told the senior Chinese officers in the National Military Council that unless the Y force moved, its April allocation of Hump tonnage would be transferred to Chennault's air force. Hearn was asked on the evening of the 12th by the Chinese to hold back this order because they were sure there would be "positive action" on the use of the Y force troops within 48 hours. Hearn agreed to wait, but insisted that the Chinese agree among themselves on a definite date and plan of attack. On the 14th General Ho, as Minister of War and Chief of Staff, formally approved the Salween crossing. Sunderland-Romanus manuscript, Vol. II.

route to India. The first units, some forty thousand, crossed the Salween River on May 10th and 11th.

Stilwell had been flinging his other troops forward with furious determination. Merrill's Marauders had been marching for days under skies so cloudy that often they could not be found by the planes carrying supplies for them. The insects pursued and the damp heat was stifling. In some places the path was so steep that footholds had to be cut even for the mules. On the 17th of May, just as the monsoon broke, the troops managed to capture the airfield at Myitkyina. The hope had been that once that airfield was captured, the whole region could be quickly cleared of the Japanese. But the Japanese gathered supporting forces. The Marauders were sick and exhausted, and the advance of the Yunnan force lagged. The rains poured down and the battle area was a dank, muddy morass. Thus the struggle for the area dragged on almost to the end of the summer. The Chinese armies which crossed the Salween were contained by the desperately fighting Japanese, by the terrible country, by the weather. The effort to gain a great and decisive victory—which Roosevelt had persuasively portrayed to Chiang Kai-shek—failed. With it went the chance that the forces in Burma might soon be brought back for the defense of East China. The Anglo-Indian forces had repelled the Japanese attack on their central front and India was saved. The air bases and air space of the Hump route had also been secured. But the Chinese, British, Indian, and American forces had to stay on in Burma through the monsoon. The campaign for the opening of the Burma Road went on through the rest of 1944 in broken steps.

In these actions and efforts, American participation was growing fast. The American combat forces were small, only the few thousands enrolled in the Marauders. But there were also the other trained thousands who carried on the dangerous work of transport over the Hump and who maintained the planes and airfields. Behind the lines there were railroad engineering troops, road construction troops, pontoon bridge troops. Americans took care of ordnance. They served in the signal, medical, and supply corps, the chemical warfare units, motor transport and maintenance sections, and the military police. They engaged in veterinary control. They were building the oil pipelines through India to Assam, and from Assam along the route of the Ledo Road. In all, according to a memo of Stilwell's of March 14th, there were about thirty-one thousand Americans doing these jobs, and more were arriving every day. Besides them, there were the other thousands of Americans operating the supply lines, the longest in the world, almost fifteen thousand miles back to the United States. We were bearing a substantial part of the work and suffering to force a way into China.

But worse trouble than ever was upon the Chinese people and the Chinese government. For during the late spring and summer—while the struggle for North Burma went on—the Japanese armies in China went into action. First they marched through Honan province in the center of China; then they began to spread out and secure control of the railroad from Peiping to Hankow, and from Hankow south. It could be foreseen that, unless stopped, they would press on to cut off Chungking from the coast and destroy many of the bases used by the American air force.[15]

That the Japanese forces might well strike out this way had often been recognized.[16] Stilwell and Marshall had long argued that for this reason most of the tonnage which could be carried over the Hump should be used to equip the Chinese ground forces, and that the Burma Road had to be opened. The Generalissimo had regarded it as a reason for not getting engaged in a doubtful struggle in Burma, and for expanding the capacity of the air transport route and the American air force in China. Chennault and those who agreed with him had been of the opinion that if the American air force was made strong enough and kept well enough supplied, it would be able with the Chinese armies to defeat any such attack. But the air force always got less than he sought and

[15] This operation, known as Ichi-Go, was planned in the autumn of 1943. Four objectives were studied. (1) to seize potential American B-29 bases at Kweilin and Liuchow; (b) to consolidate forces to meet possible Allied advance into South China via India, Burma, and Yunnan; (c) to establish a reliable land-transport system from Northern China to the Japanese armies in Southern Asia; (d) to weaken the Chinese government by destroying its army. The first objective was, however, given priority.

On January 24, 1944, orders were issued directing that in April 1944 the North China Area Army was to seize the portion of the Peiping-Hankow railroad south of the Yellow River; then in June 1944 operations were to be begun in the Hankow-Wuchang area; in July or August another army was to begin operations in the Canton area; the two armies were to crush the Chinese between them, occupy Kweilin and Liuchow, and mop up along the Hunan-Kwangsi and Canton-Hankow railroads. These operations were expected to take about five months. "Imperial General Headquarters Army High Command Record, Mid 1941 to August 1945." Japanese Monograph No. 45. Military History Section. Headquarters United States Far East Command.

[16] The probability was widely discussed in the press in both China and the United States. See, as an example of speculation on the subject, an article by Brooks Atkinson, correspondent of the *New York Times* in Chungking, in the *New York Times* Magazine Section, February 20, 1944. One passage read, "The [American air] bases are so important that Japan is expected sooner or later to make a coordinated attempt to neutralize them or to occupy those within reach of her ground troops. The highly creditable and encouraging showing of the Chinese army at Changteh in December gives reason for hoping that it will be able to defend the bases against land attacks."

usually less than he was promised.[17] Several times during April and May Chennault warned Stilwell and the Generalissimo that unless quick and drastic steps—which he specified—were taken, the security of the American air bases would be imperiled, and the 14th Air Force in China might not be able to give effective air cover to the Chinese armies. Chennault's suggestions would have required the curtailment or cancellations of the Salween offensive and Matterhorn bombing operations.[18]

The basic fact was that by June 1944 the situation which had been allowed to develop in the China and SEAC theaters was insupportable against strong Japanese counteraction. Too much was being tried with the means granted and in prospect; and these were divided among too many demands.[19] In particular, the multiple and competitive demands made both on the Indian transport system and the air transport route were excessive. Estimates of risks were too optimistic, and no margin was left to call on in a crisis. Partial failure occurred all the time, and marked failure was almost certain if the Japanese struck hard.

The Generalissimo appealed to Roosevelt for emergency help.[20] In explaining the seriousness of the situation, he said that he was informed that the Japanese had transferred fourteen divisions from Manchuria to China. This estimate was thought in Washington to be much exaggerated; but how much so the War and State Departments found it hard to determine from the widely ranging reports they received.

Stilwell, worried and intent, lingered on in Burma, leaving the de-

[17] Diversion of tonnage from the 14th Air Force had been particularly large during January-February-March 1944 in order to (1) provide help for the Anglo-Indian divisions which were stopping the Japanese advance into India, (2) support the Burma campaign, and (3) maintain Operation Matterhorn. Chennault, in *The Way of a Fighter*, page 290, wrote that of the total strength of 500 planes, 200 were immobilized by the Joint Chiefs of Staff to defend the Chengtu area and that Stilwell ordered another 150 to support the offensive in North Burma, leaving him only 150 planes to defend Southeastern China. He wrote further that the supplies of fuel, bombs, and other equipment were enough for only thirty days of all-out maximum operation; thus in the course of the fighting through the summer and autumn of 1944 the 14th Air Force became dependent on its current allowance of tonnage brought in over the Hump, and possible allocation from the reserve accumulated at Chengtu. In addition, trucks needed to carry supplies from Kunming to the other bases of the 14th Air Force in East China were diverted to other uses.

[18] Chennault messages to Stilwell, April 6, 8, 10, and his estimate to Chiang Kai-shek, April 15th. Sunderland-Romanus manuscript, Vol. 11.

[19] The main competing operations which we were trying to sustain during the first half of 1944 were (a) North Burma campaign in connection with which we were building the Ledo Road and pipeline, (b) protection of India, (c) the 14th Air Force in China, (d) the long-range bombing operation from China, (e) equipping of the Chinese armies. The maintenance of the air transport service over the Hump itself required considerable effort and tonnage.

[20] Memo to President Roosevelt, delivered by General Shang Chen, head of the Chinese military mission in Washington, May 31, 1944.

fense of East China to the Chinese commanders. Probably he thought there was nothing he could do to save it. Chiang Kai-shek called him to Chungking for consultation on June 5th. He stayed one day, and reported to Washington that he had advised the Generalissimo to use all of China's ground and air resources in the emergency. The Generalissimo at that time did not suggest that the Chinese divisions fighting in Burma be sent back to China. But he asked Stilwell with intense earnestness to provide the 14th Air Force with the combat means specified in the note given the President a few days before. Stilwell agreed to do much, but not all that was asked of him. His answer was in accord with that which the War Department was making to the Generalissimo's request. The Joint Chiefs did not want to give up the reserves for Matterhorn, and thus delay the bombing of Japan which they thought would benefit China more than Chennault's use of these resources. This was, as is remarked in the Sunderland-Romanus study, ". . . faith in strategic bombardment at its highest pitch."

Neither the War nor the State Department seems to have shared fully the Generalissimo's excitement or anxiety. Perhaps this was in part because they felt that they had earlier tried their best to get the Chinese armies prepared for this crisis. Perhaps in part because they were slow to realize the gravity of the Japanese threat; or in any case did not think the peril crucial to the whole war effort.[21]

While these battles were going on in Burma and China, the American government again became worried about the strains between the Chinese government and the Communists, and of a new surge of fear in Chungking in regard to future Soviet intentions. Harder than before it strove to calm and reconcile.

[21] This appears to have been the judgment of the China Affairs Division of the State Department as expressed in a memo written by Vincent on May 15, 1944, for the guidance of the Secretary of State in an anticipated call of the Chinese Ambassador.

Messages, Marshall to Stilwell, May 27 and June 7. Sunderland-Romanus manuscript, Vol. II.

CHAPTER 14

Again the Communists: Chinese and Russian

DURING this period of sag in China (February-June 1944) the Communists thrived. They treated the bids of Chungking with defiant unconcern. Observers in the Embassy and on Stilwell's staff thought that they were becoming surer that the Kuomintang regime would collapse as the people in their part of China grew more miserable. The Japanese columns marched without hindrance through country where both regular and guerrilla Communist forces were clustered. They traveled on railways which the Communists could have made unusable.

The dominant elements in the Kuomintang became more certain than ever that the Communists would sooner or later seek to get control of all of China—probably not, they thought, until the Chinese government was further worn down by war and Soviet troops were in occupation of adjacent territory. The temptation to try to eliminate the danger thus remained strong. But the Generalissimo faithfully maintained the position he had announced in the past September: that the dispute was to be settled by peaceful means. The Minister of Information, Liang, confirmed that attitude in February 1944, telling the foreign correspondents, "It is our declared policy to be unified and to solve the difficulty by political means. There is therefore no reason to have foreign countries make out that this matter could not be solved in a political way. It is the sincere, earnest desire of the Chinese Government to solve it in a political way, and therefore we do not want to talk about it."

But the government maintained, perhaps extended, its blockading force of government and provincial troops. Their numbers had been estimated (as of January) by our Embassy as about four hundred thousand, some among them the best trained and equipped in China. The division within China was thus both reducing the Chinese effort in Burma and weakening its ability to defend the American air bases in China. At the same time, as has been told, the Chinese were asking the American government for more help. Inevitably the question again came to the front: could no way be found to bring these opposed Chinese forces together in battle against the Japanese? Stilwell and the War Department both thought another attempt to do so should be made.

During May-June, while the Burma effort was at its hardest and the Japanese advance gaining momentum, the American government entered on a linked effort—both direct and indirect—toward that end.

It tried to convince Chiang Kai-shek that it was essential that all Chinese forces be used to fight the Japanese. At the same time it strove to enlist Stalin's help in bringing about an easing of the conflict within China which would aid the same purpose. This dual effort was, however, lax and dispersed. The White House, the State Department, and the War Department all took part in it; but they were loose in consultation and careless about keeping each other informed.

The whole range of Sino-Soviet relations had by May-June again become streaked with suspicion. The President and Secretary of State both were wondering whether the work they thought they had done at Moscow, Cairo, and Teheran was about to come undone.

One of the chief American purposes at these conferences had been to prepare the way for a Sino-Soviet agreement, which would ward off Soviet interference in Chinese affairs. Chiang Kai-shek was as dubious as ever that the Soviet Union would really leave China alone and whole. He and most of his group were the more afraid, perhaps, because of the worsening of their plight, the falling away of popular support, and the defects of their armies. They were convinced that there were close and secret relations between Moscow and the Chinese Communists. This fact they thought accounted for the stubborn refusal of the Communists to subordinate their army and political organizations to the National Government. The range of their fears and suspicions is well exemplified in a letter written by Chiang Kai-shek to the President on March 17th: ". . . though the Chinese Communist Party have outwardly professed support of the Chinese Government's policy of resistance against Japanese aggression, since February they have been secretly assembling their guerrilla units from various places and concentrating them in North Shensi, evidently preparing for an opportune moment to rise in revolt and take Sian, the base of our operations in the Yellow River Valley. The indications are manifest. Considering the matter objectively, it does not seem likely that the Chinese Communist Party would dare to make such a move without some understanding having been reached between the Soviets and the Chinese."

Then there had been the incident in Sinkiang. Along the border between this province and Mongolia, Soviet planes had in March fired at and killed Chinese troops. These troops, our Embassy in China had reported, were pursuing fleeing Chinese who according to the government were rebels. The Soviet government had claimed that the Chinese government forces had crossed the border of Outer Mongolia. The

Chinese government had denied this. Whatever the facts, the Soviet action was tough and had seemed to portend a generally hostile purpose. Chiang Kai-shek had so construed it in messages to the President. He had asked for the President's advice. Both the President and Secretary of State had thought that the incident was probably being magnified out of proportion.[1] The President's answer, sent on April 8th, had been noncommittal. It pointed out there had been no further clashes since the middle of March. It deplored any action or attitude by either the Soviet Union or China which might affect the unity among the United Nations. It suggested as a matter of practical realism that the ". . . recent incidents be placed on ice . . ." until the end of the war, without the abandonment by anyone of any sovereignty or right.

Washington's treatment of the episode had seemed justified by the way in which the trouble in Sinkiang had simmered down. The government had met no trouble in moving more troops into the province; these were cautioned by Chiang Kai-shek to avoid any conflict with the Mongols either in Sinkiang or along the border. But the Soviet government had advanced claims for compensation for Soviet property left behind in the province. More obstructively, at the same time it had demanded payment for supplies and equipment sent to China during the early years of the war against Japan. This payment was sought in the form of returned shipments of strategic materials over the land route through Russian Turkestan, which the Allies were trying to organize.

Many bright schemes for such a route had come to nought—now for one reason, now for another. Then in the first half of 1944 the Soviet government had been asked to consent to the sending of a large convoy of trucks over this route for supplies for the American 14th Air Force fighting in China. The operating crews were to be Americans and they

[1] The American Embassy in Chungking and the Chinese Affairs Division of the State Department were inclined to interpret the Russian action in striking at the Chinese troops, and stubborn Russian defense of this action, as indicating a Soviet intention to make it plain that they would not allow China to try to reextend its authority over Outer Mongolia, and to make it clear that they would support complete independence of Outer Mongolia.

The Chinese motives in making so much of the incident were construed variously:

(a) To establish undisputed control of the National Government over Sinkiang.

(b) To test Soviet policy in regard to Outer Mongolia, and possibly also as regards the future attitude of the Soviets towards the Communist Party in China, Sinkiang, and Manchuria.

(c) To try to stimulate anti-Soviet feeling in China and abroad.

(d) To rally Chinese nationalism and divert attention in China from the failings of the government.

These were all systematically stated in a memo prepared for the China Affairs Division (Clubb, May 19, 1944), entitled "American Policy with Respect to Sino-Soviet Relations."

were to remain in China as part of the combat force. This request had been made by Harriman to Molotov on April 22nd. But the best answer that could be gotten was that the Soviet government was considering it; that there was little chance that it would agree; and that one reason was because the Chinese government had been behaving badly.

Still another cause of the Chinese mistrust was the signature on March 30th by the Soviet Union and Japan of an agreement in regard to Sakhalin fisheries. This the Chinese government had taken as a sign that these two powers agreed not to go to war against one another— especially since the Soviet Union moved troops westward out of Siberia, allowing Japan to move its troops southward into China.[2] Both the White House and the Secretary of State had been reserved on this as on the other counts. They did not believe that any accord of significance had been reached between the Soviet Union and Japan. Hull could find no supporting evidence of any connection between the accord about Sakhalin and Japanese troop movements or Japanese appeasement of the Soviet Union.[3] Furthermore, both the State and War Departments —after study of the reports of the Embassy and military attaché in Chungking—thought that the estimates passed on by the Chinese government regarding the transfer of Japanese troops from Manchuria to China were unsubstantiated and exaggerated.[4]

In short and sum, the President and the State Department had not been convinced that these several complaints of the Generalissimo about the Soviet Union were well based, or his fear well enough evidenced. They had been inclined to agree with Gauss that Chiang Kai-shek was giving free rein to his excited worry to arouse us to give him greater help and active support. Thus, they had sought during April and May to calm the Generalissimo; they drilled him in the need for getting along with the Soviet Union for the sake of the whole war effort. But the Generalissimo in turn had not been calmed. He had remained obdurately fearful that the Soviet Union would, when it could, come to the aid of the Chinese Communists and extend its influence on or control over the regions along the frontiers—Inner Mongolia, Sinkiang, Manchuria.

[2] Memos of talks with Wu Teh Chen, Secretary General of the Kuomintang party, with the American Embassy, and between the Chinese Ambassador in Washington and Secretary of State Hull, both in April.

[3] Telegram from the Secretary of State to the American Embassy in Moscow and Chungking on May 3rd, summarizing talk between the Secretary of State and the Chinese Ambassador on April 29th.

[4] Telegram, Secretary of State to Ambassador Gauss, June 15, 1944. As told in Chapter 13, the various Chinese estimates differed much from each other, and the Americans were distinctly skeptical of all of them.

The President had been troubled enough to conclude that he must give the matter more energetic attention. In his view there was no fundamental opposition between the Soviet Union and China. Therefore it ought to be possible to draw them into friendly understanding, and it was most important for the United Nations that this be done. Thus he had asked Vice President Wallace to go to China to talk with Chiang Kai-shek. And when Harriman was in Washington in May he had asked him upon his return to Moscow to talk to Molotov or Stalin.

Harriman talked with Stalin and Molotov on the evening of June 10th.[5] This was four days after the first Allied landings in Normandy: days that had displayed the great vigor and force of the invasion, and established the second fighting front for which the Soviet Union had longed. The Ambassador began by recalling that Roosevelt had said at Teheran that Chiang Kai-shek was the only man to hold China together. Stalin agreed that this was so. Harriman then said that the President felt that Chiang Kai-shek should be encouraged first to seek a settlement with the Communists in the north so that they could unite in the fight against Japan, and, second, to liberalize his internal policies. Stalin commented, "That is easier said than done." Then he seems to have let his thought run freer than usual. He reaffirmed his opinion that Chiang Kai-shek was the best man under the circumstances, and must therefore be supported. But he found that best, poorish. He thought that China under the Generalissimo was not fighting well, and gave instances which may or may not have been fair. He had the impression that a good many of the men around Chiang Kai-shek were crooks, perhaps even traitors, for the Japanese seemed to know everything that went on in Chungking. He found fault with what he called Chiang Kai-shek's failure to use the Chinese Communists in the fight against the Japanese instead of disputing with them on ideological grounds. This he thought stupid. For, he went on—the memo says, with a laugh—"The Chinese Communists are not real Communists. They are 'margarine' Communists. Nevertheless, they are real patriots and they want to fight Japan."[6]

[5] The account given here of this important talk is taken from a memo made by Edward Page of the American Embassy in Moscow, who acted as interpreter, and from a paraphrase of the report sent by Harriman to the President on June 11th.

[6] There is room for speculation as to whether Stalin's comment on the Chinese Communists, which he repeated at various later times, was genuine. It may well have been, reflecting past differences with Mao Tze Tung, the Chairman of the Chinese Soviet Republic, over both the theory and tactics of revolution in China. See Benjamin Schwartz, *Chinese Communists and the Rise of Mao*. Mao's program, in contrast to the

Harriman asked Stalin what he thought should be the combined American-Soviet policy vis-à-vis China. Stalin seemed to deed us the problem. He said the United States should and could take the leadership in this field, for neither Great Britain nor the Soviet Union could. We should, he suggested, bring Chiang Kai-shek more fully under our influence, insist that he eliminate his dishonest aides and grant authority to the younger men who wanted to fight. In all these matters our policy should be flexible, ready to support good new men if they turned up. Then Stalin went at some length into the recent trouble between Sinkiang and Outer Mongolia. While the situation there was at the moment peaceful, he said that in the event that the incidents recurred the Soviet Union would feel called on again to give armed support to Outer Mongolia. Finally, he accused the group around Chiang Kai-shek of spreading false reports that the Soviet Union had made secret deals with Japan regarding China. He dismissed these reports as nonsense. The Soviet position toward China, he reaffirmed, remained based on its 1924 Treaty of Friendship with China.[7]

Harriman sent a summary report of this talk to the President at once. But the State Department did not learn about the conversation with Stalin for some ten days—in which interval it had transmitted to Gauss (on June 15th) a broad statement of its own ideas about saving the critical military situation in China and bettering Sino-Soviet relations.

This instruction of June 15th had been slowly compounded in the State Department, as it became impressed by the gravity of the Japanese offensive in China and by the widening of the rift between the Soviet

---

agricultural collectivism within the Soviet Union, was based on redistribution of land among the millions of poor peasants.

This adjective, "margarine Communists," was only one of several, all suggesting soft imitativeness, which Stalin used in describing them from time to time to the bemusement of American visitors. To the members of the group of Congressmen, headed by Representative Colmer in September 1945, he spoke of them as "cabbage" Communists. The translator was reliable. On still another occasion he spoke of them as "radish" Communists, that is, red outside and white inside.

[7] The Soviet newspapermen in Washington were at this time taking a similar line. They were expressing concern over the friction between the Kuomintang and the Communists, pointing out that the areas under Communist control were of strategic importance in Soviet military operations against the Japanese and that it would be natural for the Soviet forces to use these areas and the Chinese Communist forces. But, their exposition continued, the Soviet government was afraid to do so as it would cause trouble with the Kuomintang and be regarded in the United States as an attempt to bolshevize China. The Soviet government did not want trouble with the American government over China. Memo, June 2, 1944, made by Stanton of the Far Eastern Affairs Office of the State Department of a talk which he and Ballantine had with Walter Lippman.

and Chinese governments. Its approach to these troubling situations was foreshadowed in a memorandum sent to our Embassies at Moscow and Chungking in early June.[8] The main points of the memo were:

1. Sinkiang province and Manchuria were part of China, to be treated as such.

2. It would be well to recognize the practical situation—the fact that Outer Mongolia was autonomous. If the Chinese government tried to assert control over that country, the Soviet Union might well contest the effort.

3. That Korea should be independent, and that its people should ultimately determine their form of government without outside interference.

4. That the National Government of China was recognized by us as the primary political authority in China. It had done much in the cause of the United Nations; and the Chinese people had endured great suffering in their resistance. But China could, then and there, be making a greater contribution in the war. The American government would like to see all Chinese forces—not merely part of them—used to fight Japan. Further, the American government was not committed to support the National Government of China in any and all circumstances. It was not concerned with doctrinal questions between contending Chinese groups; it was concerned with the effectuation in China of a program that would benefit the Chinese people.

5. The American government wanted the Chinese and Soviet governments to remain friendly allies. Thus it hoped each would give generous consideration to the position and interests of the other.

This was the hazy and benign aura out of which emerged the responses to the requests made by the Chinese government for greater American military aid and the use of American influence to win Soviet favor. The most forceful and precise of these, Gauss sent to Washington on the 1st of June. This transmitted word of the extreme anxiety of the Chinese Minister of War over the "desperate" Chinese military situation, and a request that the American military authorities consider whether measures could not be taken to persuade the Soviet government to take some action

[8] This is the memorandum of the China Affairs Division of May 19th entitled "American Policy with Respect to Sino-Soviet Relations," to which reference has already been made. It was sent by airmail to Harriman on June 3rd after the State Department learned that the President had requested the Ambassador to discuss Sino-Soviet relations with Stalin and Molotov, particularly Molotov's purported complaints against the Chungking government. But it is doubtful whether Harriman saw it before his talk with Stalin on June 10th. Another copy was sent, likewise by airmail, on June 7th, to Ambassador Gauss.

on the Siberian border which would make it impossible for the Japanese to continue to transfer forces from Manchuria to China. Another effort was in order, Stettinius apprehensively told Grew, former Ambassador to Japan who was briefly serving as Director of the Office of Far Eastern Affairs, to try to allay the growing tension between China and the Soviet Union, and to check the development within China of strong anti-Soviet feeling.

Gauss was prompted on June 15th to make the attempt. He was told to back up the efforts of the War Department to stimulate the Chinese defensive effort and to discourage Chinese propaganda against the Soviets. The State Department, he was advised, did not think it opportune to suggest that the Soviet Union make diversionary movements with the intention of hindering Japanese troop transfers from Manchuria; that it was doubtful whether the Soviet Union could do so and whether the bluff would work if tried. Instead, the Department felt that he could point out to Chiang Kai-shek and others how much the Chinese situation would be improved if the Chinese General Staff saw fit to confront the Japanese with the whole available Chinese military strength. Accordingly, he might urge among other measures (1) the more adequate use of the better equipped units of the Chinese army against the Japanese, (2) an agreement between the Kuomintang authorities and the Chinese Communists which would bring the blockade of the Communist areas to an end and release troops of both sides to fight the Japanese, and (3) steps to be taken by the Chinese to effect a closer understanding and cooperation with the Soviet Union. This counsel was to be given weight by a statement to the effect that the United States, because of what it had to do in Europe, could not increase its military help to China quickly or substantially. It was to be given point by the observation that as long as the tension lasted, it could not be expected that the Soviet Union would help the National Government in any way.[9]

This advice to the Kuomintang government to help itself and to try to make up with the feared Communist regimes—Chinese and Russian

[9] This radio instruction to Gauss was drafted in the China Affairs Division (Clubb) and approved by Grew, Stettinius, and Hull. Two purposes seemed to have been combined in it: to soften Sino-Soviet ill feeling; to help the War Department in its disposition of Chinese requests for greater immediate military aid, and its wishes for more adequate use of all Chinese forces. The contents were discussed with the War Department, and Gauss was instructed to clear the points of military significance with Stilwell's headquarters. On the same day, June 15th, the State Department radioed Harriman in Moscow the substance of Gauss' recent reports and of this instruction for guidance in his talks with the Soviet government. But Harriman had already left Moscow to meet Wallace.

—was certain to seem flinty to its recipients. By the time Gauss had cleared the military features with Stilwell, Vice President Wallace had arrived in Chungking. As directed by the State Department, Gauss made the contents of this message known to Wallace, and awaited the outcome of Wallace's talks with Chiang Kai-shek. In these he was only a by stander.

Before Harriman left Moscow to meet Wallace at Tashkent he informed Molotov that he would tell the Vice President of his talk with Stalin. He thought Wallace would be extremely interested in the Marshal's views, particularly in regard to the "margarine" Communists. On one other matter, too, Harriman tried to ease the way for Wallace. For some time—as will shortly be told—the American military headquarters in China had been trying to get Chiang Kai-shek's consent to the dispatch of a small group of American official observers to Yenan. Harriman told Molotov that we were trying to arrange for this, and said that if it were arranged, we would share the information obtained by the group with the Soviet government. Harriman, it may be surmised, was trying to guard against possible Soviet objections; perhaps also trying to find out whether, if the American government sent such a mission to Yenan, the Soviet government would claim the same right. Molotov appears to have made no comment.

Harriman met Wallace at Tashkent and told him of the talks he had just had with Stalin and Molotov.[10] The next step was underway to try to smooth Sino-Soviet relations and heal the internal trouble in China by peaceful means.

[10] Harriman spent June 15th and 16th at Tashkent, and the 17th at Alma Ata with Wallace, who then went on to Chungking.

CHAPTER 15

The Wallace Mission

WHEN first in early March the President suggested to Wallace that he go to China and see what he could do to straighten out the situation there, Wallace did not think the request serious. But when convinced that the President had a real need in mind he agreed to go. He wanted to go to Moscow and to India as well. The President thought this inadvisable, but said it might be all right for him to visit Siberia and have a look at agricultural and industrial activities in that region.

Secretary Hull was uneasy about the trip. He hinted that he would be happier if Wallace did not go. But when Wallace wrote that it would help him greatly to have along someone who knew the Chinese language and was recently familiar with Chinese affairs and personalities, and asked that the State Department assign some officer with these qualifications to accompany him, Hull consented. John Carter Vincent, who had served in Chungking not long before, and who was then Chief of the Division of Chinese Affairs, was chosen. The other members of this mission were John N. Hazard, a Russian-speaking member of the Soviet Supply Section of the Foreign Economic Administration, and Owen D. Lattimore, who was then an official of the Office of War Information. He had studied long and written much about those interior regions of Asia which were on the Sino-Soviet frontiers.

Wallace was being sent to calm and encourage Chiang Kai-shek, and to plead for trust among the United Nations. The President, explaining that for the first time he was really afraid that China would not hold together to the end of the war, told him to do what he could to get the Chinese Nationalist and Communist armies to stop fighting.[1] For the rest, Wallace was left to be guided by his perceptions. He had no authority to give promises or make decisions, only a chance to interpret and advise. When they met at Tashkent, Harriman repeated in full Stalin's and Molotov's remarks about the Chinese situation.

Wallace toured provinces of Eastern Siberia and Outer Mongolia

[1] Wallace testimony before Internal Security Committee of the Senate, October 17, 1951. This impression is confirmed by the memorandum which Acting Secretary Stettinius sent to Grew on or about May 24th, which recorded the explanations which the President had given at the last cabinet meeting of his reasons for sending Wallace and what he hoped Wallace would achieve. This memo gives a stumbling account of what may have been a stumbling explanation.

first. There he visited farms and agricultural stations which he viewed as a fellow farmer. He spoke cordially of the friendship between the Russian and American people and thought his audience shared his feeling.

After this short and enthusiastic tour he hurried on to China. The government and the people were eager for the proof of American support and friendship that Wallace's coming was taken to be. They were being battered by hardship and their armies were scattering before the Japanese. There were many signs of discontent among the peasants; and students, intellectuals, and government officials, suffering badly from the inflation, were turning toward the regime in the north. The Americans were making an immense exertion to keep supplies coming in over the Hump, and the 14th Air Force was flying day and night in the attempt to break up the Japanese advance. Stilwell was back in Burma, struggling to keep that campaign going during the rains.

Wallace's conversations with Chiang Kai-shek were cordial and comprehensive. They began at the first bow and went on till the Generalissimo saw him off at the airport for home.[2] The talks were not systematic. They went over and past subjects without any prepared order. A topical summary, therefore, may be misleading in two opposite ways: it may make the talks seem more consecutive and conclusive than they were; and it may fail to convey the basic consistency of the attitudes of the two men, and the continuity, loose as it was, of their series of talks. Yet I know of no better way of identifying essentials.

RELATIONS BETWEEN THE GOVERNMENT
AND THE COMMUNISTS

Wallace introduced this subject in a fashion that must have seemed a little fatuous in his first meeting on June 21st with Chiang Kai-shek and Soong. He said that Roosevelt had talked with him about the Com-

[2] What I tell about these conversations is derived (1) from the summary notes of conversation between Wallace and Chiang Kai-shek, June 21-24, 1944, made by John Carter Vincent, which are published as Annex No. 43, in *United States Relations with China*; (2) a telegram in two parts which Wallace wrote in Kunming on June 26th, sent to the President from New Delhi on June 28, 1944, reporting the main points in his talk and his main impressions. This was published in paraphrase as an attachment to Wallace's letter to President Truman of September 19, 1951, *New York Times*, September 24, 1951; (3) Wallace Report to President Roosevelt, July 10, 1944, *New York Times*, January 19, 1950; (4) Wallace testimony, *Hearings: Institute of Pacific Relations*; (5) Wallace letter to President Truman, September 19, 1951; (6) Wallace letter, *U.S. News and World Report*, January 9, 1953.

munists in China; that the President had assumed that inasmuch as the Communists and the members of the Kuomintang were all Chinese, they were basically friends and that "nothing should be final between friends." Further, he said that the President had indicated that if the government and the Communists could not get together they might "call in a friend," and had implied that he, Roosevelt, might be that friend.

Chiang Kai-shek at this first meeting did not pursue the subject, allowing Wallace to continue with other features of his statement. But in the next talk, on the next day, the Generalissimo, in the language of the notes, "launched forth into a lengthy complaint against the Chinese Communists." In his view the United States did not understand the question; and some Americans—he gave examples—were being swayed badly by Communist propaganda. It was not, he said, merely a matter of his own opinion of the Chinese Communists; the Chinese people did not regard the Communists as Chinese, but as "internationalists," subject to the orders of the Third International. He blamed the Communists for much of the suffering and present difficulties in China; their subversive activities were harming morale among the people and the army. Even more, he thought that the Communists actually wished Chinese resistance against Japan to break. When Wallace showed himself puzzled at this comment, Chiang Kai-shek explained it. He did not mean that the Communists did not wish Japan to be defeated; but they were sure it was going to be defeated even though China fell apart. Thus they sought to cause a collapse of the Kuomintang before the end of the war, a collapse which would bring them into power. They knew they would lose their chance if the Kuomintang were still in control when peace came.

Wallace had told the Generalissimo something of Harriman's talk with Stalin, and Vincent had told Soong something more. So it was not improbable that Chiang Kai-shek had Stalin's phrase "margarine" Communists in his mind in his next comments. He remarked that the Communists, with clever purpose, were seeking to spread the impression that they were not true revolutionaries, nothing more than agrarian democrats; and that they were not tied to the Soviet Union. All this, he said, was untrue; on the contrary, the Chinese Communists were more communistic than the Russian Communists.[3] Wallace did not dispute this interpretation of the real nature and intentions of the Chinese Communists. He seems to have let the subject rest, perhaps with wondering

---

[3] This, the memo of the talk tells us, he said laughingly. The same adverb had been used to describe Stalin's manner when he called them "margarine" Communists.

disbelief and uncertainty, as he went on to discuss the possibility of an accord with them.[4]

Chiang Kai-shek summarily reviewed recent negotiations; he said that he thought the two decisive points in an acceptable agreement—and these he maintained to the very end—were: that the Communists should give up their independent army and allow it to become part of the Chinese National Army; and that they should give up their independent control of Chinese territory and allow it to become an integral part of Chinese national administration. If they would do these two things, he said, then he would guarantee the Communists political amnesty, the same treatment as other Chinese, and the right to act as a legal political party, with freedom of assembly and of discussion. He would, he affirmed, continue to seek settlement on these terms. If and when an agreement was reached, he could carry out his program for democracy earlier than expected. He urged Wallace to let the President know that he had the greatest respect for Communist propaganda—which was trying to use American opinion to force the Kuomintang to yield to Communist demands.[5] It would help most, he said, if the United States showed itself cool and aloof to the Communists.

Wallace turned the talk on this point by asking whether even though no general political accord could be reached, it might not be possible to make some arrangement "at a lower level" that would mean a maximum use of Chinese armed forces in the north. This was in line with

[4] The *New York Times* of October 10, 1951, reports that Wallace, in speaking to the press after a closed meeting with the Senate Internal Security Committee, described his talks with Chiang Kai-shek as "somewhat at cross purposes" because he found it hard in the "win-the-war" atmosphere that prevailed to understand why the Nationalists and Communists could not work together.

[5] The propaganda, it may be remarked, was the more effective because the relations of many of the American correspondents in Chungking with the Chinese government were strained, while those with the headquarters maintained by the Communists in Chungking were congenial. Many of the correspondents had come to mistrust the statements of the government and resent its repression and censorship. In contrast, the Communist representatives were able to create a deceptive atmosphere of openness in talk and reliability of statement. Interesting details of this situation are given by G. H. Moorad in his book *The Lost Peace*, 1949, pages 40-41. He comments that the chief Communist representative and negotiator, Chou En-lai, who was often in Chungking, was much liked, being intent, unpretentious, and with a quick wit. Wedemeyer later spoke of him as "a charming individual, disengaging, . . . he speaks English quite well." He was, Wedemeyer added, an avowed and proved Communist. Testimony, *Military Situation in the Far East*, Hearings before the Committee on Armed Services and the Committee on Foreign Relations, United States Senate, Eighty-Second Congress, First Session, United States Government Printing Office, 1951, to Conduct an Inquiry into the Military Situation in the Far East and the Facts Surrounding the Relief of General of the Army Douglas MacArthur from his Assignments in that Area, page 2300. This will hereafter be cited as *Joint Committee on Military Situation in the Far East*.

the known wish of the War and State Departments. Chiang Kai-shek answered, "Please do not press; please understand that the Communists are not good for the war effort against Japan." When on the next day (June 23rd), Wallace again raised the issue—in terms of the need for taking all steps that might hasten the end of the war and save American lives—Chiang Kai-shek's answer was the same. The attitude of the United States army, he remarked, supported the Communists. As he had already said the day before, he thought the army did not realize how much of a threat the Communists were, and that it overestimated their utility against the Japanese. The United States government, especially the United States army, was, he went on to complain, bringing much pressure on the Chinese government to settle with the Communists, but none on the Communists to come to terms with the government. Would not Wallace, when he returned to the United States, make it clear that they should do so?

On the last day of the talks, June 24th, while riding to the airport with Wallace, Chiang Kai-shek renewed their talk on the various aspects of relations with the Communists. He seemed to feel the need for excusing his resistance to Roosevelt's wishes. The Communists, he repeated, were not men of good faith; their signature was not good; and they did not carry out promises. But, he continued, he wanted the President to be told that if after mature consideration he wished to help to bring about a settlement, he, Chiang Kai-shek would not regard it as meddling in Chinese internal political problems. The President ought, however, to know what he might be getting into. In any event, the Generalissimo wished the President to be told again that he wanted a political solution of the situation, and that he would use only political measures in dealing with it. This was a refreshed promise.

Wallace, in reporting to the President, concluded that the talks in Chungking between the government and the Communists were "so imbued with prejudice" that he could see little chance of a satisfactory long-term settlement.

SINO-SOVIET RELATIONS

Chiang Kai-shek was sure that the Chinese Communists were in intimate association with their fellow-conspirators in Moscow. But he did not for that reason dismiss as useless or impossible the chance of arriving at an understanding with the Soviet government. The flow of talk on this subject leaves the impression that he approached it with a sense of China's weakness.

The Vice President began it by remarking on June 21st that all questions which might result in a conflict between the Soviet Union and China ought to be settled; he did not think that the Soviet government had any territorial ambitions in the Far East.[6] Chiang Kai-shek answered at once that he wished for a settlement. Perhaps, he hurried on, beyond Wallace's words and thoughts, President Roosevelt might act as arbiter or "middleman" between them. This ready response puzzled Wallace. He thought it over. Then he told Chiang Kai-shek that the President had not suggested to him that he might act as arbiter; nor did he think that the American government could act as "middleman," nor become a party to or guarantor of any agreement. But he went on to say that he thought the American government would be willing to use its good offices to get them together. Both Roosevelt and Truman were to find out how hard it was to mark and keep any line between good offices, brokerage, and arbitration.

The Generalissimo revealed an almost eager wish to make terms with the menacing neighbor to the north. He said that the Chinese government would not bargain away its sovereignty to avoid conflict. But, recognizing the desirability of agreement, he would seek an early chance to have discussions with the Soviet government. He would, he said, continue to hope that ways could be found whereby the United States could help to see that the discussions turned out well. This expressed wish was, it may be interjected, the passport to Yalta.

The memo of the conversation on this point (June 23rd) reads:

"President Chiang asked Mr. Wallace to inform President Roosevelt as follows: 'If the United States can bring about better relations between the U.S.S.R. and China and can bring about a meeting between Chinese and Soviet representatives, President Chiang would very much welcome such friendly assistance.' If the United States would 'sponsor' such a meeting President Chiang would go more than halfway in reaching an understanding with the U.S.S.R. A conference with regard to Pacific affairs was desirable and the United States would be the logical place for such a conference. Madame Chiang interpolated to suggest that it be called the 'North Pacific Conference.' Mr. Vincent inquired whether they were not speaking of two related but separate matters, that is, dis-

[6] Wallace amended this remark two days later by reference to the Soviet wish expressed to Roosevelt for a warm-water port in the Far East. Chiang Kai-shek, as he told Wallace, was already acquainted with this matter and had told Roosevelt at Cairo that he was in agreement, provided the U.S.S.R. cooperated with China in the Far East and that there was no impairment of Chinese sovereignty. Neither seems to have mentioned the other Soviet wishes of which the President had informed the Pacific War Council soon after his return from Cairo and Teheran.

cussions between Chinese and Soviet representatives in regard to their problems, and a conference of nations bordering on the North Pacific to discuss more general problems. He said that it would seem desirable to have the Sino-Soviet discussions prior to any North Pacific conference. Dr. Soong said that a North Pacific conference might be used as a cloak for discussions between Chinese and Soviet representatives. Mr. Wallace said that Dr. Soong would be of value in Washington in laying the foundation for such a conference. President Chiang said that he could not be spared from Chungking and added, laughingly, that with Dr. Kung gone and Madame Chiang planning to go abroad, Dr. Soong was his only mouthpiece in speaking to Americans."

Wallace's effort, it may be said in passing, was in beat with his colleagues. Harriman, under the President's orders, was similarly seeking out ways and chances of bringing the Soviet and Chinese governments together. So was Secretary of State Hull. He was striving to turn the statement of principles, approved at Moscow when he was there, into a new system of political relations and ethics—through the United Nations. He emphasized to the Chinese Ambassador in Washington his belief that an agreement between China and the Soviet Union was essential to all postwar security projects. He thought the differences between them small, and he told Wei he thought that Stalin's attitude was favorable. He suggested that more might be accomplished in private talks than in formal meetings.[7]

MILITARY SITUATION

Wallace made clear that the United States government was disappointed at the fight being made by the Chinese armies. He found Chiang Kai-shek distressed but not disposed to admit faults or accept blame. Wallace alluded to reports that government troops had fled without fighting in the Honan campaign. Chiang Kai-shek admitted that they had done poorly there, but explained their conduct by their worry over the suffering of their families and the inadequacy of their equipment. Moreover, he implied that if his forces sometimes gave up it ought not cause much surprise; for they had been fighting for seven years under conditions of great hardship, and having gotten so little help from abroad they felt deserted. He went on to recall that at Cairo he had told Roosevelt that he thought it essential that there should be during that spring an all-out campaign in Burma which would have brought relief

[7] Memo, talk, Hull with Ambassador Wei Tao-ming and Dr. H. H. Kung, June 24, 1944.

to the Chinese army. Otherwise, this reminiscent version of his attitude continued, he had told the President not to count on a continuance of effective Chinese resistance to the Japanese. This all-out offensive—including an amphibious entry into Burma from the south—had been settled at Cairo; but it had been reversed after Teheran; the offensive was not a knockout one, and the Burma Road still was not open. If there had been the type of campaign he wanted, the Chinese armies would not have suffered their current defeats. "Recent developments," he construed, "had proved him correct in his estimate. . . . He was . . . not criticizing President Roosevelt for his decision; but . . . he wished to remind President Roosevelt that the prediction which he, President Chiang Kai-shek, had made at the time was sound." This view of the matter may have taken Wallace, poorly informed at what had gone on at Cairo, somewhat by surprise. He does not seem to have pursued the question of whose the fault, or what the reasons, for the military failure.

On the ride to the airfield before Wallace's departure, Chiang Kai-shek reverted to the subject in a more composed way. He asked again that the President be reminded that after the Cairo plans were changed he had foreseen what was now happening; but that China had not collapsed, that the situation actually was not as bad as he had then feared. This view of the situation confirms the impression which Stilwell and Gauss had—that Chiang Kai-shek was more worried over the Chinese Communists than over the chance that the Japanese could crush them.

THE AMERICAN ARMY IN CHINA

Discussion of the military situation led Chiang Kai-shek naturally to the subject of the American army in China. He made his critical feeling evident. American army officers in China, he observed, have no faith in the Chinese army, and this attitude had an adverse effect. It also, he thought, was encouraging the Communists. He himself, he said, "continued to have full confidence in his army." And he wished Wallace to so tell the President. Wallace responded by commenting on the remarkable degree of faith which China had in the Generalissimo. He did not make the point that the lack of faith among many of the Americans serving in China seemed to be not in the fighting ability of the Chinese soldiers—if properly fed, organized, and led—but in the command.

The Generalissimo took his chance to make clear how unsatisfactory his relations with Stilwell were.[8] As the last of his long list of troubles

[8] Stilwell remained in Burma during Wallace's visit to China. He felt he ought not to leave Burma at this time when a crucial battle was still going on to keep control of

with the man whom the American army had imposed on him, he cited Stilwell's refusal during the early stages of the Honan campaign to respond to his request that gasoline flown in over the Hump be diverted from other recipients to the Chinese air force. He found it hard, he said, to operate in the face "of such an uncooperative attitude." It should be noted that Stilwell, in reporting to Washington, stated that in his opinion it would be a waste to do what Chiang Kai-shek asked, since the Chinese air force had proven itself incapable of effective action.

Coming down flatly, Chiang Kai-shek told Wallace "he lacked confidence in General Stilwell's judgment." But perhaps because he remembered the uproar caused by his previous attempt to have Stilwell replaced, he did not directly repeat it. His remarks eventuated instead in a request that the President send out to China some top emissary who could presumably control and correct Stilwell. The Generalissimo wanted a connection with the White House that did not run through the War and State Departments. Churchill had attached a personal representative to him, General Carton de Wiart, who handled both political and military matters. Why could not Roosevelt, Chiang Kai-shek asked, choose someone like this? "He could perform an invaluable service. Today military cooperation is very difficult because of personnel. He feels that Chennault is most cooperative. Stilwell has improved, but has no understanding of political matters—he is entirely military in outlook." Stilwell —to glance again at his notebook and radios—was writing that by "cooperation" Chiang Kai-shek meant "obedience." His orders from Washington stated that his assignment was to carry out the military aims of the American government in the Chinese Theater; these were not always in accord with the purposes or schedules of Chiang Kai-shek.

Wallace was impressed by the Generalissimo's tales of his troubles with Stilwell. As he recalled later, ". . . I was deeply moved by the cry of a man in distress."[9]

MILITARY OBSERVERS TO YENAN

On a matter of both military and political significance Chiang Kai-shek surprisingly gave assent. He agreed to allow an American military mission to go into the Communist areas of the northwest. Of this project,

the airfield at Myitkyina, and there was trouble with Wingate's exhausted raiders. Wallace thought he might visit the Burma front, but his time was short, and bad weather prevented him from trying to go there.

[9] *Hearings: Institute of Pacific Relations*, page 1368.

which was of great interest to both Stilwell's headquarters and the War Department, there is more to tell presently.

AMERICAN CRITICISM OF THE CHINESE GOVERNMENT

Chiang Kai-shek made repeated references to the criticisms of the Chinese situation that were appearing in the American press. These, he hinted, were largely due to Communist propaganda. They were, he observed, depressing the Chinese people and causing them to lose hope of getting help from abroad. What was needed, he asserted, was not criticism, but help in relieving the economic distress that was causing the situation.

DIVERSE GENERAL IMPRESSIONS

Records of the overflowing stream of Wallace's talks with Chiang Kai-shek leave a few other noteworthy impressions of the Generalissimo's frame of mind.

1. That Chiang Kai-shek was greatly worried but still fairly sure he could hold the situation together until the war was won.

2. That in regard to military matters, he had no important new steps in mind for reinvigorating his army or for new offensive actions. If any were to be undertaken, it would be because the United States urged them and gave the necessary training, equipment, and direction.

3. That he was sincere in his wish and intention to shape the policy of the Chinese government along a democratic path; and also in his plans for agrarian reform—such as a better system of land ownership and reduced interest rates. But these measures he thought postponable. He did not regard them as essential to keep control of China during the war or to win the war. He preferred to wait until it would be safer and easier to go ahead with them at a gradual rate acceptable to his party.

When the Vice President arrived at Kunming on June 26th, he cabled the President the gist of his thoughts about his talks with Chiang Kai-shek. This report was written in consultation with Alsop and Vincent.[10] Davies was in Kunming also, having been sent by Stilwell to represent

[10] Joseph Alsop, *Atlantic Monthly*, April 1952. "The Strange Case of Louis Budenz" recounts that the cable rose out of a talk among the three; that Wallace took heed of Alsop's pleas that something be done; that Vincent seconded his pleas and convinced Wallace; that Alsop typed out the cable and Wallace filed it. Further interesting details and thoughts about this message are given by Alsop in his column in the *Washington Post*, September 10 and 12, 1951.

him and to invite the Vice President to visit Burma. But he saw little of Wallace.

Wallace described the Generalissimo as bewildered in regard to the economic situation, unsure in regard to the political situation, and, though expressing confidence in his armies, distressed about military developments. This anxiety Wallace thought more than justified. The situation in China seemed to him extremely discouraging in all its aspects.

Wallace wrote in favor of responding to the Generalissimo's wish that the President appoint a personal representative to act as liaison between them. With sober emphasis he summarized the reasons why the appointment should be made, and why it should be followed by more far-reaching measures. There was, he informed the President, a strong probability that East China, including the American air bases, would soon be lost to the Japanese army, as soon perhaps as three or four weeks. This would nullify our military effort in China. But beyond that, it would be a violent economic and political shock to the already weakened Chungking regime. The President should therefore be prepared to see China lose all value as an Allied military base unless determined steps were taken to halt disintegration. It was necessary, he advised, to consider not only military measures but political actions also. Otherwise, he observed, there might result a political vacuum "which will be filled in ways that the President will understand."

The Generalissimo, Wallace added, was fully alarmed, anxious for aid and guidance, and ready to make relatively drastic changes if wisely approached. Affairs, he also thought, were in a more fluid state; and the right man should be able to bring about the semblance of a united front. Wallace has subsequently explained that by this he meant not a coalition with the Communists—of which he thought there was so little chance—but "a coalition, recruited from within the area controlled by the Chungking government consisting . . . of progressive banking and commercial leaders . . . the large group of western trained men whose outlook is not limited to the perpetuation of the old landlord-dominated rural society of China; and the considerable group of generals and other officers who are neither subservient to the landlords nor afraid of the peasantry."[11] The situation needed, Wallace suggested, an American gen-

[11] Wallace letter, *U.S. News and World Report*, January 9, 1953. This statement corresponds closely with his report to the President on July 10, 1944.

There is a perplexing variation between this version of a "united front" or "coalition," and the one which the notes on his talks with Chiang Kai-shek indicate Wallace then had in mind—one which seemed to contemplate inclusion of the Communists. The General-

eral officer in whom political and military authority would be temporarily united. General Stilwell, Wallace said, could not do the job; first, because he was so immersed in the offensive in Burma and, second, because he did not have the confidence of the Generalissimo. The new appointee might either be Stilwell's deputy in China with authority to deal directly on political questions with the White House, or he might be separated from Stilwell's present command.[12]

The report concluded by stating that time was of the essence; that the new man should reach Chungking before East China was lost once and for all.

---

issimo so understood him. The development of Wallace's thought may well have been due to recognition that Chiang Kai-shek was so set in his attitude toward the Communists that there was no use of pursuing that line.

[12] According to a story in Arthur Krock's column in the *New York Times,* October 11, 1951, Wallace told the press "his first choice to replace the late General Stilwell . . . was Major General Claire L. Chennault, head of the American air force which was giving the Chinese Nationalist troops the only protection they had against the mounting Communist [sic] military power." Further, that Vincent concurred in his choice, that Alsop opposed it, and that Wallace then fixed on Lieutenant General Wedemeyer. In the Wallace letter just cited, he states that he recommended Wedemeyer but that "Unfortunately Roosevelt, within 10 days of my Wedemeyer recommendation, went in exactly the opposite direction."

CHAPTER 16

After the Wallace Mission

CHIANG KAI-SHEK, despite his feeling that the Communists were implacable enemies of his regime, had agreed to allow an American mission to enter their areas in the northwest. His consent, as has been told, was abrupt. Perhaps he was genuinely impressed with the military reasons given. Perhaps, and more probably, he wanted to please the President and the War Department so that they might give friendlier heed to his needs.

The American request for entry into the Communist areas was not a sudden impulse. As the prospect of American air operations over the Communist area and of American landings on the coast at nearby points grew closer, the wish for information of military use grew more definite. And as the Communists became a more important force and element, the wish to find out what their part of China was like grew stronger. From time to time members of the Embassy talked with Communist officials who came to Chungking. But the contact was not continuous, and there was no way of testing what the men from Yenan said.

The first official suggestion that we ought to try to establish direct liaison with Yenan seems to have been advanced by Davies, in a memo which he had sent to Stilwell in January 1944. This, in brief, gave two main reasons for sending an American mission into the Communist areas: first, to obtain for ourselves essential information about the Communist forces, and Russian operations in North China and Manchuria, if it should enter the war, and about the Japanese military position in that part of China; second, to break down the isolation of the Communist areas, since the government blockade was forcing the Communists into dependence on the Soviet Union. In that connection, Davies observed that the presence of an American mission in the area would be a deterrent to the impulse of the Kuomintang to try to liquidate the Communists by force and thereby bring on civil war. He noted that the Chinese Communists had said that they would welcome American observers. But he pointed out they might change their minds, and so he urged that we act at once. He forecast that the Generalissimo would not want us to establish independent contact with the Communists, and would consent only if the President used the ample American bargaining power.[1]

[1] Davies' memo, January 15, 1944. Subject: Observers Mission to North China.

Hopkins, to whom Davies had sent a copy of this memo, found the proposal sensible. The President had asked General Marshall and Admiral Leahy to study it. Then on February 9th he had put the question to Chiang Kai-shek. A message was delivered through Stilwell, asking the Generalissimo to cooperate in the sending of a group of American observers at once to North Shensi and Shansi provinces and such other places as might be necessary. The President emphasized that it was becoming most important that we should get all possible knowledge about the large Japanese forces in North China and Manchuria in order to guide future operations, air and ground.

The State Department may not have known of the President's message. In any case, while the Generalissimo was considering it, the State Department had also taken up the project. On February 16th it had asked Gauss what he thought of the idea of sending such a mission, and on the next day, the 17th, Under-Secretary Stettinius had asked the Far Eastern Division to consult the War Department about it. Gauss had answered that it was unlikely the Generalissimo would agree, but he thought the effort worth making. The group to be sent, he advised, should be essentially military, but he suggested that John Service (another Foreign Service officer assigned to Stilwell) might be taken along.[2]

Gauss was right. Chiang Kai-shek had been unhappy over the idea. In his answer to the President (sent on February 22nd) he had tried to give satisfaction without giving consent. He said that he was ready to aid in the gathering of more accurate information about Japanese forces in North China and Manchuria. Thus he was telling his Secretary of War to get in touch with Stilwell "with a view to mapping out a prospective itinerary for the mission in all areas where the political authority of the National Government extends and where the Chinese army is located."[3] It is safe to surmise that Chiang Kai-shek knew that Stilwell's headquarters were behind the request, and that he associated it with an impending proposal that American aid be extended to the Communists.

The President's acknowledgment on March 1st had been low-toned. He thanked the Generalissimo for the steps he was taking to facilitate the entry of American observers into North and Northeast China. This area ought to be, he agreed, a very fruitful source of military information in regard to the Japanese. He did not, as he was being urged, insist that

---

[2] Davies had proposed in his original memo a "military and political observers mission," and in a later one of March 20th he had recommended that Service be included in the group.

[3] Memo, Generalissimo to General Hearn for the President, February 22, 1944, Sunderland-Romanus manuscript, Vol. II and memo Stimson to Hull, March 7.

the mission be allowed to enter Communist areas. Other matters, already reviewed, had then been in the forefront of his correspondence with Chiang Kai-shek—Burma, the American air endeavor in China, dollar payment. And Chiang Kai-shek had been trying along lines already traced to convince the President that there was a real danger, a close danger, of Communist aggression in China, with Soviet support. The President, as told, had sought to quiet Chiang Kai-shek's fear of Soviet intentions and advised him not to do anything that might hurt cooperation among the United Nations.

The idea of sending an American mission to Communist headquarters at Yenan had not been given up. On March 22nd Roosevelt had repeated his request, making the additional point that the mission might be able to get useful information about the Sinkiang border troubles which were so disturbing to Chiang Kai-shek. Stilwell, on finding out that the Chinese Minister of War was still resistant, had once again resorted to the type of pressure he thought necessary to get the Chinese to do anything. He delayed the departure of Chinese air cadets to the United States, where they were to receive training. Hull and Stimson had talked it over in Washington. The Secretary of State concurred fully in the proposal. But he had thought an appeal to Chiang Kai-shek based on wide grounds of international amity might be more persuasive than the military argument. The matter had been left for Wallace to take up during his visit. Harriman, it will be recalled, sounded out Molotov about it.

While holding out against the dispatch of an official American mission to Yenan, Chiang Kai-shek had allowed another group to pass through. Chinese and foreign press correspondents had been asking for permission to visit the Communist areas. The foreign correspondents, grouped together with Brooks Atkinson of the *New York Times* as their spokesman, had formally presented their request to the Minister of Information on February 16th. It had been granted after considerable delay. When Stilwell's headquarters had asked why the Chinese government was willing to allow this visit to the Communist regions, but would not agree to have American military observers go to the same places, the Minister of War had answered that the meaning of the two visits would be quite different. The press correspondents, he explained, were civilians; their visit would not have any official significance and their views would not be taken to represent official policy. But if an American military mission were to go to Yenan, it would be believed that the United States was about to cooperate with the Communists.

The correspondents had finally gotten away for the Communist center at Yenan in the middle of May. The Communist leaders waved their hands over the scene of their rule, as they spoke soothingly of their devotion to democracy and to the unity of China. Thus, in his first interview, Mao Tze Tung told them, "The Chinese Communist Party has never wavered from its policy of supporting Generalissimo Chiang Kai-shek, the policy of continuing the cooperation between the Kuomintang and the Communist Party and the entire people, and the policy of defeating Japanese imperialism and struggle for the building of a free democratic China. . . . But China has draw-backs and they are serious ones. They can be summed up in one phrase—the lack of democracy. . . . It is democracy too that can insure China's post-war unity. . . . Democracy must be all-sided—political, military, economic, and cultural, as also in Party affairs and internationally. All these spheres must be democratized and everything must be unified. But this unity must be based on democratic foundations."[4]

Most of the correspondents felt at home with such language, these names for political and social ideals. Many were also pleased or impressed by the enthusiasm, simplicity, and sense of purpose which they found about them. Their newspaper stories, articles, and books smoothed down or over the extreme and wilful revolutionary intentions behind these phrases and attitudes. And in greater or less measure they praised the tenacious resistance being made against the Japanese.[5]

[4] Interview, Mao Tze Tung, June 12, 1944, printed in *Political Affairs*, January 1945. The Communist leader was at the same time in messages and statements to his party conferences restating that the whole party and its leadership were convinced and faithful believers in the Marxist-Leninist doctrines, and devoted to the ultimate achievement of Communist programs. Recognition of Chiang Kai-shek's leadership was only a temporary political expedient, and, it is safe to conclude, known by his Communist colleagues to be such.

[5] It would require a separate study, and almost a separate book, to examine and state in detail the many reports which the correspondents who went to Yenan published during the following months in newspapers, magazines, and books. A brief illustration of the prevailing character of what they wrote may be borrowed from the telegram sent on July 19, 1944, by the State Department to Ambassador Gauss in order to inform him of the stories being sent in by these correspondents.

"The correspondents in dispatches to *New York Times*, *New York Herald Tribune*, and *Christian Science Monitor*, praised Communists' industrial and agricultural achievements, and applauded fighting spirit and military achievements of Communist troops. *New York Times'* correspondent on July 1 reported finding in Yenan 'hatred of Japanese and determination to defend their achievements against all interference.' Same correspondent stressed finding realization of nearness of counteroffensive against Japan, in which Communist armies and guerrillas want to participate to fullest. He reported seeing how formerly barren country has been transformed into area of intensive cultiva-

On the very day that Wallace began his talks with Chiang Kai-shek, Stilwell's headquarters in Chungking had transmitted word to the War Department that General George E. Stratemeyer (Commander of the Army Air Force in India and Burma, a deputy for Mountbatten) and General Kenneth S. Wolfe (Commander of the 20th Bomber Command, the Matterhorn Operation) felt it essential to get more information in regard to the Japanese order of battle, weather, airfields, location of friendly troops, and other matters; and were urging that the American government ask again for permission to send a military mission into the Communist areas. In passing on this message to Marshall, General Ferris, Stilwell's deputy in Chungking, concurred. He suggested that the President ask Wallace to discuss the matter again with Chiang Kai-shek. Wallace, it will be recalled, had already heard about it from Harriman. The President at once radioed Wallace to see what he could do. But Wallace had secured the Generalissimo's consent before he got this message.

On the day before, the Generalissimo had said that he would not agree to this mission unless the Communists met his terms. When Vincent tried to quiz him about the matter, he had shown plainly that he did not like it. But on the next morning, the 23rd (Chungking time), Vincent and Wallace brought the subject up again. The Generalissimo, to Wallace's surprise, reversed his position. He said "That can be done." His only conditions were that the group should go under the auspices of the Chinese National Military Council rather than of the United States Army, and that Chinese officers should go with them. In giving his consent, Chiang Kai-shek again emphasized the fact that the Communists would not obey his orders and again urged Wallace to make it clear when he got back home that the Communists should come to terms.

Later that day, Wallace, accompanied by General Ferris, who brought Service along, talked further to Chiang Kai-shek and Soong about the project. The Generalissimo confirmed his assent. He was willing to have the group leave as soon as it was organized; he agreed also that

---

tion, stock breeding, and handicraft industry. Harrison Forman in *Herald Tribune* on June 23 described Yenan as 'magnificent symbol of tenacity and determination of people of this border region of China.' He described how this border area, forced by circumstances to become wholly self-reliant since it was cut off from outside world three years ago, 'encourages any and every industry, small or large, even subsidizing some which admittedly would be unprofitable if products they yield could be imported.' Gunther Stein in *Christian Science Monitor* on June 27 declared that any Allied commander 'would be proud to command these tough, well-fed, hardened troops whose exercises show both skill and spirit.' "

it should be allowed to communicate directly with the American army command in China and have freedom of movement. Whether or not the subject was discussed, it was probably understood that Service would be going along with the soldiers.

The group was ready to start and flew off a month later to Yenan in an army transport plane escorted by fighters. In charge was Colonel David Barrett, who had been military attaché at Chungking. They were enthusiastically received. Chiang Kai-shek was right in thinking that the Communists would consider it a sign of American sympathy with their cause and wish to cooperate with it. As described by one of the news-papermen, close to the Yenan regime, who watched the arrival of the mission, "The Yenan people, too, were mighty glad. Within two months the door to their blockaded, forbidden areas had opened for the second time. And with all due respect to us, these guests obviously carried more weight than the representatives of the world's most important news-papers. Evidently the United States Army realized that the Chinese Communists had a role to play in the war against Japan. . . . At the government Guest House the national flag of the Chinese Republic, the same that flies in Chungking, greeted the first Allied officers to visit Yenan. And among those who received them was Major-General Chou, the Generalissimo's resident representative with the 8th Route Army in Yenan, smiling and apparently more pleased than embarrassed at the new phenomenon of Chungking-Washington solidarity with the Communist 'bandits.' It all seemed somewhat unreal, almost too good to be true."[6]

After the group had been in Yenan for a few weeks, Mao Tze Tung confided to Service, "Finally, any contact you Americans may have with us Communists is gold. Of course, we are glad to have the Observer Section here because it will help to beat Japan. But there is no use in pretending that—up to now at least—the chief importance of your com-ing is its political effect upon the Kuomintang."[7]

The Generalissimo's consent to the dispatch of this Observer Mission did not in fact indicate any improvement in his relationship with the Communists. Wallace had activated the subject, but his visit had not brought the opponents any nearer together. Their negotiations revolved in the same circle as before, and with the same dark grit of suspicion.

[6] This is a brief extract from a vivid account of the arrival of the Observer Group, the start of its work, and its response to its reception, in the book *The Challenge of Red China*, by Gunther Stein, 1945, pages 347-353.

[7] Report No. 15, John S. Service, Title: Interview with Mao Tze Tung, August 27, 1944.

The attitude of the government remained unchanged. As reaffirmed by the Minister of Information, Liang, a few days after Wallace had left on June 28th, "A settlement through political methods is simple. So long as the Communist Party agrees to abide by law and so long as its troops obey the orders of the Supreme Command, all questions will be solved automatically." If the Communists accepted these basic provisions, then the government would call a conference of all political parties to decide how a democratic and constitutional system of government would eventually be established.

This was the government bid to the defiant Communists, its offer of a chance to pursue the Communist program under the regular rules of political contest. While waiting for circumstances to induce the Communists to accept these terms, the government seemed to most American reporters to be doing little or nothing effective to correct its own faults and enlist popular support. In particular, and this may have been its great failure, it was making no telling changes in the conditions or relationships of the workers on the farms. They were being left to listen to the Communist clamor for reduced taxes, low interest rates, and possession of the land. Few men who work long and hard on farms can ignore the appeal of such benefits. The government professed its firm intention of doing much about these matters once the war emergency was over. But it went on thinking that until then it could not manage the great adjustments, economic and social, which these reforms would entail.

The Communists did not tire of saying over and over that all they wanted was a democratic party arrangement. But they continued to insist on major conditions before assenting to the terms offered by the government. They asked that the Communist troops should be kept together in eighteen divisions within the government army, and that these be equipped and cared for by the government in the same way as other Chinese forces. They demanded that the government recognize the "popularly elected" governments in the areas which they controlled, and that the government should end its blockade of these areas. They wanted the government to release at once all political prisoners.[8]

The maneuvers of the opponents at this time caused Ambassador

[8] The Communist terms and conditions frequently changed and had variations. These are the main features of the Communist position as summed up by Lin Tsu-han, Chairman of the Border Region Government, in talk at Chungking on June 30th with Robert S. Ward. Ward's memo of June 30th was sent to State Department by dispatch, July 5, 1944, signed by Gauss. A good account of Kuomintang-Communist discussions during this period is in *United States Relations with China*, page 55 and Annexes 40 and 41.

Gauss to reach the morose conclusion that "in its essence the struggle is one in which the Central Government is apparently seeking by political means to encompass the destruction of the Communists, while the latter are by the same means struggling to insure their survival." Chiang Kai-shek had told Wallace that if the President wanted to try to moderate this struggle, he would not resent it. At the same time he warned that the President was likely to get hurt and fooled. Neither the White House nor the State Department were ready to accept the conclusion that the struggle could not be adjusted by a fair deal which would allow both sides to live together.

Thus began their effort—which was to become more and more active —to induce or compel an agreement. They felt it imperative for the conduct of the war. Beyond that, they were worried by the threat that when the war ended, China would be in disorder and unable to play the part given it at Cairo. Worse still, there might be prolonged civil war in which the United States might feel compelled to be on one side while the Soviet Union was on the other. Then the whole plan of organizing the world for peace would crumble in the dust of China.

The Kuomintang regime by then had lost the sympathy and admiration of some elements of the American government, both civil and military. A memo written by Service while he was waiting to go to Yenan exemplifies the view of the situation that at this time was spreading in the American Embassy and army in China and in the State Department.[9] This stated in essence that the situation in China was critical, that a progressive breakdown was taking place. The Kuomintang, the analysis continued, was proving itself incapable of averting the collapse; in fact, its policies were hastening and forcing the crisis. The main reason was that, having lost popular support, it was allowing the wish to keep in power to rule its actions. In sum, the crux of all Chinese problems was democratic reform. Since the collapse of the Chinese government would greatly injure the United States, the American government ought to base its support on a policy of attempting to further the needed changes.

[9] There are two reasons for believing that the views presented in this memorandum of June 20, 1944, were widely held: (1) American policy during the summer of 1944 followed the suggested lines, (2) the memo was given exceptional attention and praise. It was approved by Gauss in the dispatch with which he transmitted it to the State Department, No. 2733 of July 1st. The Division of Chinese Affairs found it to be a timely and valuable discussion. The State Department sent Service a special letter of commendation for his "timely and able analysis" and "constructive suggestions." September 13 to Gauss. Stilwell's headquarters showed its approval by selecting him for the mission to Yenan.

This memo is printed in full in *State Department Employee Loyalty Investigation*, pages 2035-2046. Title: The Situation in China and Suggestions regarding American Policy.

This view of the situation, it may be remarked, is an open door that might lead along any of many different tactical paths. The one on the right would be a policy of friendly persuasion with the Chinese government. The one on the left might mean an effort to force the government to accept so much of the Communist terms and program that it might gain control of the whole of China. American policy during the next two years moved unsteadily over the area between these two paths.

CHAPTER 17

The American Emergency Proposals:
Summer of 1944

DURING this summer of 1944 the Japanese pushed on with dogged purpose. They were coming toward the American air bases at Liuchow and Kweilin. Should they get that far, the whole American combat air effort in China would be marked down to little. From there, the Japanese troops would be able, unless Chinese forces not then in sight were brought against them, to press on either to Kunming or Chungking or both.[1]

Stilwell, frustrated in Burma, did not spare regret about the military scene in China. He—his diaries and notebooks record his grim thoughts —regarded what was happening as proof of his unheeded warnings: that when the American air offensive in China really began to hurt the Japanese, they would try to capture the American air bases; and they would do so unless the Chinese armies were in every way reanimated. The Generalissimo, in his opinion, was not doing even what he could easily do, and his management of the campaign was ruinous.[2] The critic under the rainy Burma skies contrasted the defaults in China with the spirit and stamina of other Chinese divisions organized and trained by Americans.

[1] As succinctly summed up in a *Biennial Report of the Chief of Staff of The United States Army*, July 1, 1943, to June 30, 1945, to the Secretary of War, "In May 1944, however, the Japanese had launched a strong drive southward from Tung Ting Lake in Hunan province. In the late summer they began a complementary drive west from Canton. These salients joined near the American base at Kweilin serving unoccupied China, and overran seven of the principal bases from which the 14th Air Force had been throwing its weight against shipping in the China Sea."
Kunming was the terminus of the air supply route to India and the nerve center of our air attacks on the Japanese in China. If that was lost, the whole tremendous Allied effort to move supplies into China and maintain effective air bases and equipment would be canceled.

[2] His views are adequately suggested by his jet-like entries in *The Stilwell Papers*.
The Military Intelligence Division of the War Department, in a report that it submitted on July 5, 1945, on the Chinese Communist movement, had this to say about the government's defense effort at this time, "The Chungking Government's policy of conserving its military strength led it to keep many of its best armies away from the front in East China, and although some of its better armies were stationed in front areas, many of the front line troops represented military units which were undesirable to the Kuomintang; some were the troops of war lords, like P'ang Ping-hsun and Wu Hua-wen, others of Nationalist leaders who had formerly fought against Chiang Kai-shek, like Li Tsung-jen of the Kwangsi Military Clique, Yu Hsueh-chung of the former Manchurian (Twangpei) army and Hsueh Yueh of the Kwantung Military Clique." *Hearings: Institute of Pacific Relations*, Part VII A, page 2355.

In sultry contrast, Chennault thought the events in both China and Burma evidence of the deep wrongness of Stilwell's course. The blame for defeat he placed upon his colleague for having devoted American and Chinese combat forces to a headstrong and unended compaign in Burma; and for having so repressed the American air force in China that it was not strong enough to disperse the Japanese armies. Chennault thought that Stilwell had wilfully ignored his warnings about Japanese plans and preparations for attack. Beyond that, he believed that Stilwell's response to the requests for help was governed by hostility to him and the Generalissimo, a wish to punish them and a ruthless will to force Chiang Kai-shek to grant him full command of the Chinese armies.[3] In that charge he discounted the extent to which Stilwell's opinions were confirmed in Washington, and how far his decisions regarding the treatment of the 14th Air Force were governed by orders from Washington.

The Generalissimo also held himself free of blame and fault. In his view the main reasons why the defense of East China gave way were because the total share of Lend-Lease supplies sent to China had been so small, and that despite this he had been persuaded against his judgment to engage so large a force in Burma. But he took a controlled view of events past and current, as he waited for Roosevelt's answer to the request he had made through Wallace: that a special representative be sent, who would keep him in direct touch with the President. It is possible to discern in his attitude the traditional Chinese bent: that after all the proper course for the Chinese army and people was to maintain a prudent strategy of retreat, to wait and to wear down rather than to seek decisive victory in quick battle.

In their definite differences as how best to defend China, American and Chinese officials were swayed by their clashing appreciations of what was being done for China, and what was asked of her. Stilwell was nagged by the conviction, as were other American military men, that the United States had given a great deal to keep China alive and fighting, and that much of this help had been wasted. They had the impression that China was waiting for the United States and Britain to do the hard fighting and win the war for it. In contrast, the Generalissimo and those about him were disappointed with the help they got, as

---

[3] Chennault's opinions of Stilwell's strategy, actions, and purpose are stated at length in his book, *The Way of a Fighter*. Joseph C. Alsop, who was then on Chennault's staff, takes substantially the same view as Chennault of the occurrences of the summer, though his version is somewhat more careful, *Saturday Evening Post*, January 14, 1950. Detailed examination of the facts, and of responsibilities and justifications, I must leave to others better qualified and more fully informed.

they had been ever since December 1941, when their great hope of combined Allied effort centering on China had come to nothing. They compared the size of the American war effort in other places to that in China and thought China poorly treated, a neglected area of battle.

The American and Chinese governments were fuming at each other. The results of weaknesses and failures of the Chinese were showing up in battle. So also were the effects of that prime decision which had governed the amount and kind of American and British military co-operation with China—to defeat Germany first. This event was coming closely into sight. Within a year it would be possible to throw vastly larger combat forces into the Pacific war. This prospect reduced the gravity of current setbacks in China both in American and Chinese eyes, and probably prevented the separation from becoming extreme.

American planning for the future stages of action against Japan was being modified. The Americans were concluding that the best route to Japan was not, after all, from or through China but up and across the Pacific. On July 8th the Marines and Army ground forces, overcoming fanatical resistance, secured the final surrender of Saipan. This was the first Pacific island base from which the American long-range bombers could roam over the Japanese home islands. A week later Roosevelt, having accepted the Democratic nomination for the Fourth Term, left for Pearl Harbor to confer with MacArthur and Nimitz. His bent up to then was to support the strategy favored by the Navy and Air Force: to make the next main landings not in the Philippines but in Formosa, and from naval and air bases there and on the China mainland deprive Japan of essential supplies from the south, and prepare to reduce it to submission by blockade and bombing.[4] But, responsive to MacArthur's proofs, he swung round and approved the plan for moving next into the Philippines.[5] MacArthur's forces and the Navy hurried their preparations forward.

[4] As stated in *Fleet Admiral King: A Naval Record*, pages 566-567, "The Navy favored a direct attack on Formosa without reference to the Philippine Islands, feeling this position would dominate the sea lanes by which Japan received essential supplies of oil, rice and other commodities from her recently conquered southern empire. The Navy had no interest in fighting the Japanese on land in the home islands, feeling that a blockade exercised by sea and air power was sufficient to win. General MacArthur, on the other hand, was strongly in favor of a return to the Philippines. There were difficulties in both plans. The Navy knew that an assault on Formosa would involve a hard struggle because the Japanese had sent heavy reinforcements of planes and troops to the island."

[5] An account, based on talk with MacArthur and other participants, of the discussions at the Pearl Harbor Conference is given in *Our Jungle Road to Tokyo*, by General Robert L. Eichelberger, 1950, pages 165-166.

[168]

Campaigns in China fell further into the background; thereafter they were not deemed vital for winning the war. But more than enough reason was still seen for enabling the Chinese to fight on, and more effectively. The Japanese armies in China still loomed as a formidable force; and if the Chinese did not keep them busy fighting, they would have to be met elsewhere by the Allies. Thus, despite the change in strategic plans, the American government from July on went further than ever in its efforts to make over Chinese military direction and effort. The President and War Department asked the Generalissimo to put into effect military measures which offended his pride, and had serious political bearing upon his regime.

The War Department from Stimson and Marshall down deeply felt that Stilwell's gifts and achievements in China and Burma were being unjustly judged. In their opinion, as expressed in a memo by General Thomas T. Handy, Stilwell's effort had been excellent, and his campaign for Myitkyina brilliant.[6] But the British with whom he had to work in Burma were also suggesting his recall.[7] Thoughts turned to the possibility of taking him out of Burma, where the future tasks would not be great, and using him to salvage the situation in China. Accordingly, on July 1st, Marshall told Stilwell of the British attitude, and asked him whether he thought Chiang Kai-shek would allow him to play a part in the fighting in China, and whether he could do any good there. Stilwell's answer was that the Generalissimo might be induced to give him a command job in China if the President firmly urged it, on the score that desperate situations required desperate remedies. But he thought that in order to do the job well, it would be essential for him to have complete authority over the Chinese armies. Even if that were granted, the damage already done seemed to him so great that there was only one chance of saving the situation—by a counteroffensive to be started from the province of Shansi in North Central China. For this operation he was of the opinion that Communist forces would be needed and should participate. In sum, he concluded that these measures, and only these measures, might salvage something in China.

In passing, it may be observed that this estimate turned out to be too black. But the main reason was probably not within China. American

[6] Memo, Handy for Marshall, June 30, 1944. Sunderland-Romanus manuscript, Vol. II.

[7] When Marshall was in London in June, General Sir Alan Brooke, Chief of the Imperial General Staff, said that Stilwell ought to be transferred since he did not get along with his colleagues in SEAC.

advances and threats elsewhere during the next few months brought saving relief to the Chinese armies. These pressures made it so hard for the Japanese forces in Southeast China that they felt compelled to restrain the action there.[8] But all this appeared clearly only some months later.

In any case, Wallace's suggestion that Stilwell be removed from the China Theater was passed over. Quite to the contrary, the American government began intently to seek to have him put in command in China. The Joint Chiefs of Staff sent a memo to the President which urged that it be done. This memo affirmed the need for drastic measures to prevent disaster to American effort in Asia. It noted that throughout the war the American government had been pressed to increase the Hump transport effort, particularly to serve Chennault's air force; the required effort it found to be immense, poorly directed, and unjustified since all that Chennault alone could do was little more than slightly to delay the Japanese advance. In contrast, it praised Stilwell's ideas and command actions in face of the negative Chinese and British attitudes. It submitted the text of a message which it recommended to be sent at once by the President to the Generalissimo. As summed up by Admiral Leahy in the short note transmitting this memo to the President, "We are in full agreement that this action is immediately necessary to save the situation in China."[9]

Roosevelt, who had long had great misgivings about Stilwell's personal ways and abilities, responded to this advice. On the 6th he sent off the message which had been prepared by the Joint Chiefs. This asked Chiang Kai-shek to confer on one individual the power to coordinate all Allied military resources in China, including the Communist forces. He was, the President had continued, making Stilwell a full general; and he urged the Generalissimo to recall him from Burma and confer this command upon him directly under himself. He should, the President thought, be charged with the full responsibility and authority to coordinate and direct all operations against the Japanese. Unless these measures were taken to meet the desperate situation, the President concluded, the common cause would meet disaster.[10]

[8] The first diversion of Japanese forces from the line of advance toward the ultimate goal of Kunming or Chungking began in late August-September. Part of the China expeditionary army was disposed near the east coast of Chekiang to thwart anticipated landing attempts by United States forces. U.S. War Department, *Japanese Monograph*, *No. 129*, "China Area Operations Record."

[9] Memo, July 4, 1944, to the President from the Joint Chiefs of Staff, Sunderland-Romanus manuscript, Vol. II.

[10] A carbon copy of a memorandum found in the offices of *Amerasia*, which stated that the information therein was supplied by John S. Service, contained the gist of this

Of all the proposals made to Chiang Kai-shek since the start of the war, these were probably for him the hardest. To place any foreigner in command of the Chinese armies, even though under his authority, was a blow to his pride. Some of the Chinese military commanders were certain to be affronted and resist. To place Stilwell in that post would be equivalent to submitting the fate of his regime to that rough and scornful critic, or to enter into a struggle with him which might break his friendship with the United States.[11] To give Stilwell, as the President was asking, freedom to use and equip any and all Chinese forces, including the Communists, would involve a risk that the rebel force would become dominant.[12] It may be deduced that these requests seemed to the Generalissimo drastic and unworkable as well.

---

message from Roosevelt to Chiang Kai-shek and an account of its presentation to the Generalissimo by General Ferris, Service acting as interpreter. Chiang Kai-shek answered this message through H. H. Kung who was then at the Bretton Woods Conference. The memo also related the essentials of the next following message sent by Roosevelt from which, it is commented in the memo, a fair indication of Chiang Kai-shek's response could be gathered. *State Department Employee Loyalty Investigation*, pages 1912-1913.

[11] Alsop in the *Saturday Evening Post*, January 7, 1950, imputes to Stilwell the deliberate intention of forcing Chiang Kai-shek into an unconditional merger with his enemies. He suggests that if Stilwell had had his way developments in China would have been the same as those that took place in Yugoslavia during the war, with Chiang in the role of the abandoned Mikhailovich. This, of course, is conjectural and disputable. Stilwell, though a person of strong and stern hates, was a disciplined representative of the American government and would have sought and acted under orders. The American government was still too deeply committed to Chiang Kai-shek to have abandoned him at this time.

[12] The testimony of Vincent before the committee, *Hearings: Institute of Pacific Relations*, pages 2072-2073, is of interest on the meaning of the President's request.

"Mr. Vincent: . . . I recall—and I think it was a War Department-White House matter—that Stilwell was authorized to go over to Chiang and see him and recommend a unified command of all troops in China.

"Mr. Sourwine: What did that mean?

"Mr. Vincent: That meant, so far as I can recollect, that Stilwell was to assume command of all forces in China.

"Mr. Sourwine: Didn't that necessarily imply the arming of the Chinese Communists?

"Mr. Vincent: If Stilwell was going to take over all command?

"Mr. Sourwine: Certainly.

"Mr. Vincent: It would imply the arming of them under his command and utilizing them as a unified army.

"Mr. Sourwine: That was, then, a proposal for arming the Chinese Communists, wasn't it?

"Mr. Vincent: If it had been carried out in the way that I understood Stilwell wanted to carry it out, it would.

"Mr. Sourwine: It was a proposal for arming the Chinese Communists, whether it was carried out or not, wasn't it?

"Mr. Vincent: It was a proposal that Stilwell would take command of all the troops, and I assume it would have followed from that that the Chinese Communists would have been utilized.

"Mr. Sourwine: It was necessarily implicit, wasn't it?

"Mr. Vincent: Yes."

Service, who went with General Ferris to translate the President's telegram to the

But the quick answer which he sent on July 8th was equable. He was, the Generalissimo said, in agreement with the principle of the President's "exacting and sincere" suggestion as a way of dealing with the emergency. But there were reasons for taking careful thought before decision. Among them he pointed to the complexity of Chinese internal political problems, and to the fact that Chinese troops did not accept direction easily. If the arrangement went wrong, he observed, it would cause great trouble between the United States and China. The Generalissimo had then gone on to renew his request that the President send out an influential person, who enjoyed his full confidence and who might collaborate constantly with the Generalissimo on all political and military matters. He wanted someone of far-sighted political ability and vision. For, and here the Generalissimo exposed the foundations of the question, military cooperation must be built on political cooperation. This answer was a way of saying that he was not refusing to do what the President thought must be done. But before doing it, he wanted to be sure of his bearings and of American intentions.

The President sent this answer to the Joint Chiefs with the remark that "There is a good deal in what the Generalissimo says." He intended to establish the direct liaison wanted by Chiang Kai-shek, but this might take some time. And the feeling prevailed that the military situation in China would not allow delay. The basic policies and working details could be settled—Roosevelt told Chiang Kai-shek in his next answer on July 15th—in the course of execution of the command assignment and of the campaign. But Chiang Kai-shek was not willing to risk a hit-or-miss outcome. He made clear that before he appointed Stilwell to command he would want: (1) an adequate definition of his authority, (2) an understanding that the Communists would not be included in his command, and (3) the transfer of control over the distribution of Lend-Lease supplies to himself. These were his three conditions.

Roosevelt's trip to Hawaii and the Aleutians (during which, it will be recalled, the decision was made to move next against the Philippines) interrupted his exchange with Chiang Kai-shek about Stilwell. But he had gone on with his search for a special representative to send to China. With Stilwell's assent, he chose General Patrick J. Hurley.[13] On August

---

Generalissimo, had the same understanding of it. "This was in effect a proposal that the Chinese Communists be armed, since it was taken for granted that if General Stilwell was to command all Chinese armies, this would include the Communists and they would therefore be eligible to receive a share of American equipment." *State Department Employee Loyalty Investigation*, page 1970.

[13] Stimson had remarked to Marshall that he was trying to find an adequate job for

10th the Generalissimo was told of the choice. A few days earlier the Japanese had broken the last valiant Chinese stand at Heng-yang and were heading toward the American air bases. The President and his military advisers thought it was more urgent than ever that Stilwell be placed at once in command of the Chinese armies. They were afraid of losing the last chance of saving the situation if Chiang Kai shek waited to talk over with Hurley the many aspects of the appointment which still worried him. So they tried to brush aside the Generalissimo's three conditions as matters of detail.

But the Generalissimo would not regard them as such, and continued to think that Stilwell's appointment could wait. He was not eager to exchange the dangers he knew for others that he could not measure. The President assured him on August 23rd that Stilwell and Hurley between them would surely understand the political problems which he faced. Roosevelt gave as his ideas: that it would not be sensible in this crisis to refuse the help of the Communists; that Stilwell's position should be that of commander in the field under the head of state; and that his title should correspond. The President added that he would relieve Stilwell of control over Lend-Lease supplies. This step was probably intended to allay Chiang Kai-shek's fear of the use that Stilwell might make of the power to decide what equipment would be given to the government forces and what to the Communist forces.[14]

Chiang Kai-shek, in the talks which he had with Hurley and Stilwell on September the 7th—just after Hurley arrived—seemed to go so far in his assent that Marshall and Stilwell thought the issue settled.[15] They put their staffs eagerly at work to figure out how the situation in China could still be saved—for Chiang Kai-shek and the whole American war and peace program. But—to foretell—the Generalissimo was not willing to put the arrangement into effect until sure that he would still be giving the orders, and until there was a definite accord in regard to the relations with Communist forces.

Concurrently the American government had been urging Chiang Kai-shek to form a combined war council to coordinate the activities of all Chinese forces against Japan. All branches of the American govern-

Hurley. This apparently put the thought of using Hurley in China in Marshall's mind, for on that same day, August 3rd, he sent an inquiry to Stilwell asking him what he thought of the idea.

[14] The main points of this message are given in *United States Relations with China,* page 67.

[15] Sunderland-Romanus manuscript, Vol. II.

ment joined this essay in persuasion: the War Department for military reasons, the State Department because it thought that this step might prepare the way for some general settlement that would unify China.

The idea was that Chiang Kai-shek should call together all factions, including the Communists, and form out of them a military council or high command. It was to serve under him, but all were to share with him joint responsibility for military operations. No version of this proposal that I have read tells clearly just how this council would function, or how differences would be adjusted.

The Counselor of the Embassy, Atcheson, had discussed the idea first on July 3 with Sun Fo, who was Chairman of the Legislative Yuan and a radical critic of Chiang Kai-shek's internal policies. Sun Fo received the suggestion with apparent enthusiasm. Gauss discussed the whole prospect of agreement with the Communists with Soong, then Foreign Minister. Soong was not hopeful that Chiang Kai-shek would change his position. He repeated to the Ambassador the Generalissimo's remark that Wallace was well-intentioned, but that he did not know China; and he remarked that although Chiang Kai-shek was worried, he doubted whether he was ready to adopt extreme measures to meet the emergency. Gauss concluded in his report to the State Department on July 12th that only radical measures to effect a united front of all parties and elements to share responsibility with Chiang Kai-shek in the conduct of the war, would hold the situation. And since this would be such an about-face for the Generalissimo only a presidential initiative would secure his attention. Accordingly he offered to step aside as Ambassador to China to make way for some special representative whom the President might send out, as asked by Chiang Kai-shek, to direct all American activities in China.

On State Department advice, Roosevelt, on July 14th, a week after he first asked Chiang Kai-shek to place Stilwell in command of all Chinese forces, had also appealed to him to try harder to reach a working arrangement with the Communists for China's defense. If that were done, he observed, it would be easier for him, the President, to use his good offices to arrange a conference between Chinese and Russian representatives.[16] It may be noted in passing that Soong, who was the person indicated for the mission to the Soviet Union, agreed with the President

[16] This message, which was sent on July 14th, is in the form of an acknowledgment by the President of Wallace's full report of his talk with Chiang Kai-shek. It is printed in *United States Relations with China*, page 560.

on this point and thought that an accord between the Chinese government and the Chinese Communists should precede his visit to Moscow.[17]

Within the next month—while both American emergency proposals, command for Stilwell and a combined war council, were being talked over—reports began to flow back from the Observers Mission in Yenan. The reports of the military observers went to Stilwell's headquarters and from there to the War Department. Others can tell more reliably of their views; in sum, they found the Communist forces to be in good shape, well-disciplined, eager and skillfully led, but poorly equipped, and not as large as the Communists made them out to be. Service's reports came in sometimes through one, sometimes through two, sometimes through three channels.[18] They were favorable to the Yenan group.[19] He concluded in sum that the Chinese Communist Party had grown to a healthy and moderate maturity and would not be easily killed. Whether Service realized the extent to which he was judging social aims and attitudes as well as facts, remains a matter of surmise. The most practically important of his proposals at this time was that the United States should give aid to the Communist armies. This he advocated for both military and political reasons. We could thereby, he thought, get more effective help against the Japanese. We could also force the Kuomintang—in competition with the Communists—to reform in order to keep the favor of the Chinese people.[20] The Kuomintang, he surmised, would obstinately object; and we would have to decide whether the anticipated gains would justify us in overcoming or disregarding this opposition.

Probably with some knowledge of what the Observer Group was doing and reporting, Chiang Kai-shek became disturbed. On August 30th, he called in Gauss to review the whole question of his relations with the Communists. He wanted to explain more fully his reasons for resisting the advice with which the American government, civilian and military, was showering him. Particularly, he said, he wanted once again

[17] Telegram from American Embassy, Chungking, to State Department, July 25, 1944.

[18] These channels were: (1) to Stilwell's headquarters, thence to the War Department; (2) to the American Embassy in Chungking, thence to the State Department; (3) to Davies and from Davies to Hopkins.

[19] Among the most interesting and significant ones were: (1) Memo No. 1, July 28, 1944, title: First Informal Impression of the North Shensi Communist Base; (2) Report No. 15, Interview with Mao Tze Tung, August 27, 1944; (3) Report No. 16, title: Desirability of American Military Aid to the Chinese Communist armies, August 29, 1944; and (4) Report No. 20, title: Need of an American Policy Toward Problems Created by the Rise of the Chinese Communist Party, September 3, 1944.

[20] Dispatch from Gauss September 28, enclosing and commenting on Service's reports Nos. 15, 16 and 20.

to explain the Communist problem in China, because he felt that despite all he had been saying, Washington still did not understand. He thought we were acting in a way which could have very serious results, for the Communists were out to dominate all of China and to sovietize it. American insistence on an arrangement with them was, he thought, causing them to be more stubborn; and the presence of the American observers in Yenan was making them arrogant. They were, he said, now making demands equivalent to asking the Chinese government to surrender unconditionally. The American government ought to stop trying to force him into an agreement; it ought rather to be telling the Communists to submit to the National Government. Finally, he added, with reference to proposals being made by Stilwell, that he thought it unwise of us to stress the need of the Communist forces to defeat Japan. For it would be useless if—in order to fight the Japanese—China were turned over to the Communists. This danger would not, in his opinion, be averted by appointing a foreign commander over the Chinese armies.

Gauss denied that the presence of the American Observer Group made the Communists harder to handle. They had, he pointed out, turned down the terms offered by the Generalissimo in the past and in his opinion would continue to do so until mutual trust was established. The American government, he tried to explain, was not suggesting that the Chinese government yield to the demands of the Communists. All that it was urging was that China rescue itself from a desperate military plight. A broad transformation of the government might not be possible at the moment, he admitted. But, he argued, the seriousness of the crisis made it most advisable to seek a limited solution, an arrangement by which all parties would join in a responsible war council for planning and carrying out resistance to Japan. Should this be formed, and should it work well, then the mistrust and hostility which was now dividing China might fade and a chance for permanent reconciliation follow. Chiang Kai-shek at the end of his talk commented that the suggestion was at any rate worth study.[21]

Hull found Gauss' report of this talk so like the one which Wallace had made as to indicate ". . . a discouraging lack of progress in the Generalissimo's thinking, in consideration of dissident developments reported in other areas not under the influence of the Communists, and in the light of Chiang's own professed desire to come to a settlement with the Communists." Gauss was authorized to return to the subject, and to tell

[21] Paraphrase of Gauss' report of this talk (August 31, 1945) is printed in *United States Relations with China*, pages 561-562.

the Generalissimo that the President and the State Department thought that the idea of a "coalition council" was timely, practical, and worth careful consideration. Further, he was authorized to say again, as coming from both the President and the Secretary of State, that if Chiang Kai-shek would arrange a meeting with the Communist representative in Chungking, that he, Gauss, would talk with him in the same spirit that he talked with the Generalissimo. He would emphasize to him, as he had to the Generalissimo, the urgent need for unity and for a spirit of good will, tolerance, give-and-take.[22]

Just how the American suggestion would have shaped up had it been tried, there is no way of knowing. For it was only a *formula*, and of the broadest kind. It did not mean, in the Ambassador's mind, a full coalition government for China, but something less: a combined war command to decide on the use of all Chinese resources for the prosecution of the war. But it is hard to see how this could have been arranged without deciding on the distribution of authority within the government as well as within the war council. Who would have been authorized to give orders to whom, and about what?

Gauss waited for a week before acting on this instruction. By then the crisis over whether Stilwell was to be put in command of all Chinese forces was nearing its climax. And Hurley had arrived in Chungking. Agreement about the several American emergency proposals was still in suspense, but not, it seemed, out of reach. Each of them required grave decisions as to how much authority the Chinese government was to devolve, share, or yield; and on what conditions. The American government wanted these matters to be settled quickly. Hurley—who had dealt well with similar issues elsewhere—was hopeful that he could manage them. He found out that China was different, and that the Chinese, with more patience than any people in the world, use time and talk as weapons.

[22] Telegram, Hull to Gauss, September 9, 1944. This was drafted in the State Department and submitted to the President. The State Department sent over to the White House along with its draft of this message, as background material, extracts from various cables and dispatches sent by Gauss and two memos prepared in the Far Eastern Division. Both of these memos drew upon dispatches and the June 20 memo written by Service concerning the causes and character of the weakness of the Chinese government and making recommendations as to American policy.

CHAPTER 18

Hurley Goes to China via Moscow

HURLEY, as personal representative with the Generalissimo, was to report directly to Roosevelt.[1] The letter of appointment stated that he was being sent to China to promote efficient and harmonious relations between Chiang Kai-shek and Stilwell, and to facilitate Stilwell's exercise of command over the Chinese armies placed under his direction. The War Department was to instruct him further in regard to various duties he was to have in matters of supply (Lend-Lease).[2] In the letter of introduction which Roosevelt wrote to Chiang Kai-shek, Hurley's assignment was stated to be ". . . to coordinate the whole military picture under you as Military Commander-in-Chief—you being, of course, the Commander-in-Chief of the whole area—to help to iron out any problems between you and General Stilwell who, of course, has problems of his own regarding the Burma campaign and is necessarily in close touch with Admiral Mountbatten."[3]

From these brief written orders and his talks with the President, Hurley gathered that he was being called on to do three jobs: to keep China in the war, to keep the Chinese army in the field, and to unify all Chinese military forces against Japan.[4] It would seem that it was left to him to decide how to deal with the Chinese Communists, and with Chiang Kai-shek's reluctance to have us deal with them at all. There seems to have been a presumption that we would use and equip Communist forces if they came as part of a unified or coordinated force under Stilwell's command, not otherwise.[5]

---

[1] The selection originated in the War Department, and the President fell in with it. He told Under-Secretary Stettinius on August 9th that he intended to make this appointment. He notified Chiang Kai-shek on the 10th. The President talked with Hurley at some length on the 18th and gave him brief written instructions. These are printed in *United States Relations with China*, page 71. Hurley informed the State Department of these on the 19th and the State Department passed the information on to the American Embassy in Chungking. Then, on the 22nd, Hurley discussed his mission with Vincent. At this time there seems to have been no difference in conception between Hurley and the State Department about what he was to try to do or how he was to try to do it. Similarity of viewpoint and purpose is indicated by the fact that Hurley was told to keep in contact with Gauss; and that Gauss was told by Hull to ask Hurley to go along with him when he talked with Chiang Kai-shek about the proposal to create a combined war council.

[2] Letter, Roosevelt to Hurley, August 18, 1944.

[3] Letter, Roosevelt to Chiang Kai-shek, August 19, 1944.

[4] Hurley testimony, *Joint Committee on Military Situation in the Far East*, page 2935.

[5] I do not know whether this and related matters were dealt with in the directive which the War Department was to have given Hurley as regards his handling of supply matters.

Hurley was under the impression—which was never clearly contradicted—that the President and Secretary of State (Roosevelt and Truman; Stettinius and Byrnes) agreed that it was essential to keep the
Chiang Kai-shek regime in control of the government of China.[6] But
his mission was disturbed by disputes as to whether this was or was not
a primary and governing rule of American policy. And, paradoxically,
in the course of his effort to arrange for military unification, he sponsored proposals which might have brought other elements into power.

Hurley, reflecting on tactics, felt it would be useful to know more
about Soviet intentions before taking up his tasks in China. He wanted
to find out how the influence of the Soviet government was going to be
used. Would it encourage the Chinese Communists to resist unification
or advise them to come to terms? Was it going to be friendly or hostile
to China; did it share Chiang Kai-shek's wish for a friendly understanding? Hull, as recounted, was doing his best to get the Soviets and Chinese
to make up and be friends for the sake of world peace. The President
was similarly inclined—as marked by the message which he had sent to
Chiang Kai-shek on July 14th, commenting on Wallace's report of his
visit to China. "I also welcome the indication given me by Mr. Wallace
of your desire for improved relations between the U.S.S.R. and China,
and your suggestion that I use my good offices to arrange for a conference
between Chinese and Soviet representatives is being given serious
thought."[7] Soong had told Gauss that he wanted to go to Moscow on
this errand, and that he was hoping that he would soon be authorized to
visit the United States, and to go on from there to the Soviet Union.

Hurley had been to Moscow and talked with Stalin and Molotov once
before, in November 1942. He had then been, according to his own
account, pleased by Stalin's manner and his clear, concise, and direct way
of stating his views. When Hurley had expressed his interest in knowing
more about the Soviet military staff and strategy, Stalin had arranged
to have him fully informed and to visit vital combat areas. He was the
first American to whom so much had been disclosed. This experience
made a durable mark upon Hurley's judgment of Stalin's attitudes and
intentions. Having been trusted, perhaps flatteringly trusted, he was
disposed to trust. The adage about the difference between the devil sick
and the devil well was not inscribed in his memory book.

When Hurley set off for Moscow in August 1944 he was ready to

[6] See Chapter 21.
[7] The letter is in *United States Relations with China*, page 560.

show and expected to find good will. Donald Nelson, former head of the War Production Board, went with him. He was being sent to Chungking by the President to help the Chinese government plan and organize production. Secretary Hull sent an advance message to Ambassador Harriman, which said that Hurley and Nelson were the President's personal representatives to Chiang Kai-shek; that they were not going to Moscow with any presidential instructions; and they understood that in any discussions with Soviet officials they were to be guided by the Ambassador.

When Hurley and Nelson saw Molotov on August 31, Nelson led off the talk.[8] He explained that the President's first purpose was to end the war against Japan quickly; and that he thought that China, as a base for air operations and otherwise, could be of help. To enable China to do so and also to take care of itself after the war, he, Nelson, was going there to see what could be done to improve its economic arrangements and prospects. But, Nelson's exposition continued, to realize these purposes China must be unified. In that regard, he asked for Molotov's advice.

This soft address drew a righteous answer. Molotov said in substance that the Soviet Union had always wanted to be friendly with China. He reminiscently claimed credit for bringing about the release of Chiang Kai-shek, when in 1936 the Generalissimo had been kidnaped by Chang Hsueh-liang, the war lord in Sian (Shensi province). But, Molotov went on with an air of accepting the fact that no gratitude was to be expected in these matters, the Chinese government had not wanted close relations. The Soviet government, he continued with indignation, was being held responsible for the internal divisions within China. This was unjust; it was in no way to be blamed for them or for the miserable conditions in parts of China. Nor should the Soviet Union be associated with the Communists in China. Then, just as Stalin had in his talk with Harriman on June 10th, Molotov seemed virtually to disclaim any interest in the Chinese Communists. In effect, he said that although they called themselves Communists, they had no true or real relation to Communism; they expressed their discontent by taking the name, but if their economic lot was bettered they would forget that they were Communists. If the American government helped them, he continued, there would be fewer Communists in China; the key to the problem was

---

[8] The sources of information about this talk are Harriman's report to the State Department, September 4, 1944, printed in *United States Relations with China*, pages 71-72, and a memo made by Page, who was the interpreter.

to provide work for them and to better their economic conditions; if Chiang Kai-shek could do these things, then they would cease to give trouble. Thus Molotov concluded—with a nod toward the tasks which Hurley and Nelson had explained they were going to China to do— he was sure that the Soviet people would be very glad if the United States helped China and the Chinese people to improve their economic conditions and achieve military unification, and to choose the best people for these tasks.

These flatly spoken statements impressed his American audience of two. They seemed to be an affirmation, almost a promise, that the Soviet government, regarding the Chinese Communists as mere seekers for better conditions, would leave them to shift for themselves. Hurley's whole later treatment of the internal division in China was affected by hearing these words. He became confident that without Soviet support the Chinese Communists would be responsive to proposals for entering a unified National Government. Further, he thought that with this cause of mistrust removed, the Chinese and Soviet governments would find it easy to reach a friendly accord.

Such beliefs now seem like ghosts escaped from a graveyard. But in their day—and it is only yesterday—they were very much alive throughout the land and had much to feed on. We and the British were carrying forward our assault on Germany's western front with the utmost vigor. The Soviet armies were thus being enabled to free their country and their people. It was easy to believe that our effort was winning its reward in the Pacific; that the Soviet government was honestly ceding to us the management of Chinese affairs—all the easier because it was anticipated that the battered Soviet people and industry would be needing and wanting help and friendship to repair the damage of war.

With such auspicious thoughts, Hurley and Nelson hurried on to Chungking. Hurley quickly told Chiang Kai-shek what Molotov had said. He thought that his account dispelled the Generalissimo's belief that the Chinese Communists were controlled from Russia and lessened his fears of dealing with them.[9] Gauss, however, was doubtful on both scores. He had no hope left that China's internal division could be settled by political means. His pessimism was due mainly to his opinion that resistant elements in the Kuomintang would continue to defeat all attempts. He thought that Chiang Kai-shek would not be able either to recapture popular support or to reach terms with the Communists unless

[9] Letter, Gauss to Secretary Hull, September 28, 1944.

he made radical reforms, and that the controlling group within the Kuomintang would never consent to such reforms. Though Gauss did not say so, it would have been logical for him to think that Hurley's report would make Chiang Kai-shek less not more inclined to make concessions to the Communists.

There was much resemblance between the impressions which Molotov professed to have of the Chinese Communists, and those which were appearing about this time in the American press and periodicals.[10] True, Molotov dismissed the Yenan group because of the moderation which he attributed to them, as disqualifying them in Russian eyes; while in contrast, most American commentators thought this entitled them to American trust and help. Moscow's show of disdain was taken as evidence that the Chinese Communists were really separate and different, closer in spirit to American than to Soviet ideals.

How did this confluence between the versions of the Chinese Communist movement given out at Moscow, current in Yenan, and diffused in the United States, come about? To what extent was it merely the result of persuading association between Americans and the Chinese Communist leaders? To what extent was it only a careless echo of a planned propaganda line? Who among the diffusers of the affiliated view that the Chinese Communists sought only democratic social justice—as understood by Americans—were acting by intention as agents of the international Communist movement?

I shall not try to give even a presumptive answer to these questions. To do so would require a rigorous and detailed examination of hundreds of reports, articles, speeches, and books written by some scores of Americans; and this I have not made. But it may not be amiss to speculate briefly on some of the possible reasons why these versions of the nature and aims of Chinese Communism were not more quickly and vigorously disputed in the press, in scholarly circles, or in the government. Why, in other words, was it possible for the deception to spread that the Chinese Communists were not true Communists—thoroughly revolutionary, ruthless, and irreconcilable enemies of liberal Western civilization?

The Yenan regime was at the time pursuing policies that could be

[10] For example, the article in the *Far Eastern Survey* of November 15, 1944, by Laurence E. Salisbury, which after alluding to various recent articles observed that "In recent months . . . a number of Americans with varying backgrounds have obtained firsthand knowledge of the Chinese 'Communists,' enough for us to realize that the term can be used correctly only in quotation marks."

thought moderate and progressive. It was using all elements of the people. It was allowing private economic activity to continue. In the countryside it was redistributing land, and reducing rents and interest rates; but it was not crushing the land-owners or money-lenders. In short, the Communist organization in Yenan was not then acting in economic matters as determined Marxists. Similarly it seemed to be allowing all elements to share in political activities, or at least in the activities of local governments. The official Chinese Communist program promised democracy, freedom, and individual liberty. Some perceived that these principles—these names for ideals—were handy weapons in the fight against the Kuomintang government; and that they were being systematically used to break down censorship and control, and to get freedom for Communist agitation and recruiting. But the actual ways in which the Communists conducted the government in the region under their control impressed various reporters as giving honest value to the principles and words. In sum, the Communist regime in China did not seem to be ruled by dogma, or rather that such dogmas as it was standing on were taken to be much like those which were popular in the United States in the year 1944.

True, the record of association of many active Chinese Communist leaders with international Communism was abundant. It was well known that many of them—civil and military—had spent long terms in Moscow being schooled. True also, they had not been taciturn. Anyone who sought to know, for example, what Mao Tze Tung wanted to do in China had only to study his articles and addresses. But no primary effort seems to have been made at the time to look into these subjects. Most of those who wrote about China did not attach much significance to them. Not many fixed on the grim conclusion that enlisted Communists could not really be half-Communists, pale Communists, though they might for a while seem to be; or on the still more somber judgment that being part of the Communist movement they must sooner or later turn out to be enemies of the West.

The United States was fighting in close association with the Soviet Union, the base and center of international Communism. Why then worry over the question of whether some of the Chinese Communists were in touch with the Soviet Union? The prevailing American wish was to believe that it would be possible to live alongside the Soviet Union itself, and work with it to maintain international peace. This pleasant supposition gained almost free passage into American thought in those summer and autumn months of 1944 when the Soviet armies were pounding Germany back from the east and the American armies were pounding it back from the west. President Roosevelt, Harry Hopkins, Secretary of State Hull, Secretary of War Stimson, all believed that it was best for human welfare to act on the assumption that it was true or could be made true. It was natural for those concerned with China to be disposed to take the same chance with the Chinese Communists.

It might be expected that more trained professional minds, especially those in the career diplomatic service, would have shown greater reserve toward this opinion and policy as it bore upon China. Some of them did, but many did not until later events alerted them. This was in part due to the fact that almost none of the government officials who conducted our relations with China day by day were well schooled about either Communist dogma or methods. Their training and experience were predominantly in the Oriental countries and in the Oriental languages. Their working life had been spent in lands with much history of their own, in which Communism up to then had played little part—in China, Japan, Indo-China, Malaya, Siam. These men did follow current Communist statements and activities not only in China but elsewhere in ways that in the past had been judged adequate for their daily work. Few had felt the need to make a thorough study of the history and tactics of Communism; and fewer still had pondered deeply over its secret inner nature and compulsions.[11] Their impressions were formed mainly during the period—pre-war and war—when the Communists were avowing a wish for a common front, and associating themselves with other political elements in the West and East. Their knowledge was not deep enough to cause them to sustain cold disbelief when it was easier to believe.

These conjectures on the opinion that Chinese Communists could be tolerable working associates pertain to an understanding of the policy which the American government pursued in China during the following year. But they have delayed the account of Hurley's efforts in Chungking to put that policy into effect.

[11] For illustration of this statement, see the answers given by John Carter Vincent, who was then Chief of the Division of China Affairs, to questions regarding his knowledge of Communist doctrine or of the record of the Chinese Communist leaders. *Hearings: Institute of Pacific Relations*, pages 1689-1690.

CHAPTER 19

The Crisis About Stilwell

HURLEY set to work with the air of a man expectant that he can put through a quick deal. The first comment Stilwell jotted down about his presence can be read straight, or with relish, or with a jeer. "Hurley and Nelson arrive full of P and V. They are going to pound the table and demand: 1. Real unification in China. 2. Unification of command. Then and only then will they talk about what the U.S. will do for China economically."[1] The Generalissimo cleared the way for his tasks with Hurley by telling Stilwell that he would give him command of the Chinese armies but that he would not consent to the use of the Communists unless they acknowledged his authority. He said the same thing to Hurley in their first talk on September 7th.

Almost every day thereafter, and sometimes more than once a day, the Generalissimo discussed with Hurley the terms on which command could be conferred on Stilwell with mutual satisfaction. He continued to avow a wish to follow the President's advice. But he contended that if he acceded to the American proposal unguardedly, Stilwell would have more power in China than he had. He wanted it clearly understood that on major matters of strategy Stilwell would act according to his orders. Most of all, perhaps, the Generalissimo wanted control over the distribution of Lend-Lease supplies. In brief, the talks concerning both the appointment of Stilwell to command and military unification dragged on. Hurley did not settle them in a day, nor in a week.

And as he tried, grave military events supervened. These sharpened all the connected questions which were at issue in this crisis over the direction of Chinese military affairs:

Would the Generalissimo see through to the end the combined operations in Burma, or would he refuse to provide such additional means as might be needed, or even call back troops to China?

Would he accept American command of his forces—giving Stilwell authority to reorganize them and use them in battle as he wished?

Would he continue to immobilize many of his divisions to maintain the blockade of the Communists?

Would he consent to having Americans equip and work with the Communist forces?

[1] *The Stilwell Papers*, page 325.

The military situation seemed to allow no more time for discussion. By the middle of that month (September), there was trouble on both the Burmese and Chinese fronts. The Yoke force, after hard fighting, had crossed over the Salween River and was struggling over high mountains toward pivotal Japanese positions in North Burma. The opposition was strong, so strong that on September 12th Stilwell told Marshall that there was a chance that the Japanese might even throw the Yoke force back across the Salween, and the whole venture might end in rout. Stilwell wanted the Generalissimo to send more troops from China in order to enable the Yoke force to carry on to the object of its march.

In East China the Japanese armies were rapidly closing in on the American air net at Kweilin. The last strong Chinese defense position had been smashed. The Chinese Minister of War and General Chennault were frantically asking for American help in the emergency— for guns, ammunition, and gasoline.[2] Stilwell thought the Generalissimo ought to bring down divisions which were standing by, blockading the Communists. On September 14th, while Hurley was still thrashing over with the Generalissimo the terms on which command of the Chinese armies was to be conferred on Stilwell, that now thoroughly disturbed General flew down to Kweilin. There he decided—if he had not already decided—that the situation was lost, and ordered the demolition of the American air base.

While flying back to Chungking, Stilwell wrote out a report to Marshall. But before sending it off, he went with Hurley to give Chiang Kai-shek an estimate of the situation. He found the Generalissimo's tactical and strategical conceptions "idiotic," but inserted them into the message to Marshall also.[3] This stated that he regarded the situation in the Kweilin area without hope; that on the Generalissimo's orders the only reliable Chinese units would try to defend Kweilin from inside the city and would be trapped there. In short, he thought that the jig was up in South China and that the trouble came from the top. Next, as for Burma, he was at odds with the Generalissimo, who was threatening to

---

[2] It was on Stilwell's treatment of these requests for aid, during and after the battle for Hengyang, that Chennault based his most furious accusations against Stilwell—to the effect that Stilwell refused help until he knew it was too late to save Kweilin, and then would not give as much as he could. Chennault attributed to Stilwell a wish to prove that he was right in his opinion that the American airfields would be lost, and a purpose of putting the Generalissimo in a position where he would have to yield command of the Chinese armies to an American commander. See pages 297-302, Chennault, *Way of a Fighter*. Stilwell maintained that he provided a good deal of help, though he was almost sure it was useless and would be wasted. This controversy I must leave to military historians.

[3] *The Stilwell Papers*, entry, September 15th.

draw back the Yoke force unless Stilwell made a diversionary move. To this he was opposed, since possession of the points for which they were fighting would give China control of the entire trace of the Burma Road. Here again was the clash between Stilwell's demand for enough Chinese troops to batter the Japanese down in Burma, and the instinct of the Chinese government to protect its situation in China until the Japanese were further worn down.

This message from Stilwell to Marshall was sent the same day (September 15th, Chungking time) that Gauss was making his final attempt to persuade Chiang Kai-shek to form a united council of all Chinese parties for the joint conduct of the war. And—to revert briefly to that initiative—the Ambassador found that the latest military reverses had not shaken Chiang Kai-shek's views. The Generalissimo concurred in principle with the idea but demurred in practice. He said that he would form this council only if all parties would obey his orders. He asked whether the suggested war council would mean a change in the structure of the government. Gauss answered in effect that it would not mean an immediate change, but that it would mean a sharing of responsibility and authority. There the subject was left. When Gauss suggested that he, himself, might talk with the Communists, Chiang Kai-shek did not object. But he wondered aloud whether they might not spread word of the action as a sign that the American government was recognizing them. And he asked the Ambassador, if he decided to venture on these talks, to urge the Communists first of all to accept unifying command under him, the Generalissimo, and to submit to the political control of the National Government. Gauss left the decision to Hurley, who from then on took over the task of achieving unification by any or all ways.

Marshall was in Quebec, where Roosevelt and Churchill and the Combined Chiefs of Staff were again conferring. Stilwell's message— the one he had begun on the plane while flying back from Kweilin and finished in Chungking—was relayed to Quebec. There it was received some time on the morning of September 16th (Quebec time). At no time before or after could his message have created so much stir. For the Combined Chiefs had just agreed on an immense plan of operations against Japan; and one of its salient elements was an extended effort over land, sea, and air to open the Burma Road by the next spring, and to expel the Japanese from all of Burma as soon as possible.[4] The

[4] The main features in this plan were stated in the directive issued to Mountbatten on

Americans had prevailed upon their British colleagues, who would rather have delayed the action in North Burma and used whatever resources became available for amphibious attack elsewhere in the SEAC area.[5]

This whole program would be deranged if the Generalissimo had his way and pulled the Chinese troops out of the Burma campaign. General Marshall and the President clamped their jaws and agreed this must not be allowed to occur.

Marshall submitted a message for the Generalissimo which said so with blunt effect.[6] The President signed it. The minutes of the Combined Chiefs of Staff of that day (the 16th) record that: "At the President's request, General Marshall outlined certain developments with regard to the Chinese forces. The Generalissimo contemplated withdrawing the Y force across the Salween unless General Stilwell advanced on Bhamo with the Ledo Force. No replacements had been provided for the Salween force, which had now dwindled to 14,000 men. A note had been sent by the President to the Generalissimo pointing out the

September 16th and printed in his *Report*, B Paragraph 260. It defined the objective of the campaign as "the destruction and expulsion of all Japanese forces in Burma at the earliest possible date. Operations to achieve this objective must not, however, prejudice the security of the existing air supply route to China, including the air staging post at Myitkyina and the opening of overland communications." The plan contemplated that the fight to open the Indian-Chinese land route would be carried forward as fast as the weather allowed; the main action in this part of Burma was to be taken by the two groups of Chinese armies, who were to be supported by American and British air forces, air supply, penetration groups, and an amphibious operation on the Arakan ·coast. In addition, Mountbatten was to prepare for a larger amphibious operation in the Bay of Bengal as soon as the fighting in Europe made it possible to transfer the necessary resources (Operation Dracula), with target date of March 15, 1945.

Other operations against Japanese forces in the Pacific and in the Japanese islands would, it was reckoned by the planners at Quebec, make it hard, if not impossible, for Japan to sustain its forces in Burma.

[5] The impending fall of Kweilin, which might open the way to Kunming, had further significance to the American military planners. The Quebec Conference had advanced the date for MacArthur's assault against Leyte, in the center of the Philippine Islands, by two months, to October 20th, bypassing intermediate points. The planners were counting on the support of the 14th Air Force in the advance that was to follow to the North Philippines. *Biennial Report of the Chief of Staff*, United States Army, July 1, 1943 to June 30, 1945, page 71. The War Department hastened to pass on Stilwell's report to MacArthur. MacArthur said that he would not need the 14th Air Force because the Japanese air force had been so weakened that it would be possible to move directly from Leyte north to Luzon.

[6] This message was transmitted in special code so that a literal copy, not a paraphrase, could be delivered. It was sent off from Quebec to the War Department in Washington sometime during the 16th. But it was received in Chungking only on the morning of the 19th, Chungking time. I am not certain of the cause of the delay. It is printed in *Joint Committee on Military Situation in the Far East*, pages 2867-2868, but incorrectly dated as February instead of September.

consequences of the proposed action and stating that the Generalissimo must accept full responsibility therefor."

The President's note was in the first person. It stated that he was convinced, after reading the last reports on the situation in China, that Chiang Kai-shek was faced with disaster unless he proceeded at once:

1. To reinforce the Chinese armies in the Salween area and have them press their offensive. If, the President said, the Generalissimo continued to attack in conjunction with Mountbatten's offensive, the land line to China would soon be open. But if he failed to do so, then this great chance would be lost, and the Generalissimo himself "must . . . be prepared to accept the consequences and assume the personal responsibility."

2. To place Stilwell "in unrestricted command" of all his forces. The defeat in East China, the President said, placed the Kunming air terminal in danger of attack, which would reduce the Hump tonnage and possibly sever the air route. Unless drastic and immediate measures were taken, all the benefit of long years of Chinese struggle and of American effort might be thereby lost.

Thus—softening the stern summons—the President said that he trusted that the Generalissimo, with his farsighted vision which had guided and inspired the Chinese people during the war, would realize the necessity of doing what was now required. He had, the note ended, stated his thoughts with such complete frankness because "it appears plainly evident to all of us here [Quebec] that all your and our efforts to save China are to be lost by further delays."[7]

This was a forceful and reproving message, relieved by a genuine note of warm attachment. Properly, this warmth would have been conducted through the person who presented it. But it was not. Stilwell himself took it to Chiang Kai-shek. On his way to the Generalissimo he stopped by to talk with Gauss.[7a] He told the Ambassador that he had a message from the President that he knew would shake the Generalissimo badly, but he did not show Gauss the text.

Talks that Hurley and Stilwell had been having with Soong during the last few days had shown that real differences still existed in regard

[7] Memo, Stilwell to Chiang Kai-shek, September 19, 1944.

[7a] On the same morning, September 19th, that Stilwell received this message for delivery to Chiang Kai-shek, he got another summarizing the main strategic decisions made at Quebec, which was marked to be delivered by Gauss and the British Ambassador to Chiang Kai-shek. The reason for Stilwell's call at Gauss' house may well have been to leave a copy of this other message. It is allowable to conjecture whether the Generalissimo's reaction to the one directly presented by Stilwell might have been modified if the other informational one had been given to him first.

to the powers to be conferred upon the American commander. Stilwell summarized his ideas in the memo which he prepared for these talks. He thought he needed "nothing less than full power, including the right of reward and punishment (summary punishment)—and of appointment and relief. He [the Generalissimo] must accept the appointment of foreigners in some positions. The Commander must be allowed to move units from one war zone to another, combine units, inactivate units, activate new units, make drafts from one unit to another, and change organization as he sees fit. . . . The Generalissimo must refrain from any interference in operations."[8] After the talk, Stilwell noted in his Diaries, "He [Soong] is appalled at gap between our conception of field commander and the G-mo's. . . . I do not want the God-awful job, but if I take it I must have full authority," and in another note, "What the Peanut wants is an over-all stooge, apparently foisted on him by the U.S., with a deputy commander for the Chinese Army."[9] He was wary lest the Generalissimo so frame the offer of command that it would be in reality a device to shift "the responsibility for collapse."

Hurley was at the Generalissimo's house on the afternoon of the 19th, when Stilwell arrived, with the President's message in the pocket of his tunic. Stilwell declined Chiang Kai-shek's invitation to join the company, which included Soong, the Minister of War, and various generals and members of the National Military Council. He asked Hurley to step out of the room. Seated on the porch, he showed Hurley the President's message. Hurley tried to dissuade him from delivering it; to allow him (Hurley) instead to tell the Generalissimo what was in it. To quote from his later testimony, "I said [to Stilwell] 'You shouldn't now because of this firm language pile it on him at the time when he has felt compelled to make every concession that we have asked. He had made them; he is ready to go; he is ready to bring troops down from the north to reinforce you on the Salween front; he is going to appoint you commander-in-chief.' "[10]

Perhaps Stilwell, because of his own experience, doubted whether Hurley's statement was correct. The point is hard to judge, for, as this narrative will show, Hurley was inclined to look on the sunny side of his negotiations with Chiang Kai-shek. Perhaps Stilwell felt that even though Hurley's estimate might be correct, he had to carry out orders.

[8] Memo, Stilwell for Soong. September 16, 1944. *Hurley Papers.*
[9] *The Stilwell Papers.* Entry September 16, 1944, Sunderland-Romanus manuscript, Vol. II.
[10] *Joint Committee on Military Situation in the Far East*, page 2868.

Or, perhaps he wanted the satisfaction of delivering this message. In any case he insisted on doing so. Again, to quote Hurley, "[Stilwell] said, 'Well, I am directed by the President to deliver this.' " Hurley observed that this remark raised the question of who had the authority to speak for the President, but he did not stand on this point.

Stilwell went in. Tea was served him. He then told Chiang Kai-shek that he was there to deliver a message from the President and he handed it to General Chu Shih-ming to translate. Hurley, thinking to save the Generalissimo from humiliation, stepped forward. He asked if there was not a Chinese translation. There was, and Hurley took it and passed it over to Chiang Kai-shek. The Generalissimo read it. Hurley's impression was ". . . that he looked like he had been hit in the solar plexus. . . ." But, showing no emotion, he said merely, "I understand." Silence followed. Chiang Kai-shek reached over to his teacup and put the cover on upside down. Stilwell, in Chinese, said, "That gesture still means, I presume, that the party is over." Someone in the audience said "Yes." Stilwell and Hurley then walked out.

Stilwell was briefly exhilarated. The entry he made in his notes that evening began "Mark this day in red on the calendar of life. At long, at very long last, F.D.R. has finally spoken plain words, and plenty of them, with a firecracker in every sentence. 'Get busy or else' "[11] But Stilwell's first report to Marshall about the episode was short and matter-of-fact, merely that he had delivered the message personally and that the Generalissimo's only answer was, "I understand."

Hurley advised Chiang Kai-shek to take time to put his thoughts and feelings in order. He continued to talk with the Generalissimo about the terms and ways of giving effect to the President's proposals. But he was so impressed by Chiang Kai-shek's revulsion against Stilwell that the next report he prepared to send to the President seemed to Stilwell equivalent to recommending his relief. Hurley revised it, before sending it on (September 23rd).[12] Stilwell remained convinced that nothing less than what the President had urged would save the military situation in China. He was all for standing fast. To Marshall he described Chiang Kai-shek as a man hesitating before taking a bitter dose— in this case acceptance of a foreigner as commander of his armies, and recognition of the Communists. But he thought that when the shock

[11] *The Stilwell Papers*, entry, September 19, 1944.
[12] Recounted by Hurley in his cable to the President of October 13th, *Joint Committee on Military Situation in the Far East*, page 2879.

wore off the Generalissimo would give in if our pressure was maintained.[13]

But as the days passed Stilwell's assurance seemed to ebb. The delay worried him as being beneficial to the Japanese. The War Department, he told Hurley, was expecting them to break the stalemate. He prepared a compromise proposal. The memo in which he formulated this acknowledged that the Generalissimo had recently been listening to American advice; he had changed his plans for the defense of Kweilin and was moving six divisions down from the Northwest. On the two matters that he thought were worrying Chiang Kai-shek most—use of the Communist forces and control of Lend-Lease materials—Stilwell proffered reassurance.[14] He suggested that he be sent to Yenan to propose to the Reds that they acknowledge Chiang Kai-shek's authority and accept his command through Stilwell; five Communist divisions were then to be equipped and used north of the Yellow River; discussion of political matters between the Kuomintang and the Communists was to be dropped until the Japanese were beaten. Hurley, despite reservations in regard to Stilwell's proposal about Lend-Lease materials, liked Stilwell's new terms. "This," he enthused, "will knock the persimmons off the tree."[15]

But Hurley now found that the Generalissimo was no longer willing to consider any program which would leave Stilwell in authority in China. He had already drawn up his answer to the President's message of the 19th; it said plainly that he was willing to place an American in command of the Chinese-American forces fighting against Japan in China, and of all Chinese field armies and air force. He was also willing to make such changes in the Chinese army staff and personnel as might be necessary to bring harmony in the relations with the American field commander. But he would not have Stilwell as the American com-

[13] The main points of Stilwell's messages to Marshall of September 22nd and 26th are printed in *United States Relations with China*, page 68.

[14] This Stilwell memo of September 23rd, the most moderate of those written by him in many a day, is printed in *Joint Committee on Military Situation in the Far East*, page 2873. Two days previously Chennault, in a letter to the President, gave it as his opinion that the United States should sponsor a new attempt to bring Chungking and Yenan together. At each twist of the landscape the opinions of these two men seemed destined to conflict. Chennault took a most gloomy view of the military outlook for China after the loss of the American air bases. He thought that the government armies could not recuperate for eighteen months; that the Communists would continue to gain popular support and relative military strength, so much so that they would have an excellent chance to defeat the government with or without Russian aid, and that therefore a foresighted arrangement should be made with them in order to avert that unsatisfactory situation when the war against Japan ended. This line of reasoning was more or less the same as that of Davies, the political adviser on Stilwell's staff.

[15] *The Stilwell Papers*, entry, September 23, 1944.

mander. "I cannot, however," his note (September 25th) to the President said, "confer this heavy responsibility upon General Stilwell, and will have to ask for his resignation as chief of staff of the China Theater and his relief from duty in this area." The Generalissimo explained his attitude by saying that he did not believe Stilwell intended to cooperate with him, but thought that he was being appointed to command him; and that he was sure that the dissension would continue as long as Stilwell remained in China.[16] But the language of this memo made clear as well that Chiang Kai-shek was not disposed to place any American "in unrestricted command." He was after all determined to keep the right to give orders to whatever American might be appointed, and he expected obedience. He wished to retain the authority to decide how, when, and where Chinese forces were used.

From then on, the debatable and debated questions in Washington were: with Stilwell out of the way, would Chiang Kai-shek prosecute hard the war against Japan and reform his government along democratic lines? Stilwell was sure that he would do neither; that he would go on waiting for the United States to win the war.[17] But he tried another step along the path of conciliation. He offered (on September 28th) to drop the idea of using Communist troops, and said he would plan to bring back the Yoke force from Burma as soon as possible.[18]

Soong was sure that the break was beyond repair.[19] He radioed Hopkins that if the tension continued, he feared for the future of Sino-American relations. He recalled that Hopkins had once before interceded to save China, and asked him to do it again. Kung, in Washington, at this juncture talked the situation over with Hopkins; then he cabled to Chiang Kai-shek that Hopkins told him that if the Generalissimo insisted, the President would replace Stilwell. Kung also said that the President had not yet discussed with Marshall the problem of Stilwell's successor, but as soon as that was settled, he would answer the Generalissimo's last note (of the 25th). Whether this was an accurate report of what Hopkins said to Kung is disputed.[20] Soong at once in-

---

[16] The text of this aide-memoire of September 25, 1944, given to Hurley for the President, is printed in the *Joint Committee on Military Situation in the Far East*, page 2874, *et seq.*

[17] *The Stilwell Papers*, entry, September 18th, and Stilwell messages to Marshall, September 22nd and 26th.

[18] *The Stilwell Papers*, entry, September 28th, 1944.

[19] Letter, Ambassador Gauss to Hull, September 28, 1944.

[20] George Moorad in *Lost Peace in China*, page 37, has written that Gauss, on hearing the news, asked Washington about it, and Hopkins said that he had been misquoted. However, no such inquiry from Gauss has come to my attention in the State Department papers. But when on October 6th, Hurley told the President of the Kung-

formed Hurley of Kung's radio, and Hurley at once told Stilwell.[21]

The Generalissimo, on the day after receiving Kung's message, revealed his intention of standing firm. He spoke to the Central Executive Committee of the Kuomintang Party, saying with deep heat that he would continue to insist that Stilwell must go. He accused him of refusing to obey his orders after the capture of Myitkyina—a charge which it may be noted Stilwell told Marshall was false. Chiang Kai-shek went on to say that he would also insist that he be given control of the distribution of Lend-Lease material; and that if there was to be an American commander-in-chief in China, that officer would have to be under his orders and maintain contact only with such Chinese military units as he, Chiang Kai-shek, put at his disposal. If the worst came to the worst, if the Americans refused, the Generalissimo told his intimate political colleagues, they could get along by themselves, they could still stand on their feet in four provinces.[22]

In Washington there was an interval of indecision. Marshall still was sure that it was necessary to stick by Stilwell. He prepared a message to go from the President to the Generalissimo. This was to state in substance that Stilwell was the only person who could conduct the planned operation in Burma and China as well; and that his removal would prejudice the American inclination to continue to help China and Chiang Kai-shek personally.[23] Stimson agreed and thought that a great injustice was about to be done. In his view, "Stilwell has been the one successful element of the three forces that have been supposed to cooperate in Burma. . . . This campaign in all the difficulties of the mon-

---

Hopkins talk, Hopkins denied having so spoken. He radioed Hurley that "I told him [Kung] . . . that I had no idea how the President would reply to the Generalissimo in regard to the latter's request for Stilwell's withdrawal." Radio, Hopkins to Hurley October 7, 1944, *Hopkins Papers*. But it seems likely on the basis of what Roosevelt recounted to Hurley when the latter was in Washington in February 1945 that Roosevelt did make a remark to Hopkins, which if passed on by Hopkins to Kung would have had this meaning. Sunderland-Romanus manuscript, Vol. II.

[21] *The Stilwell Papers*, entry October 1, 1944.

[22] Letter, Gauss to Hull, October 5, 1944, transmitting stenographic transcript of an oral communication made to him by a participant in the CEC meeting.

[23] These are the main points in the draft of a message prepared by Marshall on September 28th for discussion with Admirals Leahy and King and General Arnold and for approval by the President. It also explained that Stilwell's action in personally delivering the President's message of September 16th to Chiang Kai-shek was in accord with the practice adopted long before in order to assure that the messages would be untampered. It also affirmed the belief that Stilwell had never sought to assume powers not assigned to him, or to undertake unauthorized activities. But the President decided not to send this message, and a far more compromising one was sent instead. *Forrestal Diaries*, entry, October 5, 1944.

soon has been a triumphant vindication of Stilwell's courage and sagacity. He has been pecked at from both sides, carped at by the British from India, and hamstrung at every moment by Chiang Kai-shek. . . . Marshall today said that if we had to remove Stilwell he would not allow another American general to be placed in the position of Chief of Staff and Commander of the Chinese armies, for it was so evident that no American would be loyally supported. I am inclined to go farther. The amount of effort which we have put into the 'Over the Hump' air-line has been bleeding us white in transport planes—it has consumed so many. Today we are hamstrung in Holland and the mouth of the Scheldt River for lack of transport. . . . The same lack is crippling us in northern Italy. This effort over the mountains of Burma bids fair to cost us an extra winter in the main theater of war. And in spite of it all we have been unable to save China from the present Japanese attack owing to the failure to support Stilwell in training adequate Chinese ground forces to protect Kunming."[24]

The President's mind was revolving. He was about to yield to Chiang Kai-shek's rejection of the proposals which, in that dramatic message sent from Quebec on September 16th, he had said were essential to save China. Further than that, he was about to suggest that the United States reduce its military responsibilities in China.

Both Marshall and Stimson were convinced that if Stilwell were withdrawn, worse failures would follow. And this was probably the main reason for the changes of policy. But the imputing mind can find other circumstances which may have influenced the decision. The Generalissimo's answer of the 25th, stubborn and almost accusatory in tone, may have given offense and seemed to show incorrigible wrongness of judgment. Then too the reasons for trying to drive the Generalissimo into a greater immediate military effort were becoming less imperative. China was no longer primary in the American plans for defeating Japan. By early October the Joint Chiefs of Staff were concluding that it would not be necessary to make an American landing either on Formosa or the East China coast.[25] Thus the strategy to which Marshall, Stimson, Stilwell,

[24] These are extracts from a memo which Stimson prepared for talking with the President on October 3rd. *On Active Service in Peace and War*, Henry L. Stimson and McGeorge Bundy, pages 536-539.

[25] This decision was shaped mainly by the way in which the war was going elsewhere; by the prolongation of the fighting in Europe, which postponed possible transfer of large forces to the Pacific; by the success of MacArthur's island operations and Nimitz' naval actions; and by the weakening of the Japanese air forces.

When Roosevelt met MacArthur and Nimitz at Hawaii in July they had decided that the next main American action in the Pacific should be, not in Formosa and the China

and others had clung since 1941 faded out. Stilwell noted this in the entry that he made in his diary October 4th, "War Department is with me apparently, but this theater is written off and nothing expected from us."[26]

The narrative may pause to emphasize that this change in strategic plans had important future consequences. The armies of the Chinese government at the end of the war were weaker and less qualified and equipped than had been hoped; and they were scattered in the far-off interior and in the south. There were no American ground forces in China. Thus, when Japan surrendered with unforeseen haste, Chiang Kai-shek's troops had to be moved great distances and American landings hastily organized. These operations took time. The Communists in China used this time to expand.

The emergent change in the American position was expressed in the President's next answer on October 5th to Chiang Kai-shek. He informed the Generalissimo that he thought the situation in China had grown so much worse that he was now inclined to think it best that the United States should not accept responsibility for the command of ground forces in China. Instead, he proposed that Stilwell should be relieved as Chief of Staff. He would remain in China, but only as commander of the Chinese ground forces in Yunnan and Burma—on the understanding that Chiang Kai-shek would maintain these armies. Someone else would be given control of the distribution of Lend-Lease supplies; and General Sultan, American Commander in India, would be

---

coast, but in the Central Philippines. Then at the Quebec Conference in September the Combined Chiefs of Staff had approved the program for the next phases of the war against Japan: (1) seize a position in Central Philippines soon, (2) occupy Luzon late in the year, (3) thereafter take other island positions for the purpose of extending the sea and air blockade of Japan, (4) conduct operations on the China coast that would contribute to the blockade and air bombardment, limited to objectives that might be obtained without commitment to extensive land campaigns. Then after further consultation the Joint Chiefs of Staff decided (on October 2nd on Admiral King's motion) that the operations against Luzon, Iwo Jima, and the Ryukus should be carried out before the seizure of Formosa, which might not be necessary or advisable at all.

[26] General Merrill of Stilwell's staff had been in Washington while these decisions were being made. On his return to China he reported to Stilwell (1) that the repeated statements made by Admiral Nimitz that the United States needed bases on the China coast were cover for other intentions, (2) that the American plans from then on assumed that the Chinese would do nothing but contain some Japanese forces, (3) that no large American ground forces would be employed in China, (4) but that the War Department would—after the trace of the road in North Burma was secure—be interested in any operations from the interior of China toward the coast between Amoy and Tsingtao, and concurrently to stiffen resistance in the entire China Theater and to hold or recover areas which were essential to American air operations.

put in control of the tonnage over the Hump. Chennault would be continued in command of the 14th Air Force. Hurley would stay as special representative in China. By these retreats from former demands, the President tried to save the Burma campaign, and Stilwell for the Burma campaign.[27]

But Chiang Kai-shek now pressed home his wish. He refused to consent to having Stilwell remain even in the limited command of the forces fighting in Yunnan and Burma. His next note to the President (October 9th) was a simple restatement of lack of confidence in Stilwell and request for his recall. But in an explanatory memo given to Hurley at the same time, he spelled out his grievances at length.[28] In evidence for his opinion that Stilwell's military judgment was poor, he reviewed their differences over Burma. Stilwell's conduct of that campaign and disregard of his warnings, the Generalissimo said, had drained off most of the properly trained and equipped troops in China and reduced incoming tonnage over the Hump for the Chinese armies. In effect, he attributed the military disaster in East China to these and related blunders and refusals by Stilwell. Thus he centered on that hated officer the blazing stream of blame for the strategic policies and decisions of the American and British governments.

The concluding paragraphs of this memo are of continuing interest, as showing that the Generalissimo recognized, despite his words of a week before, that American support was vital:

"In his last telegram the President asserted that the China situation has deteriorated so far that he is now inclined to feel that the United States Government should not assume responsibility involved in the appointment of an American commander [of the Chinese forces].

"I do not altogether understand this statement for two reasons:

"First. No matter what has happened, no matter what command arrangements are adopted, I cannot personally escape the ultimate responsibility for the future in the Chinese theater. Even the responsibility of General Stilwell's errors must be borne by me, since I allowed myself to be over-persuaded against my own judgment to countenance them.

[27] Stilwell thought this message "rather encouraging," noting that "It might have been a soft capitulation." *The Stilwell Papers*, entry, October 7, 1944.

[28] The text of Chiang Kai-shek's memo of October 9th is printed in the *Joint Committee on Military Situation in the Far East*, pages 2869-2872. Hurley testified that he refused to deliver an earlier version to the President and after talking with him, Chiang Kai-shek changed it, particularly in regard to the statements made about Stilwell. But Stilwell had the impression that the result of Hurley's effort was merely to help the Generalissimo prepare a message which Washington would find hard to handle. *The Stilwell Papers*, entry, October 9, 1944.

"Second. I cannot feel that the deterioration is so serious as the President suggests. After long years of experience and firsthand knowledge of the Japanese methods and strength, despite the defeats in east China, I cannot foresee any disaster fundamentally incapacitating China.

"The statement was also distressing to me in another sense. While I do not anticipate disaster, the situation in China is indeed critical. Aid is most needed in this hour of crisis. Yet the statement I have referred to appears to imply that aid will be withheld precisely because this crisis of the hour is upon us.

"I am disturbed by the fact that the President had expressed regret at my reversal of agreement with respect to the appointment of General Stilwell in command of the Chinese forces. My telegram to the President, of August the 24th, showed great readiness to meet his wishes, as far as humanly possible. . . .[29]

"I am wholly confident that if the President replaces General Stilwell with a qualified American officer, we can work out together to reverse the present trend and to achieve a vital contribution to victory in China."

Stilwell shrugged off the Generalissimo's version of what had occurred. The only real issue, he told Marshall, was whether China would make any more effort in the war. Hurley up to then had been trying to do what he was sent out to do—adjust relations between the Generalissimo and Stilwell. But now he accepted the verdict. He concluded that the time had come for Stilwell to depart. On the 13th he sent off to the President a message which smashed any remaining doubts in Washington.[30] Hurley told the President that he thought that the Generalissimo was open to persuasion and leadership; but that Stilwell was convinced that he never acted unless forced to do so, and on this basis Stilwell's every move was toward the subjugation of Chiang Kai-shek. The Generalissimo would never submit. As Hurley had come to view the situation after a month in Chungking, ". . . There is no issue between you and Chiang Kai-shek except Stilwell. . . . My opinion is that if you sustain Stilwell in this controversy, you will lose Chiang Kai-shek and possibly you will lose China with him." On the other hand, his estimate concluded, if the United States sent out the proper officer for the task, Chiang Kai-shek was ready to entrust him with command and adequate

[29] This date is erroneously given in the printed paraphrase. The correct one, as given in the original message, is August 12th.

[30] Hurley showed Stilwell a draft and, after listening to Stilwell, took out some statements that Stilwell thought were barbed. *The Stilwell Papers*, entry, October 10th. Hurley testimony, *Joint Committee on Military Situation in the Far East*, pages 2878-2879. Hurley's message of October 13th is printed, *ibid.*, pages 2879-2881.

authority; and he would be able to harmonize, reorganize and retrieve the American position in China.[31]

[31] Later, in May 1945, Hurley acquainted President Truman with the circumstances of Stilwell's recall. He said that he had advised the Generalissimo that with an American Chief of Staff, who would also be commander of all American forces in China, and an American commanding all the air forces, and an American in charge of the Service of Supply, with American officers helping to train the Chinese army, and with himself as representative of the President near the Gimo, we could in cooperation with the Chinese still stop the Japanese attack and prevent the collapse of the Chinese National Government. The Generalissimo was persuaded, according to his reminiscent version, that under these arrangements American and Chinese activities in China could be harmonized, and he accepted the advice. *Hurley Papers*, telegram, Hurley for Truman, May 20, 1945.

CHAPTER 20

Stilwell Goes and Wedemeyer Takes Over

A WEEK passed before the President made his decision known, during which many messages went back and forth between Washington and Chungking. He gave in to Chiang Kai-shek's wish though he denied its justice. All those plans and decisions about Burma for which the Generalissimo blamed Stilwell had been made by the Combined Chiefs of Staff and approved by Churchill and himself. The President made that amply clear in the answer he sent on October 18th. Further, the President contended, these projects were sound and to the best benefit of China. Even so, the President went on, he was issuing orders at once for the recall of Stilwell. But, he added, under the circumstances he did not feel that an American should assume responsibility in a command position for the operations of Chinese forces in China. He would, however, provide one to serve as the Generalissimo's Chief of Staff— General Albert C. Wedemeyer, one of three American officers whom Chiang Kai-shek had named for the assignment. He asked for the Generalissimo's assurance that the two Chinese forces would continue to play their part in conjunction with Mountbatten's offensive operations in Burma.

Before the world the President treated the change in command as merely a "case of personalities." In response to many questions seeking to elicit details, he insisted that it did not involve matters of strategy, distribution of supplies, or relations with the Chinese Communists.[1] This was an expedient but quite inadequate explanation—as the record will have shown.

The Generalissimo henceforth would not be as exposed to rough American admonition. He would be able to make the decisions for China at greater ease. But he would still have to remain mindful of our judgment, since the American government would also feel freer to decide whether or not to give needed means for his armies.

---

[1] The questioning was stimulated by a front-page story in the *New York Times*, October 31, 1944, by Brooks Atkinson, its Chungking correspondent, which stated that Chiang Kai-shek had demanded (1) that Stilwell must go, (2) that he would not be coerced by Americans into helping to unify China by making terms with the Communists, (3) control of Lend-Lease; and that if the American government did not yield on these matters, China would go back to fighting Japan alone. This forceful and indignant article went on to observe that "Inside China it [the relief of Stilwell] represents the political triumph of a moribund anti-democratic regime which is more concerned with maintaining its political supremacy than in driving the Japanese out of China."

The Joint Chiefs of Staff issued the pertinent orders. Stilwell was withdrawn from China. The China-India-Burma Theater was divided into two parts, under separate commands: (a) the China Theater, (b) the India-Burma Theater.[2] Wedemeyer was appointed Commanding General of the United States forces in the China Theater. He was authorized to accept also the position of Chief of Staff to the Generalissimo. Simultaneously General Daniel Sultan was appointed to the same post in the India-Burma Theater; actual control of the Chinese troops fighting in Burma passed to him. Sultan and Wedemeyer were mutually enjoined to work closely together. Under these arrangements Wedemeyer's command relationships were much simpler than those under which Stilwell had tried to operate.

Wedemeyer hurried to China while Stilwell was on his way back to Washington. That combative general continued to speak his mind in the final report which he submitted to the War Department about his mission. The central seam of his opinion, the seam along which the division had come, was marked clearly in one paragraph of this report:

"Nowhere does Clausewitz's dictum that war is only the continuation of politics by other methods apply with more force than it did in CBI. In handling such an uncertain situation as existed in that theater of war, the Americans would have done well to avoid committing themselves unalterably to Chiang, and adopted a more realistic attitude toward China itself. We could gain little by supporting the attitude of the Chiang regime. We could have gained much by exerting pressure on Chiang to cooperate and achieve national unity, and if he proved unable to do this, then in supporting those elements in China which gave promise of such development."[3]

Wedemeyer took over on October 31st. In temperament, training, and behavior he was a very different person from Stilwell. He had been one of the most keen and active members of Marshall's planning staff. A year before, Marshall had reluctantly let him go to become Deputy Chief of Staff of the SEAC. Mountbatten had used him to present his ideas to the Americans and to work out difficulties between himself and the Americans. Wedemeyer had done well, both in making plans and in steering them through the stormy upper regions of Anglo-American staff conferences. He had also shown vigor in the organization of mili-

[2] The boundaries of the China Theater included the mainland of China and Indo-China and the Chinese islands immediately adjacent such as Hong Kong, but excluded Formosa and Hainan.

[3] *United States Relations with China*, page 70.

tary action. Ordinarily he sought to effect his purposes by being flexible and conciliatory, rather than insisting rigidly on a few essentials—as had been Stilwell's way.

On October 24th the Joint Chiefs of Staff issued to him a new directive which was to remain the governing order for American military activity in China until the end of the war. It specified:

1. That in regard to the United States combat forces under his command his primary mission was to carry out air operations from China.

2. He was also to continue to assist the Chinese air and ground forces in operation, training, and logistical support.

3. He was to control the allocation of Lend-Lease supplies delivered into China, within priorities set by the Joint Chiefs of Staff.

4. In regard to the Chinese forces he was authorized to advise and to assist the Generalissimo in the conduct of military operations against Japan.

5. He was not to use United States resources to suppress civil strife except insofar as necessary to protect United States lives and property.

When later Chinese government forces moved toward the north and the Communist forces spread out, Wedemeyer was not going to find it easy to give effective aid without infringing upon this last provision of his orders. Also, as time went on, he had trouble finding in these orders full answers to the question of what he was supposed ultimately to accomplish. Within three months he was asking Washington whether his mission was only to contain Japanese forces, or whether it was to move toward rearming China so that she could be a strong Asiatic power, or whether it was also to unify China under Chiang Kai-shek.[4] Later pages will tell how hard it was for Washington to make up its mind about the answers, and how it several times changed its mind.

Chiang Kai-shek sped warm welcome to Wedemeyer. In response to the message informing him of the appointment, the Generalissimo assured the President that he would go through with the military effort which was required of him. Specifically he said that he would:

Delegate command of the Chinese forces in India and Burma to General Sultan and give Sultan discretion in their use, subject to consultation with him;

Provide the necessary replacements for the Chinese forces fighting in Burma and for the Ramgarh training center;

Maintain the efforts of the Yoke force and also keep it up to strength.

[4] Memo, meeting, Forrestal-Stimson-Grew, January 16, 1945.

These promises were in denial of Stilwell's assertion that Chiang Kai-shek did not intend to fight any longer. The Generalissimo, in further refutation, told the President that he thought that firm and energetic action might still enable China to hold the remaining vital air bases in the east. Soon after Wedemeyer arrived, Chiang Kai-shek offered him command of the Chinese armies.[5] The Generalissimo was politely told that it seemed best to the American government that he should not accept.

As soon as Wedemeyer had a chance to talk with his Chinese staff, he sent Marshall an estimate of the situation, which was less despairing in tone than Stilwell's. But his list of reasons for past defeats was the same as those which had spattered Stilwell's notes: lack of comprehensive plans with sound military objectives—which meant that the Chinese forces had been committed at random and in piecemeal fashion. Absence of unity of command, failure of senior commanders in adjacent districts to cooperate, the attempt to control operations from Chungking—these, he thought, hindered field commanders and resulted in many useless and tiring marches and countermarches. Poor leadership in divisional and higher command, and poor training and replacement systems, inadequate food and equipment for the troops—these were the reasons why he found the armies "quite lethargic and apathetic . . . quite discouraged."[6]

The combat situation, he reported to Marshall on November 10th, was bad and getting worse, while the muddle in the Chinese plans and operations exceeded understanding. He soon confirmed the conclusion which Stilwell had reached almost two months before—that Kweilin, with its airfield, was lost. The Japanese would, he thought, almost certainly gain control of the whole Kweilin-Liuchow-Nanning sector, with its other American air bases. From there, it was his best guess, they would try to move against Kunming in the west. They would have, he reckoned, five divisions to send on this mission while the Chinese might well have nothing to stop the drive except the 14th Air Force and rough terrain.

He exerted himself to organize the defense of the Kunming area. The plans he proposed to Chiang Kai-shek gave this priority, leaving the defense of Chungking in second place. For some time the Generalissimo wavered. He wanted to remain in or near Szechwan province,

[5] There are statements to this effect in the Alsop article in the *Saturday Evening Post* for January 21, 1950, and in Leahy's book, *I Was There*, page 272.

[6] Wedemeyer Testimony, *Joint Committee on Military Situation in the Far East*, page 2304.

should worst come to the worst; and he did not want to have to take refuge in Kunming in the province of Yunnan, whose governor he did not trust. Without Wedemeyer's knowledge he went so far once as to order divisions out of the Kunming area. But presently he mastered his fears and concentrated forces to defend Kunming, among them five divisions of troops moved by air from Sian on the Communist borders.[7]

The Generalissimo also wished, despite the assurances given to the President, to hustle all Chinese troops out of India and Burma. Wedemeyer argued with him that this would wreck the Burma campaign and expose the supply line over the Hump. He persuaded the Generalissimo to order out, at this time, only two divisions.[8] General Sultan was not pleased to lose even these, and he tried to hang on to them as long as he could. By the middle of December both the American and British Chiefs of Staff agreed that they should be released, and they were. It turned out that they were not crucially needed in Burma.

Within a few months after Wedemeyer took over, reports from all sources agreed that some improvement was taking place in the condition and morale of the Chinese armies. They were better organized and more sensibly located. The command in both staff and field was more satisfactory. Americans and Chinese cooperated in all branches of work. A system of supply, in charge of an American general, was beginning to work fairly well.

At the beginning of the new year, 1945, the situation was still precarious. But the fear that Chinese resistance might collapse was waning. The American air terminus and air base at Kunming remained operative. Wedemeyer got time and chance to reorganize, train, and equip the Chinese army. It was still thought then that they would have to fight their way against strong Japanese forces back to the coast. But they were never put to that hard test. There is no need to guess as to whether they would have won out, or whether they would have relapsed to the condition in which Wedemeyer found them. From Japanese participants, it has since been learned that by this time the main forward campaign of the Japanese expeditionary force in China was disappointingly halted; and that in Imperial Headquarters it was regarded as a failure despite the capture of seven American airfields. Any further attempt to advance in force upon either Kunming or Chungking was thwarted by the need to repel American attacks elsewhere.[9]

[7] *Ibid.*, page 2299.
[8] Mountbatten, *Report*, Section B, Paragraph 333.
[9] The advance of the China Expeditionary Army came to a stop because it was called on to perform so many other tasks at the same time, while it had more and more trouble

Hopes of quick victory were reviving. New plans began to sprout. News of Japanese defeats elsewhere gave cheerful impetus to the efforts of both the Chinese and the Americans. Our forces were coming closer and closer to Japan. They were capturing control of Luzon (the Northern Philippines) and preparing to move to Iwo Jima and Okinawa. Our bombers were beginning to pound the home islands hard. It was becoming plain that soon the Japanese armies in China would have to begin to retreat. The tonnage being flown in over the Hump was beginning to reach the volume so long the object of desire.[10] And, not least, the Japanese in Burma were broken; it could be foreseen that before the next rains the road across Burma into China would be open.

These improvements in the military outlook did not, however, dispel once and for all one subject: whether or not to work with the Communists. Wedemeyer tried to arrange for some coordination between the action of their forces and those of the government. But neither side responded to his suggestions. The Army Observer Mission at Yenan was cooperating with the Communists to get military intelligence and weather information, and to rescue American fliers. Some of Wedemeyer's staff while he was temporarily absent from his headquarters composed a summary plan for the operation of American paratroops under American officers in Communist territory. They were also to lead Communist forces, guerrilla and regular, against the Japanese; and the United States was to provide the weapons for these forces and control their use. This plan seemed to its authors a promising way to capture at small cost important but lightly guarded objectives in North China. The sponsors broached the project to Soong and the Minister of War about the middle of December. Then without waiting for Chiang Kai-shek's assent, members of the Army Observer Group

---

in bringing up supplies and shifting troops because of American air and sea attacks. Among the other calls upon this force were (a) to protect the captured Hankow-Canton Railway and air bases, (b) to guard the coast against expected United States landings, (c) to prepare to destroy other United States air bases in North China (Chengtu), (d) to provide strength to the Kwantung Army in Manchuria. U.S. War Department, *Japanese Monograph No. 129,* "China Area Operations Records."

[10] The tonnage brought in over the Hump by all carriers had markedly increased as follows:

January 1944	14,472
June 1944	18,235
September 1944	29,625
December 1944	34,777
January 1945	46,482

and of the O.S.S. in Yenan took it up with the Communists.[11] They were enthusiastic.

But when Hurley, who had not known what was afoot, heard of this plan, he protested to the President, and it was dropped. Hurley thought that the episode did real damage; that it was the fundamental reason why the Communists rejected the latest offers made to them by the government—of which I am about to tell. In his opinion the Communists took it to mean that the American government was ready to recognize them as armed belligerents and to deal directly with them. Whether or not the Communists attached so much meaning to this sketchy proposal is not to be known. But during this period they did have the hopeful impression that the American government was sympathetic to them and felt a need to work with them. This impression could have been derived from the whole range of American contact with them, of which this military project was only an episode—beginning with the dispatch of the Observers Mission, the daily working touch with the Mission, and Hurley's current attempts to induce them to enter the Chinese government. Then it is probable that as the Communists learned that the American government would after all have nothing to do with them until or unless they reached an accord with the Kuomintang, they were the more resentful. In the rejection of what they regarded as offers of cooperation they could find cause for being anti-American.[12]

Thus Wedemeyer, for all his care, was briefly tangled in the Chinese internal dispute. Thereafter, as he went on with his military assignments, he tried his best, in accord with his orders, to keep clear of it. In exercising control of the Lend-Lease inflow he took care not to do anything which the Generalissimo might oppose; the only supplies provided the Communists were a small quantity of medicines. As offset, he tried to make sure that the government armies which he was helping to develop

[11] References to the interviews between U.S. Military Headquarters and Chinese government officials and between members of the Observers Mission and Office of Strategic Services in Yenan and the Communists are made in *State Department Employee Loyalty Investigation*, page 1903. This is probably the plan of which Service later told Jaffe, the editor of *Amerasia*, with the warning that it was "very secret"—in the conversation recorded by the F.B.I. *Ibid.*, page 1404.

[12] Some interesting details on these matters are to be found in a statement which Michael Lindsay (Lord Lindsay of Birker) sent to the Senate Sub-Committee investigating the Institute of Pacific Relations: *Hearings, Institute of Pacific Relations*, pages 5367 *et seq*. Lindsay, an English scholar and radio technician, was working for the Chinese Communists in Yenan during this period and seems to have followed closely the contacts between the American Observer Group and the Chinese Communists. His comments and judgment are colored by the belief that we were untrue to implied promises made by Hurley and the Observer Mission.

would not be turned against the Communists. In short—after a brief period of criss-cross—he strove to see that what he did fitted with Hurley's attempt to bring about the unification of China by peaceful political means. This attempt, in which by this time (January 1945) Hurley was deeply engaged, is now in order for review.

CHAPTER 21

Hurley Goes On with His Assignment
(October 1944 to February 1945)

HURLEY had failed to reconcile the Generalissimo and Stilwell. Since he thought their quarrel due mainly to personal traits, he was not greatly depressed. The President had told him also to try to coordinate or unify the government and Communist forces to fight Japan. He soon perceived that this could be done only as one feature of an accord on political affairs.[1]

Ambassador Gauss turned over the job to him with little regret. He thought his term of service in China a fretful failure. His opinion of the Chinese government was akin to Stilwell's. His manner and habit of mind were roughly direct. He was judgmatical, at times cranky, and could not be beguiled. It is not to be wondered, then, that his relations with the heads of the Chinese government had remained businesslike and nothing more. The advice he gave Washington was usually based on the belief that it would prove foolish to confer free favors on the Chinese government; that if we wished results it was necessary to bargain for them.

Washington had passed him by in the main crises. The President had used other agents. He and the Generalissimo had usually dealt with one another, not through the Embassy, but through Soong and Kung in Washington, through Hopkins, and through the special emissaries who were sent out to China from time to time. The War Department fought out its issues with the Chinese without consulting Gauss. Stilwell came to him now and again in hours of trouble, but the touch between the two had been only occasional.

The Secretary of State and staff of the State Department had made an effort to keep the Embassy advised and active. But they themselves had often been out of the know when main Chinese matters were decided. They were informants, consultants, and commentators rather than makers of decisions. In the autumn of 1944 Hull was ill, unable to carry the full burden of his office, and remaining only at the President's re-

---

[1] Letter, September 28th, Gauss to Hull. The agenda which Hurley drew up on September 8th for his early discussions with Chiang Kai-shek began (1) "The paramount objective of Chinese-American collaboration is to bring about a unification of all military forces in China for the immediate defeat of Japan and the liberation of China. . . . (3) The unification of all military forces under the command of the Generalissimo. . . . and (5) Support efforts of the Generalissimo for political unification of China."

quest. The Under-Secretary of State, Stettinius, knew little about Chinese affairs except what he was quickly told. He was disposed to look for orders rather than to make policy. A wish to do the right thing and to please did not make up for this lack of experience. At the end of November Hull gave up his office, and Stettinius was put in his place. The choice was correctly taken to indicate that more than ever the President and Hopkins would direct our foreign policy. At the same time Joseph C. Grew, who had been keeping a general watch over Far Eastern Affairs within the State Department, was named Under-Secretary. A few days later (December 12th) Hurley, who was already deep in our Chinese business and had been named Ambassador, formally took charge of the Embassy. This was the group of men, who, guided by their divisional staffs, and in association with their military colleagues, directed our effort in China during the closing phase of the war.

In following Hurley's first efforts from October 1944 on we must bear in mind the view of China which was being put before Washington by a cloud of witnesses whose minds were excited by what they saw and feared. Radios and dispatches rained in from the American Embassy and military headquarters in Chungking, from Burma and India, from Chennault, from the American observers in Yenan—who were the most diligent writers of all—and from American consular officials in widely scattered parts of China: Kweilin, Kunming, Chengtu, Sian, Lanchow and Amoy. These reports were crammed with detailed observations and rumors. They were by no means the same in tone or judgment, and they revealed many variations in conditions prevailing in the different parts of China. But even so, in total effect, this continuous symposium about China conveyed—and still conveys—a few transparent impressions:

1. That the entire front in China was threatened. Kunming was in danger. Chengtu, the northern base for our long-run bombing operations against Japan, might also be captured. The government might be forced to leave Chungking—bombed out if not driven out. All these were reported to be critical possibilities, until roughly the end of December; by that time the Chinese forces of resistance were somewhat restored and the Japanese advance began to seem fatigued. How seriously the dangers were taken is indicated by the fact that in early December the Embassy repeated previous warnings that all American civilians in Central China who did not have to remain there, should leave.[2]

[2] Telegrams, American Embassy, Chungking to State Department, November 23, 29 and December 5, 1944.

2. That the Chinese war effort had lost vitality; that the Chinese armies were in poor shape and their will to fight mostly gone. But again, from December on, some signs of recuperation were perceived, and it was anticipated that the decisive battle probably would be fought in February.

3. That the economic suffering had become worse and more general; that inflation was more rapid than ever and that many Chinese intellectuals, officials, and members of the middle class were being beggared.

4. That the conservative elements within the Kuomintang were in control and that the Generalissimo felt compelled to keep their support.

5. That the government administration was becoming less effective and more corrupt.

6. That the talks between the government and the Communists were dragging, and some three hundred thousand government troops were still being used to maintain the blockade.

Such then was the situation in China, as viewed by American observers, with which Hurley, in team with Wedemeyer, had to reckon. He disregarded Stilwell's tactics of pressure. He relied on persuasion, and acted on the belief that the best way to gain trust and influence with both the government and the Communists was to show an almost boisterous goodwill. His words acquired weight from the knowledge that the American government retained the power to decide the ways and extent to which it would support the Chinese government or any other faction. They acquired gravity from the perception that the Soviet Union would soon be in a position to take a more prying part in Chinese affairs.

In regard to the very active effort which the American government now began to bring about military unification, a bold surmise may be ventured. Its original impetus came from the deep wish to have all Chinese combat strength engaged in the fight against Japan and from the impatient feeling that unless they were, American soldiers and airmen would needlessly have to give up their lives. This remained a constant incentive. But each passing month the need for using the Chinese armies, any or all, was waning. The American power to destroy came closer and closer to Japan. The forces of the British Empire would be released after the defeat of Germany. And—as will be told later—it was definitely settled that the massive armies of the Soviet Union would also march against the Japanese. True, in the event of American landings on the China coast north of Formosa, the Communist troops could have done much to disrupt the Japanese armies. But projects for such landings were put farther to the side; and even if it was decided to attempt them, reports from China made it clear that the Communists would on their own account join in the action as a way of extending their areas. In sum, the Chinese could still play a useful part in completing the defeat of Japan. They could help to make the end quicker and less costly. But that end ceased to be in doubt, and the Chinese contribution ceased to be essential. Objectives outside the range of military necessity came to the fore.

But the officials in the State Department and in the Embassy in Chungking, including Hurley, appear to have been slow to grasp this evolution in the military prospect. If that impression is justified, several possible reasons suggest themselves. These officials were closer to the Chinese scene, and hence perhaps more sharply aware of how much more China could be doing for itself and the war effort, if unified. On the other hand, they were not informed in advance of American military intentions; in regard to the decisions about landings in China, Pacific island operations, and arrangements for Soviet entry in the war their knowledge lagged. They seem usually to have been left to evaluate for themselves the military need for full engagement of Chinese forces, including the Communists.

Or, perhaps the main reason why they were slow to adjust their views was of another sort. Chinese military unification was inseparably linked with other elements of policy that were in the ascendant. It thus remained important as the wedge of purpose after it ceased to be itself a major one. The political need for unity within China, which could begin with conjunction of the opposed Chinese armies, was becoming more urgent. Internal unity began to emerge as an essential condition of peace not only within China but among the powers. Unified, China at the end of the war would be able to play its assigned part in the Pacific, and as one of the great powers in the United Nations; divided, it would be able to do neither. Unified, the Chinese government would be able to settle its many pending questions with the Soviet Union; divided, it was probable that it could not. And unless these questions were settled, the Soviet Union might—by arrangement with the Chinese Communists or otherwise—take and keep control of Manchuria and parts of North China. The United States might then be drawn into the resultant quarrels unless—repeat unless—the American government should be willing to accept a peaceable division of China as the only manageable arrangement. But this it would not consider.[3]

---

[3] As summed up in a memo prepared in the State Department on January 9th for the

It was, I believe, some such general awareness as this which gave so much impetus to the wish to unify in some way or other the government and Communist forces in China—and thereby at least cause a suspension in their conflict. The White House, the State Department, and the War Department were at this time all in favor of making more of an effort to bring this about. So were Hurley and Wedemeyer and the staff of the American Embassy at Chungking, and the American observers at Yenan, and even Chennault. Churchill and Eden were saying that they were of the same mind, though some of the British representatives in the Far East may have been of the opinion that it would be best that China should stay divided; at least Hurley felt they thought so.[4] Stalin and Molotov were also saying that they thought the two Chinese parties ought to get together.

In sum, all elements within the Allies' circles of officialdom were in favor of some kind of accord or merger between the forces of the National Government of China and the Communists and other dissenting elements. All professed to want to see this come about peacefully. All thought that the American government should use its influence to that end. But what a variety of ideas there were as to how and on what terms unity would or should be brought about!

Thus it came about that American policy in and toward China at this time centered on a formula, in which the quantities were undefined—*unification by peaceful means.* In one respect and only one it was clear and conclusive: that neither Chinese side should use force against the other and that the American government would do its best to see that

---

possible use of the President in talking with Churchill and Stalin at Yalta: "It is of course highly desirable that embarrassment and difficulties, political or military, be avoided in the event of Russian military operations in North China. The obvious and reasonable solution would be a working agreement between the Chinese government and the Communists which would establish a unified Chinese military command to work with the Russian Command." The memo expressed doubt, however, that such an agreement would be reached. As alternative it suggested an overall American command of all Chinese troops—as an advantage in the event that the Soviet Union entered the war, and as a stabilizing influence after the war. There is no indication in the file copy as to whether or not this memo was actually sent to the White House, or whether the President read it. Memo, Chinese Affairs Division, January 9, 1945.

[4] See Leahy's condensation of his notes of "the many conversations I had with the President . . . in January 1945" on reports received from Hurley and others on British, French, and Dutch activities in China and Southeast Asia. *I Was There*, pages 287-289. Hurley—to whose mind Britain and imperialism were synonomous—was sure that the British-Dutch-French propaganda was directed toward defeat of American efforts to unify China and to use Chinese and American forces and Lend-Lease to reconquer their colonial territories. This last purpose he thought both wicked and against the Atlantic Charter, and it kept him constantly upset.

they did not. For the rest, the task of finding the terms and quantities which might make the formula work was mainly left to Hurley.

Neither the White House nor the State Department seems to have given Hurley an explicit statement of American policy in regard to the most trying question he was to encounter—how far would we stand by and support the Kuomintang government? Nor was any sent to him upon his appointment as Ambassador. On December 24th, about two months after he had begun his mediating activities, in answer to a query from Stettinius, he stated his idea of American policy in that regard. "In all my negotiations," he answered, "it has been my understanding that the policy of the United States in China is: (1) to prevent the collapse of the National Government; (2) to sustain Chiang Kai-shek as President of the Republic and Generalissimo of the Armies. . . ."[5] This statement was not questioned or corrected by the Secretary of State either in the personal acknowledgment that he sent to Hurley or in the report that he sent to the President on January 4, 1945 in regard to Hurley's ideas and activities.[6] Nor was it denied or qualified when Hurley repeated his understanding in a message to the President a few weeks later.[7]

But in reality there were many shades of difference among the American officials concerned as to how essential it was to preserve the authority of the Kuomintang government, headed by Chiang Kai-shek. There were some, like Hurley, who regarded that as a settled principle of our policy. To others it was merely a provisional preference.[8] They thought that we should cling to the Kuomintang regime only if it qualified itself to be the ruling element by reforms, greater regard for popular welfare, and cooperation with other Chinese parties. Or in other words, that we should let Chiang Kai-shek go if necessary to get a unified, popular government. There were still others who had concluded the Kuomintang government was finished; and that the people of China wanted to get rid of it and would, no matter what we did. They thought that it was

[5] Telegram, Hurley to Stettinius, December 24, 1944, in *Joint Committee on Military Situation in the Far East*, pages 2908-2910. (Dated in Hearings the 23rd.)

[6] This acknowledgment sent by Stettinius on January 2nd was intended to be responsive to Hurley's telegrams of December 24th and 30th and to the letter in which Hurley congratulated him on the "new team in the State Department."

[7] Hurley to President on or about January 15th, 1945. He averred that his directive was "of course" to prevent the collapse of the government and sustain Chiang Kai-shek, while unifying the military forces of China, and as far as possible helping to liberalize the government and promote a unified, free, and democratic China.

[8] For example, Vincent, in commenting on Hurley's summary of American policy, said that while he thought the five points in which the Ambassador outlined his mission were basically sound, it was "desirable to maintain sufficient flexibility in our attitude toward the political scene in China to avoid embarrassment in the unlikely event that Chiang with his government is ousted. . . ." Vincent memo, December 26, 1944.

therefore not in the interest of either China and the United States to make great exertions to save the Kuomintang government; that we should instead be getting ready to deal with the Communists as the future destined government of China. These divergences of attitudes within the American government became more and more marked as Hurley's efforts to bring about unification went on. Of the issues and the disputes they caused, more will be told as the narrative continues.[9]

Hurley started out with a whoop—Oklahoma style. He tried to corral both sides within a fence of general principles, and turn them into a committee for law and order.[10] He stressed to Chiang Kai-shek the need and benefits of a unification of all Chinese military forces. Soon after Hurley's arrival in China, the Communists had invited him to visit Yenan. Although of the opinion that no good would come of it, the Generalissimo said he was willing to have Hurley talk to them, but asked that he postpone going to Yenan. Hurley agreed to do so; he stayed on in Chungking and went into the subject further with the official committee that the Generalissimo had created to study the reconstitution of the National Government. He found that this committee, referring to Sun Yat-sen's precept that China was to remain under one-party rule during a period of tutelage while it became ready to run a democratic government, thought that the time had not yet come for that next big step. But on consultation with this committee and in touch with Soong and the Generalissimo, he evolved five points of possible accord with the Communists. These were found acceptable by the representatives of the Communist Party who were in Chungking. In Hurley's phrase, they were "rather innocuous."

Thereupon, after conferring with Chiang Kai-shek and Wedemeyer, he flew off on November 7th to Yenan. He was warmly greeted at the Communist capital. During two days and nights, as he informed the President, "We argued, agreed, disagreed, denied, and admitted in the most strenuous and most friendly fashion and pulled and hauled my five points until they were finally revised. . . ."[11] Mao Tze Tung, as chairman of the Central Committee of the Communist Party of China, signed

---

[9] Chapter 24.

[10] This account of the early phases of Hurley's mediation is mainly based on his telegrams to the Secretary of State of December 24, 1944, and January 31, 1945, in *Joint Committee on Military Situation in the Far East*, pages 2908-2911 and 3669-3672. His historical review of the negotiations between the government and Communists and of his part in them was continued in two other telegrams sent February 7th and 17th and three telegrams sent February 18th. *Ibid.*, pages 3672-3679.

[11] Telegram, Hurley to Secretary of State, January 31, 1945. *Ibid.*

the statement in which they were set forth. Hurley also signed, as "Personal Representative of the President of the United States."[12] He did this, by his own account, as witness, not sponsor. He then flew back to Chungking. Chou En-lai went back with him in order to be on hand to continue discussion of these points with the National Government.

This was the first of many offers and counteroffers which during the next few years American intermediaries helped to devise. For that reason mainly, its features remain of interest:[13]

(1) The Government of China, the Kuomintang of China and the Communist Party of China will work together for the unification of all military forces in China for the immediate defeat of Japan and the reconstruction of China.

(2) The present National Government is to be reorganized into a coalition National Government embracing representatives of all anti-Japanese parties and non-partisan political bodies. A new democratic policy providing for reform in military, political, economic and cultural affairs shall be promulgated and made effective. At the same time the National Military Council is to be reorganized into the United National Military Council consisting of representatives of all anti-Japanese armies.

(3) The coalition National Government will support the principles of Sun Yat-sen for the establishment in China of a government of the people, for the people and by the people. The coalition National Government will pursue policies designed to promote progress and democracy and to establish justice, freedom of conscience, freedom of press, freedom of speech, freedom of assembly and association, the right to petition the government for the redress of grievances, the right of writ of habeas corpus and the right of residence. The coalition National Government will also pursue policies intended to make effective the two rights defined as freedom from fear and freedom from want.

(4) All anti-Japanese forces will observe and carry out the orders of the coalition National Government and its United National Military Council and will be recognized by the Government and the Military Council. The supplies acquired from foreign powers will be equitably distributed.

(5) The coalition National Government of China recognizes the legality of the Kuomintang of China, the Chinese Communist Party and all anti-Japanese parties.

This statement seems to have visualized a coalition arrangement through which some kind of democratic multi-party system was to be evolved. It was a prospectus of intentions—which told nothing about points crucial in determining how the program would be worked out or how it would work. Who could tell on reading it how power within the

---

[12] A paraphrased text of this proposed agreement is printed in *ibid.*, page 3669.
[13] *United States Relations with China*, page 74.

coalition was to be shared and exercised; or how the struggle between the Communists and the government would be carried on?

Most of the principles endorsed in this proposal were traditional in the United States; even the more vaporous of them, such as "freedom from fear," were warmly approved at the time as objects for political endeavor. It may be wondered how Hurley conceived they could be genuinely reconciled with Communist practices. Various guesses may be made as to his thoughts on this point. He was under the impression that the Chinese Communists were not true-blue Communists, that the name was more or less of a misnomer.[14] He might have thought it expedient to credit the good faith of the Communists; that they might think it to their advantage to justify that trust. Or, he may even have thought that it made little difference what principles were affirmed, provided both sides accepted them and proceeded to work together.

The government firmly declined the program which Hurley brought back from Yenan. Soong's comment was, "The Communists have sold you a bill of goods. Never will the National Government grant the Communist request." The Generalissimo said that he thought that the proposed agreement would eventually result in giving the Communists control of the government.[15] Hurley tried to convince Chiang Kai-shek that he understood that the National Government had to be maintained; that its collapse would cause chaos. He tried to assure him by reporting that the Communists had authorized him to say that they pledged themselves to uphold Chiang Kai-shek's leadership both as President and Generalissimo. But Chiang Kai-shek was neither convinced nor reassured. He referred to what he called the peculiar Chinese psychology which would interpret acceptance of this coalition offer as total defeat.

But Hurley remained sure that Chiang Kai-shek personally was anxious for a settlement.[16] Hurley besought him to reformulate terms that would bring unity without giving the appearance of defeat to any of the major factions. The government drew up a counterproposal which compressed its terms in three points, as follows:[17]

(1) The National Government, desirous of securing effective unification and concentration of all military forces in China for the purpose of accomplishing the speedy defeat of Japan, and looking forward to the post-war recon-

---

[14] In the report which he made to the President on November 16th after he had been in Yenan, he still referred to the Communists in one place as the "so-called Communists."

[15] Telegram, Hurley to President, November 16, 1944, *Hurley Papers*, Book I, Item 97.

[16] *Ibid.*

[17] *United States Relations with China*, page 75.

struction of China, agrees to incorporate, after reorganization, the Chinese Communist forces in the National Army who will then receive equal treatment as the other units in respect of pay, allowance, munitions and other supplies, and to give recognition to the Chinese Communist Party as a legal party.

(2) The Communist Party undertakes to give their full support to the National Government in the prosecution of the war of resistance, and in the post-war reconstruction, and give over control of all their troops to the National Government through the National Military Council. The National Government will designate some high ranking officers from among the Communist forces to membership in the National Military Council.

(3) The aim of the National Government to which the Communist Party subscribes is to carry out the Three People's Principles of Dr. Sun Yat-sen for the establishment in China of a government of the people, for the people and by the people and it will pursue policies designed to promote the progress and development of democratic processes in government.

In accordance with the provisions of the *Program of Armed Resistance and National Reconstruction*, freedom of speech, freedom of the press, freedom of assembly and association and other civil liberties are hereby guaranteed, subject only to the specific needs of security in the effective prosecution of the war against Japan.

The two proposals glaringly show how far apart the two sides were. The Communists were demanding substantial participation in the government at once, the thorough reorganization to be made by joint agreement. The Kuomintang was to become merely one of several political parties in the coalition. The struggle for control over the government and the country was to go on without constraint. In contrast, the government rejected the idea of coalition. It offered to receive back the Communist rebel armies into its ranks and to treat them in the same way as other government forces, and to allow the Communist Party to function as a legal party within the constraint to which all parties in China were then subject. When it thought the time ripe, it would proceed to reform itself along democratic lines.

Many another man might have been dejected, but not Hurley. He had tried to persuade Chiang Kai-shek that the program written in Yenan would strengthen the government both morally and politically. He had failed. With similar earnestness he next tried to induce the Communists to accept the government offer. But they slammed it down hard. On December 8th Chou En-lai, who had returned to Yenan, informed Hurley that his party thought it impossible to find any common basis in the Three Point Proposal made by the government. Therefore, he said that he did not think it was any use for him to return to Chungking to continue the discussion. In his view the Communist Party was being asked to surrender; and he thought that its rights could be safe-guarded only if it was accepted on a basis of equality and a genuine coalition government was formed.[18]

Still the sap of hope ran in Hurley's spirit. His view of the situation, as reported to Secretary of State Stettinius on December 24th, was:

". . . We are in daily conferences with the Generalissimo and members of his cabinet endeavoring to liberalize the counter-proposal made by the National Government to the Communists. We are having some success. The Generalissimo states that he is anxious that the military forces of the Communist Party in China and those of the National Government be united to drive the invader from China. The Communist leaders declare this is also their objective. I have persuaded Chiang Kai-shek and others in the National Government that in order to unite the military forces of China and to prevent civil conflict it will be necessary for him and the Kuomintang and the National Government to make liberal political concessions to the Communist Party and to give them adequate representation in the National Government. Chiang Kai-shek has appointed a new Committee, which is now working out a plan that he believes will be feasible and on which he hopes a working agreement can be reached with the Communists. The Kuomintang is trying to avoid the use of the word "coalition," they do not want to admit that they had formed a coalition with the Communists. The Kuomintang still hopes to keep China under one-party rule. Notwithstanding all this, you should bear in mind that the Communists have acknowledged the leadership of Chiang Kai-shek and have accepted nearly all his avowed principles. There is very little difference, if any, between the avowed principles of the National government, the Kuomintang, and the avowed principles of the Chinese Communist Party."[19]

Thus Hurley drew assurance from the similarity of expressed desire, while he continued to contend with all four groups whom he identified as the opponents of unification. These were (1) the extremists in the Kuomintang, (2) the extremists among the Chinese Communists, (3) foreigners who thought their national interests in Asia would be better served if China were divided against herself, (4) some American officials and diplomatic officers, "who believe that the present Chinese government will eventually collapse and that there can be no military or political unification of China under Chiang Kai-shek and his 'die-hard' supporters

[18] Hurley's message to the President, December 12, 1944. *Hurley Papers*, Book I, Item 124. Hurley telegram to the Secretary of State, February 7, 1945.

[19] Telegram, Hurley to Stettinius, December 24, 1944.

in the Kuomintang." Hurley concluded his comments on these points by saying that none of these arguments against what he was doing had impressed him, but that he was transmitting them to Washington so that "you [the Secretary of State] may have them definitely before you and give them what weight you think they deserve."

Hurley's belief that he was making progress did not collapse even when, on December 24th, Mao Tze Tung said that the National Government had not shown enough "sincerity" to warrant continuation of the talks; or when, four days later, Chou En-lai laid down four new conditions. He asked that the government should (1) release all political prisoners, (2) withdraw all the forces that were surrounding the Communist area, (3) abolish all oppressive regulations which restricted the people's freedom, and (4) end all secret service activity. The government. of course, regarded these conditions as equivalent to allowing the Communists to carry on their revolution without opposition or hindrance. In the interval it may be recalled, an American military project for arming the Communists had been broached to their leaders in Yenan; and Hurley later had the impression that this episode made them bold and more stubborn.

All the while the Japanese were marching on; and Wedemeyer was trying to rally the government forces to hold them back.

It is not easy to know or to tell what the White House and the State Department were thinking at this juncture about the way to handle the Chinese internal quarrel. They were unsure and wavering. Stettinius acknowledged Hurley's reports with the anemic comment that "The information you have given me and your comments thereon affords me a valuable insight into the problems with which you are faced, and for which you are seeking solutions with characteristic energy and acumen."[20]

The China Affairs Division of the State Department marked Hurley's reports with marginal notes which seemed to suggest that the situation could best be resolved—perhaps only be resolved—if Chiang Kai-shek gave in much more. As expressed in a memo sent by Stettinius to the President on January 4th, "Chiang is in a dilemma. Coalition would mean an end of Conservative Kuomintang domination and open the way for the more virile and popular Communists to extend their influence to the point perhaps of controlling the Government. Failure to settle with the Communists, who are daily growing stronger, would invite the

[20] Telegram, Stettinius to Hurley, January 2, 1945, in *Joint Committee on Military Situation in the Far East*, page 2908. (This is dated January 4th in the Hearings.)

danger of an eventual overthrow of the Kuomintang. Chiang could, it is felt, rise above party selfishness and anti-Communist prejudice, to head a coalition government which might bring new life into the war effort and insure unity after hostilities." The political reporters on Wedemeyer's staff (particularly Davies and Service) also were shrilly sure that there was no chance of agreement unless Chiang Kai-shek yielded more, yielded enough to risk Kuomintang control of the government.

But what if the Generalissimo did not take this way out of the bedeviling dilemma? Then it was suggested that an alternative way of stabilizing the internal Chinese situation would be to have an American placed in command of all Chinese armies, including the Communist. This was a reversion to the main issue on which Stilwell had gone aground. The President in October had given in about it; and he had thereupon said that he did not want to assume the responsibility of having any American officer in command of *any* Chinese armies. "It is understood that both Chiang and the Communists would agree to this," the sponsors in the State Department remarked, when advancing this suggestion.[21] It is hard to know precisely what kind of arrangement they thought might be mutually acceptable;[22] surely neither the Chinese government nor the Communists would have agreed to put its forces under the unified command of an American except on terms which each thought to its own advantage.[23]

Hurley managed to persuade the two sides to resume their talks. Going against the more unyielding elements in his party, the Generalissimo was offering more liberal inducements to the Communists if they

[21] As stated in the memo which Stettinius sent to the President on January 4th, 1945, commenting on Hurley's telegram of December 24th. This solution had been proposed in various memos, e.g. that of December 26th, which the China Affairs Division (Vincent) sent to the Secretary of State. The interest of the State Department in this proposal grew more definite and urgent later on, as the efforts at negotiated unification failed and the prospect of Soviet entry into the war came closer. The idea came to be regarded as a possible route toward unification, with joint American and Soviet pressure and promise to cooperate only with the combined force. See Chapter 27.

[22] In January the Nationalist government proposed that an American army officer responsible to Chiang Kai-shek be placed in command of the Communist troops, *United States Relations with China*, pages 79-80. The Communists were unwilling to accept Kuomintang control of their forces even indirectly, but might have accepted American command as a feature of cooperation with the American army. There is a puzzling ambiguity in Hurley's reference to the subject in his telegram to the State Department of February 7th, in which he stated that both sides desired that the Communist troops be under the overall command of a U.S. Army officer. *Joint Committee on Military Situation in the Far East*, page 3673.

[23] This appears clearly in the account of the negotiations, as summarized in *United States Relations with China*, pages 79-80.

would subordinate themselves to the authority of the government. Hurley sent a series of messages to Yenan assuring the Communist leaders that the concessions were genuine. Mao Tze Tung climbed down from his cliffs. He agreed to have Chou En-lai go back to Chungking once again.

Hurley was invited by both sides to referee in this new bout of talk.[24] The student of political dialectics will get rewarding instruction from both Soong's and Chou En-lai's able exposition of their views—as I shall allow him to find out for himself.[25] All the barriers were still in place. The government was unwilling to agree to a coalition arrangement in which its power to prevail might be shaken or lost. The Communists were unwilling to consent to anything else. But neither side wanted to turn its back conclusively on the other, or to appear plainly as the obstinate one. Thus they agreed upon a measure which obligated them to nothing at the moment but could lead to a settlement at a later time. Hurley played an effective part in inducing both sides to try out this new route to accord rather than to separate.

Chiang Kai-shek made known that he was willing to convoke a con-

[24] Hurley construed a remark made by Acting Secretary Grew in a press conference at Washington on January 23rd in regard to "The exercise of friendly good offices when requested by the Chinese" as a signal that the State Department was trying to restrict his role in the negotiations. He prepared a protesting telegram but did not send it. Just before he left to visit Washington, on February 18th, he sent a message to the Secretary of State, telling him of this, and giving his opinion that mere use of friendly good offices would not be effective, as shown by the outcome of Gauss's earlier attempts. He said that he was leaving the subject for personal discussion after his arrival in Washington.

[25] A summary of the main train of their arguments is to be found in Hurley's telegram of February 18th to the Secretary of State, printed in *Joint Committee on Military Situation in the Far East*, pages 3676-3679.

Soong was acting president of the Executive Yuan as well as Foreign Minister. His appointment to these offices was one of several changes in the Generalissimo's circle, which the State Department thought promising. They were taken to connote that Chiang Kai-shek was now trying hard to improve his government and to reach an accord with the dissenting liberal groups.

The top changes were (1) the appointment of General Chen Cheng as Minister of War. Chen was a vigorous advocate of reform in army administration. (2) The appointment of O. K. Yui to take the place of H. H. Kung as Minister of Finance. Yui was reputed to be honest, though not of exceptional ability, and to be close to the Generalissimo. (3) The appointment of Wang Shih-Chieh as Minister of Information. He was regarded as an able man, who had shown himself openminded in the talks with the Communists and who would, if allowed, relax censorship. Vincent memo to Stettinius, December 6, 1944.

H. H. Kung, who was in the United States, resigned his posts as Vice President of the Executive Yuan and Finance Minister. He was ill, and for that reason refused Chiang Kai-shek's request to reconsider. He also turned down the suggestions that he become Ambassador to the United States. But he wanted to remain in this country for medical treatment and also to continue to handle economic and financial matters. Important issues in this field were being discussed with the American government.

ference "to take steps to draft a constitution to pass control of the National Government to the people and to abolish the one party rule of the Kuomintang." After much talk back and forth, in which Hurley participated, the government submitted a definite proposal on February 3rd.[26] Its main points were (1) the National Government was to invite the representatives of the Kuomintang and other parties and some non-partisan leaders to a Consultative Conference. (2) This conference would consider (a) steps to be taken to end the period of tutelage under one-party rule and establish constitutional government, (b) the common political program to be followed in the future, (c) the unification of the armed forces, (d) the form in which members of parties other than the Kuomintang would take part in the National Government. If the conference reached a unanimous conclusion, this was to be submitted to the National Government for enactment.

Before leaving Chungking to return to Yenan, Chou En-lai told Hurley that he believed that his party would take part in this Consultative Conference. But there was no agreement as to how the conference was to be composed; or how many of its members would be supporters of the Kuomintang, supporters of the Communists, or independents. Further, as Hurley pointed out to Chou En-lai, that while this program sounded very nice, it did not accomplish the immediate unification of the armed forces of China. Still, Hurley could feel that at least there would not be open civil war right away and that at most reconciliation might follow. His optimism survived on what others might think a thin diet of belief. As rather wearily expressed in the report he sent on this agreement, "I pause to observe that in this dreary controversial chapter two fundamental facts are emerging: (one) the Communists are not in fact Communists, they are striving for democratic principles; and (two) the one party, one man personal Government of the Kuomintang is not in fact Fascist. It is striving for democratic principles. Both the Communists and the Kuomintang have a long way to go, but, if we know the way, if we are clear minded, tolerant and patient, we can be helpful. But it is most difficult to be patient at a time when the unified military forces of China are so desperately needed in our war effort."[27]

Chiang Kai-shek remained convinced that ". . . fundamentally the National Government has the support of the people and the Communists

---

[26] The course of these talks and negotiations was reported by Hurley in his telegrams of February 7th and February 18th, 1945, *ibid.* A good summary account is given in *United States Relations with China*, pages 79-81.

[27] *Ibid.*, page 86.

could never control China."[28] Hurley thought so too. But other American observers did not. They got the impression that Communist obstinacy was based on the confident belief that their cause could and would win over the Chinese people. This view was well represented by a report made to the State Department by one of its officers after four months of travel in the Shansi-Suiyuan and Shansi-Chahar-Hopei Communist base areas. This transmitted impressive evidence for the conclusion that while "additional and more wide-spread investigations in Communist base areas thus far unvisited by American military personnel are advisable . . . until such time as reliable evidence to the contrary is forthcoming, there is no valid reason to doubt but that popular support of the Communist armies and civil administration is a reality which we must consider in future planning. Evidence of popular support of the Communists in North China is so wide-spread that it is impossible longer to believe that it is a stage-setting for the deception of foreign visitors."[29] Another report by the same observer gave ominous meaning to this impression of strength. The Communists, he wrote, were frankly outspoken in regard to their plans for territorial and military expansion. "These plans," to quote from the summary of this report, "envisage the eventual development of connected series of Communist Base Areas extending from the Great Wall to the East River. . . . As the Chinese government forces withdraw in the face of the Japanese advance chaotic conditions create a political vacuum which the Communists are in a position to fill, and they propose to do so whenever and wherever possible. . . ."[30]

All the time that the government and Communist representatives were talking with one another, each had the thought of the Soviet Union in the back of his head. But neither knew during the negotiations which have just been reviewed that Roosevelt was on his way to meet Stalin; and that they would then, that early and that definitely, enter into an accord on the terms of Soviet entry into the Pacific War. There is no evidence that either Chinese side was swayed by secret knowledge that the Soviet government was promising to enter into a treaty of friend-

[28] Hurley memo, Book II, Item 35.
[29] Dispatch of February 12, 1945, from the American Embassy, Chungking, enclosing a memorandum for the Assistant Chief of Staff, G-2, February 2, 1945, by Second Secretary of Embassy Raymond P. Ludden, detailed to the Headquarters United States Forces, China Theater. Subject: Popular Support of Communists as Evidenced by People's Militia Organization in Shansi-Chahar-Hopei Communist Base Area.
[30] Dispatch February 16, 1945, from the American Embassy in Chungking transmitting another memo by Ludden, February 7, 1945. Title: Communist Plans for Expansion.

ship with the Chinese government if its wishes were met in other respects. It is unlikely that any secret cautionary word passed from Moscow to Yenan and influenced the Communist acceptance of the proposal for a consultative conference; but it is not out of the question.[31]

Hurley left Chungking for Washington on February 19th in a mood of mingled satisfaction and pugnacity. He had the feeling that he had managed to bring the two sides together in a step which, if properly managed from then on, could unify China and insure its postwar future. This he thought he had accomplished without spoiling his relations with either side, and without proposing any principle or method which would weaken the leadership of Chiang Kai-shek or the National Government.[32] He carried with him a letter from Chiang Kai-shek to the President which showed that the Generalissimo regarded him as a friend.

"I count it as my great good fortune to have General Hurley here. . . .

"On the occasion of his going home, I have asked him to report to you in detail on the latest political developments in China, the general policy pursued by the National Government and also my own opinion on the outstanding problems.

"The achievement of the Crimean Conference [Yalta] is a lasting tribute to your great and inspiring leadership. I hope you may be disposed to acquaint me with any decisions which may have been taken regarding the Far East."

But along with this sense of an effort well conducted, there was resentment at what he regarded as efforts to undo or defeat his work. Some of the military men in China, as already told, had proposed direct dealings with the Communists. Not long before Hurley left, the Communists had made another attempt to arrange this; the senior Communist commander, General Chu Teh, had sent a request directly to Wedemeyer asking for a twenty-million-dollar loan for arms for the Communist forces with the suggestion that Hurley not be told of it.[33] Wedemeyer had, of course, informed Hurley, and the request was refused. But it was another irritant. For Hurley was convinced that various members of the American diplomatic mission in China and various officers in the Far Eastern Division of the State Department were critical both of

[31] As early as February 3rd, Chou En-lai told Hurley that for the first time he had a feeling that a basis for cooperation was being reached. Hurley's telegram to the Secretary of State, February 18, 1945. The first talk between Roosevelt and Stalin on this subject was on February 8th and the agreement between Roosevelt, Stalin, and Churchill was signed February 11th.

[32] Hurley's telegram to Secretary of State, February 18, 1945.

[33] Telegram to State Department, February 17, 1945.

him and the way he was handling the situation in China. Of this more will be told shortly.

There may have been also in his mind a tinge of feeling that he ought to have been present at the Yalta Conference. He had traveled to Moscow before coming to China in order to prepare the way for an agreement between the Chinese and Soviet governments. He had kept the President reminded of its utility.[34] It would have been natural for him to think he should have been called on to advise on China's situation and needs, especially since he did not know of the rapid march of plans for Soviet entry into the war, which crowded Roosevelt into the Yalta accord on the Far East. Of these plans and of this accord it is now time to give an account. To do so we must leave Chungking, Yenan, and Washington for a while, and go first to Moscow and then to Yalta.

[34] His latest reminder of the sort had been sent on January 14th, at a stage in the negotiations with the government when the Communists were refusing to budge and Mao Tze Tung was saying that he saw no purpose in going back to Chungking to resume the talks. Hurley suggested to the President that he should seek Stalin's approval as regards (1) the immediate unification of all military forces in China, (2) a postwar unified and democratic China. Hurley, message to President, January 14, 1945.

CHAPTER 22

The Syndrome of the Yalta Agreement

As FAR back as June, it will be recalled, Chiang Kai-shek had told Wallace that he wanted an understanding with the Soviet Union; and that he would welcome the friendly touch of the United States to bring this about. He went on the alert for a good chance to send a special personal envoy to Moscow to see whether an acceptable agreement could be had. He watched for signs of Soviet good will, which he hoped the President might manage to evoke.

The American government had remained wary about accepting the part of mediator. But it had sought ways to dispose the regimes in Chungking and Moscow to take a friendly view of one another, as allies in the war and partners in the making of the peace. Hurley's visit to Moscow on his way to Chungking had been prompted by a wish to find out Soviet intentions toward China. He had left persuaded that the Soviet government (a) did not want civil war in China, (b) did not recognize the Chinese Communist Party, and (c) did want more harmonious relations with the Chinese government. These impressions he had imparted to Chiang Kai-shek in an effort to quiet his fears about dealing with the Chinese Communists and the Soviet government.[1] Cognately the American government had continued to keep the Soviet government aware of our determined intention to treat and sustain China as one of the four main members of international political society. We had also let it know that we were giving calming advice to the Chinese government about Soviet attitudes.

Toward the end of 1944 it became clear to Roosevelt that it would be risky to allow Sino-Soviet relations to remain unsettled any longer; and that it would be better to strive to bring the two powers together sooner rather than later. The Soviet government could be expected to give more heed to American wishes while still in great need of American help than it would thereafter. It would not wish to lose benefits still to be had; while no one ever knew it to be grateful for benefits already received. Further and incisively, the Soviet government was saying that its armies would not begin to move against Japan until its claims against Japan were discussed and settled; and a Sino-Soviet accord was in that connection highly desirable if not essential.

[1] Hurley telegram of December 24, 1944.

At the Teheran Conference Stalin had stated the Soviet Union would enter the Pacific war as soon after the defeat of Germany as it could. The British and American governments had received this declaration in good part. But they had not in the interval budgeted for that coming event. When on September 23, 1944, the American Ambassador Harriman and the British Ambassador Clark-Kerr had called on Marshal Stalin to tell him of the plans approved at the second Quebec conference for carrying on the war against Japan, he brought the subject up. Stalin seemed puzzled because the program did not appear to take more account of the part that the Soviet Union might bear in the fighting. He had remarked that ". . . there had been no change in the Russian attitude, but if the United States and Great Britain preferred to bring Japan to her knees without Russian participation, he was ready to agree."[2] Harriman and Clark-Kerr had answered that both the President and the Prime Minister expected the Soviet Union to come in. But they explained that the Americans and British thought they had to rely on doing the job themselves until the Soviet government was ready to join in planning for the best use of the combined resources of all; and this the Soviet government had not thus far been willing to do. I leave to others the long conjecture as to what the future course of events in the Far East would have been had the British and American governments at this juncture answered otherwise: had they told the Soviet government then that they were ready to finish the war against Japan by themselves.

Stalin had then said that he was ready to begin the needed joint planning. He would, he volunteered, instruct his military leaders to begin work with the American military missions in Moscow. The Joint Chiefs of Staff had thereupon proceeded to define their ideas of the tasks which Russia should be asked to perform. General Deane, head of our military mission, had been ordered to work them out with the Soviet military authorities. But he and Harriman had found that, despite Stalin's expression, the Soviet military organization was in no hurry to begin actual planning for combined operations. While they were puzzling over this, it had been learned that Churchill was, on his own initiative, soon to visit Moscow in order to talk over with Stalin a wide range

[2] Deane, *The Strange Alliance*, page 240. General Deane was head of the American military mission in Moscow and he had accompanied Ambassador Harriman on this talk, as he did on almost all of the talks with Stalin, Molotov, and the Russian military leaders about Soviet entry into the Pacific war. This book is one of the main sources of the account given of this subject during this and later periods. The other main source is Harriman's reports to the President.

of political and military matters. The President, the Joint Chiefs of Staff, Harriman, and Deane had all thought this might be a good chance to expedite the combined planning.

They had a brief twinge of anxiety lest Stalin and Churchill in their talks might either neglect the subject or throw it out of line. On October 10th, the day before Churchill arrived in Moscow, Harriman had cabled the President that there seemed no further need for general talk about the Soviet participation, but that it would be of great use to know what Russian combat capacities would be in the Far East and what their supply needs would be. He suggested that the Prime Minister in his talk with Stalin therefore ought to emphasize the importance of the American-Soviet staff talks that were in suspense. He added that he would try to see that the Prime Minister did so.[3] Whether or not the President sent some word to the Prime Minister, Churchill and his advisers had been most cooperative. They had agreed that since the direction of the Pacific war was in American hands, Ambassador Harriman should be present at the military talks with Stalin, as representative of the President; and that General Deane should be assigned the task of exposing military views concerning the conduct of the war against Japan and the part it was hoped the Soviet Union would undertake. "Churchill agreed to back our play to the limit, but would otherwise leave the matter in our hands."[4]

The Joint Chiefs of Staff had informed Deane of the two points on which they particularly wanted answers from the Soviet government: how long after the defeat of Germany before the Soviet Union would begin active measures against Japan; and what were the Russian capabilities? Almost as soon as the talks with the Russians got underway, Harriman and Deane had asked them these questions. The answers had been impressive both in their military meaning and in their bearing on Soviet-Chinese relations.

On October 14th, General Deane had expounded the ideas of the American military authorities to the Russians and British. He had told them that the Joint Chiefs of Staff hoped that the Soviet Union would enter the Pacific war as soon as possible and in all available strength; and that they wanted to start the necessary planning for combined operations at once. He enumerated those particular actions which it was thought the Soviet Union could advisedly carry out—in number, five:

[3] Telegram, Harriman to President, October 10th, 1944.
[4] Deane, *The Strange Alliance*, page 243; telegram, Harriman to President, October 11, 1944.

1. To secure the Trans-Siberian Railroad and the Vladivostok Peninsula.

2. To conduct American and Soviet air operations against Japan from the Maritime Provinces and Kamchatka.

3. To interdict the sea lines of communication between Japan and the Asiatic mainland.

4. To secure the supply route across the northern Pacific to the Soviet Union.

5. To destroy Japanese ground and air forces in Manchuria. This was to be the principal and ultimate job of the Soviet forces.

The exposition of Soviet plans and intentions had been full and revealing. They had opened the prospect of immense intervention. General Antonov, Chief of Staff, had explained that the Soviet Union had at that time thirty divisions on the Trans-Baikal and Manchurian fronts; that it wanted to have thirty more, sixty in all, in position there before entering the war; and that it also wanted to accumulate in advance the supplies that would be needed for these forces. The extent of these provisions indicates, it may be noted in passing, that the Soviet military authorities were at one with their American associates in expecting at this time that Japanese resistance on the mainland of Asia would be strong and determined. This talk (of October 15th) touched on the fact that the Russian estimate of the prospective Japanese forces to be encountered—forty-seven large-size and well-equipped divisions—was greater than any American forecast.[5]

Stalin had actively entered in the discussion. He had remarked, after Antonov had finished his general exposition, that he thought that within three months after the end of the war in Europe enough supplies could be accumulated to maintain the Soviet forces for a combat period of between one and a half and two months. Within that short time he reckoned that it would be possible "to deal a mortal blow to Japan." In answer to a question asked by Harriman as to whether he was to be understood as meaning that the Soviet Union would be ready to go into action against Japan within three months after the collapse of Germany, the Marshal answered, "Yes—in three months. After the building of supplies, in several months."[6]

[5] Actually, the Kwantung army in Manchuria was being depleted, and by the end of 1944 was only about half as strong as the year before. Divisions had been taken away for the defense of the Philippines, Formosa, and other Pacific islands and for use in the planned offensive in China. But it was increased later by a variety of emergency measures. Japanese Monograph No. 45, pages 234-235.

[6] A very large amount of the supplies which the Soviet government stated that it

In regard to the part which the Soviet Union was to play in the final defeat of Japan, the Soviet military authorities had on the whole fallen in with the ideas of the Joint Chiefs of Staff. But they had placed greater emphasis on ground operations, and were considering movements which might carry Soviet forces beyond Manchuria, down to the Great Wall in China, or even farther. As pointed up by Stalin himself, "If we are thinking seriously of defeating the Japanese, we cannot be limited to the Pacific region. We shall strike direct blows from different directions in Manchuria. But to have real results we must develop outflanking movements—blows at Kalgan and Peking, otherwise the assaults in Manchuria alone will produce no important results. I do not believe that the major battles will be so much in Manchuria as in the south where Japanese troops are to be expected to be found when they withdraw from China. The problem that faces us is to prevent the Japanese from withdrawing from China into Manchuria. Our objective is to see to it that the Japanese forces in China cannot be used by the Japanese in Manchuria."[7]

One other passage in the talk had thrown even stronger light on the breadth of Stalin's conception of the part that his forces would play. Harriman explained that the United States was planning to make landing operations on the China coast to take airfields, but that it did not contemplate any other operations in that area of China. Stalin had said that he agreed that this was the proper plan; that the Americans would cut off the Japanese garrisons in the Southern islands and that the Russians would cut off their land forces in China.

Stalin had indicated that he had a political agreement in view. After making his statement, at the meeting on October 15th, that the Soviet Union would prepare to enter the Pacific three months after Germany collapsed, he had paused, and then gone on to say that he was not

___

would need for these operations was to be provided by the United States. The list presented later was astounding. It was computed, the Soviet officials said, to provide a two months' supply of food, fuel, transport equipment, and other materials for a force of one and a half million men, three thousand tanks, seventy-five thousand motor vehicles, and five thousand airplanes. The total tonnage of what was asked of the United States mounted up to about 860,410 tons of dry and 206,000 tons of liquid cargo. These supplies were to be in addition to the other great shipments being made under the current Lend-Lease program. General Deane, from whose book this information is taken (pages 248-249), states that the list was revised, but apparently it was not greatly ⁻reduced in total. The United States succeeded in delivering about eighty per cent of the supplies which it had undertaken to furnish for this Far Eastern Soviet force by June 30, 1945.

[7] Memo of meeting, October 17, 1944.

ready to set a precise date, since there were also certain political aspects which would have to be taken into account. The Russians would have to know what they were fighting for; they had certain claims against Japan. Harriman and Deane had waited for him to enlarge on the subject but he had not done so.

It may be safely guessed that Stalin thought it would be best to reserve discussion of these claims for his coming meeting with Roosevelt. In talking with Harriman, he had referred to conversations which, with the knowledge of the President, the Russian Ambassador in Washington, Gromyko, had been having with Hopkins. He had said to Harriman that he understood that Hopkins had told Gromyko that the President thought it would be possible to meet with him, Stalin, in the Black Sea area toward the end of November. He had asked Harriman to assure the President that he would be very pleased if this was arranged, and that he thought the two of them would be able to arrive at an agreement with regard to Japan.

The narrative may briefly pause for surmise on some of the ways in which it would have been natural for these October conversations to have entered into the reckoning of the President. It is easy to believe that this preview of Russian offensives reduced the intensity of his interest—and that of the Joint Chiefs of Staff—in the Chinese military situation; that it induced a more relaxed attitude toward the danger that the Japanese might take Kunming and Chungking; and that it seemed less important to have an American in command of the Chinese forces. It is also hard not to believe that the records of these Moscow talks—contrastingly—quickened anxiety over the internal division in China. For every line about Soviet strategy must have suggested the question as to what the situation would be if China was still miserably divided when the vast Russian troop movement began, and if a rebellious Communist army was roaming over the northern regions of China which the Soviet forces might reach. In sum, there is no great risk in the surmise that the reports received from Moscow in October made it seem more urgent than ever that the internal division of China be composed as soon as possible. Also that they imprinted more blackly the need of an agreement which would restrain the impact on China of Soviet entry into the Pacific war. Whether or not the reflections of the President followed the trail of these surmises, from that time on these two lines of American diplomatic effort were intertwined.

The Generalissimo had been told nothing of these secret talks about Soviet plans to enter the Pacific war. He was on the edge of sending his oldest son, Chiang Ching-kuo to Moscow, encouraged by the fact that the Russian chargé d'affaires in Peking had spoken to this son about the idea of arranging a meeting between the Generalissimo and Stalin. Chiang Kai-shek had sent word to Roosevelt through Hurley on November 7th that he wanted the President to be fully informed of every step he took in this matter, and that he wished to cooperate with the President.

On November 18th (shortly after Hurley had reported that the Generalissimo would not subscribe to the five-point proposal which he had brought back from Yenan), the President had asked Hurley to tell the Generalissimo that—not only from his point of view but also from that of the Russians—a military agreement between all Chinese forces would greatly expedite the ejection of the Japanese from China. Since, the President had added, he could not at that time explain his thoughts more fully, Chiang Kai-shek would simply have to take his word that this was so. Hurley was told that when giving this message to the Generalissimo, he might emphasize the word "Russians"; that was as near as Roosevelt came to hinting of Russian plans to enter the war.

Chiang Kai-shek had not been sufficiently impressed by this hint to accept in haste the Yenan proposals. But he, as already told, had set his staff to work on a counteroffer. And he had gone ahead with his efforts to begin negotiations with the Soviet government. He had decided on Soong rather than his son for this mission to Moscow, and he had asked Stalin to receive Soong. The Soviet government had answered that it would be glad to do so—but not till the latter part of February or the first part of March.[8] Though no exact date had yet been set for the meeting of Roosevelt, Stalin, and Churchill, it was practically certain that it would be held within a few weeks. Thus it would appear that Stalin chose to postpone Soong's visit until after he had tested American and British opinion of the claims which he was going to make as payment for entering the Pacific war.

On the President's orders, Harriman had investigated these claims in a talk with Stalin on the evening of December 14th. Harriman had told Stalin that the President wanted to know more about the reference which Stalin had made in October that he thought there were political questions to be clarified before Russia entered the war against Japan. Stalin

[8] Hurley telegram to Stettinius, December 24, 1944.

proceeded to state his wishes at length and in detail. As told to Harriman, they were in summary enumeration:

1. That the Kurile Islands and Lower Sakhalin should be returned to Russia. This, Stalin said, was to make sure that Russia could protect the port of Vladivostok.

2. To lease both Port Arthur and Dairen and the surrounding area. Harriman recalled that when this subject was discussed at Teheran, the President had in mind an international free port and not a Russian lease on this area; and that the President had thought that this method, while giving the Soviet needed protection, was more in line with current concepts of how international questions of this kind could best be handled. Stalin had answered cryptically, "This can be discussed."

3. To lease the lines of the Chinese Eastern Railway from Dairen to Harbin, thence northwest to Manchouli and east to Vladivostok.

4. To recognize the status quo in Outer Mongolia, by which he meant the maintenance of the Republic of Outer Mongolia as an independent entity.

The conversation had also touched upon the situation in China. But Stalin's comments were slight and noncommittal. He made no remark at all regarding the negotiations between Chiang Kai-shek and the Communists.

Harriman concluded his detailed report of this talk to the President with an ominous statement. The Ambassador said that he believed, although he was subject to being wrong, that if there was no arrangement between the Soviet and Chinese governments before the Soviet Union entered the Pacific war, the Soviet forces would back the Chinese Communists in the North and turn over to them the administration of the Chinese territories which the Red Army would liberate; and then the Generalissimo would find himself in an increasingly difficult situation.[9]

Between these December talks and the meeting at Yalta in the following February, there seems to have been no further discussion of the Russian desires in the Pacific. In any case, it is clear that all the main subjects which were to figure in the Yalta Agreement were well in mind before Roosevelt and Stalin met.

Neither the Generalissimo nor Hurley, nor anyone in the State Department except perhaps Secretary of State Stettinius, knew that the

[9] Telegram, Harriman to President, December 15, 1944.

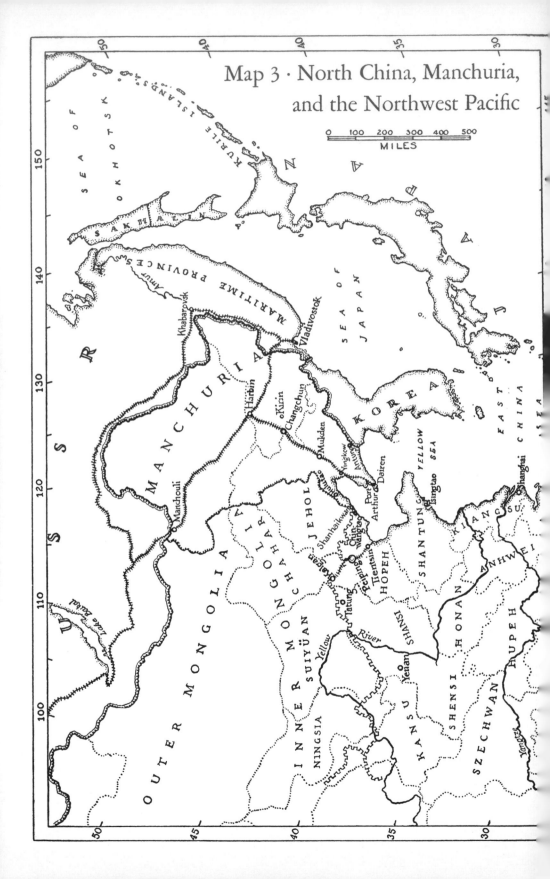

Map 3 · North China, Manchuria, and the Northwest Pacific

0   100   200   300   400   500
MILES

SEA OF OKHOTSK

KURILE ISLANDS

SAKHALIN

MARITIME PROVINCE

Amur

Khabarovsk

Vladivostok

SEA OF JAPAN

R

U

S

S

MANCHURIA

Manchouli

Harbin

Kirin

Changchun

Mukden

Antung

Yingkow

Dairen

Port Arthur

KOREA

YELLOW SEA

Tsingtao

EAST CHINA SEA

Shanghai

OUTER MONGOLIA

INNER MONGOLIA

CHAHAR

JEHOL

Shanhaikwan

Chinwangtao

Kalgan

Peiping

Tientsin

HOPEH

SHANTUNG

KIANGSU

ANHWEI

HONAN

Lake Baikal

Selenga

SUIYÜAN

Tatung

NINGSIA

Yellow River

SHANSI

Yenan

SHENSI

KANSU

SZECHWAN

HUPEH

Yangtze

President was on the verge of an agreement with Stalin about China.[10] On February 4th, the day of the first formal session at Yalta, Hurley reported again to Washington on the ideas of the Chinese government in regard to an agreement with the Soviet Union.[11] Hurley said that both the Generalissimo and Soong had told him that the Soviet government had confirmed that it would receive Soong in Moscow either during the last days of February or the first days of March.[12] Soong showed Hurley the provisional agenda which was being prepared for this visit, and Hurley repeated it with the statement that the Generalissimo said he would be glad of comment and cooperation. Continuing, Hurley recalled the comments which Molotov had made to him in the previous September about the Soviet attitude toward the Chinese Communists; and said that he and Chiang Kai-shek very much wanted to know if that attitude remained the same. During these first days of February, it should be borne in mind, Chou En-lai was back in Chungking; terms of coalition were being discussed; and the Generalissimo was wavering in regard to how far he would go.

The State Department answered Hurley's radio on February 6th. The reader—knowing what he knows but what the drafters and signers of this cable did not know—may well find some of its "tentative comments" odd. ". . . We find, and I think you will agree, while we are always anxious to be helpful to the Chinese Government, we should not allow it to get the impression that we are ready to take the responsibility as 'adviser' in its relations with the Soviet Union. As Vice President Wallace, and his statement was subsequently approved by the President, informed Chiang Kai-shek clearly last summer, the United States

[10] The State Department had been aware, however, that a meeting of Roosevelt, Churchill, and Stalin was in prospect, and had prepared various background and position papers for possible use by the President. The prevailing view is probably exemplified in an extract of a memo which one of its senior divisional officials circulated within the Department on January 8th, outlining various proposals which Roosevelt might put before Churchill and Stalin regarding the future international security organization, European and Far Eastern political questions. "We must have the support of the Soviet Union to defeat Germany. We sorely need the Soviet Union in the war against Japan when the war in Europe is over. The importance of these two things can be reckoned in terms of American lives. We must have the cooperation of the Soviet Union to organize the peace. There are certain things in connection with the foregoing proposals which are repugnant to me personally, but I am prepared to urge their adoption to obtain the cooperation of the Soviet Union in winning the war and organizing the peace."

[11] This telegram of February 4th was relayed by the State Department to Stettinius at Yalta. But apparently neither he nor the President while at Yalta sent an answer, leaving that to the State Department in Washington.

[12] But a few days later the Soviet government requested a further delay of Soong's visit until the latter part of March or early April.

could not be expected to act as 'mediator' between China and Russia."[13] As regards the Chinese agenda which Hurley had sent on, the State Department thought it best not to take the responsibility of either eliminating or sponsoring any particular item. But it questioned the advisability from the Chinese point of view of raising the question of Soviet entry into the Pacific war. Finally, it said that it had no information in regard to the Soviet attitude about the Chinese internal struggle counter to that summed up by Hurley.[14]

Hurley did not receive any further advice on this subject until after the Yalta Conference, when he returned to Washington and talked with the President. The State Department learned nothing more for some time after that.

The Joint Chiefs of Staff on January 23rd, just before the President left for Yalta, again formally recorded their views about Soviet entry into the Pacific war as follows:

"The Joint Chiefs of Staff have been guided by the following basic principles in working toward U.S.S.R. entry into the war against Japan:

"Russia's entry at as early a date as possible consistent with her ability to engage in offensive operations is necessary to provide maximum assistance to our Pacific operations. The United States will provide maximum support possible without interfering with our main effort against Japan.

"The objective of Russia's military effort against Japan in the Far East should be the defeat of the Japanese forces in Manchuria, air operations against Japan proper in collaboration with United States air forces based in eastern Siberia, and maximum interference with Japanese sea traffic between Japan and the mainland of Asia."[15]

By that time the American and British military organizations were sure that if need be they could defeat Japan without Soviet assistance. But they thought that it might well be necessary to fight two extremely hard and costly military campaigns: (1) the invasion of the Japanese home islands and (2) against the large Japanese armies on the mainland of Asia. General Marshall later recalled the line of reckoning

---

[13] This answer was drafted by Vincent (then Chief of the Division of Chinese Affairs) and Ballantine (then Director of the Office of Far Eastern Affairs), approved by Assistant Secretary of State Dunn, and signed by Acting Secretary Grew.

[14] There is no indication that this message of February 6th from Grew to Hurley was sent to Stettinius or the President at Yalta.

[15] The Joint Chiefs of Staff memo is printed in Ambassador Harriman's statement to *Joint Committee on Military Situation in the Far East*, page 3332. This statement is the most informative printed account of the military and diplomatic ideas and circumstances which influenced the negotiation of the Yalta Accord.

followed by the Chiefs of Staff: that the Japanese Kwantung army would put up a strong fight in Manchuria and probably in Korea; that it was important that the Soviets should carry out the campaign against them in both places in order that these forces could not be used to strengthen resistance against invasion; that the American troops were having a terrific fight in every island in the Pacific and having to exterminate all the Japanese defenders; that the Chiefs of Staff were then considering the landing in Japan, where there were supposed to be two and a half million Japanese troops; and that the United States seemed confronted with the necessity of landing three army corps in three different places with the anticipation of very heavy casualties.[16]

The fight which the Japanese were making to hold the Pacific islands was leaving its impression also on the American commander who was to be in charge of the invasion of the Japanese home islands, General MacArthur. As recorded by Secretary of the Navy Forrestal, who talked with him in Manila, just after his reentry into that Philippine capital, "On the . . . question of the war against Japan . . . [MacArthur] expressed the view that the help of the Chinese would be negligible. He felt that we should secure the commitment of the Russians to active and vigorous prosecution of a campaign against the Japanese in Manchukuo of such proportions as to pin down a very large part of the Japanese army. . . . He said he felt that our strength should be reserved for use in the Japanese mainland, on the plain at Tokyo, and that this could not be done without the assurance that the Japanese would be heavily engaged by the Russians in Manchuria. He expressed doubt that the use of anything less than sixty divisions by the Russians would be sufficient."[17]

There were dissenters among the American military men on this foreview of the situation. There were some senior officers, especially in the navy and air force, who were sure that the Japanese home islands could be forced to surrender by air bombardment and naval blockade; and that thereafter the Japanese armies in Asia would not long be able to sustain their resistance. But both the American and British staffs felt that it was essential to plan against the grimmest possibility. How grim they thought this might be is shown, if I may anticipate, by the agreed summary of the conclusions that they jointly reached at the Yalta Conference. They resolved (a) upon the defeat of Germany—

[16] Marshall testimony, *Joint Committee on Military Situation in the Far East*, pages 562-564.
[17] *The Forrestal Diaries*, edited by Walter Millis with the collaboration of E. S. Duffield, 1951, entry February 28, 1945.

in cooperation with the other Pacific powers and Russia—to direct the full resources of the United States and the United Kingdom to bring about the unconditional surrender of Japan at the earliest possible date; (b) this was to be done by sea and air blockade, intensive air bombardment, and "invading and seizing objectives in the industrial heart of Japan"; (c) the dates on which planning should be based were that the war against Germany would end at the earliest by July 1, 1945, and at the latest by December 31, 1945. "We·recommend," this report stated, "that the planning date for the end of the war against Japan should be set at eighteen months after the defeat of Germany." They were playing safe. They wanted to take time to prepare for an overwhelming defeat. Still, this planning schedule reveals how stubborn the military organizations of the two countries thought Japanese resistance might be.

To anticipate further, the President and the Prime Minister approved this report of the Combined Chiefs of Staff (February 9th). But Roosevelt seems to have been actively hopeful that it would not be necessary to go through with the whole program. The day before, he had said to Stalin that, "He hoped that it would not be necessary actually to invade the Japanese islands and would do so only if absolutely necessary. The Japanese had four million in their army and he hoped by intensive bombing to be able to destroy Japan and its army and thus save American lives."

Based on this scrutiny of the pertinent circumstances, surmises regarding the aims that guided the American diplomatic activity toward China at the time of the Yalta Conference may be summed up at this point. They were:

1. To help China to repossess at the end of the war, in accordance with the Cairo Declaration, all the territories which Japan had detached from it.

2. To help China gain and hold the place assigned to it in the postwar political organizations, as one of the four great powers, or "policemen," as they had been called at Teheran.

3. To bring internal peace and unity to China by peaceful means.

4. To assure Soviet entry into the Pacific war as soon as possible—while guarding against undue Soviet demands for rights or territory as a reward for doing so.

In the background was the effort which was being made, under General Wedemeyer, to prepare Chinese government forces for whatever part they could play, with limited help, in expelling the Japanese from China. Greater means for that effort would, it was anticipated, soon become available over the Hump and the Burma Road, and then be continued before the war ended through ports of the southern coast of China. In the foreground was the prospect that large Soviet armies would presently be marching into Outer and Inner Mongolia, Manchuria, and perhaps North China; that Soviet ships would be in the China seas and Soviet planes over the Japanese home islands.

This was the landscape, as far as I can reconstruct it, spread out before the President when his thoughts turned to Sino-Soviet relations on the way to the Yalta Conference. It is hard in the changed sight of elapsed time to be sure of its tones. Even as meadow and mountain look different in every passing hour of day and night, so does the land of historical decision. Bright and dark places, slopes and depressions, are apt to dance about as we voyage through time.

To try to see the prospects as they conceivably appeared to Roosevelt on his way to Yalta. Should Soviet claims in the Pacific conform to Chinese and American conceptions of what was safe and fair, there was much to be gained from an understanding with the Soviet Union. Should they turn out to be excessive, the American government would be faced with a most crucial problem of decision. It could pass them by and allow the Soviet Union and China to quarrel over them. Or, it could accede to them as less harmful than leaving the Soviet Union unbound at the end of the war. Or, it could resist them with diplomatic protests. Or, it could even contest them by military countermeasures; it could stop sending supplies for the Soviet armies in the Far East, and even try to put American forces first in the places which it did not want the Soviet Union to have. But as this story will soon tell, Roosevelt at Yalta did not feel called painfully to choose among these courses. The span of dispute was small and brief.

CHAPTER 23

The Agreement Made at Yalta: February 1945

THE President and his company set off for Yalta with a sense of excitement tempered by knowledge that many hard problems awaited them. They were used to making great decisions. But this time they were facing all the complexities of a smashed Europe. They wondered whether the understanding reached with Stalin at Teheran would turn friendlier or be lost in a battle of purposes. The experience of the year in between left doubt. The Soviet government had carried out its main military promises. But it had often been demanding, suspicious, and quick to advance grievances. Churchill's visit to Moscow in October had been useful in keeping the lines of war cooperation clear, but had settled nothing else. Every mile that the Allied armies from the west and the Soviet armies from the east traveled toward one another had made greater the need for a meeting among all three.

In the search for a mutually convenient spot to meet, American and British suggestions had ranged all the way from Northern Scotland to Jerusalem. But Stalin was not to be budged out of the Soviet Union. So the President and Churchill finally agreed to go to the Crimea, where the ruins left by the German army were to be plain to their sight. This was the limit of time and space within which the President could keep in necessary touch with the operations of the American government. A cruiser, the U.S.S. *Quincy*, brought him across the ocean to Malta. He left it there and flew on to Yalta, while the ship took station in Great Bitter Lake, near the Suez Canal. A navy communication ship, the U.S.S. *Catoctin*, was moored alongside a seawall in the harbor of Sevastopol, eighty miles away from Yalta.

Roosevelt struck many of those who saw him as looking tired, overtired, even at the end of an easy sea voyage. All photographs taken at Yalta explain this impression. Age had struck with cruel speed. But still he seemed to those about him as active-minded and eager as always to take on the work ahead. Hopkins was sick, kept alive only by great care. He stayed away from the dinners and the regular meetings and played his part, a leading part, from bed. Secretary of State Stettinius was along, wishful as always to do the right thing. No desperate doubts or stubborn opinions sent him on lonely walks or kept him awake at night. The President and Hopkins told him what they thought it was useful for him to know, and no more. They made the ultimate decisions on the disputed points which arose in his discussion with the other foreign ministers.

The mood in which the American delegation entered the conference is expressed in the words used by the President on opening the first formal meeting on February 4th: "He felt that we understood each other much better now than we had in the past and that month by month our understanding was growing."[1] The British and Soviet delegations seemed to feel the same way.

The main and most urgent business of the conference was not the Far East. The President, Churchill, and Stalin came together to discuss primarily European problems; and they devoted almost all of their time and talk to these problems. So did the military staffs of the three countries. How little attention could have been left over from these items: arrangements for the occupation and control of Germany; the future frontiers and government of Poland; the treatment of states liberated from the Nazis; the organization of a new government for Yugoslavia; and, along with these, such general questions as the form and charter of the security organization to be created in San Francisco, and plans for the future periodic meetings of the foreign ministers; as well as most extensive military plans for the further conduct of the war in Europe, the Pacific, and the Far East.

These matters took up virtually the whole attention of the formal sessions of the conference. The large assembled delegations did review military prospects and plans in the war against Japan. But they did not discuss Far Eastern political questions. These were dealt with in private talks among the three heads of state, with Molotov, Harriman, and Eden acting as aides. This arrangement suited the need for secrecy. Perhaps also there was a wish to minimize the risk of offending Chiang Kai-shek. China was not in the conference; and although Chiang Kai-shek had told the President he would be glad of help in arranging a meeting with Stalin and an agreement with the Soviet Union, he might resent it if his business were discussed in open conference in his absence. Actually, the arrangement seems to have been worked out almost entirely just between Roosevelt and Stalin; and the consultation with Churchill seems to have been incidental. Perhaps this was because of the feeling that Churchill had little interest in China and was too deeply attached to conservative notions of imperial rule. But this verges on conjecture, an attempt, which cannot be verified, to supplement records

[1] American memo of first formal conference, February 4, 1945.

[241]

which state only that the uppermost purpose was to keep dark the Soviet promise to enter the war.

Stalin had given notice that he was going to raise the question of the political conditions under which the Soviet Union would enter the Pacific war. On meeting in the harbor of Valletta (Malta) on their way to Yalta, Stettinius and Eden had touched on them passingly. Eden remarked that he thought the Russians would enter the Pacific war under their own momentum and he did not think there was any need to pay a high price for their participation. In his view, he added, if the Americans and British agreed to the claims which the Soviet government was advancing, they should ask a good return in other fields. Stettinius gave his usual affable assent.

On the afternoon of the fifth day of the conference (February 8th) Roosevelt and Stalin discussed the military outlook in the Pacific. Harriman and Molotov took part. The President was trying to hasten Russian cooperation in the establishment of American air bases in the Maritime Provinces of Siberia and along the lower reaches of the Amur River. Now Stalin once again said this would be effected, as would the other operational plans which had been discussed with Churchill in October.

Then he alluded to the Soviet claims—the political conditions of Soviet entry into the war against Japan. These he had allowed time to ripen and his armies to confirm. The President remarked that Harriman had reported to him in full. He then went on to state what he thought the Soviet Union could ask with just title. His instinct, it may be surmised, was to try by this show of free and ready assent to make it a little harder for the Russians to press for more. The President said that he saw no difficulty in regard to turning over to Russia at the end of the war the Kurile Islands and the southern half of the island of Sakhalin. In regard to the Soviet wish for a warm-water port in the Far East, the President recalled that when he had talked with Stalin at Teheran, he had suggested that the Soviet Union be given "the use of a warm-water port at the end of the Manchurian railway, possibly at Dairen, on the Kwantung Peninsula." This might be arranged, the President went on, in either one of two ways: the port might either be leased outright to the Soviet government as it was suggesting, or it might be made into a "free port" under some form of international control. Of the two, the President said, he preferred the free port arrangement. Stalin, after an interval in the talk, remarked that the Russians would not be difficult about the matter.

There was another question, Stalin said: the Soviet Union wanted the use of the railways of Manchuria. The word "use" is, I am assured, a correct translation of the word used by Stalin. The Czars, Stalin mentioned, had had the use of the line running from Manchouli, on the Siberian border, to Harbin, and then southward to Port Arthur, as well as the line running east from Harbin to connect with the line to Vladivostok. The President did not contend that the Soviet Union could get reliable "use" of these lines by some usual sort of trade and traffic agreement with China. He accepted the idea that a special arrangement was necessary to make sure that the Soviet Union would have full use of these railways. He answered that there were two possible methods of dealing with this matter also: these lines might be leased by the Soviet authorities and operated directly by them, or they might be placed under a joint Chinese-Russian commission. The question was not further pursued at this talk.

Stalin found a way of working on the American wish for Soviet entry into the war. "It was clear," he said, "that if these conditions were not met, it would be difficult for him and Molotov to explain to the Soviet people why Russia was entering the war against Japan . . . they would not understand why Russia would enter a war against a country with which they had no great trouble." The President did not comment on the unusual respect which Stalin was showing for public opinion within his country. His answer was indirect. He remarked that he had not yet discussed these matters with Chiang Kai-shek; and that it was hard to do so, since anything told the Chinese was known to the whole world in twenty-four hours. Stalin agreed, and added that he did not think it necessary to speak to the Chinese yet. Still, Stalin went on, he thought it would be well if the three powers should before leaving Yalta agree in writing on the conditions of the Soviet entry into the war. The President indicated that he thought this could be done.

He may well have believed that he would only be putting his name on a script that events had already written or would soon write. Or, more literally, that there would be no practical way of preventing the Soviet Union, once its armies were in Manchuria and its warships in the Sea of Japan, from realizing all these claims or greater ones. However that may be, by this assent he assumed responsibility for the script—chapter and verse. For doing so he has since been called into account both in the quiet aisles of history and the loud halls of partisanship. What charges of error, foolishness, even of treason, have not been made against him? It is safe to say that he perceived that he was exposing himself to such charges and took the risk—regarding it as necessary.

Roosevelt and Stalin on this same occasion discussed the internal situation in China. The President said to Stalin that for some time the United States had been trying to keep China alive. Stalin dryly replied that "China would remain alive." He added that new leaders were needed around Chiang Kai-shek, that although there were some good people in the Kuomintang they were not brought forward—for reasons he did not understand.[2] The President said that General Wedemeyer and Ambassador Hurley were having much more success than their predecessors, and were making much more progress in bringing the Communists in the North together with the Chungking government. He added that it seemed to him that the fault lay more with the Kuomintang and the Chungking government than with the so-called Communists.[3] Stalin merely said that "he did not understand why they did not get together, since they would have a united front against the Japanese. He thought for this purpose Chiang Kai-shek should assume leadership."

Quickly scanned, the record of this almost ceremonious dialogue gives the impression that each was making a show to the other of benevolent impartiality toward the internal Chinese quarrel. But it is not easy to be sure of all that either may have had in mind, or to know how this exchange of comment may have colored their valuation of the accord which they signed.

The Russians took the initiative in converting spoken assent into a written agreement. Two days after this plain talk—February 10th—Molotov gave to Harriman a memo with the heading, "Draft of Marshal Stalin's political conditions for Russia's entry in the war against Japan." This was far from plain, reading, as follows:

The leaders of the three Great Powers—the Soviet Union, the United States of America, and Great Britain—have agreed that in two or three months after Germany has surrendered and the war in Europe has ended the Soviet Union shall enter into the war against Japan on the side of the Allies on condition that:

[2] Sherwood, *Roosevelt and Hopkins*, page 868, in referring to Stalin's statement writes "He [Stalin] said there were some good men in the Comintern [sic] and he did not understand why they had not been brought forward." But it may be assumed this is an error.

[3] Here Sherwood writes, "He [the President] said that the blame for the breach lay more with the Comintern and the Kuomintang than with the rank and file of the so-called Communists." *Ibid.* This is a puzzling variation.

(1) The status quo in Outer-Mongolia (The Mongolian Peoples Republic) should be preserved;

(2) The former rights of Russia violated by the treacherous attack of Japan in 1904 should be restored viz:

(a) The southern part of Sakhalin as well as all the islands adjacent to this part of Sakhalin should be restored to the Soviet Union,

(b) Possession of Port Arthur and Dairen on lease should be restored,

(c) The rights possessed by Russia before the Russo-Japanese War to the operation of the Chinese-Eastern Railroad and the South-Manchurian Railroad providing an outlet to Dairen should be restored on the understanding that China should continue to possess full sovereignty in Manchuria;

(3) The Kurile Islands should be handed over to the Soviet Union.

The Heads of the three Great Powers have agreed that these claims of the Soviet Union should be unquestionably satisfied after Japan has been defeated.

For its part the Soviet Union expresses its willingness to conclude with the National Government of China a pact of friendship and alliance between the U.S.S.R. and China in order to render assistance to China with its armed forces for the purpose of liberating China from the Japanese yoke.

This Soviet text, it need hardly be pointed out, had some features more pleasing to Stalin than to anyone else. It covered Soviet claims with a cut-to-order mantle of historic justice. It followed the line of treatment of Manchurian ports and railways desired by the Soviet government and thus far resisted by the President. It sought to obligate the President and Prime Minister to support the Soviet claims unconditionally—no matter whether the Chinese government found them acceptable or not, and no matter how the Soviet government behaved.

Harriman said at once to Molotov that he thought the President would object to three points in the draft. He proceeded to explain the changes which he thought the President would want, to wit:

1. That Port Arthur and Dairen should be international free ports and not Soviet leaseholds.

2. That an alternative arrangement for the Manchurian railways should be specified—joint operation by a Chinese-Soviet commission.

3. That he was sure the President would not wish to dispose finally of these two matters in which China was interested without the concurrence of the Generalissimo.

Harriman reported at once to the President. Roosevelt agreed that these three features of the Soviet proposal must be corrected, and he approved the amendments for that purpose which Harriman drafted. The first two bore out what Harriman had said to Molotov. As regards the third, concerned with the provision stating that Soviet claims should be "unquestionably satisfied," a new qualifying sentence was to be inserted in the text. This was to read, "It is understood that the agreement concerning the ports and railways referred to above requires the concurrence of Generalissimo Chiang Kai-shek." Harriman was not convinced that this would take care of the matter. But the President was satisfied that it would. He regarded this provision as restricting the other, as ruling over it. Besides, he placed stress on the fact that he had often told Stalin that under the American Constitution any agreement that he entered into with foreign governments must be provisional and subject to the approval of Congress.[3a] This, it may be observed, might have been pertinent as regards the legal validity of the agreement, or perhaps even as regards his ability to carry out the agreement. But it was not conclusive in regard to the moral or personal obligation which the President assumed.

Harriman at once sent these amendments to Molotov. That same afternoon, February 10th, after the formal meeting of the conference adjourned, Stalin walked across the room to Harriman. He said that he was entirely willing to have Dairen a free port under international control. But as for Port Arthur, that was to be a Russian naval base, and therefore Russia required a lease. Harriman said that the President would have to decide the question. Stalin thereupon took it up with the President. The President agreed to Stalin's revised proposal regarding the Manchurian ports. Stalin in turn agreed that it would be more appropriate for the Manchurian railways to be operated by a Chinese-Soviet Commission. And he also agreed on the need for getting Chiang Kai-shek's concurrence in regard to the ports and railways. He added that he thought that the Generalissimo should also give his concurrence to the status quo in Outer Mongolia.

There is nothing in the available record to indicate whether or not the President and Stalin discussed what would happen if Chiang Kai-shek did not concur. Were the President and Churchill obligated to overcome any resistance the Generalissimo might make? Or would they be free of obligation—then leaving the Soviet Union free to enter the Pacific war or not as it saw best, and also leaving the Soviet Union free to deal with China as it saw fit? But these contingencies were, the whole talk suggests, thought unlikely by both Stalin and the President.

[3a] The most flat notice of the possible limit to the President's power to carry out agreements with foreign governments that I have found is in the letter Roosevelt wrote Stalin on April 1, 1945, on the Polish question: "You are, I am sure, aware that the genuine popular support in the United States is required to carry out any government policy, foreign or domestic. The American people make up their own mind and no government action can change it."

They went on to discuss how and when Chiang Kai-shek should be told of the accord. The President asked Stalin whether he himself wished to take it up with Soong when he got to Moscow, or whether he wished him, the President, to take it up with the Generalissimo. Stalin answered that as he was an interested party, he would rather have the President handle the matter. Roosevelt agreed to do so. He then asked Stalin when he thought the subject should be discussed with the Generalissimo. Stalin replied that he would let the President know when he was ready to have this done. They agreed that secrecy for the time being was advisable for military reasons; Stalin particularly wanted to have twenty-five more divisions in place in the Far East before informing Chiang Kai-shek.

At this point Churchill interrupted the discussion between Stalin and the President. But a little later Harriman asked Stalin whether he would undertake to write out the further revisions. The Marshal said he would. The text which he produced overnight, in addition to incorporating the amendments agreed upon, contained some entirely new language. This I have italicized in the text of paragraphs 2(b) and 2(c), as they came back from Stalin.

(b) the commercial port of Dairen shall be internationalized, *the preeminent interests of the Soviet Union in this port being safeguarded* and the lease of Port Arthur as a naval base of the U.S.S.R. restored,

(c) the Chinese-Eastern Railroad and the South-Manchuria Railroad which provides an outlet to Dairen shall be jointly operated by the establishment of a joint Soviet-Chinese company it being understood that *the preeminent interests of the Soviet Union shall be safeguarded* and that China shall retain full sovereignty in Manchuria.

The practical application of the phrases I have italicized was not talked out. As far as is known, Roosevelt accepted them without further discussion with Stalin. His view was that their meaning was well understood as between himself and Stalin, that the "pre-eminent" interests recognized were only towards (a) having Dairen an internationalized free port and (b) having unimpeded use of the Manchurian railways for Soviet transit traffic. His willingness to forego further argument over these or other particular phrases may have been in part due to his sense that the accord being signed was of broad political scope and that its ultimate interpretation and value would depend on the whole main set of political relations, rather than on the precise language used. This was lax treatment of matters on which for almost half a century grave quarrels had centered. It left a hazy corridor open to later dispute as to the nature or extent of the Soviet interests to be safeguarded; the dangers against which they were to be safeguarded; and as to who should be responsible for safeguarding them. Later the Soviet and American governments were to take quite different views of what was intended.

Harriman, after consulting the President, went on to find out whether the defense departments might see something wrong with the accord. He showed the text to General Marshall, and to Admirals Leahy and King, individually. He asked each to read it carefully and said he would pass on any comment to the President. None had criticisms. It may be surmised that they were pleased with its immediate military object—that the Soviet Union would enter the war at an early date—and that they did not feel called on to judge its political soundness. Their assent cannot fairly be construed as approval. But it can be taken as an indication that they were not disturbed from a military point of view, short or long gauge.

This agreement regarding the Far East, like all the others made at Yalta, was finished and signed in an urgent whirl. The last few days of the conference were extremely busy. Some of the most important European issues were still being disputed. The delicate tasks of preparing an official summary of decision and the public statement regarding the work of the conference had barely been begun. On the afternoon that the President and Stalin had their final talk about the Far Eastern accord, Roosevelt said that he would have to leave the next day at three o'clock. Churchill voiced doubt as to whether it would be possible to get the undone work finished by then. Stalin suggested that the great dinner scheduled for that evening be canceled. Instead it was agreed that the drafting committee should report to the foreign ministers and the three heads of state that night after dinner. During the dinner Stalin again said that he thought more time was needed to consider and finish the business of the conference. The President answered that he had three kings waiting for him in the Middle East, including Ibn Saud, but if necessary he would stay over another day. It was arranged that there should be a full meeting of the conference at twelve noon the next day, Sunday, and that after the meeting Stalin would lunch with the President and the Prime Minister.

The work went on through the night and the next morning. Then the various final formal papers and the communiqué were brought to the luncheon table. They were put down among the plates and the glasses. The President and Stalin signed the agreement about the terms of the Soviet entry into the war with the sense that it would serve not only their own country but the world as well. Churchill signed because he thought it necessary. Eden had tried to persuade him not to. Churchill answered that the whole position of the British Empire in the Far East might be at stake. "He was going to sign," he said, "in order that Great Britain might stay in the Far East," and added "that he had great faith in President Roosevelt and felt that he could rely completely on the President's judgment in this matter."[4]

Though it is printed in many places, readers may want the full text of the agreement, as signed, before them. It bears the somewhat vagrant title: "Agreement Regarding Japan."

The leaders of the three Great Powers—the Soviet Union, the United States of America and Great Britain—have agreed that in two or three months after Germany has surrendered and the war in Europe has terminated the Soviet Union shall enter into the war against Japan on the side of the Allies on condition that:

1. The status quo in Outer-Mongolia (The Mongolian People's Republic) shall be preserved;

2. The former rights of Russia violated by the treacherous attack of Japan in 1904 shall be restored, viz:

(a) the southern part of Sakhalin as well as all the islands adjacent to it shall be returned to the Soviet Union,

(b) the commercial port of Dairen shall be internationalized, the pre-eminent interests of the Soviet Union in this port being safeguarded and the lease of Port Arthur as a naval base of the U.S.S.R. restored,

(c) the Chinese-Eastern Railroad and the South-Manchurian Railroad which provides an outlet to Dairen shall be jointly operated by the establishment of a joint Soviet-Chinese Company it being understood that the pre-eminent interests of the Soviet Union shall be safeguarded and that China shall retain full sovereignty in Manchuria;

3. The Kurile islands shall be handed over to the Soviet Union.

It is understood, that the agreement concerning Outer-Mongolia and the ports and railroads referred to above will require concurrence of Generalissimo Chiang Kai-shek. The President will take measures in order to obtain this concurrence on advice from Marshal Stalin.

The Heads of the three Great Powers have agreed that these claims of the Soviet Union shall be unquestionably fulfilled after Japan has been defeated.

For its part the Soviet Union expresses its readiness to conclude with the National Government of China a pact of friendship and alliance between the

[4] Stettinius, *Roosevelt and the Russians*, pages 94-95.

U.S.S.R. and China in order to render assistance to China with its armed forces for the purpose of liberating China from the Japanese yoke.[5]

Roosevelt left late that afternoon, the 11th, to spend the night on board the *Catoctin* at Sevastopol. He had promised to do so; and when advised to remain at Yalta and spend the afternoon and evening resting, he said he did not want to hurt the feelings of his naval friends. According to a worried observer of the fatigue that showed through his mood of deep satisfaction (described by Sherwood as "supreme exultation") it would have been much wiser had he not gone. The eighty-mile drive from Yalta to Sevastopol over a curving mountain road was tiring, the dinner hearty, the night on board the ship breathlessly hot.[6] Suddenly General Watson fell ill. Then the next morning the President flew to Egypt to board the *Quincy*—after an unpleasant small boat ride—and to travel on for his talks with Ibn Saud, Haile Selassie, and then Farouk. Along with the other troubles between the peoples of the earth that beset him, he was inviting both the Jews and Arabs to discuss with him in close intimacy their sad, angry struggle.

The Protocol of the conference—which is the official signed summary of the discussions and decisions—did not include the understanding regarding the terms of Soviet entry into the Pacific war.[7] Nor was it mentioned in the joint communiqué published at the end of the conference.[8] Nor did the President refer to it in the report on the conference he made to a joint session of Congress after his return (March 1st). In fact, he went out of his way to give the impression that the political problems of the Pacific had not been discussed. He said—and he was formally correct—that the conference ". . . concerned itself only with the European war and with the political problems of Europe—and not with the Pacific war." But he added that at Malta the Combined American and British Chiefs of Staff had made their plans to increase the attack against Japan. No allusion was made to any arrangements for bringing the Soviet Union into the war.

This thorough secrecy served several purposes:

1. The military one. If Japan had been sure that the Soviet Union was going to enter the war, it might have closed the port of Vladivostok.

---

[5] *United States Relations with China*, pages 113-114.

[6] In the letter he dashed off to Mrs. Roosevelt on the morning of the 12th, he most exceptionally confessed to "fatigue." "We have wound up the conference—successfully, I think. . . . I am a bit exhausted but really all right."

[7] It was regarded as a separate accord, not as a part of the regular conference business. The text of the Agreement regarding Japan was made publicly known in 1946; the Protocol of the Conference was published in March 1947.

[8] Report on the Crimea Conference, released by the White House, February 12, 1945.

Certainly it would have hastened its counterpreparations to meet the Soviet attack in Manchuria and Korea. However, had these things occurred, it may be noted, the Japanese retreat from south China probably would have taken place sooner and quicker. Thus it would seem that the military advantages of secrecy redounded to the Allies fighting Germany, particularly to the Soviet Union, and not to China.

2. It postponed any possible reaction to the agreement by either the Chinese government or the Chinese Communists.

3. It averted what almost certainly would have been a very active debate within the United States about the terms of the agreement. Such a debate at that time might have impaired the unity of the Allies, not only in the Pacific but in Europe.

In the perspective of time it is clear that it would have been wiser to have given up the advantages of secrecy. Perhaps on the balance of military considerations, it would not have been sensible to have published the agreement. But such risk as would have been incurred by informing the Generalissimo at once should have been taken. Even though he was known to be eager to have the President represent his views to the Soviet government and agreeable to most of the points of this accord—as the President understood them—he had the right to know without delay what had been signed by Stalin, Roosevelt, and Churchill. It is true that later events in the Pacific war might not have gone differently. The accord between the Soviet and the Chinese governments a few months after (August) might have been the same. But the air that surrounded the Yalta Agreement then and ever since would have been clearer and healthier. The facts bearing on the making of the agreement and its terms would have been less subject to distortion. The secrecy in which the agreement was made and kept has ever since interfered with the effort to judge it in the round.

Of the great reasons and calculations which moved the President to enter into this accord there is no need again to tell. Engrossed in these, he may well have judged that certain detail of form and substance were of secondary importance. But the later flow of events in the Far East has brought out the flaws like a stone under the hammer. These also may be reckoned up by aftersight.

1. The discoloration of history now affects unpleasantly American thought. It was a mistake to allow the Soviet act of expansion to be phrased as a gesture of fair redress for past injuries.[9]

[9] A long and detailed historical essay would be needed to bring out the degree in the

2. The admission in paragraph 2(b) of the phrase "the preeminent interests of the Soviet Union in this port [Dairen] being safeguarded" opened the way for unknown future claims and troubles.

3. Similarly, the admission into the language of paragraph 2(c) having to do with the Manchurian railway, "It being understood that the preeminent interests of the Soviet Union shall be safeguarded," opened the way to Soviet claims of undefined scope in or upon Manchuria. The paragraph as written could be construed to mutilate historic American policy: the unqualified defense of Chinese territorial and administrative integrity and the principle of equal opportunity for the commerce and industry of all nations throughout the territory of China.

It is to be doubted, however, whether the language used in regard to the ports and railways had any significant effect on the later conduct of the Soviet government. Even if the troubling clauses had been omitted, the Soviet government would still have sought to extract the rights wanted in much the same way that it did. Power, not language, was its guide.

The really important faults to be found with the Yalta Agreement are of different kind:

1. It hardened the decision, proclaimed at Cairo, to reduce Japan to a dependent power in the Pacific.

2. It did not give conclusive form to one of the main, if not the main, justifying purposes of the accord—to secure Soviet cooperation with the Chinese government. The final paragraph held a promise to that effect but did not clinch it. "For its part the Soviet Union expresses its readiness to conclude with the National

---

discoloration in the introductory statement to paragraph 2 of the Yalta Accord, to wit; "The former rights of Russia violated by the treacherous attack of Japan in 1904 should be restored. . . ."

Russia had given up its claims to the Kurile Islands in 1875 in return for Japanese renunciation of claims to Sakhalin. Then in the Treaty of Portsmouth, September 5, 1905, which had ended the Russo-Japanese War, Russia had ceded the southern half of Sakhalin to Japan.

The rights to the ports and railways in Manchuria had been originally secured by force and rested on force. Japan took them over also in the Treaty of Portsmouth, acquiring leaseholds to Port Arthur and Liaotung Peninsula and railways and mining rights in south Manchuria. The American government had denied and contested the validity of these rights. So had the Chinese government in later years—as illustrated by the protest it made when in March 1935 the Soviet Union sold to Japan its share in the ownership and control of the Chinese-Eastern Railway. "While Russia may have deemed fit to surrender her own interests in the Chinese-Eastern Railway to a third party—be it real or fictitious—China can never recognize any party as a successor to any of the rights and interests of the railway. No railway can be held or operated by any persons or organizations in the territory of China without her explicit consent." *China Year Book*, 1935, page 139.

Government of China a pact of friendship and alliance between the U.S.S.R. and China in order to render assistance to China with its armed forces for the purpose of liberating China from the Japanese yoke."

This was only an avowal of readiness, not an obligation, which left the Soviet government free to bargain about both the cost and the value of its friendship. The actual words used seemed to contemplate an arrangement for the conduct of the war, which might or might not settle any issues that remained after the war. The Soviet government thus remained in effect free to determine later whether or not it would stand by the Chinese government in its internal conflict. Maybe some such inconclusive statement of attitude was all that the President could have obtained from Stalin at this time. But it proved to be not enough for the purposes which Roosevelt had in mind. Perhaps, when it was written, it was thought that before the war ended the Chinese government and the Chinese Communists would have reached an accord; that there would be a unified government speaking for the whole of China.

Or, failing that, it might have been adequate if at the end of the war the Chinese government and its armies had been more equal to their tasks. In this connection other queries arise: should we not, after signing the Yalta Accord, have provided them with greater means, either by air or over the Burma Road? Should we not have revised our military program and strategy? This much is clear: that if at the time of the Japanese surrender, the government armies had been in better shape, the Yalta Accord might have worked out as Roosevelt thought it would.

These reflections are written with the ink of the present. There are good witnesses to what Roosevelt and his associates felt about what had been done at Yalta. Ambassador Harriman, who was closely associated with the President in this matter, has written, "President Roosevelt felt that he had achieved his principal objectives. He had obtained the agreement of the Soviet Union to enter the war against Japan within three months after the defeat of Germany. . . . [He] had also obtained Stalin's pledge of support for Chiang Kai-shek, and recognition of the sovereignty of the Chinese National Government over Manchuria."[10] More than that, the President felt that a trustworthy general understanding had been reached with the Russians. As told by Hopkins to Sherwood, "We really believed in our hearts that this was the dawn of the new day we had all been praying for and talking about for so many years. . . .

[10] Harriman Statement: *Joint Committee on Military Situation in the Far East*, page 3334.

The Russians had proved that they could be reasonable and farseeing and there wasn't any doubt in the minds of the President or any of us that we could live with them and get along with them peacefully for as far into the future as any of us could imagine."[11] But dark shadows began to fall upon this belief before spring came around. Within a few months Hopkins, almost deathly sick, was to make another flight to Moscow to test whether it was still supportable.

This is indeed another day with other judgments. The Yalta Agreement has since been condemned in many moods and ways. The President's action in signing this accord has been indicted by many as having hurt China, and by the more extreme as having betrayed it. Some, with an excited lack of proportion, have named it as the cause of the downfall of the Chiang Kai-shek regime and the Communist triumph in China. The final irony which so often emerges in dramas of historical change has sounded. On January 26, 1952, T. F. Tsiang, speaking for the Nationalist Government of China, in the course of charges against the Soviet Union before the Political and Security Committee of the United Nations Assembly in Paris, said, "Although the price that China had to pay for the Soviet absence of ill will was indeed high, it was felt that the price was not without compensation. It was under such psychological conditions that my Government yielded to the pressure of the Government of the United States in accepting the substance of the Yalta agreement. Today we must pronounce the Yalta agreement a great mistake, a disastrous mistake. Without the Yalta agreement the whole history of China and Korea in the post-war period would have been different and happier."[12]

Defeat and pain smother and twist. They write harsh and poor history. But when Roosevelt accepted the role of mediator, of mutual friend between the Soviet Union and the Chinese National Government, he accepted the chance that someday such words would be spoken. They are wholly unfair to his intention. Almost as certainly, they are unfair in regard to the consequences of his actions. But whoever trusts, risks; and whoever, in his pride, makes decisions for others, exposes himself to reproach. Roosevelt did that. Perhaps, if he had not died in April two months afterwards, he could have turned the Yalta Accord into the triumph of compromise which he conceived it to be.

[11] Sherwood, *Roosevelt and Hopkins*, pages 869-870.
[12] *New York Times*, January 27, 1952.

CHAPTER 24

Differences about Policy: The Seams Traced

THE voyage home from Yalta was a sad one. Hopkins had felt forced to seek rest from work and care, and had stayed behind in the African sunlight. General Watson, the President's military aide whose hearty and good-natured strength had so often lightened the day's worries, died aboard ship on the way home. Yet as far as the country knew, Roosevelt turned to the tasks of his office with the same sense of command as ever.

A few days after his return, Hurley appeared in Washington. China still remained the most distant and troubling border of the war. Four hundred million suffering and divided Chinese were a radioactive mass which we did not know how to shape. The Ambassador hurried into talks with the State and War Departments. They were marked by animated and confusing differences. There was personal discord in the circle of American officials concerned with China, and hot-tempered dispute as to what the United States ought to be doing. Among some of the career officers in the State Department and in China there was dislike, with a tinge of contempt, for the President's personal representative and his policies. Hurley, for his part, had come to distrust these officers, thinking they were trying to defeat his efforts.

It is hard even to identify the complex and variable currents of thought in regard to our China policy which ran through the government at this time. It is harder still to give any brief account of them with assurance that it is either correct or fair. There are several reasons why this is so.

First, many individuals were—in some way or degree—at odds with Hurley. Their accounts, set forth in telegrams, letters, dispatches, and memos, were most voluminous. Some were factual and calm, others opinionated and excited. Together they made a monsoon of reports which soak the mind. Their authors did not think wholly alike. Each observed, theorized, advised on his own, and each had his own traits of thought and feeling. There was a sympathetic and mutually influencing exchange of impressions and ideas among some of them. There was much similarity in certain conclusions among those who differed from Hurley, but they were by no means all of one mind.

Second, Hurley's reports of his thoughts and actions were not as systematic as could be wished. Some went to the White House and some to the State Department. They did not narrate what happened in brief, well-arranged sequences. Hurley excused this method of reporting on the score that he did not have a qualified staff to assist him.[1] There were officers in the Embassy well trained for such work, but Hurley did not use them. He had already quarreled with them, and did not trust them; he was sure that several were keeping the Communists secretly informed.

Third, Hurley and the Foreign Service officers agreed that it was urgently desirable to end the division in China by peaceful means, by political measures. All eagerly wished first to unify all Chinese military forces, and then to reconcile the quarreling political regimes. They were alike, but not alone, in placing too high a military value on that objective. Hurley seems to have expressed the opinion of all when he advised the Secretary of State, "A unification of the military forces of the Communist Party and the National Government would have a battle effect, equal at least, to one fully equipped American army. The result of unification of the Chinese military forces is worth much more consideration than it has hitherto received from Americans."[2] But they were far apart as regards how to proceed to get unification, and most particularly how to treat, and how to treat with, the two opposed sides.

The special position of that group of Foreign Service officers with whom Hurley's relations grew most strained must be appreciated—the group attached to American military headquarters in China. Their assignment to the staff of the United States commanding general in China had been an unusual step. Stilwell's command had been farflung, extending into China, Burma, and India. It had business with all three of these peoples and governments, as well as with their military organizations. In order that Stilwell might be able to concert policy and action among the various parts of his command, it was deemed necessary for him to have his own liaison and advisory staff. They would also be able to represent him in his dealings with the various local political authorities.

The first officer designated for this work, John P. Davies, went out to China about the same time as Stilwell. He was assigned to the American Embassy at Chungking, and then detailed to the American military mission in China, which became the headquarters of the United States army forces in the China-Burma-India Theater. He was instructed to act under the orders of the commanding general. Stilwell used him in all three countries, and he had offices in both Chungking and Delhi. He

[1] Hurley, telegram to State Department, January 31, 1945.
[2] *Ibid.*

traveled freely back and forth, and made several trips to Washington. From the start his reporting aroused interest because of its search for essentials, its vividness, and its audacity. All recipients of Davies' memos read them with alert attention.

Then in August 1943 other Foreign Service officers had been sent to expand the work. There was a plan afoot in Stilwell's headquarters at the time to obtain intelligence and conduct special kinds of warfare in outlying areas. As explained to the State Department by Davies, who was then in Washington, a composite staff was being formed to direct this program, which was to be under his supervision. Various other branches of the government in Washington were providing experts for American military headquarters in the CBI Theater: the Office of Strategic Services, the Board of Economic Warfare, and the Office of War Information. These were to form boards of research and analysis at Chungking and New Delhi to report to Stilwell. Foreign Service officers were, it was thought, needed to give political direction to both the staff and such activities as might be undertaken. The plan, it may be interjected, was never realized. The representatives sent out to China by the many branches of the American government were never formed into a joint cooperative corps. They performed in six or so separate rings, until the band played "Home, Sweet Home."

Stilwell through the War Department had asked by name for four officers.[3] John K. Emmerson was wanted at Chungking as an expert on Japanese affairs. Raymond P. Ludden was to serve in Yunnan, along the borders of Burma, Thailand, and Indo-China. John S. Service was sought because of his excellent command of the Chinese language and his wide acquaintance with Chinese officials. He, it was contemplated, would spend most of his time in Chungking but would probably also be sent on special trips of investigation to the interior. Kenneth C. Krentz was to be assigned to the New Delhi headquarters.

Stilwell's request had been approved by all the officers of the State Department concerned with China. But Gauss, who was then in a hospital in California, was not consulted. Three of the four additional Foreign Service men had been sent on their way quickly; Krentz was not sent. Stilwell gave them the same freedom of movement and expression which he himself enjoyed, and did not worry over the tangles into which they might get. They were absorbed in their job, had fast and bright

[3] War Department memo to Secretary of State, June 29, 1943, in *State Department Employee Loyalty Investigation*, pages 1994-1995.

pens, and were deeply devoted to the welfare of the people with whom they mingled.

It soon came about that their far-ranging reports to Washington aroused more interest than those which came in from the Embassy at Chungking. While Gauss was Ambassador, he did not mind that fact. After a run-in with Davies over the question of who was to advise Washington on political policy, he restricted their access to the files of Embassy business. He neither assumed responsibility for them nor tried to control them. He sent on many of their reports to the State Department, usually with brief, neutral or sympathetic comment. In the main he thought the group was doing sound and significant work and that their opinions had the right inclination. But Hurley became speedily disturbed at their activities. He soon differed with some of their impressions and opinions and resented their independence.

The papers written by this group of officers had unusually diverse range for their kind. The regular official circulation was in itself wide. Copies were sent to the commanding general's headquarters in China, to the American Embassy at Chungking, and to Davies' headquarters in New Delhi. In each of these places they were well read, circulated, and passed on. American military headquarters sent them on to the War Department. The Embassy at Chungking sent them on to the State Department, where, either in full or in summary, they had an assortment of readers. A few—thought to be novel or important—were sent directly by letter or messenger to Harry Hopkins in the White House, who now and again drew the President's attention to one.[4] Nor was this the whole range of official distribution. Extracts were transmitted to American diplomatic missions in other countries. Selected reports, in whole or part, were sent by the State Department to the Treasury, Office of War Information, and Office of Strategic Services. In sum, the written work of this group of advisers was widely read within the authorized circle which was a loosely formed one. When they were in the United States—particularly Davies and Service—there were many in and out of the government who wanted to hear what they had to say.[5]

[4] For example, on September 6, 1944, Hopkins passed on to the President a copy of Service's report No. 1 of July 28, 1944. Subject: First Informal Impression of the North Shensi Communist Base, with the comment that "Here is Mr. Jack Service's preliminary report on the Communist situation in North China. Service is a member of the State Department staff. He certainly makes some arresting observations."

[5] Service, in his testimony, *State Department Employee Loyalty Investigation*, pages 1971-1972, tells in detail of his many meetings and contacts inside and outside the government, observing that, "I was spending full time being available to officials and others who had a responsible interest in China and wanted recent background, particu-

I know of no way of judging how much influence the reports and advice of this group had on American policy, as traced in this narrative. Stilwell was a set and sheathed man on whom, in the words of one of his closest subordinates at this time ". . . when [he] made up his mind no one had a marked influence . . ."[6] Wedemeyer found the information they provided "helpful and constructive" in some regards, but unbalanced in others.[7] After getting caught in one mix-up with Hurley about arming the Communists, he seems to have become leery of listening to any political comment. Hopkins was receptive, as he was to other bright and closely informed reporters of the China scene. Their influence was probably greatest in the State Department, where their studious and earnest zeal was most at home. To venture a risky surmise, it seems to me probable that their analysis of the defects of the Kuomintang government was more convincing and persuasive than their interpretations of the regime at Yenan. The main effect of their reporting was, to continue the surmise, to weaken faith in the power of the Generalissimo and his group to govern China.

Some time or other, this loosely controlled and more or less competing channel of advice was certain to be upsetting to any chief of mission. This would have been true even if all members of the group had been discreet and modest in advancing their opinions, and they were not; even if their views were usually in harmony with those of the Chief, and they were not. The man responsible for the outcome of any tough and delicate diplomatic task is almost sure to feel entitled to be able to control all reporting that bears on his mission. In other words, Hurley's grievance against the set-up was legitimate—irrespective of the individuals and their opinions.

It is the duty as well as the pride of our diplomatic staff in the field to record their observations and judgments fully and frankly, even when they are critical of current official policy. Those who refrain are not doing the whole of their job. But experience indicates that there is only one way this can be done without serious risk of trouble; that is, to and through the chief of mission, relying on him to see that the policy-makers in Washington are informed. A good chief of mission will not

---

larly on the Communists. My superiors knew that I was expressing my own personal opinions freely and apparently considered that I had sufficient judgment and discretion."

They were mistaken. Service's zeal led him into the *Amerasia* circle, to whom he gave confidential information, oral and written, imprudently and beyond the bounds of usual exchanges even with tested and trusted newspapermen.

[6] Testimony of Colonel Frank A. Dorn. *Ibid.*, page 2166.

[7] General Wedemeyer reviewed his relations with this group in a letter printed in *Hearings, Institute of Pacific Relations*, pages 2534-2536.

repress such activity. He will appreciate the value of having his attention called to facts and conclusions that differ from his own. He will consider them with care and when they seem of merit consult with Washington about them. But his must remain the ultimate power to decide how the flow of information and advice from his post is to be conducted, and how far contradiction is to be allowed.

There are ways within a congenial diplomatic family to manage such matters—by trust, mutual consideration, skill in drafting, and good temper. In China these ways were not well used. Even if they had been they might have failed; for by the time Hurley took over, the opinions of the Foreign Service officers may have been too wilfully set for any amiable adjustment.[8]

The main seams of the terrain of difference between Hurley and the Foreign Service officers can be briefly traced.

1. Hurley was disposed to take a friendly and favorable view of the plight and intentions of the Chinese government. In his opinion it merited support and help. If aided, he thought that it would in time correct its faults and failures. He felt esteem for Generalissimo Chiang Kai-shek, and he found the company and ways of the members of the government agreeable. In contrast, many of the Foreign Service officers, moved by the misery, privilege, and corruption they observed, were repelled. They formed an aversion to Chiang Kai-shek and for those with whom he worked. They concluded that this group, left to themselves, would never give the Chinese people a decent government. This feeling colored their views of official action. It caused those who visited Yenan to be impressionable; they were longing to find a healthy contrast and thought that they found it among the leaders and followers of the Communist movement.

2. Hurley thought, and Wedemeyer gradually came to agree, that,

---

[8] This group of advisers to the commanding general was only one of several American official groups in China whose reports and letters were not subject to the Ambassador's supervision. The Treasury, the Office of War Information, the Office of Strategic Services, and other branches of the government had representatives in China who also carried on communication with Washington. Of these, the Treasury attaché, Solomon Adler, seems to have been both the most zealous and the most unfriendly to Hurley. By letters sent to the Assistant Secretary of the Treasury, Harry D. White, he kept up a scathing flow of comment as regards Hurley, Chiang Kai-shek, and other members of the Kuomintang government. His scent for troubling news or gossip was strong and his taste for communicating it was well formed.

Hurley tried to coordinate the activities of all these groups with each other and with the civilian and military staff of the Embassy by calling them together frequently and explaining American policy to them. But the effort was not markedly effective.

everything considered, the government was making a fair effort to fight the Japanese, and wanted to do more. The critics thought the government forces had virtually stopped fighting, that they were waiting for us to win the war, meanwhile hoarding their reserves to fight the Communists. In reverse, Hurley thought that the Communists were doing little since their forces never engaged large bodies of Japanese troops. The critics consistently lauded the guerrilla warfare conducted by the Communists.

3. Curiously enough, there was no vigorous clash of impressions between Hurley and the Foreign Service officers as to the nature and aims of the Communist movement in China. Hurley remained of the opinion that the Chinese Communists were not really Communists, were not deeply devoted to the principles of Communism. During and after his visit to Yenan he was impressed by the Communist verbal endorsement of Lincolnian mottos and principles of government, and was often heard to say that the Chinese Communists in the main spoke the same political language as Americans.[9]

Some of the critics, especially Service, agreed with this characterization of the nature and aims of the Chinese Communist movement.[10] Others

[9] As for example in a press and radio conference in Washington on April 2nd before leaving to return to China, he said, "You gentlemen should know this though—I believe you all do know, that it is a matter of common knowledge that the Communist Party of China supports the principles of Dr. Sun Yat-sen. That was generally referred to as the Peoples Three Principles of China. . . . The three principles are government of the people, by the people and for the people. All the demands that the Communist party has been making have been on a democratic basis. . . ." A transcript of parts of this interview is published in the *Joint Committee on Military Situation in the Far East*, page 2896.

His interpretation of the "Three Principles of the People" formulated by Sun Yat-Sen and known as San Min Chu I was rough and elliptic. A good brief summary of the essentials of these is given in *United States Relations with China*, page 39, as follows: (1) "people's nationalism," under which China was to regain its national integrity and full freedom from foreign control, (2) "people's democracy," under which the people would exercise the four political powers (suffrage, recall, initiative, and referendum) by which they control the government, and (3) "people's livelihood," a form of socialism involving equalization of land ownership, regulation of capital, and avoidance of the class struggle.

Hurley testified that he was influenced in making these comments in part by his observations in Soviet Russia and China and in part by the President's admonition to say anything favorable he could about the Communists, so as to maintain a basis for unification. Hurley testimony, *Joint Committee on Military Situation in the Far East*, page 2906.

[10] As summed up by Service in a talk with a group of government officials while in Washington in December 1944: the Communist leaders believed that their principles of democratic organization and operation of industry could be applied with success throughout China. They were convinced that China needed foreign investment and seemed willing to accept the principles of private property not only for the foreigner, but for the Chinese as well; they see no way forward except by means of the moderate development

took a more worldly view of Communist democratic professions, as expressed in the first paragraph of a memo written by Davies on November 7th, "The Chinese Communists are back-sliders. They still proclaim the infallibility of Marxian dogma and call themselves Communists, but they have become indulgent of human frailty and confess that China's Communist salvation can be attained only through prolonged evolutionary rather than immediate revolutionary conversion. . . . They have come to accept the inevitability of gradualness."[11]

Neither Hurley nor the Foreign Service officers at this time thought that the Chinese Communists were inseparably welded or even closely allied to Moscow.[12] But they differed in the practical conclusions they

---

of relatively small privately owned industries; and although in the areas that they dominate, they have reduced interest rates and rents, they have helped to assure the money-lenders and the landlords of the regular receipt of the income; in sum that the Communist activities were much closer to a government of, for, and by the people than has ever existed in any part of China. Memo, C. F. Remer, December 11, 1944.

[11] Davies' memo, November 7, 1944. Subject: How Red Are the Chinese Communists? *State Department Employee Loyalty Investigation*, pages 1435-1436.

[12] Hurley's view, of which he thought for a time he had convinced Chiang Kai-shek, was that (1) the Soviet government did not recognize the Chinese Communists as real Communists and (2) was not supporting them. In other words he thought they had no foreign entanglement.

The Foreign Service officers knew there had once been a close kinship and connection, but most of them seemed to think that the connection no longer amounted to much and would not prevent friendly cooperation with the United States. The most unguarded expression of this opinion that I have come across is in the first sentence of the summary of a memo which Service had written on September 28th, title: The Orientation of the Chinese Communists Towards the Soviet Union and the United States. "Politically, any orientation which the Chinese Communists may once have had toward the Soviet Union seems a thing of the past." *State Department Employee Loyalty Investigation*, page 1363.

Mao Tze Tung does not ever appear to have in any official utterance changed the attitudes summed up in the pamphlet he wrote in 1941, entitled "The New Democracy." His views, which appeared in early 1940, were a deliberate attempt to unify the thinking of the members of the Communist Party and to make definite the party's doctrines which had been somewhat confused during the period of participation in the united front with other Chinese political parties. It is regarded by students as an attempt to make a genuinely new contribution to Marxist-Leninist theory; to provide a particular theoretical analysis of the Chinese situation in the light of its "historical peculiarities." The statement formulated the position of the party in terms of minimum and maximum aims. Pertinent extracts touching on the relations with the Soviet Union were: "First, the revolutionary, or new, genuine Three People's Principles must be for alliance with the Soviet Union. The facts of today are extraordinarily clear. If there is not a policy of alliance with Russia, of co-operation with the socialist state, then there must be a policy of alliance with imperialism, of co-operation with imperialism. Did not this sort of thing happen after 1927? . . ." and "Secondly, the revolutionary, new or genuine Three People's Principles must be for alliance with the Communists. . . ."

These are taken from page 270 of *A Documentary History of Chinese Communism*, by Conrad Brandt, Benjamin Schwartz, and John K. Fairbank.

The American career officers in China seem to have been more impressed by the statement of immediate rather than by that of ultimate aims. Perhaps this was in part because in his talk with Americans in Yenan, Mao Tze Tung spoke often as though he thought friendship with the United States possible, and solicited American help.

drew from this shared impression. Hurley took it to mean that if the American government, while keeping in friendly touch with the Chinese Communists, refused to aid them in any way as long as they were in rebellion, they would yield to a recreated National Government. Or, in other words, he thought that if they were left by us to fight their own battle, they would presently choose to accept the best of a hard bargain. In contrast, the Foreign Service officers took it to mean that if shown friendship by us, the Communists would align their actions to the policies of the West; or if they failed to do so and broke with the United States, they would lose the support of Chinese democratic public opinion. While, their forecast continued, if we turned our back on them and our arms against them, they would go over to Moscow; and with or without Soviet aid might well come into power in China. This line of reasoning was substantially the same as that which Churchill, and his lieutenant in Yugoslavia, MacLean, were following in their dealings with Tito.

4. This divergence reflected different estimates of the strength and vitality of the Communist movement among the Chinese people. Hurley did not think it had great or lasting support. Several of the Foreign Service officers were thoroughly convinced that it had. The reasons Davies dramatically summed up:

"The Chinese Communists are so strong between the Great Wall and the Yangtze that they can now look forward to the post-war control of at least North China. They may also continue to hold not only those parts of the Yangtze Valley they now dominate but also new areas in Central and South China. . . .

"The Communists have survived ten years of civil war and seven years of Japanese offensives. They have survived not only more sustained enemy pressure than the Chinese Central Government forces have been subjected to, but also a severe blockade imposed by Chiang.

"They have survived and they have grown. Communist growth since 1937 has been almost geometric in progression. From control of some 100,000 square kilometres with a population of a million and a half they have expanded to about 850,000 square kilometres with a population of approximately ninety million. And they will continue to grow.

"The reason for this phenomenal vitality and strength is simple and fundamental. It is mass support, mass participation. The Communist governments and armies . . . have this support because the governments and armies are genuinely of the people."[13]

[13] This is an extract from a memo of Davies entitled: Will the Communists Take China? dated November 7, 1944. *United States Relations with China*, page 566.

The Foreign Service officers were impressed by the fact that to the ordinary people of China the regime promised or practiced by the Communists seemed progressive, compared with the poverty and compulsions under which they lived; that the Communists seemed to them to be conferring benefits which the Chinese government was failing to bring, and which American ideas could not, at any rate quickly, achieve in these regions. Some of the military men in China were similarly impressed by the popular appeal of the Communist program and by its growing strength. They also thought the Communist army might well prove the stronger of the two.[14]

5. Still another cause of difference concerned the need for improvement in government administration and policies. Both favored and urged reform. But Hurley, impressed by the obstacles which made it hard for the Generalissimo to take unusual measures, was not downcast by the signs of lethargy. The others were convinced that only thorough and rapid reform could save the government. To arrest the transfer of support to the Communists, they thought it essential that no matter what the opposition, the government should at once enforce great changes in farm ownership, rents, taxes, food distribution, and methods of conscription. In their view real reform could not wait on peace and unification, while Hurley accepted the conclusion that it must.

[14] As affirmed by Hurley in his telegram to the Secretary of State, January 31, 1945, "There was honest opposition among some of our own military on the ground that the Communist Armed Party is stronger than the National army. . . ."

The Military Intelligence Division of the War Department in the special study which it submitted on July 5, 1945, entitled, "Report on the Chinese Communist Movement," concluded, "The consensus of opinion of U.S. observers is that the Chinese Communist Regular Army is a young, well fed, well clothed, battle-hardened volunteer force in excellent physical condition, with a high level of general intelligence, and very high morale. Training of these troops may be rated as fair for their present capabilities even though it is woefully inadequate judged by American standards. Military intelligence, for their purposes, is good. The most serious lack of the Communist forces is in equipment.

"The outstanding weaknesses of the Communist forces include lack of sufficient small arms ammunition, lack of artillery, lack of engineers and other technical personnel, lack of signal equipment in general and especially of radio communication below regiment level, complicated and irregular organization, and heavy casualties among officers with consequent weakness in junior leadership." Hearings: *Institute of Pacific Relations*, page 2446.

CHAPTER 25

The Focal Issue Argued: Should the United States Enlist the Chinese Communists?

ALL these seams of differences converged on the issue as to whether the American government should cooperate with the Communists in any way while they remained in rebellion against the Chinese government. This question presented itself during the winter of 1944-1945 in various forms.

The one episode which had open political significance was disposed of without dispute. Just before Hurley left for the United States, announcement was made of a conference to be held at San Francisco to write the charter for the future United Nations organization. Chou En-lai at once wrote Hurley, claiming that the Chinese Communists ought to be invited. He argued that a delegation appointed by the government would not represent either the Chinese in the Communist areas or the will of the broad masses of the Chinese people outside these areas. Hurley answered that the Generalissimo had been recognized as the representative of China at the conference and would select the delegation; and explained that the Communist Party was only one of the political parties of China, different from the rest only because it was armed, and if the conference recognized any armed political party in China other than the National Government, it would destroy the possibilities of the unification of China.[1]

After his arrival in Washington, Hurley received another argumentative message on the subject from Chou En-lai. He suggested to the President that it might be possible to use the situation as a way of fostering Chinese unity. He thought it would be of advantage if some representatives of the Chinese Communists and other Chinese political parties were included in the Chinese delegation. Stettinius agreed and the President made a recommendation to this effect to the Generalissimo on March 15th. Chiang Kai-shek answered that he was glad of the suggestion and that he would include in the Chinese delegation of ten, one member each of the Communist Party and of two other opposing parties, and three distinguished leaders without political connection. The Chinese delegation to the San Francisco Conference was com-

---

[1] Chou En-lai's letter to Hurley of February 18th and Hurley's answer of February 20th are printed in *United States Relations with China*, pages 576-577.

posed in this way and made a favorable impression. In the conference it served harmoniously under the general direction of the National Government and the chairmanship of Soong. But the Communists were not impressed or made more reasonable by this gesture. They used their stay in the United States to expound their cause. Various junior members of the American delegation and of the State Department talked with them about the situation in China, but no attempt was made to start negotiations.

But the argument as to whether we should provide the Communist forces with equipment and establish direct military contact with them was not so smoothly settled. Stilwell had favored such action. Various American officials in China—military and civilian—had continued to do so since his departure in October. Toward all suggestions to that effect Hurley maintained the position stated in his telegram of January 31st to the Secretary of State, "In all my negotiations with the Communists, I have insisted that the United States will not supply or otherwise aid the Chinese Communists as a political party or as an insurrection against the National Government. Any aid to the Communist Party from the United States must go to that Party through the National Government of China." Wedemeyer briefly strove to maintain a neutral position, but presently fell in line with Hurley. As he explained at a press conference in Chungking on February 15th, after expressing the wish to avoid involvement in Chinese politics, "I would like to let you all know my feeling. It is quite strong on the subject of political matters here. I have required every officer to sign that he understands my policy with reference to the China theatre. Every American officer is required to sign this indication that he has read and understands it. My policy is this, that we will not give assistance to any individual, to any activity or any organization within the China Theatre, we American officers, we American military people. . . . Obviously we get requests from time to time for assistance from various sources but I am ordered to support the Central Government and I am going to do that to the best of my ability. The Central Government is recognized by my Government. . . . I add just this one thought—I hope with all my heart that the Chinese get together and resolve their differences before the war is over. . . . I hope that they will, because it will strengthen the military effort considerably. . . ."[2]

[2] Telegram from American Embassy, Chungking, February 18, 1945. Hurley on the 17th in the last paragraph of a cable commenting on Chu Teh's direct request to Wede-

But various Foreign Service officers—some on Wedemeyer's staff and some in the Embassy—maintained their dissent. They urged in substance that the American government should (a) cooperate with the Communists in the war against Japan with or without Chiang Kai-shek's consent, (b) equip the Chinese Communists to the extent necessary to make that cooperation effective, (c) use these measures to induce or compel the Chinese government to come to terms with the Communists so that there could be some kind of unification. As summarized by Service in later testimony about this clash of opinion, "At the first we all agreed that [persuasion] had to be tried, but eventually as the negotiations had gone on for some time with no success ... some of us believed that we had to take more direct action and in effect tell Chiang Kai-shek instead of asking him. ... Basically the point at issue was the use of the Communist armies ... I always argued that you can't stop aid to an ally in the middle of a war, so that the only way we could attack the question of the use of the Communist armies if Generalissimo Chiang wouldn't agree was to simply tell the Generalissimo, as we did in the case of Yugoslavia, we are going to arm any forces that are in a position to actively engage and resist the Japanese."[3]

The arguments advanced in favor of that course branched into both military and political considerations. The military reasons, cited in various dispatches, were definite: that the Communist position extended into the geographic center of the inner zone occupied by the Japanese, and therefore we could use it well as a base for American paratroop operations; that if we provided the Communists with minor supplies they could do great damage with their skilled methods of penetration; and finally that in the event of an American landing on the China coast the Communist forces could join the attack and make it less costly.

But what of the political import of any attempt to secure these supposed military advantages? On this Hurley and the critics, each of them pursuing the lines of reasoning already denoted, fell far apart.

---

meyer for a twenty-million-dollar loan remarked (in paraphrase) "I am working in closest cooperation with Wedemeyer in this matter. His officers have been finally ordered by him to refrain from any part in discussion of political matters at least until the quarrel between the Government and Communists has been settled."

[3] Service testimony, *State Department Employee Loyalty Investigation*, page 1991. Or, as expressed in a memo which Davies gave Wedemeyer and Hurley, and sent by letter to Hopkins on December 13, 1944, "It is time we unequivocally told Chiang Kai-shek that we will work with, and within our discretion, supply whatever Chinese forces we believe can contribute most to the war against Japan. We should tell him that we will not work with or supply any Chinese unit, whether Central Government, Provincial or Communist, which shows any inclination toward precipitating civil conflict. We should tell him that we propose to keep him, as head of the recognized government, informed of what supplies we give the various Chinese forces."

A few days after Hurley and Wedemeyer got to Washington, a group in the Embassy at Chungking sent a telegram which brought the whole dispute sharply to the fore. It was a bid more challenging than any previous one for a new decision. Experienced officials would know that it might cause the Ambassador to have to justify his policies. Some career diplomats might have taken the incident as a matter of course. But Hurley thought it was an attempt to put him "on the spot."

The stimulus for this particular message seems to have been the return of one of the political officers on Wedemeyer's staff, Ludden, from an arduous trip in Communist territory and behind Japanese lines. In his report on this trip (telegraphed to Chungking on December 4th and sent by airgram to the State Department from Chungking on December 13th), he said among other things, ". . . In North China the Communists occupy positions from which, with modest supplies of small arms, ammunition and demolition material, they could seriously interfere with Japanese communications." The report further observed that the war planning of the Communists was concentrated on offensive action against the Japanese then judged possible, since they considered such action the best means of presenting the Communist case before China and world opinion. Other members of Wedemeyer's staff and of the Embassy had talked the report over with Ludden. Service and Ludden, on February 17th, prepared a memorandum which became the basis for a telegram. A sense prevailed among them that Hurley's reporting of the negotiations between the government and the Communists had been "incomplete and non-objective." George Atcheson, who was in charge of the Embassy during Hurley's absence, suggested the preparation of a telegram summarizing the situation as viewed by the sponsoring group and making recommendations to overcome the impasse.[4]

Few would care now to follow the full course of the reasoning in this message or find it novel. In most condensed form, its substance was: that American support was making Chiang Kai-shek unwilling to compromise, oversure; that the Communists were increasing their strength and preparing to face us with the dilemma of accepting or refusing their help when we landed in China; that they were talking of seeking Soviet support; and that if the situation was allowed to drift civil war was probable. Thus—assuming that the American military authorities agreed that it was desirable or necessary to cooperate with the Communists—

---

[4] Service's testimony, *State Department Employee Loyalty Investigation*, page 1974. Signed by Atcheson, it stated that the telegram had been drafted with the agreement and assistance of all the political officers of the staff of the Embassy and was endorsed by General Gross, Wedemeyer's Chief of Staff, then in acting command.

it was proposed that the President should ". . . inform Chiang Kai-shek in definite terms that we are required by military necessity to cooperate with and supply the Communists and other suitable groups who can aid in this war against the Japanese, and that to accomplish this end we are taking direct steps. . . ." But Chiang Kai-shek, the stream of advice went on, can be assured "that we do not contemplate reduction of our assistance to the Central Government. . . . We may include a statement that we will furnish the Central Government with information as to the type and extent of such assistance [.to other groups]. In addition we can inform Chiang Kai-shek that it will be possible to use our cooperation and supplies as a lever to restrict them to their present areas and to limit aggressive and independent action on their part. Also we can indicate the advantages of having the Communists assisted by the United States instead of seeking direct or indirect help or intervention from the Soviet Union."

At the same time that we confronted Chiang Kai-shek with this firm statement of what we proposed to do, the authors of this recommended policy thought we would be well advised to assure him that we still favored Chinese unity and coordination of military command. Thus we would be willing to lend our good offices in support of the creation of a war cabinet or supreme war council in which the Communists and other groups would be effectively represented. Also the proponents felt that the Communists and other selected forces should be incorporated into the armies of the Central Government, ". . . under the operational command of United States officers designated by Chiang Kai-shek upon General Wedemeyer's advice, upon agreement by all parties that these forces would operate within their existing' area or areas which have been specifically extended."[5] The American decision to cooperate with any forces able to assist the war effort was not, however, to wait upon or be contingent upon the completion of such internal Chinese arrangement. On this point, it may not be necessary to recall, Hurley strongly held the opposite position.

All this was to be told the Generalissimo in private. But, the proposal in this telegram wound up, he ought to be made clearly to understand that if he refused assent the American government might take the much more drastic step of a public expression of policy such as that made by Churchill with reference to Yugoslavia. Even if not made public, it was

[5] This is similar to a suggestion in the proposal made by Chiang Kai-shek to the Communists on January 24th, but it does not explicitly state, as had Chiang Kai-shek, that the American commander was to see to it that the Communists would obey government orders.

observed, our action would soon become known through China; and it would stir up the tremendous internal pressure that existed in China for unity based upon compromise with the Communists, and a chance for self-expression for the repressed liberal groups. In sum, the authors submitted that such a policy would: secure the cooperation of all Chinese in the war; hold the Communists on our side instead of throwing them into the arms of the Soviet Union; convince the Kuomintang that its apparent plans for eventual civil war were undesirable; and advance the cause of unification within China.[6]

Considering time and the down-drain of the vitality of the Chinese government, these proposals were in order as a needed fresh attempt to manage the situation before the war ended. But on vital points they were obscure. Would the Generalissimo retain ultimate authority in the proposed war council? How could it be assured that the Communists would use the arms to be supplied them against the Japanese? If the Communists were thus treated as partners in the war, would they have to be similarly regarded in the making of the peace?

The proposals were also predictive, as any and all policies toward China at this juncture had to be. But what if the assumptions turned out to be wrong? Suppose the shock to Chiang Kai-shek's prestige and position were so strong that his supporters left him, that armies in the field deserted him. Or suppose the Communists equipped by us, with their skilled tactics of expansion and penetration, found ways around the written word and took over new areas? As regards these real possibilities, the message was silent. Perhaps because they were regarded merely as risks that had to be taken. Perhaps because it was thought that if no measures such as those proposed were tried, the struggle would go against the government anyhow, as a result of popular will. Or perhaps also because of the opinion which Service had bluntly ventured in an earlier (October 10th) memo to Stilwell: "Our dealings with Chiang Kai-shek apparently continue on the basis of the unrealistic assumption that he is China and that he is necessary to our cause. It is time for the sake of the war and also for our future interests in China that we take a more realistic line. ... With the glaring exposure of the Kuomintang's failure, dissatisfaction within China is growing rapidly. The prestige of the party was never lower, and Chiang is losing the respect he once enjoyed as a

[6] A paraphrase of the text of this cable is printed in *United States Relations with China*, pages 87-92.

leader. In the present circumstances, the Kuomintang is dependent on American support for survival. But we are in no way dependent on the Kuomintang." . . . [Hence] "we need not fear the collapse of the Kuomintang Government" . . . [and] "Finally we need feel no ties of gratitude to Chiang."[7]

Acting Secretary Joseph Grew sent a copy of the message of February 28th from Chungking to the White House on March 2nd with an accompanying note that should have given it favorable entry. He said that the telegram presented very clearly the dangers of a failure of the Kuomintang and the Communists to get together; that the State Department had been becoming more worried by recent signs that Chiang Kai-shek was being intractable; and that developments indicated the need for "flexibility" in applying American policy toward China, which presumably meant that we should avoid exclusive or rigid liaison with any party. At the end Grew's note remarked that the expected presence of both Hurley and Wedemeyer in Washington would provide a good chance to review the whole situation, and in particular the recommendations made by the Embassy in Chungking.

Hurley had it out with the staff of the Far Eastern Office of the State Department on March 5th. In his sense of the occasion, he was "put on the carpet in the State Department."[8] He was not a person who would ordinarily let others force him into a posture of defense. In summary, Hurley's attitude was: that the sending of this telegram was an act of disloyalty by his staff toward him; that it reopened questions which he thought had already been decided, compelling him to fight out all over again the issue of recognizing the Communists as armed belligerents.

[7] Extract from Service memo, October 10, 1944: Subject: The Need for Greater Realism in Our Relations with Chiang Kai-shek. In *State Department Employee Loyalty Investigation*, pages 1987-1990. Of all Service's reports this one seems to have upset Hurley most. He construed it to be ". . . a general statement of how to let the Government that I was sent out there to sustain, fall. . . ." Hurley testimony, *Senate Foreign Relations Committee*, December 1945.

[8] In the press release made by Hurley on August 7, 1949, following on the publication of the volume entitled *United States Relations with China*, which was generally called the China White Paper (cited herein under its real title), he expressed his feeling more forcibly and accusingly ". . . I was called on the carpet with a full array of the pro-Communists in the State Department as my judges and questioners to defend the American policy in China against every official of the American Embassy in China." *Joint Committee on Military Situation in the Far East*, page 3256.

A memo was written of the talk between Hurley and the State Department officials on March 5th but I have not been able to locate it. But Ballantine on March 6th wrote another memo of a long telephone talk with Hurley on that day in which he records that Hurley went over much the same ground as on the day before.

The State Department officials denied any tinge of disloyalty; and they argued that the gravity of the situation made it not only proper but imperative to reexamine every element of American policy and consider every possibility. They looked at the situation in much the same way as their colleagues in Chungking—though not sure whether it was feasible to make military connection with the Communists unless and until the Americans landed in China.[9]

Hurley went on to talk out these issues with Stettinius, Marshall, Stimson, and the President. While he was doing so, Vincent called on Wedemeyer and tried to quiz him about the military importance of arming and using the Communists. Wedemeyer's answer, while not conclusive, leaned away from the idea. Possibly he did not feel free to tell Vincent that plans for major landings on the China coast had been filed. He said that his information was not firm enough to warrant an opinion as to whether or not the Communist guerrillas could really prove useful, but that he was against building up the Communist forces. He indicated a belief that no matter what arrangement was made, Soviet Russia would, when it could, aid the Chinese Communists. The record of this talk indicates that neither Wedemeyer nor Vincent had any knowledge of the agreement that had been signed at Yalta some four weeks ago.[10]

In the upshot the President upheld Hurley. It was again decided that we would not help the Communists unless and until Chiang Kai-shek consented. We would sustain and work with the National Government and pivot our plans around it while striving to change it for the better. There are few harder stunts of statesmanship than at one and the same time to sustain a foreign government and to alter it against its fears and inclinations.

As a consequence of this clash—of which the telegram that has just been reviewed was only one major incident—several members of the Embassy in Chungking to whom Hurley objected were transferred and

[9] Their views were clearly shown by the memos they wrote during this period. For example (1) memo January 29th by Vincent, prepared for the use of the Acting Secretary of State in answering inquiries of the Secretaries of War and Navy, (2) memo, Vincent on March 1, 1945, title: The Situation in China, and (3) memo of March 2nd by Drumright, Stanton, and Vincent called American Policy with Respect to China.

At the end of his March 1st memo Vincent added, "Since preparing the foregoing I have read Atcheson's telegram of February 28th and feel it should receive the most serious consideration." In the chit by which Ballantine forwarded these memos to Under-Secretary Grew he observed, "You will of course wish to consider in this connection the contents of Mr. Atcheson's telegram of February 28th. . . ."

[10] Vincent memo, talk with Wedemeyer, March 12, 1945.

the corps of political officers assigned to the commanding general in China was disbanded. The senior member, Davies, was already out of China. Service, Hurley found out while he was in Washington, was in Yenan again on another mission; Hurley protested and Service was brought back to Washington.[11] The other Foreign Service officers on Wedemeyer's staff were shortly thereafter assigned to other jobs. From then on Wedemeyer looked to the Ambassador for political and economic advice. Atcheson and other regular members of the Embassy staff who had approved the offending telegram were also replaced.

The dissenters in the State Department thought a mistake had been made. There was ebbing in their criticism of Chiang Kai-shek and his government, and more frequent expression of the thought that the American government ought to bring pressure on the Communists as well as on the National Government.[12] But gleams of difference between Hurley and Foreign Service officers both in the State Department and in China keep appearing. The Far Eastern specialists went on advocating "a flexible and realistic approach"—that is, deal with all factions to fight Japan—in contrast to what they regarded as "blank-check" support of the Generalissimo. They still were bothered by Hurley's tactics.[13] He in turn remained of the belief that their activities encouraged, perhaps incited, the Communists to refuse to compromise. This professional group, moving back and forth between the Embassy and the State De-

[11] Service had been sent to Yenan by General Gross, who wished that he be allowed to remain there. He informed Marshall that the purpose of the trip was to obtain essential military information bearing on planned American military operations, and that Service's departure would be a great loss. General Wedemeyer also wrote a letter to the Secretary of State in which he spoke well of Service's performance of duties. When questioned about this letter by a Senate Committee, Wedemeyer added, "Yes, I have stated, sir, I never had any feelings that there was anything wrong with these men." But he also remarked that he did not pay as much attention to their work as he probably should have as theater commander. *Joint Committee on Military Situation in the Far East*, pages 2553-2555.

[12] As for example the memo of March 24th, written by Vincent, Ballantine, and Stanton. Vincent had just talked with Hurley; the State Department expected that the President would also see him that same day to give him instructions before his return to China; and this memo was probably intended as a follow-up of the scheduled talk at the White House. However, it was not sent to the White House, probably because the President left Washington unexpectedly and did not see Hurley again before his departure. One paragraph of this memo read, "Measures to compel unity would call for a different approach from that hitherto used. We might be able to use some measure of compulsion on Chiang to reach an agreement with the Communists but we have no apparent means of using compulsion to cause the Communists to reach an agreement with Chiang. Any steps we might take to compel Chiang to reach an agreement should be predicated on a clear understanding that the Communists would abide by reasonable terms for cooperation in the Government."

[13] See for example the memo written on this subject by Stanton to Grew and Dunn, April 28, 1945.

partment, were, he continued to suspect, in league to defeat his policy and humiliate him. Despite changes in personnel, later frustrations in China caused him to grow more bitter in this belief. When, near the end of 1945, he laid down his assignment, he placed blame for the failure not upon any fault in his own reasoning or on the hard facts of the China situation, but on this group. But that story must wait.

American policy during the rest of the spring of 1945 roughly fitted both the mold of public opinion and the view taken of the curve of circumstances. Despite articles in press and radio which portrayed Chiang Kai-shek's regime as poor, selfish, and failing, most Americans remained attached to it, or rather to their image of it. They continued to think of brave suffering China whose cause we had upheld against Japan, as Chiang Kai-shek's China. They would have felt uneasy at turning away from him and consorting, no matter how cautiously, with his mistrusted opponents. But they also would have been sorry if, instead of going on with the fight against the Japanese, he had provoked civil war.

The trend of events during this period made it easier to believe that our current policy would work out well in the end. The campaign in the Philippines was almost over. Japan was at the mercy of our bombers. The Japanese thrust in the south and southeast of China was stationary; before long, it could be foreseen that Japan would be forced to draw its troops out of these regions. The air transport route over the Hump was at last attaining much expanded capacity.[14]

At last the battle for Burma was all but won. Chinese, Indian, and British troops had converged on the battered Japanese forces in North Burma. The Chinese divisions, trained under Stilwell, had in this campaign fought with the stamina and bravery he was sure they would show. On January 26th, the Chinese troops who had marched west across the high mountains from Yunnan had met with those other Chinese troops who had fought their way east from India. The road into China was open. The first convoy of trucks had crossed the frontier on the next day. At times as its builders had struggled against rock, heat, and jungle, and its advocates had struggled against those who thought the effort wasted, it had seemed as though it might be easier to build a road to the moon. Even Roosevelt's message to Chiang Kai-shek, now read again, seems sobered by fatigue. "After two years of struggle and grueling work, we have succeeded in opening the road to China . . . of which

[14] The net tonnage brought in over the Hump expanded from 14.5 thousands of tons in January 1944 to 46.5 thousands in January 1945.

there is no equal. This will help our common cause much. It is a great tribute to our armies and will be a lasting bond between our people." Chiang Kai-shek had broadcast a message to the United States which began, "We have broken the siege of China," and which ended, ". . . Let me name this road after General Joseph Stilwell, in memory of his distinctive contribution and of the signal part which the Allied and Chinese forces under his direction played in the Burma campaign and in the building of the road."

The opening of the road brought assurance that China and the Chinese armies could be adequately sustained. But if we may pause to foretell, the road was completed too late for the purposes which had driven Stilwell. Before it could serve as a main route of supply, more time and work were needed.[15] From Kunming out, the roads to other parts of China were still very bad, and mechanical means of transport scarce. Thus, to glance ahead, the main immediate use of the Burma Road was to provide security, an easier flight route, and better bases for the air transport service into China and for the American combat air forces in China. Tonnage actually brought into China during the rest of 1945 over the Burma Road (and the parallel pipe line) was much smaller than that carried by air, which grew with great rapidity.[16] Then by the summer of 1945 action was underway to capture ports on the South China coast and open a seaway into China. After V-J Day goods and soldiers came over the ocean into the liberated ports.

The Chinese military organization was beginning to respond to Wedemeyer's direction and the brightening outlook. The broken and scattered Chinese armies were being regrouped and re-equipped, and regaining

[15] General W. D. Styer, Chief of Staff, Army Service Forces, reported to Marshall on January 23, 1945, that it ought to be possible by April 1945 to bring 16,000 tons of freight over the road to Kunming and to increase its capacity progressively to a maximum of 80,000 by April 1946. To do this he reckoned that there would be needed in the India-Burma and China Theaters, 58,200 American troops, 7,840 trucks, and 8,000 trailers.

[16] Tonnage brought into Kunming, China (thousands of short tons):

1945	Over Burma Road including weight of truck	Over "4" Pipe Line	All air carriers over the Hump
January	—	—	46.5
February	5.2	—	42.5
March	6.7	—	49.0
April	15.4	0.4	46.5
May	28.0	5.5	51.4
June	28.0	5.1	58.2
July	23.3	11.6	73.7
August	15.9	10.8	63.1
September	18.6	12.4	49.2

combat usefulness. They would, it could be foreseen, soon be augmented by the experienced divisions which would come back from Burma. A good prospect was emerging that by the end of the year there would be in China a reinforced, well-trained, and effective army corps—equipped with artillery. But the struggle ended before this was accomplished.

But to return to the events of the spring: while differences over our policy in China were being argued in Washington, the Chinese government had been making a new effort to tempt the Communists into cooperation on its terms. Chiang Kai-shek on March 1st had moved on his own. He had announced plans to convene a People's Congress in the coming November to prepare for the introduction of constitutional government.[17] When this was done, he promised that all political parties would have legal status and enjoy equality. Acting Secretary Grew had hastened to praise this initiative. He told the press that he thought Chiang Kai-shek's statement indicated that the trend in China was toward political unity and a democratic government and concluded, "President Chiang's statement offers hope of a future unity as a consequence of the promised National Assembly meeting in November, and we may hope that, during the interim period, agreement among the Chinese may be reached for a unity of military effort to meet the crucial situation in the months to come." But the Communists had rebuffed the whole program. Chou En-lai in a letter which he sent to the National Government on March 9th called the announced People's Congress in advance "deceitful, China-splitting and one-party controlled."[18] He had sought to enlist Hurley's interest by a message telling him of the reasons for his rejection of the Generalissimo's program. Hurley's answer to Chou En-lai, sent from Washington, had been temperate. He urged the Communist

[17] Important parts of his interesting statement of that date are printed in *United States Relations with China*, pages 83-84. In this address the Generalissimo reminded his auditors "I have long held the conviction that the solution of the Communist question must be through political means." He announced (1) the assembly of a People's Congress, the next November 12th to inaugurate constitutional government, (2) that upon the inauguration of constitutional government all political parties would have legal status and enjoy equality, (3) that the next session of the People's Political Council with a larger membership and more extensive powers would soon meet; and that the government would consider with it the measures in regard to convening the People's Congress and all related matters.

These proposals thus did not define the composition of the council that would determine the form and conditions of the People's Congress. The membership of the People's Political Council whom he proposed to consult was at this time dominated by the Kuomintang.

[18] This was on March 12th relayed by the American Embassy in Chungking to Hurley in Washington. *United States Relations with China*, pages 84-85.

leaders to reach no final conclusion until he had returned to China and could discuss the matter with both sides.

Service, who was in Yenan at the time, had interpreted the rejection of this proposal as a sign of the increasing self-confidence among the Communists. They were, he repeated, becoming more defiant and less inclined to listen to Chiang Kai-shek. The trend, it seemed to him, was toward separation, not unity. But Hurley and those who decided policy did not share this gloomy view of the situation. They thought Chiang Kai-shek's new measures showed an increasing wish on his part to form a government in which all parties could function, and that the Communists would presently find it more expedient to take part in that government than to continue armed resistance. One other factor in this hopeful train of thought was the anticipation that the Chinese government would reach an agreement with the Soviet government. The accord that had been signed at Yalta was still a most closely kept secret. But Hopkins and Hurley and others knew of it, and thought that it would affect the future balance of negotiations between the Chinese parties.

Hurley started back to China with unchanged instructions. The President, after assuring him of support, had told him, "Now make it as easy as you can on them [the Communists] and say everything favorable you can and don't destroy your basis for a possible unification of the armed forces in China."[19] He, Hurley, was determined to stand by the Chinese government while continuing to strive for unification by peaceful means. The better to bring this about, he went by way of Moscow.

[19] Hurley testimony, *Joint Committee on Military Situation in the Far East*, page 2906.

CHAPTER 26

The Soviet Side

EVEN now the origins of Hurley's trip to Moscow are hard to trace and its purpose hard to identify. The White House never commented on it; and Hurley's explanations are as puzzling as they are dramatic, or perhaps I should say dramatized. A legitimate guess is that Hurley, supposing that he would have to win the Generalissimo's concurrence for the accord reached with Stalin at Yalta, wanted to put himself in a position to interpret Stalin's intentions as well as Roosevelt's.

Chiang Kai-shek and Soong had shown themselves eager to know what had happened at Yalta and what would happen next. On February 27th, the American Embassy in Chungking had reported that the Chinese Foreign Office was preparing a Treaty of Amity which Soong might submit to the Soviet government when he went to Moscow.[1] On March 6th, Soong had cabled Hurley that the Generalissimo wished him to make a quick trip to Washington to discuss international and economic questions with the President. He also had more fully explained his purpose in another message to Harry Hopkins. He observed that the President had already seen the Foreign Ministers and the Prime Ministers of Great Britain and the Soviet Union at Yalta—and no member of the Chinese government had been present. He thought that it had never been as essential as it was at that moment to get the President's advice about "our joint strategy" including "our relations with Soviet Russia, the Communists, and plans we have for dealing as best we can with our desperate economic problems."[2] Hurley had answered on the 9th that both the President and the Acting Secretary of State felt that the time remaining before the conference at San Francisco was too short for such a visit; they also were afraid other governments might misunderstand.[3]

[1] It is of incidental interest to note that the Embassy thought this effort on the part of the Chinese government unrealistic. Its reasons for thinking so were that the Soviet government was not likely to sign any such treaty until the current trouble in Sinkiang was adjusted, and while the dominant groups in the Chinese government had such hostility and mistrust of Chinese Communism and the Soviet Union. The members of the China Affairs Division of the State Department shared this opinion. Thus it would appear that neither knew that President Roosevelt had already dug a channel into which the negotiations might more easily flow.

[2] Soong cable to Hopkins, March 10th, 1945, *Hurley Papers*, Book II, Item 47. This was in reference to requests which Kung was making of the American government for gold shipments and other economic help, of which full account will be given in a later section. Soong cable to Hurley, March 12th, 1945, *Hurley Papers*, Book II, Item 48.

[3] Soong cable, March 6, 1945, *ibid.*, Item 45; and Hurley cable, March 9, 1945, *ibid.*, Item 46.

Thus Soong's visit had been put off. Whether by intention or not this postponement allowed the President to defer questions about what had been done at Yalta, and granted Hurley the chance to equip himself to explain the Yalta Agreement to the Generalissimo.

But these conjectures do not jibe with the accounts which Hurley gave later of the thoughts which impelled him on this hard trip to Moscow. These may be read in different versions. The contemporary one was set out in a cable to Truman on learning, en route to Moscow, of Roosevelt's death. After offering his resignation, Hurley said that President Truman could command him for any service; and then went on to say that the purpose of the mission he was on was to obtain cooperation from the British and Soviet governments for the American policy of supporting the Chinese National Government and all reasonable efforts of the Chinese leaders to create a free, united democratic China.[4] But much later (in 1951) with the knife of memory he etched in quite a different and more detailed version.[5] He related that while he was still in China, before returning to Washington in February 1945, he had heard all sorts of rumors about a secret agreement reached at Yalta; that in fact he knew of its existence through the Chinese Armed Communists. On getting back to Washington he had asked the State Department about it and had been told that the Department knew nothing. But even before securing an authentic version of its details, he had concluded that something wrong had been done. Off he had gone to the White House ". . . with my ears back and my teeth skinned, to have a fight about what had been done. When the President reached up that fine, firm, strong hand of his to shake hands with me, what I found in my hand was a very loose bag of bones. Then I looked at him closely, and the skin seemed to be pasted down on his cheekbones; and you know, all the fight that I had in me went out."[6] But he had argued with the President that the United States had surrendered the territorial integrity and political independence of China. The President had denied that he had given up anything. The next day, the President had allowed him to read the agreement and had given him a copy. And then—some days later—the President had admitted to him that there were some features in the accord which justified his fears. Thereupon the President had said he would like Hurley to go and talk with Churchill and Stalin and see if he could ameliorate the agreement or set it aside.

[4] Telegram, April 13, 1945, Hurley to President Truman, *ibid.*, Items 66 and 67.
[5] Hurley testimony, *Joint Committee on Military Situation in the Far East*, pages 2883-2888.
[6] *Ibid.*, page 2884.

Such is the contradicted account last given by Hurley of the reasons for his trip to London and Moscow. Ambassador Harriman, who was in Moscow throughout the whole of Hurley's visit, has commented on it: "At no time did he [Hurley] indicate to me that President Roosevelt was disturbed about the understanding reached at Yalta or that he desired that this understanding be ameliorated. On the contrary the purpose of Ambassador Hurley's visit to Moscow, as he stated it to me and to Stalin, was to find out from Stalin when Chiang could be told about the Yalta understanding and to help further cement the relations between the Soviet Union and the Chinese National Government."[7] The subject may be left with the note that Hurley's own current reports of the talks he had with Churchill and Stalin do not contain mention of direct suggestions for changing the details of the Yalta Agreement.[8] But some such intention may have guided the pleas which he made in both London and Moscow for observance of the principles of the Atlantic Charter; these can be read as an oblique way of trying to make sure that the obscure phrases in the Yalta Accord would not apply so as to impair Chinese sovereignty or independence. It may also be observed that not many weeks later qualms were felt within the American government about the wisdom of going through with the Yalta Accord until its meaning was clarified. Of this more will be told presently.[9]

Hurley left the United States for London and Moscow on April 3rd. Even before he went, the mould of mistrust was defacing the agreement reached by Roosevelt, Churchill, and Stalin in the Crimea regarding the liberated states of Europe. While Hurley was on his way the decay became marked. As well summarized by Dexter Perkins, "Less than a month after Yalta, Andrei Vishinsky appeared in Bucharest and without consulting Russia's allies, imposed on the Rumanian people a government of Communist orientation. In theory the powers stood together on the question of the future of Germany, but in practice the Russians

[7] Harriman's statement, *Joint Committee on Military Situation in the Far East*, page 3335. A pertinent passage in the memo made by Edward Page, Secretary of the American Embassy in Moscow, who acted as interpreter of the talk between Hurley and Stalin on April 15th, records that Stalin asked Hurley whether there were any plans to tell Chiang Kai-shek of the Yalta Accord and recalled that Roosevelt had suggested that this should be done either by or through Hurley; and that Hurley remarked that this question was the main purpose of his visit. This accords with the explanation of his purpose in visiting Moscow which Hurley gave to President Truman in his letter of May 20, 1945: that President Roosevelt had directed him to bring about close harmony in the relations between Russia and China.

[8] Telegram, April 17, 1945, Hurley in Moscow to State Department. In *United States Relations with China*, pages 94-96.

[9] See Chapter 28.

pressed the question of reparations. . . . At the same time the Soviet Union made clear that it intended to extend the Polish frontier far to the west, without much regard for the views of the United States or of Great Britain as to the future of the Reich. In theory the way was cleared for the building of the United Nations, but what Russia thought of the whole project was to be revealed before long by their acts."[10]

The Soviet attitude toward the composition of the government for Poland became a foremost cause of doubt as to the value of all the Yalta accords. Roosevelt was beginning to realize that the Soviet government was determined to place its friends and agents in control of that country, ignoring both our ideas and the wishes of the Polish people. On April 1st, he had sent a message of firm accent on this subject to Stalin. It began, "I cannot conceal from you the concern with which I view the development of events of mutual interest since our fruitful meeting at Yalta," and ended with the remark that "I wish I could convey to you how important it is for the successful development of our program of international collaboration that this Polish question be settled fairly and speedily. If this is not done all the difficulties and dangers to Allied unity which we had so much in mind in reaching our decisions at the Crimea will face us in an even more acute form. . . ."

Then there had also been a startling burst of accusation from Moscow in connection with an intimated chance that the German army in Italy might surrender. Unconfirmed word had been received that some German officers were considering surrender of their troops opposing the British-American forces in Italy. General Alexander, the field commander in Italy, was authorized to send a representative to Switzerland to find out whether the report was true, and if so, to arrange a conference at his headquarters in Italy to work out the details of surrender. The Soviet government was promptly told of this project, and told also that if a surrender conference was held Soviet representatives would be welcome. Molotov had sent an answer drenched with suspicion lest a deal in violation of the principle of unconditional surrender was in the making. He asked that any further step be suspended. The President had radioed Stalin a full explanation of what had occurred. And again on April 1st, he had repeated in another message that the possible meeting at Berne was solely for the military purpose of arranging contact with competent German military officers and not for negotiations of any kind. Stalin had refused to trust either the explanation or the assurance.

[10] Dexter Perkins, Review of Edward Stettinius, *Roosevelt and the Russians*, Yalta Conference. *Journal of Modern History*, September 1951.

He had answered on April 3rd that he thought the President was misinformed. He said that his Russian military colleagues "have no doubt that negotiations have taken place and have ended in an agreement with the Germans on the basis of which the German Commander on the Western Front, Marshal Kesselring, had agreed to open the front and allow the Anglo-American troops to advance to the east and the Anglo-Americans have promised in return to ease the peace terms. I think that my colleagues are closer to the truth. . . . As a result of this the Germans on the Western Front have in fact ceased the war against Britain and the United States."

The President, on April 5th, had denied all this with astonished indignation. He suggested that Stalin's information must come from German sources who were trying to create trouble. His answer closed with the reflection that ". . . it would be one of the great tragedies of history if at the very moment of the victory, now within our grasp, such distrust, such lack of faith, should prejudice the entire undertaking after the colossal losses of life, material and treasure involved." Stalin had not yielded either in regard to the facts or conclusions he drew from them. In his next response to the President, on April 7th, he had broadly hinted that the British, whom he thought to be the prime movers in the deal, were fooling the President. The taste left by this answer was not made more pleasant by an instance given to show how superior his sources of information were; Stalin recalled that General Marshall had once sent reports to the Soviet general staff about German army plans that turned out to be wrong, and hinted that this error may have been due to a deliberate enemy intelligence trick.

While Roosevelt and Stalin were exchanging these messages in early April, Harriman was warning that the Soviet government, once freed from the struggle against Germany, was going to be hard to deal with; that it viewed all matters from the standpoint of its own selfish interests. This was a regretful comment by a man who had tried so hard and ably to bring help to the Soviet people and armies during the war. He had slowly reached the conclusion that the generous and considerate attitude adopted by the United States was regarded by the Soviet government as a sign of weakness and that it was not possible to bank general good-will in Moscow.[11]

Roosevelt, on his last stay in Warm Springs, studied these matters with grim attention. Experience was dealing harshly with the impression that he had shared with the American people on Christmas Eve of 1943,

[11] Harriman cable to the President and Secretary of State, April 6, 1945.

just after his return from Teheran: "To use an American and ungrammatical colloquialism, I may say that I 'got along fine' with Marshal Stalin. He is a man who combines a tremendous, relentless determination with a stalwart good humor. I believe he is truly representative of the heart and soul of Russia; and I believe that we are going to get along well with him and the Russian people—very well indeed."[12] But he was still determined to preserve, if it could be done in tolerable ways, good working relations with the Soviet Union for the sake of a firm world peace. On April 12th, there were forwarded to Stalin his final words about the surrender incident in Italy. That, Roosevelt wrote, now appeared to have faded into the past without having accomplished any useful purpose; but "in any event, there must not be mutual distrust, and misunderstandings of this character should not arise in the future." Mistrust, he had not yet grasped, was the governing element in Soviet behavior. The events of early April were not passing incidents of misunderstanding, but signals of greater trouble.

By the time this message was read by Stalin, Roosevelt was dead. The multiple tasks of peace-making, unsettled and rather deranged, passed into other hands. From then on, the Americans and British would have to deal with a Politburo which no longer felt it essential to have their help or accord. The Soviet armies were within thirty miles of Berlin and pounding their way forward. Soon they would be able to flow freely and relentlessly east as well as west.

Among the unsettled tasks was that of bringing into effect the still secret Yalta Accord regarding the conditions of Soviet entry into the Pacific war. The incoming President, Harry S. Truman, knew nothing of this pact before entering office. He had to have a search made for its text, which had been kept by Admiral Leahy in a special file. Hurley, as already told, on hearing of Roosevelt's death, paused on his way to Moscow to explain to Truman what he knew about the making and meaning of this Yalta Accord. Truman at once sent him word that he would stand behind what Roosevelt had done.

In his talks with Churchill and Eden in London, Hurley thrust out on his own. He was ridden by the conviction that despite the outward agreement of the British government with American policy in China, its true bent was otherwise. He correctly detected that the British did not share either the American belief that China could play an important

---

[12] Roosevelt broadcast from Hyde Park, December 24, 1943, State Department Bulletin, January 1, 1944.

part in the Far East or the American fervor for unification. While in China he had gotten the impression that some British officials thought it might be best if China were divided into two parts; and that this would make the position of Hong Kong and other British imperial possessions more secure.[13]

The conversation became lively when Churchill called the American long-range policy in regard to China "the great American illusion." It erupted into argument when Hurley remarked that if the British failed to observe the principles of the Atlantic Charter and continued to hold Hong Kong, Russia might well make demands in regard to areas in North China. To which Churchill answered, first, that Britain was not bound by the Atlantic Charter in regard to its colonies, and, second, that Hong Kong would be taken out of the British Empire only over his dead body. Only a few unsystematic remarks seem to have been exchanged about the terms of the Yalta Accord for the Pacific. The flare-up of argument proved to be the prelude to amiable agreement between Hurley and Churchill, neither of whom ever minded a touch of friction. Churchill repeated what he had said to Roosevelt: that he would support American policy for the unification of the Chinese armed forces and creation of a free, unified, democratic China. Eden added he would recall any British agent or official in China who opposed American policy. Hurley felt that his chief purpose in London had been achieved by these affirmations.[14]

Hurley flew on to Moscow, to step into Stalin's parlor. While his plane was on the way, Harriman called upon Stalin to tell him officially of Roosevelt's death. He reported that Stalin seemed deeply distressed at the news, and remarked "President Roosevelt has died, but his cause must live on. We shall support President Truman with our forces and our wills." Then, in response to Harriman's suggestion that he make this intention plain by sending Molotov to the San Francisco Conference, Stalin consented.

Hurley saw Stalin on the night of April 15th. Harriman and Molotov were present. This singular talk swirled about. Hurley recalled earlier statements made by Stalin that the Chinese Communists were not true Communists. He then gave a résumé of the recent negotiations between

[13] Admiral William D. Leahy, *I Was There*, pages 288-289, gives a condensation of his notes on Hurley's views and reports on this subject.

[14] This summary of Hurley's talk with Churchill and Eden is based on Hurley's message to President Truman, dated April 13, 1945. The talk had taken place before Roosevelt's death, and the message may also have been written before Hurley learned of it. But he had had the news by the time the message was sent off and in this same message he offered his resignation to Truman. *Hurley Papers*, Book II, Items 66, 67.

the Kuomintang and the Communists. Stalin said that he was ready to help in any way he could to bring about the unification of military forces in China. Hurley said that this was the best news that he had received. Hurley passed on the information that the United States was equipping and training thirty-six Chinese divisions. But, he continued, it would also like to train and equip the Communist troops and combine them with the National troops under the control of the National Government and leadership of Chiang Kai-shek. "Stalin," the memo of this talk reports, "highly approved this proposal." He repeated his ideas of why the Chinese army was so weak, saying that all Chiang Kai-shek needed was forty good divisions, that Wedemeyer was now training thirty-six and if the Communist divisions were brought in there would be over forty. He seems to have been thinking of the battles still to be fought against the Japanese.

Stalin brought up the subject of informing Chiang Kai-shek of the accord signed at Yalta. Hurley said that Roosevelt had told him to keep the matter most secret until Stalin authorized its communication to Chiang Kai-shek, and that Truman had told him to carry out Roosevelt's orders. Stalin seems to have been disposed at first to think that it would be all right if Hurley told Chiang Kai-shek as soon as he arrived in Chungking. But later he remarked that Russia would need two or three months more to concentrate its force for the war against Japan. Then it would seek a pretext to take the offensive; and he wanted to settle certain political matters before seeking the pretext. In brief, he would be ready in two or three months, and then would not be afraid if the secret were divulged. It was agreed to leave it to Hurley to choose the best time, on the understanding that he would not inform Chiang Kai-shek without first checking with Stalin. The Marshal said that he would not therefore discuss the document with Soong.[15] The visit of the Chinese

[15] This summary of the talk regarding the question of when and how to tell Chiang Kai-shek of the Yalta Accord is based on the memo by Page. It is confirmed by the later and more detailed account of this point which Hurley sent to President Truman from Chungking on May 10th. In this Hurley wrote, "Both Roosevelt and Stalin advised me that it was agreed between them that I would not open the subject of the Yalta decision with Chiang Kai-shek until the signal was given me by Stalin. Stalin said that he would give me carte blanche and let me use my own judgment as to when and how to present the subject. However, both Harriman and I were of the opinion that it would be best to delay the presentation because of the possibility of leakage which in turn might bring undesirable results. I explained this to Stalin and it was finally decided that I am not to present the subject to Chiang Kai-shek until we have advised Stalin that, in our opinion, the time is opportune and until we have received the signal from him." *Joint Committee on Military Situation in the Far East*, page 3337.

Foreign Minister, having again been postponed, was expected in Moscow in May.

There are faint signs in this talk that Stalin may no longer have been deeply concerned as to just when Chiang Kai-shek was told of this agreement. Perhaps this was because he thought that the Japanese had read his intention from the notice given ten days before by the Soviet government that it wanted to end its Neutrality Pact with Japan; and that they knew large Soviet forces were being moved eastward.[16] Or, was the always wary Stalin unsure as to whether the American government really would follow through Roosevelt's promise to secure Chiang Kai-shek's concurrence; and therefore inclined to have us do so at once, even at the risk that the Japanese would learn of the accord?

No such queries marked Hurley's report to Washington of this talk with Stalin. It shone with satisfaction. As summarized by him, "The Marshal . . . wished us to know that we would have his complete support in immediate action for the unification of the armed forces of China with the full recognition of the National Government under the leadership of Chiang Kai-shek. In short, Stalin agreed unqualifiedly to America's policy in China as outlined to him during the conversation."[17]

Harriman, who had taken part in the Stalin-Hurley talks, was not impressed in the same way. He had flown back to Washington almost as soon as the last word was spoken. There he told President Truman and the State Department—in effect—that he thought that Hurley was taking Stalin's assurances too trustfully. His opinion was that this talk would make little difference one way or the other, that Stalin would not

[16] The termination of the pact was widely interpreted in the world press as having this meaning. For example, the lead editorial in the *New York Herald-Tribune* on April 6, 1945, right after the event, began, "Russia is preparing to enter the war in the Far East. This is the only interpretation which can be given the denunciation of the Russian treaty of neutrality with Japan."

[17] This message of April 17, 1945, is printed in *United States Relations with China*, page 96. Hurley reaffirmed this summary of Soviet policy in a press conference which he held on April 28th, soon after reaching Chungking, when he said, "Finally all the United Nations, of which China is one, endorse China's aspirations for a free, united, democratic China. I have made this statement before and I have repeated it and the policies toward China in Washington, London and Moscow and [sic] found all in agreement on the Chinese policy." Telegram, Hurley to State Department May 4, 1945. In a talk which he gave to the assembled representatives of American agencies in China on May 8th, he concluded his remarks on the subject by saying that the U.S.S.R. had "now joined Britain and the United States in a United Nations policy toward China which endorses Chinese aspirations for the building of a free, united and democratic China and for the unification of all anti-Japanese military forces under the National Government of China." Dispatch from American Embassy, Chungking, May 15, 1945.

cooperate indefinitely with Chiang Kai-shek; that if and when the Soviet Union entered the Pacific war, it would make full use of and would support the Chinese Communists—unless by that time a united Chinese government "friendly" to the Soviet Union was brought into existence. His darker view of the probable line of Soviet policy, however, led him to the same practical conclusion as Hurley's brighter one: that we should continue to try to promote unity in China and harmony in Sino-Soviet relations. He was disturbed lest Hurley's evaluation of Stalin's words might mislead Chiang Kai-shek and cause him to fail to perceive how imperative it was to strive for an agreement with the Communists.[18]

George Kennan, who was in charge of our Embassy in Moscow during Harriman's absence in Washington, was similarly disturbed. He convoyed Hurley's report by one of his own. This pointed out that Stalin could in good faith from his own standpoint affirm the principle of unifying the armed forces of China, since he knew that unification was feasible only on conditions acceptable to the Chinese Communist Party. It expressed the judgment that within the scope of a fluid, resilient policy, the Soviet government would seek to reacquire all the diplomatic and political assets on the mainland of Asia that Czarist Russia had once possessed; to dominate the provinces of China contiguous to the Soviet frontiers; and to secure sufficient control of all areas of North China now dominated by the Japanese to prevent other foreign powers from repeating the Japanese incursion. "It would be tragic," Kennan observed, "if our natural anxiety for the support of the Soviet Union at this juncture, coupled with Stalin's use of words which mean all things to all people and his cautious affability, were to lead us into an undue reliance on Soviet aid or even Soviet acquiescence in the achievement of our long term objectives in China."[19]

This analysis of Kennan's was more than the dismissal of Hurley's impressions. It amounted to an almost flat statement that the Soviet

[18] Harriman's talk with Stanton of the Far Eastern Division of the State Department is summarized in *ibid.*, page 97.

[19] This message from Kennan, of April 23, 1945, is printed in *ibid.*, pages 96-97, with one excision of some interest, to wit: "That the Soviet Government would find it easier to achieve the three enumerated aims if it had the cooperation of a unified government 'friendly' to it. It would prefer not to have to demonstrate its power in China conspicuously or in a way which would engage Russian prestige or commit it to a rigid program. It would rather work through others and veil the means by which it exerted the real power. Thus it would prefer to work through an inwardly strong and nominally independent Chinese Government sufficiently reliable and subservient to be an effective sphere of influence. If this was not achievable, however, the Soviet Government was ready to operate, as it was then in Sinkiang, through local forces which will not hesitate, when necessary, to challenge central authority."

government would not be content unless it secured domination in Manchuria, Mongolia, and North China; and that its support of unification was merely one of the routes by which it thought it might accomplish this purpose. It was easier to have faith in Hurley's estimate of Soviet intention than in this more somber one. For if the Soviet Union· was bent on expanding its influence and control as far as Kennan predicted, how were we to prevent it? We were already using our full diplomatic influence to avert any such attempt. We might have abruptly altered our course, and tried to build up the forces of the Chinese government with greater vigor and speed, and perhaps even send American combat divisions into China. Or, we might even have hurried into plans for landings on the North China coast, Manchuria, or Korea. But such preventive measures would have required a great adjustment of programs and prolonged involvement in the affairs of the remote regions along the Sino-Soviet frontier. To Secretary of War Stimson and General Marshall, the uppermost wish still was to draw Soviet forces into the war in time to shorten it and ease the battle strain upon the United States.[20]

In any event, these differing reports about the meaning of Hurley's talk with Stalin brought no change in our treatment of the China situation. But Stettinius on April 23rd sent a prudential notice to Hurley, who had just arrived in Chungking. This hinted broadly that Stalin's remarks might only be dues paid to circumstances; and that after the war in Europe was won, he might change his mind and tactics. "Consequently," it advised, "I believe that it is of the utmost importance that when informing Generalissimo Chiang Kai-shek of the statements made by Marshal Stalin you take special pains to convey to him [this] general thought . . . in order that the urgency of the situation may be fully realized by him. Please impress upon Generalissimo Chiang Kai-shek the necessity for early military and political unification in order not only to bring about the successful conclusion of the Japanese war but also to establish a basis upon which relations between China and the Soviet Union may eventually become one of mutual regard and permanent friendship."[21] The officials in Washington were at this time begin-

[20] Entry, *Forrestal Diaries*, April 23, 1945, giving gist of notes made by Bohlen of meeting at White House.

[21] Telegram, Stettinius to Hurley, April 23, 1945, *United States Relations with China*, page 98. This message to Hurley was sent before the President saw Molotov that same day. Just before seeing Molotov, the President convened a meeting of Stettinius, Stimson, Forrestal, Marshall, King, Leahy, Harriman, and Deane to discuss the tendencies which the Soviet government was showing toward domination in Europe. At the end of the meeting the President said he would inform Molotov that if one part of the

ning to get seriously worried as to whether Stalin would carry out any of his accords with Roosevelt in an honest way, and a few weeks later Hopkins was to be sent to Moscow to find out.[22]

Yalta Accord were breached, he would consider all as no longer binding. Forrestal memo in *Forrestal Diaries*, entry April 23rd.

[22] See Chapter 28.

CHAPTER 27

Blurred American Policy: Late Spring 1945

POLITICAL

HURLEY's belief in what he had been told at Moscow was not quenched by Stettinius' message from Washington. Three weeks later, in reviewing the past for the new President, he wrote ". . . We have been instrumental in bringing about closer and more harmonious relations between Russia and China. . . . We have obtained the approval of Britain and Russia for the unification of the armed forces of China, support of the American policy to endorse the aspirations of the Chinese people to create for themselves a free, united democratic government."

Nor did Hurley allow himself to be dismayed by the long report which on April 24th Mao Tze Tung made to the Seventh National Congress of the Chinese Communist Party—a candid statement which still commands attention.[1] It began with an avowal of the need for unifying all political parties in a democratic provisional coalition to deal with the current crisis and make democratic reforms. It then reviewed the history of relations with the "reactionary" Kuomintang in a most accusatory way, and the rise of the "peoples movement" led by the Communists. The liberated areas of China, Mao Tze Tung asserted with pride, went as far north as the border of Inner Mongolia and as far south as Hainan. Ninety-five million people lived in them. Everywhere in these vast liberated areas, he avowed, governments elected by the people were being set up, regional coalitions were being formed, and the people mobilized. These areas thus were being made into a model of democratic China and the center of the fight against the Japanese aggressors, in spite of the Japanese, the Kuomintang blockade, and the lack of outside help. The Communist leader declared that in contrast the Kuomintang was exercising a harsh rule over domestic policy which the people resisted, and that for this reason the Kuomintang armies had shrunk and lost their ability to fight. A deep chasm was seen between the Kuomintang government and the Chinese people, causing poverty, discontent, and revolt because of incompetence, corruption, starvation, and bankruptcy. As long, Mao Tze Tung expounded, as the requisite

[1] A Political Report by Chairman Mao Tze Tung to the Seventh National Congress of the Chinese Communist Party. April 24, 1945. Yenan. A good analysis of the meaning of this report and extensive parts of the main official papers of this conference and of Mao Tze Tung's address are in *A Documentary History of Chinese Communism*. Pages 285 *et seq.*

conditions for socialist economics were still absent, the Chinese people could not, and therefore should not, attempt to build a Communist state. They should seek a system of government based on a coalition of democratic parties and groups. The people would exercise their power in various assemblies, while at the same time state affairs would be dealt with "in a centralized manner with the various government agencies doing the work entrusted to them by the people's assemblies and safeguarding the necessary democratic activities of the people." At the present stage of the Chinese economy, Mao Tze Tung thought that "Every tiller should have his own land, but all monopolies for enterprises of a scale beyond the means of private interest, for example, banking, railroad, and shipping should be managed and controlled by the state." This program he defined in comparison with the future and ultimate program as a "minimum program." Observing then that "We Communists never conceal or disguise our political views," he concluded that ". . . our future, our ultimate program is to push China forward to Socialism and Communism; this is definite and beyond question." But the meaning of this affirmation was somewhat obscured by other passages in his report, for example, "Some people wonder if the Communists, once in power, will establish a dictatorship by the proletariat and a one-party system, as they have done in Russia. Our answer is that a new democratic state of a union of several democratic classes is different in principle from a Socialist state of a proletarian dictatorship. . . . Chinese history will create the Chinese system. . . . China's historical conditions prescribe a coalition government."

These statements could have been read to mean that there was no use trying to reach terms with the Communists. Or, they could have been read as only a definition of ends which the Communists could pursue by peaceful means if they were drawn into a unified government. The second is the view that Hurley took. He drew the conclusion that the Communists were not familiar with the decisions made at Yalta; and that Communist objectives appeared in general to be the same as those of the Kuomintang, the chief difference between the public statements of the two sides being over procedure.[2] Thus the premise of his working effort remained unchanged: that both the government and the Communists could be led to see, must be led to see, that compromise was better than civil war.

Nor did Mao Tze Tung's statement make any deep impression in the State Department. Before it could be fully known and weighed, the

[2] Telegram from American Embassy, Chungking, May 6, 1945.

Department had reformulated its ideas in a memo for the use of Stettinius at the San Francisco Conference, a summary of which was sent out to Hurley on May 7th.[3] Its main features were:

1. We seek to promote a "broadly" representative Chinese government which would bring about unity, including the reconciliation of the differences between the Communists and the Kuomintang.

2. We continue to support the government headed by Chiang Kai-shek as the still generally recognized central authority which thus far offers the best hope for unification and avoidance of chaos in China's war effort.

3. However, against the possible disintegration of the authority of that government, we aim to maintain a degree of flexibility to permit cooperation with any other leaders who may give greater promise of assuring unity and contributing to peace and security in East Asia.

4. We want an effective joint prosecution of the war. Thus we are preparing and arming Chinese forces and urgently seeking to bring about Chinese military unity.

5. We would logically expect to assist China to build an effective military organization after the war. In view, however, of the uncertain Chinese political situation and its potentialities for civil war and complications with Soviet Russia, we are not prepared to commit ourselves with the present Chinese government to give such assistance until we are convinced that the government is progressing toward the achievement of unity and solid popular support.

Hurley was told that it was deemed most important that we maintain complete flexibility with regard to the means of reaching our ends. He was told also to be sure to make it entirely clear to Chiang Kai-shek and his government that our support was not a blank check; that they must

[3] The memo was prepared on April 18th. On May 2nd William Phillips, who was briefly serving in the Department, called a meeting to discuss a new instruction for Hurley, which might provide a more positive approach to the problem of inducing or influencing political unity in China under a "coalition" government (Vincent memo, May 2nd); and it was apparently decided that a summary of the memo of April 18th was adequate for this purpose.

The first knowledge of Mao's report in Washington seems to have been derived from a brief digest of a broadcast from Yenan on May 1st, which was picked up by the Federal Communications Commission. On the basis of this, Drumright wrote a short memo (undated) calling attention to the report and concluding that it dimmed any hope that might be held for the achievement of Chinese internal unity in the foreseeable future and observing that there might be read into this report a hint of defiance with respect to United States policies in China. But it is probable that this Drumright memo was not read by the group which actually drafted the instruction to Hurley till after this was sent.

share their power and mend their ways, to the end that internal unity and stability might be achieved as soon as possible, that the prosecution of the war might be facilitated, and that a sound basis could be laid for firm and friendly relations with Russia.[4]

To interpret, the American government saw no way of dealing with the problems of China and of Chinese-Soviet relations except by bringing about a conversion of the Chinese government into one which would give representation to all political elements of China, and through which they would all get along peacefully. Up to then it had relied on exhortation to bring this about. Henceforth it leaned toward the use of our power to give or refuse our support as an aid to persuasion. This inclination grew stronger as time passed and China still remained divided. But we never dared to follow it fully or decisively.

When Hurley resumed his talks with the government and Communist leaders he found that both still clung to the same positions in which he had left them in February. The political spokesmen remained apart, each group quick to blame the other when their troops clashed. Most of the Foreign Service officials thought the main trouble was the rigid unwillingness of the Kuomintang to share its power, and that American support was allowing them to pursue this harmful course. But Hurley thought that the Generalissimo was making a real effort to deal fairly with his opponents, and that we ought not to lessen our aid nor be perturbed by Communist reactions.[5] As though to bear out his opinion, suddenly in June both the government and the Communists showed a refreshed disposition to meet again with one another. A new chapter of talk was begun. But before telling about this, there is much to be known about other decisions that bore upon the course of events in China. While Hurley, during this mid-April to mid-June period was trying to bring the two sides together again, Washington was

---

[4] Telegram, May 7, 1945, Grew to Hurley.

[5] During this period of balked effort, another alienating episode occurred between Hurley and the career officers in his Embassy. Two members of the Embassy staff prepared a report which in main substance said that fighting between the Kuomintang and Communist forces was spreading fast, that the attitude of the "ruling clique" was dead-set against a peaceful settlement with the Communists. It added the opinion that as long as the United States gave "unlimited" support there was no chance of a peaceful settlement. Hurley tore the report apart in his comment to the State Department, made after a special staff meeting attended by Wedemeyer. He contradicted the statement that the fighting was growing worse and the danger of civil war greater. He denied that Chiang Kai-shek and the group about him were bent on provoking a civil war. He virtually accused the authors of a die-hard effort to bring about the collapse of the National Government.

measuring the aid—military and economic—to be given the Chinese government.

MILITARY

In March, in the course of setting future schedules of airplane production, the need had been presented of deciding what military support was to be given China in the future. The Assistant Secretary of War had asked the question: how large and what kind of army, air force, and navy would the American government be helping China to have after the defeat of Japan? The query had been referred to the inter-departmental committee known as the State-War-Navy Coordinating Committee—symbol SWNCC—which was composed of senior representatives of the three departments, each of whom was expected to consult with his colleagues and submit decisions to his chief. The committee had close working relations with the Joint Chiefs of Staff, and operated the usual mill of special committees and subcommittees.

On request the State Department had produced a paper for SWNCC analyzing our problems and aims in China.[6] Its recommendations on military aid conformed to the trail of thought which the State Department was at this time following. They were:

That the equipping and training then going on of the forces of the National Government for use against the Japanese was justified and should be continued until the Japanese armies in China and Manchuria were destroyed.

That the American government should not at that time assume any obligation to the existing National Government to aid it in developing and maintaining a postwar military force. However, this question should be reconsidered when (a) internal political unity and stability shall have been achieved in China, (b) the Chinese government has attained the support of the Chinese people, and (c) the Chinese economy, with whatever assistance it might be practical for the United States and other states to give, could support a modern army and air force.

This left the whole matter up in the air; and there it stayed until after V-J Day. But the SWNCC Committee adopted these conclusions in its final report dated May 28th; the heads of all three departments concurred in them; and the Joint Chiefs of Staff said they had no objec-

---

[6] This memo of April 3, 1945, drew heavily upon an earlier one which had been sent to the Secretaries of War and Navy on or about January 29th. The text of this earlier memo is printed in *Joint Committee on Military Situation in the Far East*, pages 2929-2930.

tion to them on military grounds.[7] Its conditional mood was expressed in this paragraph: (a) "No commitment looking toward the implementation of a military policy of assisting the Chinese Government to create and maintain a modern post-war army and air force should be made until the interested departments of the United States Government have been consulted and have expressed the opinion that certain necessary political and economic conditions have been fulfilled by the Chinese Government."

It ought to be recalled that the makers of this decision thought that the war against Japan would go on quite a while longer, and that they would have ample time to review the matter in the light of intervening events in China. Germany was down. But the planners, both civilian and military, thought it prudent to expect and prepare for a long, hard struggle against Japan.

The way in which the civilian agencies were thinking is shown by the report on "The War: Phase Two," prepared by the Office of War Information in collaboration with other government agencies and sent to the President on May 10th by Fred M. Vinson, Director of War Mobilization and Reconversion. In this, the first basic factor was said to be that the "(1) War against Japan will probably grow in severity over a prolonged period. Unconditional surrender of Japan, as of Germany, is our goal and it is hardly likely that Japan will yield her home islands to occupation by our forces short of successful and complete invasion. . . . Experience has shown that any effort to forecast definitely the duration of such war activities usually fails. All our effort toward war and toward production will be needed up to the last instant."

The military planners were thinking similarly. They reckoned that it would take four to six months to redeploy the American forces for full action in the Pacific. The target date for the first phased step in the invasion of Japan (Operation Olympic) was still November 1, 1945. True, the chance that Japan might be brought to give in sooner by bombing and blockade was being admitted, but official planning remained basically conservative. It was only on June 14th that the other possibility was significantly recognized in an order sent to MacArthur, Nimitz, and Arnold which stated that "Although there is at present no evidence that the sudden collapse or surrender of Japan is likely, the Joint Chiefs of Staff direct that plans be made to take immediate advantage of favorable

---

[7] This report is SWNCC 83-1 in which the State Department memo of April 3rd is incorporated as an appendix.

circumstances such as a sudden collapse or surrender to effect our entry into Japan proper for occupation purposes."

Meanwhile the Americans had been working hard, first to salvage and then to repair the Chinese army. Wedemeyer's position was easier than Stilwell's, and his ways of correction were more adept. He relied on persuasion and, no matter how tried, kept a friendly temper. He praised whenever he could, and criticized with deference. He managed to draw close to the government group without loss of independence. But he did not during this period have to face Chiang Kai-shek with any crucial decision.

Wedemeyer, as Stilwell before him, urged the government over and over again to reduce the size of its armies. Out of the three hundred and twenty-seven divisions nominally in existence in the winter of 1944-1945, he judged almost none to be effective combat divisions. He advised Chiang Kai-shek to reduce this vast and ragged troupe to eighty-four; and of these, he thought, the United States would train and equip thirty-nine and China the rest. Were this done, his plea continued, it would become possible for the Chinese government to feed, pay, and train the smaller force much better; and its soldiers would be physically stronger and much readier to fight. He also urged that the officer corps be thoroughly culled, that the command be drawn together, and that the armies be relocated.

On all these matters something was done, but less than Wedemeyer thought could or should be done. As late as May he found himself compelled to tell Chiang Kai-shek, "If we perpetuate the conditions that prevail today and perpetuate the vast number of divisions which in my opinion from a military and political standpoint are unjustified, we cannot marshal this country's strength to create effective forces of the military standard that you and I desire." Gradually American officers were placed in all branches of service within the Chinese army. A senior American general was assigned as adviser to each senior Chinese commander. Other general officers were attached to each section of the Chinese combat command. American colonels were made advisers and liaison officers with each division commander. Under each senior American officer attached to those divisions which the United States were sponsoring, there was a group of juniors to help in training and to observe in action. By the summer of 1945 this program was roughly in effect. About five hundred American officers and five hundred enlisted men were serving with (it might be almost as correct to say serving *in*) the Chinese forces. Also, the American air force was reorganized. The 10th Air Force was transferred from India and combined with the 14th, and both were put under the command of Stratemeyer. Chennault, survivor of more dangerous days, was relieved.

The Japanese advance against Kunming and Chungking that had been deemed almost certain a few months previous was never made. Some fear that it might still be attempted lasted throughout the spring.[8] In April-May, the Japanese made a last serious thrust toward Chihkiang in western Hunan, one of the few remaining American air bases. The Chinese divisions, though inadequately trained and equipped, stood fast against the Japanese columns. American planes pounded them. They were thrown back with heavy losses. Wedemeyer saluted the action; he found it a telling sign that the Chinese armies would be able to play their due part in the final expulsion of the Japanese from China. Hardly less impressive, he thought, as indicative of the cooperation growing between American and Chinese officers, was the supporting movement by air that was carried out. He suggested to Chiang Kai-shek that word be passed on to the Chinese commanders, units, and personnel that "These events together may prove in history a decisive turning point in the prosecution of the war in China. . . ."

This was the last offensive that the Japanese were able to try in China. Soon our reports began to teem with news that the Japanese troops were starting toward the coast and the north. The Chinese forces came on behind them. Wedemeyer found it necessary to dissuade the Chinese commanders from premature and piecemeal local offensives which would use up limited resources. His mind was set and his efforts bent on creating a small but powerful striking force to attack in vital areas when ready, and when the situation favored.

The optimism reached the War Department. A sample of it was the report made by Under-Secretary of War Patterson to his colleagues. At a meeting held to decide whether or not to send scarce trucks and textiles to China, he said, "The fighting in China is, we believe, going to take a rapid change for the better and they are for the first time conducting a real offensive. . . . And the hopes of our army people over there are

[8] The China Expeditionary Army had wanted to invade westward across the Kweichow plain. But the Japanese General Staff overruled it. Instead, on January 22nd it was ordered to begin to concentrate, especially about the lower Yangtze and along the coast to meet expected American attempts to land. It was instructed not to start any actions westward of a specified line, except raids by small forces, without special orders. Japanese Monograph No. 45.

high in getting a real effective effort against the Japanese in China. . . .
For the first time now in three and a half years they are on the go."[9]

There was a plan underway with the code name Rashness. Its object
was to gain control of the Canton-Hong Kong area and open a port or
ports through which the United States could send supplies and weapons,
and possibly troops. This area was to be captured by the Chinese marching overland from the interior to the coast. American air force and technical troops—increased by transfers from Burma—were to take part in
this action. Wedemeyer had approved this plan in February, with the
idea that it would start in May. Chiang Kai-shek had promised to carry
it out. The Joint Chiefs of Staff had assigned it a priority just below
that given MacArthur's operations in the Pacific. But delays had still
occurred, both in the arrival of supplies and in the preparations of the
Chinese forces.

Then—to carry the account of this project ahead of the rest of the
story—the Japanese retreat seemed to open the way to an easier action.
It was decided to form and send an advance expedition to take a smaller
port, close by to the south, Port Bayard. Through this there could be
hurried in the heavier weapons wanted for the assault on the Canton
area. In June, Marshall approved this operation and Nimitz concurred.
The time-table for the beginning of the Chinese offensive in China called
for the recapture of the air bases of Liuchow and Kweilin in early July,
the occupation of Port Bayard by August 15th, and then the assault from
four sides on the Canton area, to begin about November 1st.

But hindrances did not end. In the words of one message sent by the
American military headquarters in Chungking on July 4th, "Sobs and
sabotage, thieves, high water, all hell seems to be gathered in an attempt
to slow down movements and operations that are now underway." But
these were kept in motion. When the atom bomb brought the war to an
abrupt end, the leading Chinese divisions were not far from Port
Bayard. An American convoy headed for the port was just a few days
away. Both the Chinese and the American military organizations in
China had to face the problems of dealing with a beaten Japanese army
and an unbeaten Chinese Communist army sooner than they had figured.
The American government did not have the time on which it had
counted to make up its mind as to what military support to give the
Chinese government after the end of the war.

[9] Memo of meeting, May 29, 1945, Morgenthau, Patterson, Crowley, Clayton.

ECONOMIC

While these military questions were being considered and these military actions were being prepared, the issue of economic aid to China had also been to the fore in Washington. The general condition in Nationalist China was poorer than ever. The food supply was reduced by the Japanese capture of important rice-growing areas. The only civilian goods coming from the outside were brought by irregular trade with the occupied areas. Except for insufficient rationed rice, local produce was bought and sold in the black markets. Prices were going up fast and inexorably; and the families of the soldiers were suffering. Tax collections fell unevenly. Those who could not escape the imposition, mainly the peasants, paid heavily. Those who could evade, and many of the merchants and land owners could, did not pay. Government revenues were far below government expenditure. Among the great expenses were those made in connection with the expansion of American military activities in China. The Chinese government was being asked to provide great sums of Chinese paper dollars to pay for the construction of airfields and the building of roads. The deficit was met by huge printings of paper money, which bought less and less. Its exchange value in terms of the dollar swooped down month by month.

No one, not even the most stern devotee of sound finance and austerity, thought that this state of affairs could be wholly corrected at once. Until the food-growing areas were recaptured, production increased, war expenses reduced, and more goods brought into China, the situation was sure to remain bad. But American observers both in China and Washington thought more could be done than was being done to ease the distress among the poor. They also feared that if inflation went on unchecked the defensive effort of China would collapse and the Chinese government with it. The soldiers might refuse to stay in the ranks. The Chinese people might refuse to carry on the war. Revolt, the breakup of free China, a deal with the Japanese—any or all of these things could happen under the strain. The problem was how to keep the situation together for the next year or so.

The American treatment was little more than a sermon in favor of endurance and good government. The Chinese dreamed about a future brightened by large loans. The Chinese government turned to expedients which might at least slow down a little the rate of depreciation of the currency. It proposed to use the unspent two hundred million dollars left from the American loan of 1942 to buy gold. The gold it then intended to sell in China for Chinese paper dollars. The idea was that this plan would extract a substantial amount of paper money from circulation, and thereby retard the rise of prices and the fall in the value of the Chinese paper dollar.

When Soong came to Washington in April, he asked the Treasury to arrange for increased shipments of gold to China to be used for this purpose. The request stirred up a storm in the Treasury, particularly among the staff headed by Harry D. White. Its members thought the plan wasteful and sure to fail. It would end only, they thought, in the dissipation of dollars that would be needed later to buy essential goods for the Chinese people.[10] Previous operations of the same general sort had not had any marked or lasting effect on the monetary situation in China. It was believed within the Treasury that they had benefited mainly a few interests and individuals, who, the records were thought to show, had been allowed to buy gold and securities redeemable in gold at a price in Chinese currency below their true value. Substantial fortunes, it was figured, had been made in this way by the inside groups. On the Treasury lists of large purchasers there appeared banks and industrial companies in which Soong and Kung were thought to have some kind of interest or connection. There were also whispered statements that some members of the Soong family had personally profited, though the evidence of that was evanescent.

The Treasury staff in strained sessions with the Secretary of the Treasury and members of the other government departments dwelt heavily on these points. On May 8th, Morgenthau gave Soong an answer which in effect, though not explicitly, rejected the request to make more gold available. It outlined what the Treasury regarded as a sound anti-inflation program. The elements of this program were admirable, but far beyond what could be brought about, in the there and then. It was suggested that the Chinese government should set aside—as basis for some future anti-inflationary program—a five-hundred-million-dollar stabilization fund; to this it was further suggested the government should devote the two hundred or so million dollars left from the American loan and other existing Chinese dollar balances. The purposes and availability of this fund were to be determined jointly. This advice was polished off by curt comment on the way in which most of the loan had up to then been used: "It is most unfortunate that the impression has arisen in the United States that the two hundred million

---

[10] They had explained the reasons for this opinion to Chinese Treasury representatives in Washington months before in connection with earlier requests for gold shipments. Memo: talk, White, Soong and others. October 2, 1944. *United States Relations with China*, pages 502-504.

of U.S. dollar certificates and bonds and the gold sold in China have gone into relatively few hands with resultant large individual profits and have failed to be of real assistance to the Chinese economy."

Soong's answer reminded the Secretary of the Treasury of an earlier note that had been forgotten. On July 27, 1943, Morgenthau had promised the Chinese government ". . . that two hundred million be made available from the credit on the books of the Treasury in the name of the Government of the Republic of China for the purchase of gold."[11] Soong did not take direct issue with or offense at the criticisms of past operations. He pointed out that they had taken place when he was not in charge in China. He stated that neither he nor the Chinese government wanted speculators or rich people to make a profit out of the gold sales. The sales price of gold for Chinese dollars had already been raised greatly, he pointed out; and he intended to tax heavily any profits made from future purchases.

Soong's justification for his requests (there were two others then before the American government for textiles and trucks) went on to broader ground. There was bitter point in his remark to Morgenthau as recorded in the Secretary's notes, "Prague was taken yesterday. . . . This country [China] that first was beaten up by the aggressor will be the last to be rescued. . . ."[12] Further, "He [Soong] threw in the fact that he had gotten along so well with the Russians and that Molotov is insisting that he go to Russia . . . and if I would strengthen his hand at this time it would make possible the success of his mission to Russia."[13]

Morgenthau, after reprimanding his staff for their failure to remind him of the promise he had given in 1943, made up his mind that he would have to consent to the program of gold sales. But he still hung back. Soong spoke to the President, who referred him back to the Treasury. There Morgenthau was still engaged in a struggle against a still opposed staff who were urging him (and continued to urge him to the last) to "wriggle out" of the earlier engagement on the score that the money had not been well used.[14] He settled the matter by telling them that while he too thought it was putting money down a rat-hole, he felt obliged to keep the word of the American government. More positively he added that Admiral King had just told him that the Chinese were really beginning to fight and Wedemeyer had to do what

[11] *Ibid.*, pages 487-488.
[12] Memo, Morgenthau-Soong talk, entry, Morgenthau Diary, May 8, 1945.
[13] *Ibid.*, entry, May 9th.
[14] Memo, Morgenthau meeting with staff, May 15, 1945. White and Coe had prepared a memorandum to that effect which Morgenthau rejected.

the Chinese would not let Stilwell do; and in the face of that he felt as though he was acting like a huckster over a matter that had been settled months ago. But he remained disturbed lest the action later would be the subject of scandal, both in the United States and China. So he went on to see whether the State and War Departments would not join with him in the decision. For reasons of their own they both agreed to do so. And then the President assented.

On the morning of the 16th Morgenthau wrote Soong of the decision. On doing so he again remarked that the Treasury thought that past sales of gold had not proven effective; and that the manner in which they had been conducted and the consequent public criticism of them in China were not conducive to achieving the purposes for which American financial aid was granted; and he repeated his hope that the Chinese government would make financial reforms and proceed to create a stabilization fund.[15] Soong, this business done, hurried back to the conference at San Francisco.

Hurley in Chungking had not been kept informed of the progress of these talks about gold sales. When they were over on May 31st, the Treasury told him what had occurred and asked his opinion in regard to the proposed stabilization fund. Hurley in his answer (June 6th) remarked that he would much rather have been consulted before the deal was made than after. He went on to say that he agreed with Morgenthau that there was little evidence that sales of gold would stop inflation, adding that, "Until there is a radical change in the present policy little can be expected. For the government to sell gold below the open market price is a denial of the objective to absorb printing press currency in the maximum amount and furthermore, it has given rise to vicious speculation and much unfavorable publicity. . . ." But, he added, neither could he see how inflation could be stopped merely by setting up a big stabilization fund from current assets. If the American government really thought so, Hurley observed, it should have made its consent to the gold sales conditional on a promise to establish a fund. He had respect, he observed, for the power of suggestion, but in this instance he would have relied on the power of two hundred million dollars.[16]

The Treasury began to make gold available. The Chinese government was able to make good on forward sales to which it was already com-

[15] *United States Relations with China*, pages 507-508.
[16] Telegram, June 6, 1945, Hurley to Morgenthau, *Hurley Papers*, Book III, Item 6. Grew in an acknowledgment to Hurley on June 11th took full blame for not keeping Hurley currently advised.

mitted. But in June, after Soong got back to Chungking, he suspended such forward sales. The Chinese dollar continued to depreciate fast.[17] Like all other features of Chinese life, improvement awaited the final defeat of the Japanese and the return of peace. Then it was thought government financing could be put in shape; and then too the American government could take curative action. On these matters, too, the Communists were found standing in the way.

While making the decisions—political, military, and economic—during the spring of 1945, the American government was mindful that Sino-Soviet relations after the war were still undetermined and that the Soviet armies would soon begin to march into Manchuria. It was on the point of seeking Chinese concurrence to the Yalta Accord; but only after a brief spell of wondering whether after all it wanted the Soviet Union to enter the Pacific war on its own or any other terms.

[17] The Chinese government had in previous years used about 260 million of the 500 million loan: about 200 of it as a fund to redeem the bonds and certificates it sold, 40 to buy gold, about 20 to pay for paper bank notes. Of the remaining 240 millions it used 180 million to buy gold in May, June and July, 1945; 35 million of what was left were used to buy more paper bank notes (the air freight cost of which to Chungking was becoming an increasingly large part of the price as the Chinese dollar depreciated), and the other 25 for textiles and other goods and services.

CHAPTER 28

Steps Pursuant to the Yalta Agreement

Now the American government had to face the fact that only weeks were left to tell Chiang Kai-shek of the secret Yalta Accord, and to have the indicated terms made effective and precise by an agreement between China and the Soviet Union. On April 5th the Soviet government had informed the Japanese government that the Neutrality Pact between them "has lost its meaning, and the continuance of this pact has become impossible." By its own terms this pact was to remain in effect for a year after such notice. But there were obvious signs that the Soviet Union did not intend to observe this stipulation. On May 1st Hitler, deep under the ruins of Berlin, killed himself; a week later Germany ended all resistance. The Soviet armies were free for other conquests. They were already moving in impressive numbers to the Far Eastern front. The promised American equipment was being hustled to them over every route—through Murmansk, Iran, and Vladivostok under the gaze of Japanese ships. If there was to be any confirmed agreement in regard to what the Russians would do and demand in the Far East before their armies moved into battle, it would have to be quickly effected.

The American government was pledged to bring this about. But at this last interval of choice, a current of uneasiness started in the minds of the officials who were face to face with the assignment. This uneasiness cannot be traced to any sense stated in the record that Roosevelt had not acted fairly and for the good of the Chinese. It came rather from the ebbing of faith in the value of Soviet promises and purposes.

Hurley was asking whether the time had not come to tell Chiang Kai-shek. On May 10th he radioed the President that since his return to Chungking he and the Generalissimo had talked over the whole range of Sino-Soviet relationships without speaking of the Yalta Accord or the Soviet promise to enter the war. He reported also that the Chinese Ambassador in Washington had informed Chiang Kai-shek of all the items in the accord save the primary Soviet promise, but somewhat incorrectly; for example, the Ambassador seemed to think that the United States government was going to join in the Sino-Soviet Agreement as a third party. Hurley said he was convinced that Chiang Kai-shek would accede to all the requirements of the Yalta Agreement, but that he would object to the use of the two words "pre-eminent" and "lease." These, Hurley pointed out, had dark meaning in China. They had been used and abused in the past to gain foreign privileges, and seemed to impinge on the territorial integrity and independence of China.[1]

News of Russia's military measures in the Far East was reaching Chungking. The Chinese government was almost sure that the Soviet Union was going to enter the war.[2] Secrecy was losing all point.[3] Thus Hurley was of the opinion that the time had come to give Chiang Kai-shek a whole and correct account of the agreement reached at Yalta. He asked the Joint Chiefs of Staff and the Secretary of State to advise him when he, Hurley, might seek Stalin's concurrence.

This message arrived just when the men in Washington to whom it was addressed, suffering the doubts described, were worrying about what our policy in the Far East was to be, on the verge of Soviet entry into the war. On May 12th, after several talks with Secretary of the Navy Forrestal and Assistant Secretary of War McCloy (Stimson being briefly absent), Grew sent them a memo.[4] Its purpose was to get guidance for Harriman, who on his return to Moscow would be talking with Stalin about the further disposition of the Yalta Accord.

This memo posed some leading questions which the student may well think ought to have been asked by the Secretary of State some months

[1] Text of this message is printed in *Joint Committee on Situation in the Far East*, pages 3337-3338.

[2] On May 7th Hurley had cabled that a Chinese official in Switzerland had reported to Chungking that thirty mechanized Soviet divisions had been ordered to the Far East, and that the Japanese in Shanghai knew of this movement. To which it may be added that the Soviets were failing to keep their own people from guessing it—as reported by the American representative in Vladivostok. Sailors from the Baltic were walking the streets of the city, anti-aircraft batteries were being installed, doctors were being told to be ready to go into war service on twenty-four hours' notice.

[3] In mid-May the Japanese Army General Staff concluded that Soviet intentions to attack and preparations for action were evident. As related in *Japanese Monograph No. 45*, pages 232-233, "It was believed that Soviet Russia would enter the war during the summer or autumn because that would be about the time when American and English forces would invade our Homeland, Southern Korea and North-Central China. In addition owing to climatic conditions in Manchuria aims would have to be achieved before the coldest season started in December."

[4] Joseph C. Grew, *Turbulent Era*, 1952, pages 1445-1446. Grew's personal thoughts regarding the alarming meaning to the United States of the newly revealed wish of the Soviet Union for domination in the Far East and Europe were running strong. They are summed up in a memo which he wrote for himself and read to Harriman and Bohlen on May 19th. One sentence of this, set down with the excited clarity of sleep-lessness read, "A future war with the Soviet Union is as certain as any thing in this world can be certain." About this sentence Grew commented that it should have been qualified with the proviso "unless we recognize the danger and take steps to meet it in time."

before, since at this time they were like rockets shot up in the air. The first of these was in substance: is the entry of the Soviet Union into the Pacific war at the earliest possible moment of such vital interest to the United States as to preclude an attempt to obtain Soviet agreement to certain desirable political objectives in the Far East before such entry? The second was: should the Yalta decision in regard to Soviet political desires in the Far East be reconsidered or carried out in whole or part? What the State Department wanted from the Soviet government, if military considerations permitted, were (1) a promise to use its influence with the Chinese Communists to assist American efforts to unify China under a National Government headed by Chiang Kai-shek; (2) a plain reaffirmation that Manchuria was to be returned to China—as declared at Cairo; (3) a definite pledge that Korea, as soon as liberated, would be placed under a four-power trusteeship; and (4) assurance that it would settle its differences with the Chinese government over Sinkiang in a friendly way.

The War and Navy Departments braced themselves to deal with the two tough questions which Grew had phrased for them. Meanwhile it was thought best to postpone the enlightenment of Chiang Kai-shek. The President told Hurley that the best time for this had not yet come; that he would be told to go ahead as soon as it was felt that full information could be disclosed to the Generalissimo without damage to the overall prospect.

Consistently, when Soong called on him the next day, May 14th, the President let the talk range wide without speaking of the Yalta Accord. After reviewing the various requests for American support which his government was making, Soong passed on to the problem of dealing with the Communists and the Soviet Union. He observed that the National Government would like to have the Communists "join in" but only if they recognized that the National Government was in supreme control in China. Neither the President nor Grew, who was present, made any direct response to this remark. Soong went on to say that he thought there had been a recent change in the attitude of the Soviet Union: that earlier in the war it had been friendly and helpful to the Chinese government, but now it seemed to be supporting the Communists rather than the government. Therefore, he thought he ought to get over to Moscow just as soon as the conference at San Francisco ended; and he would appreciate it if the American government would provide a plane to take him there and then bring him back to the United

States, then on to Chungking. The President began to assent to this request, but Grew asked for time to think it over. Soong pointed out that the Russians were using American planes; and he added that he thought it would be helpful to have the Russians gather that after visiting them he would be returning to Washington to see the President. This matter was left open.[5] Soong returned to San Francisco.

There ensued a week of thought-searching among the State, War, and Navy Departments. Stimson and Marshall were not upset by the queries that the State Department had posed. But they agreed that it was not practical to answer them conclusively at the moment, or even to discuss them with anybody. For they had a momentous secret they could not reveal. The latest reports on progress in the making of an atomic bomb had been distinctly hopeful; they indicated an excellent chance of success. The final proving tests were soon to be held. The results would greatly affect the answer to the first question asked by Grew: how vital was the American interest in having the Soviet Union enter the war as soon as possible? Stimson saw a reason beyond that for letting our actions speak for us for the time being. If, his thought ran, it was deemed necessary to thresh out with the Soviet government these questions about Manchuria and China, it would be better to wait until the American government had this new master weapon, and the world knew it. Thus, when the Cabinet officers (Grew, Stimson, Forrestal, Harriman, and McCloy) met on the 14th, Stimson said that the War Department was not yet in a position to answer the questions asked. It was decided that Harriman should defer his return to Moscow until our course was clearer.

Stimson and Marshall did not give any sign of the secret in their heads in the perplexed answers which they presently (on the 21st) sent to Grew. These remind at least one later reader of a towline hauling too many barges.[6] But the drag of their involved thought can be followed, to wit: (1) That the Soviet Union would pay little heed to any political action the United States might take in deciding whether or not to enter the war against Japan. (2) That Soviet entry would have a profound military effect, in that almost certainly it would materially shorten the war. (3) That it had the choice of waiting until American forces had all

[5] This summary is drawn from Grew's memo of Soong's talk with the President and himself at 2:00 p.m. of May 14th, *Turbulent Era*, pages 1460-1461. A copy was sent to Hurley.
[6] Stimson and Forrestal sent their comments on Grew's memo of May 12th to him on May 21st. Stimson's letter, in which Forrestal concurred, is given in Grew, *ibid.*, pages 1457-1459.

but destroyed the Japanese, or of entering the war sooner and of saving American lives. (4) That either way it would have the military power to take what had been granted at Yalta—unless the United States was ready to go to war to prevent it. (5) That they did not object on military grounds to a review of the Yalta Accord, looking toward fuller understanding; but doubted whether "much good will" would come of it. (6) That unless there was some agreement between the Chinese government and the Chinese Communists, American military problems in China would become very complicated as the Soviet forces advanced to areas in contact with the Communists; and that such an agreement seemed a necessary preliminary to a Sino-Soviet accord.[7]

The whole consultation ended in a mild conclusion: we would not try to revise the terms of the Yalta Accord; but before asking Chiang Kai-shek to concur we would try to get Stalin to re-endorse protective principles. We would again test whether the Soviet government honestly intended to allow the Chinese government to exercise unimpaired sovereignty over all of China and Manchuria, and whether it would fall in with our lead in the effort for unification. In effect, this was a belated resolution to clear up any possible dual reading of the Yalta Accord.

While divisional draftsmen were still buffing the surfaces of these subjects, Hopkins set off to talk them over with Stalin. Truman, who was taking up the task of finding out whether he could work with the Soviet Union, a task which had worn away the last weeks of Roosevelt's life, had asked Hopkins to risk the journey. It was thought that he, if anyone, could on the one hand reassure Stalin that Roosevelt's policies

---

[7] On the same day that this Stimson-Forrestal answer was sent to Grew, the State Department sent them a second memo which suggested in detail terms and methods, political and military, for unifying China militarily, with Soviet and British cooperation. This was directed towards getting the Soviet government to accede to a definite program and to help to bring it about and make it effective.

Both Stimson and Forrestal were disturbed by these detailed suggestions about military matters, and stressed the need for further study (particularly McCloy's analytical letter of May 27th).

Hopkins and Harriman saw the first papers before leaving for Moscow on the 23rd, and Bohlen, who left the same day, took with him the second State Department memo. Then on June 2nd Grew cabled Harriman to let him know that the War and Navy Departments were expressing concern as to (1) approaching the Soviets in such detail on the military aspects before knowing the Chinese reaction, (2) possible effect on American military plans and operations. Hopkins and Harriman answered on the 4th that the outcome of their talks with Stalin had been reported to the President, and they did not plan to go further at that time nor to discuss any other subjects in the State Department memo. Harriman and Hopkins felt that they did not have enough knowledge of prospective American military plans or of Washington's views as to the way in which the Manchurian situation should be handled. Stalin could be concrete when it suited him, and on these points they could not be.

would be continued, and on the other induce Stalin to carry out faithfully with Truman the agreements reached with Roosevelt. The mission was regarded as a crucial attempt to restore the trustful working accord which Roosevelt and Hopkins thought had been formed at Yalta, particularly in regard to whether Stalin would act fairly toward Poland and adhere to the American understanding of what had been arranged for the Far East.

Most of the many talks between Stalin and Hopkins (scattered between May 26th and June 6th) were devoted to European affairs, especially Poland. Hopkins was direct from first sentence to last. He began by referring to Roosevelt's confidence that the United States and the Soviet Union could work together in peace as well as in war. The American people had shared this opinion. But now, he went on, even those who had strongly supported Roosevelt were seriously perturbed over the present trend of relations with the Soviet Union. President Truman wished to continue Roosevelt's policies, and intended in fact and spirit to carry out all the arrangements which Roosevelt had made with Stalin. But, and Hopkins made the point plain, the President too was now disturbed and that was why he had asked Hopkins to make the hard journey to Moscow. Stalin did not long remain on the defensive. He brought forward his own table of grievances against the United States. While the talks were softened by a mutual friendly regard and a prudential wish to avoid a definite break, they exposed rather than settled the clash of ideas and purposes as regards Poland and several other issues in Europe. Churchill had reason for remarking, when on June 4th he urged another meeting among the three heads of state, that, "Nothing really important has been settled yet. . . ."

In contrast, the talks about Far Eastern affairs went swiftly and smoothly.[8] Hopkins devoted his effort to securing Stalin's affirmation that the Yalta Accord meant what Roosevelt had thought it meant. He

---

[8] At the third meeting on May 28th, an important segment of the long talk was devoted to Japan. Others will tell of this more adequately than I can here. In brief, Stalin was of the opinion that Japan would not surrender unconditionally until utterly beaten. He told Hopkins that certain Japanese elements were putting out peace feelers, and he thought they might try for a conditional surrender in an attempt to divide the Allies and save a military nucleus. This seemed to him to make it urgent that the United States, Great Britain, and the Soviet Union decide their joint attitude toward Japan and work together. Harriman said that the American government did not intend to modify the unconditional surrender. Stalin said he was glad to hear it, and agreed with us. The talk brought out the fact that Stalin expected that the Soviet Union would share in the actual occupation of Japan and wanted an agreement with the United States and Britain as regards occupation terms and zones.

entered the subject by saying that General Marshall and Admiral King would find it most helpful to know the approximate date of the Soviet entry into the Pacific war. Stalin answered that the Soviet armies would be prepared and in position by August 8th. But he explained that the decision as to when actually to start operations would depend on the execution of the Yalta Accord. In other words, he said, the Soviet armies would begin to advance in early August if China by then had accepted the terms of this accord. What would happen otherwise, he did not say. After some talk as to how much longer it would be possible to conceal Soviet plans, it was agreed that it would be all right to consult the Chinese government early in July. Soong was to be haled to Moscow not later than July 1st; the Soviet government would take the matter up with him there, while Hurley at the same time was to take it up with Chiang Kai-shek in Chungking. It may be observed in passing that Japanese Imperial Headquarters was by this time convinced that the Soviet Union would enter the war and was taking such measures as it could in the face of American attacks to meet the further danger.[9]

As the talk about China flowed on, Stalin said once more he agreed that it was desirable that China be unified. When Hopkins asked his view as to how this could be done, Stalin said he had no special plan. He added that he did not think that China would soon become industrialized and that he thought that the United States must play the largest part in helping China to come back, since the Soviet Union would be occupied with its own internal needs and Great Britain would be busy elsewhere. He explicitly said that he agreed with the American Open Door Policy in China.

Harriman asked what would happen if the effort to unify China had not succeeded by the time the Soviet troops entered Manchuria. Would Stalin then consider it possible to make the necessary arrangements with the Generalissimo? Stalin answered that the Soviet Union did not pro-

---

[9] During the early months of 1945, the Japanese High Command had become so alarmed by the American victories in the Philippines and elsewhere in the Pacific that they drew heavily on the Kwantung army to strengthen their forces in Formosa and elsewhere in the Pacific, Coastal China, and the Japanese home islands. Then, as the signs of Soviet intentions to enter the war became more conclusive, they tried to make up for the weakening of the Kwantung army by concentration of their forces. *Japanese Monograph No. 45*, pages 190-191. As further related in "History of the Army Section, Imperial Headquarters," *Japanese Monograph No. 72*, page 198, "Toward the end of May the changing situation on the continent convinced GHQ of the urgent necessity of quickly strengthening the defensive preparations in Korea and Manchuria against the Soviet menace, and on May 28th they issued an order telling the Commanding General of the 17th Area Army . . . to operate under the direction of the Commander in Chief of the Kwantung Army to battle against the U.S. forces and the preparation of anti-Soviet defenses in North Korea."

pose to alter the sovereignty of the Chinese over Manchuria or any other part of China. He emphasized that the Soviet Union had no territorial claims with regard to China, either in Sinkiang or elsewhere. He went on to say (1) that the Soviet people would not hinder Chinese unity but would help to achieve it, and (2) that he did not know the Chinese leaders well, but that he thought that Chiang Kai-shek was the best of the lot and would be the one to undertake the unification of China—in fact he saw no other possible leader, and he did not believe that the Chinese Communist leaders were as good or as fit for the job. Finally, he added—and this had not been said before—that if Soviet troops entered Manchuria, he would ask Chiang Kai-shek to organize the civil administration within the areas of occupation. Chiang Kai-shek could send his representative to set up the Kuomintang regime in any places where the Red Armies were; he was quite prepared to accept them.

Who, except those most schooled in mistrust, on hearing these statements, would not have found in them relieving assurance? It will long be wondered whether they were a true expression of Stalin's thoughts at the time, or cover for his real thoughts. The only certainty is that he was careful to say nothing which might have prevented the completion of the Yalta Accord. He knew that there would be a long later chance to take guidance from circumstance; to work along with the United States and the Chinese government if that was advantageous, to slip away if it was not.

Both Hopkins and Harriman concluded that Stalin genuinely intended to work with the United States to bring about a unified China under Chiang Kai-shek's leadership, and that he would abide by the Yalta Agreement as understood in Washington. As summed up at the end of their report to the President on their talks with Stalin, "We were very encouraged by the conference on the Far East."[10] And in view of the fact that Stalin had made plain that he intended to attack during August, they thought it important that Soong should go to Moscow before the 1st of July.

The President was impressed by their report. Despite the position and rights in the Manchurian ports and railways to be accorded the Soviet Union, he regarded Stalin's promise that Manchuria should remain fully Chinese as firm and clear. Hence he concluded the way was open for China to reach an agreement in Moscow giving effect to the Yalta

[10] The main substance of that report is in Sherwood, *Roosevelt and Hopkins*, pages 902-903.

Accord which would not be offensive to American interests and principles. The thought that it might be necessary to have a showdown in
this realm with the Soviet government was smothered by Stalin's assurances; and with it any possible idea of postponing further discussion
of the execution of the Yalta Accord until the outcome of the atomic
bomb tests was known.

Soong, who was still at the San Francisco Conference, was planning
to return to Chungking before he went to Moscow. The President, on
hearing from Hopkins, asked Stettinius, who was also at San Francisco,
to tell Soong orally that Stalin wished to talk over "important matters"
with him in Moscow before July 1st, and that we would fly him there.
Stettinius—who knew that Soong already knew much of what was in
the Yalta Accord—urged that he should be told all by us before he left
for Moscow. Otherwise, in acknowledging his instructions, he remarked
Soong would certainly feel that we had not been frank with him. But
the President stood by the arrangement made between Stalin and Hopkins: that Soong was to be told when he got to Moscow, and Chiang
Kai-shek was to be told at the same time by Hurley. Thus on June 5th,
Grew informed Stettinius that the President did not yet think it wise
because of security reasons to tell Soong of the agreement; but that he
had it in mind when Soong came to Washington to give him a general
indication of our position and grasp of the subjects which Stalin wished
to talk over.

On this same day, June 5th, but before he had heard from Grew,
Stettinius had another talk with Soong. Soong again sought information
in regard to the Stalin-Hopkins talks and Soviet entry into the war.
Stettinius put him off with the answer that either he or the President
would want to talk with him before he went to Moscow on the general
subject of Sino-Soviet relations. Soong remarked that China's only hope
of keeping out of the Soviet orbit was a strong connection with the
United States. On that same calendar day, June 5th (but Chungking
time, ahead of our time) Hurley sent word that the Soviet envoy in
Chungking had talked with Chiang Kai-shek some days before about
various aspects of China's territorial integrity and political independence.
Chiang Kai-shek had told Hurley of the discussion. Hurley took note
of the fact that the Soviet Ambassador had not mentioned the Soviet
decision to enter the war. Both parties, Hurley added, were pleased by
the talk.

On the next day, Stettinius relayed Stalin's message to Soong: Come before July 1st. He told him also of our willingness to provide a plane to take him to Chungking, thence to Moscow, and then back again to Washington. He also said that the President wanted to talk with him within the next few days. Soong tried to quiz him further. But Stettinius said that he could not answer his questions at San Francisco; they must wait until he saw the President in Washington. Soong hurried along to Washington. While he was on his way, the President, through Grew, again consulted Stettinius as to how much to tell Soong. Stettinius again advised complete frankness.

The President talked with Soong on June 9th in the presence of Grew and Leahy.[11] He wrapped up the Yalta package attractively, imparting the information without making each and every phrase exactly known. His way of doing this was to show Soong a copy of a message which was being sent to Hurley.[12] The first part of this message set out in full the assurances which Stalin had given Hopkins. Then it specified the conditions laid down by the Soviet Union for its entrance into the war—in the phraseology of the Yalta Accord. Hurley was told to tell Chiang Kai-shek on June 15th of all the foregoing; and to explain that President Roosevelt had promised to support the Soviet claims and that President Truman was in agreement. Hurley was asked to obtain Chiang Kai-shek's approval of the accord and to see that Soong got to Moscow by July 1st.

Soong read the copy of the message to Hurley with care. But he did not say much, just enough to indicate disquiet about one or two points. After the meeting Grew took a paraphrase of this message to Soong's house so that he might study it thoroughly. Then two days later (June 11th) Grew and Soong talked more fully about the particular Soviet demands. Soong's comments were tentative, mainly in the nature of review of the several ways in which most points in the accord could be interpreted and applied; some would be objectionable, others not. He asked Grew what the term "pre-eminent interest" meant. Grew said he was not present at Yalta and thus could not interpret the agreement. He assumed, he said, its details would have to be ironed out at the next meeting of the Big Three; and Soong himself would soon have the chance to discuss them with Stalin. He repeated that the American government was committed to support the agreement as it stood. Soong answered, and not impertinently, the question is, just what have you agreed to support?

[11] Grew's memo of this talk is in *Turbulent Era*, pages 1465-1466.
[12] White House telegram No. 285 from the Secretary of State to Hurley, June 9, 1945.

Grew's answers did not quiet the queries in Soong's mind. So he sought and was granted another interview with the President before setting off for China. This took place on June 14th. The President reviewed in an optimistic way the assurances which Stalin had given to Hopkins, saying that they were more categoric than any previous ones. Soong acknowledged pleasure at learning of this. But he again asked about the meaning of various particulars. The President did not attempt to interpret, and the talk glided to broader ground. The President pointed to our interest in having the Soviet Union enter the war soon enough to help shorten it and thus save American and Chinese lives, but he assured Soong that he would do nothing which would harm China.[13]

Soong set off for Chungking. There Hurley was waiting for June 15th to come around so that he could tell Chiang Kai-shek what had to be told. He was irked at the fact that Soong was being told so much while his own tongue was tied. His justified understanding was that it would be left to him to handle the talks with the Chinese government. He also felt that it was pointless to wait any longer since, as he informed the Secretary of State, the Soviet Ambassador had the day before submitted to Chiang Kai-shek the conditions upon which the Soviet Union would enter the war—without however making any reference to the assurances which Stalin had given Hopkins.[14] Still Hurley waited out the set time before entering into formal talk with the Generalissimo about the Yalta Accord.

When he did, Chiang Kai-shek had three suggestions:

1. That the United States and Great Britain should become parties to whatever agreement China might sign with the Soviet Union. This, he said, would make it more certain that the Soviet Union would comply with its terms.

2. That Port Arthur should be designated as a joint naval base for four powers: China, Soviet Union, United States, and Great Britain.

3. That the transfer of Sakhalin and the Kuriles to the Soviet Union should be discussed by the same four powers rather than by China and the Soviet Union alone.[15]

[13] Grew memo, June 14, 1945, in *Turbulent Era*, pages 1466-1468.
[14] Telegram, Hurley to Stettinius, June 13, 1945.
[15] Telegram, Hurley to Truman, June 15, 1945.
None of the Hurley Papers or cables that I have seen gives information as regards the way in which Chiang Kai-shek reacted to this notification about the Yalta Accord. They informed Washington of the Generalissimo's questions and proposals, but passed over his attitude. Perhaps this was due to the fact that Chiang Kai-shek already knew everything that was in the Yalta Accord. But General Wedemeyer, who went along with Hurley for

These proposals, Grew and the President figured, could not be answered without consulting the Soviet and British governments. Truman observed in their talk that Chiang Kai-shek and Soong now knew as much as he did about the Yalta Accord, and that while he was committed to it, he was not qualified to expand on its interpretation.[16] Hurley was told to tell Chiang Kai-shek that the American government could not consent either to share in the joint use of Port Arthur as a naval base or to become a party to whatever agreement the Chinese government might decide to sign with the Soviet Union. He was told also that it seemed very doubtful whether the Soviet Union would consent to the arrangements that Chiang Kai-shek had in mind, since the purpose of the pact with China would be regulating Sino-Soviet relations.[17]

Hurley reviewed with Soong his mission as envoy to Stalin. He repeated (in his talk with the Generalissimo and Soong on June 22nd) that President Truman approved and supported the Yalta decisions, and Roosevelt's position in regard to them.[18] Although it had been made plain to him that the American government would not become a co-sponsor, the Generalissimo continued to want a protective agreement with the Soviet Union. Both he and Soong saw the uses of it, and accepted the great need for it. But they remained uneasy as to what China and their own regime might be made to pay in order to get it. They longed for other defenders of China's integrity and independence against the brutish bear. Despite these anxieties, Soong got ready to leave for Moscow. Hurley was optimistic as to what would follow. "I am convinced," he said, "that the Soviet Union and China will be able to reach an agreement quickly."[19] Through Harriman, Washington had been keeping Stalin informed of the talks with Chiang Kai-shek and Soong, trying to ensure that China would be decently treated. Soong got to Moscow early in July.

The Chinese Communists followed his flight to Moscow no less intently than the government. A new inning of negotiations between

---

this talk, later gave his impressions of the occasion. He recounted that the Generalissimo did not ask any questions; that he was silent for about a minute and then asked that the interpreter repeat what Hurley told him, and it was repeated, and then he just said that he was terribly disappointed, or words to that effect. *Joint Committee on Military Situation in the Far East*, pages 2416-2417, and page 2431.

[16] Grew memo of conversation with President, June 16, 1945.
[17] Grew cable to Hurley, June 18th, 1945.
[18] Telegram, Hurley to State Department, June 23, 1945.
[19] Hurley telegram to State Department, June 27, 1945.

them had opened in which Hurley took an active part.[20] The terms forwarded by the Communists were equivalent to asking the government to accept a minority place in the conferences about the future form of government in China. Still, Hurley inferred that progress was being made. The Kuomintang, he thought, now clearly recognized the need to change both the form of government and many of its policies. Soviet influence, he forecast, would control the action of the Communists; they still believed that they would have the support of the Soviet Union, but he predicted that when they learned that they did not, they would settle with the National Government if it made generous concessions to them. Both sides, he thought, were waiting to learn the results of Soong's visit to Moscow.[21]

On the same day, July 10th, that Hurley sent this report, Wedemeyer sent one of grimmer import to Marshall. If unification was not soon achieved, he predicted that the clashes between government and Communist forces, already numerous, would extend in scope and severity as both sides moved into country evacuated by the Japanese. These might turn into general civil war which would bring revolution and chaos in China. He did not think that polite appeal would bring about unification; but that coercion, jointly exercised by the United States, the Soviet Union, and Great Britain might do so—coercion on both the Kuomintang and Communists to make realistic concessions to form a coalition. Wedemeyer did not have to spell out the great questions raised: was the American government willing to stand aside while the condition and control of China was settled by civil war? Would, as Hurley hoped, peace within China come out of Moscow? There Soong was having a hard time.

Soong's talks with Stalin and Molotov had begun in the tremor of coming events. It was known that in about a month Soviet troops might be coming down through Mongolia and Manchuria into China and Korea, within easy reach of the Communist zone. It was also known that Stalin would in about a fortnight be meeting with Truman and Churchill. Whether secret information that while they were meeting, an atomic bomb would be exploded at Alamagordo in New Mexico affected the ideas of Stalin is not easily known.[22]

[20] For details of Hurley's talks with the various political groups at this time, see *United States Relations with China*, pages 99-105.

[21] Hurley telegram to State Department, July 10, 1945, *ibid.*, page 99, and Smyth memo of talk Hurley and Wang Shih-Chieh.

[22] That the Soviet Intelligence knew of the coming test and the approximate time of

Stalin without scruple demanded rights and privileges in Manchuria that went well beyond any claims revealed before or at Yalta. He began by making clear that all other questions would have to be settled in advance before the Soviet Union would enter into a pact of friendship with the Chinese government. The issue that figured most troublesomely in the first phase of their talk, and may have worried Soong most to the last, was Outer Mongolia. Stalin insisted adamantly that China formally recognize its independence.[23] Soong said that Chiang Kai-shek could not agree to cede territory by executive act; if he did so, his government might fall and the Chinese Communists would be among the most active critics. Stalin dismissed these anxieties with the remark that there would be nothing to fear if the Chinese and Soviet governments stood together.

Stalin then submitted to Soong prepared drafts of three agreements: A Treaty of Friendship and Alliance; An Agreement Regarding the Ports at Dairen and Port Arthur; An Agreement Regarding the Manchurian Railroads. The first, in carefully worded and arranged phrases, offered Chiang Kai-shek what he so eagerly wanted—a degree of assurance that the Soviet government would work with his regime and refrain from aiding his enemies. The other two specified the price which the Soviet Union wanted to exact for this promise. The arrangements which were proposed in these memos would have in effect allowed the Soviet Union to control the whole of Manchuria. The Soviet government proposed the creation of a military zone which was to include not only the ports of Dairen and Port Arthur but adjacent land and sea areas. It was to have the right to keep naval and air forces in this zone. A naval base was to be established in one of the inner bays of Dairen for the exclusive use of the Chinese and Soviet navies. The Manchurian railroads and connected enterprises ·(factories, workshops, lands, coal mines, timber tracts) were to be exclusively owned by the Soviet Union, which also was to have the governing voice in their management and operation.

---

this momentous test, seems almost beyond doubt. But whether Stalin foresaw that it would greatly hasten the end of the war against Japan, remains unknown. As for Soong, he had nine months before told Gauss that the war would be won by a secret weapon which the United States was developing. But how much he knew is unknown—at least to me.

[23] Coincidentally, another visitor from the east arrived in Moscow and was greeted by Molotov—Marshal Choibalsan, Premier of the Mongolian People's Republic. Choibalsan wore the medal of the Order of Lenin for "conspicuous services in organizing material aid to the Red Army in the Mongolian People's Republic." *Time*, July 16, 1945.

At this point the historian cannot reject a speculation: that Stalin thought himself free and able to extract from Chiang Kai-shek's regime terms more favorable to Russian expansion than he would have thought wise to seek from the Chinese Communists. To have asked of them what he asked of the government might have caused a schism in the whole international Communist group in the Far East. Further than that, it might even have led to a patriotic reconciliation between the Communists and the government in resistance to Russian demands. If this surmise is valid, it is not hard to see why Stalin sought the softer bargain: a confirmed position in Mongolia and Manchuria in return for a promise that would not have to be carried out if the Communists eventually proved the stronger. And by giving this promise, he could lull the fears of the United States and cause it to take a more trusting view of other postwar settlements. Such, rather than his professed indifference to the Chinese Communists, might well have been the trail along which his instinct guided him. The appearance of coldness toward his Chinese associates served both to make his course convincing, and to leave him free. But, to repeat, this is only speculation.

Soong tried to give the drafts back to Molotov, but Molotov suggested that he had better keep them. So Soong took them and at once transmitted them to Chiang Kai-shek. His message was crossed by one from the Generalissimo which set down the maximum concessions which he thought China ought to be called upon to make. These were near the opposite bargaining boundary. The Generalissimo said that in return for full Soviet recognition of China's sovereignty in Manchuria and a definite agreement to withdraw all moral and material aid from the Chinese Communists and rebellious groups in Sinkiang, he would agree to preserve the status quo in Outer Mongolia until the end of the war, when a plebiscite would be held.[24] He would also (a) agree to grant

---

[24] The Chinese government was again greatly anxious about the situation in that vast border province of Sinkiang. A serious revolt had begun in the previous February and was still unsettled. The Chinese government was sure that the Soviet Union inspired the insurrection, and that the rebels were getting arms and ammunition from across the Soviet border. The evidence of this was vague. The American Embassy in Moscow thought that the Soviet Union was not out to get direct control over the province, but did mean to get a governing influence over its official policies, and to assure itself of a friendly regime in the province which would encourage the resumption of trade with the Soviet Union and favor Soviet penetration. Hurley had discussed this situation with Stalin and Molotov when he was in Moscow in April. Stalin at that time commented that only five per cent of the province was Chinese, and that he thought that it was the constant refusal of the Chinese government to make concessions to the members of other races that was causing the trouble.

The revolt had dragged on. Then in June the Chinese government had asked the local Soviet Consul-General to use Soviet good offices to settle it. The Soviet official

the Soviet navy the right to use Port Arthur as a base along with the Chinese navy, but the port was to be under Chinese administration. (b) He was opposed to the inclusion of Dairen in the naval base area. But he was willing to turn it into a free port under Chinese administration, giving the Soviet Union a lease on docks for merchant shipping and free and full right to import and export through the port. (c) He agreed to turn over the direction and management of the Manchurian railroads to a joint Sino-Soviet company, the title to rest with the Chinese government.

So far apart were these two sets of terms that Harriman did not think that any agreement would be reached unless the American government intervened. He suggested that Washington should prepare at once an official American interpretation of the terms of the Yalta Accord, and that President Truman should discuss the issues with Stalin when they met at Potsdam. He advised Soong not to come to an impasse with Stalin at this time but rather to have a friendly adjournment. The Ambassador's impression was that Soong would cede more to Stalin than the Generalissimo would, if the form of the settlement saved the face of the National Government, and if he was convinced that the Soviet government would really support the National Government in unifying China.[25]

While Soong was wondering whether he dared suspend the talks and return to Chungking, the Russians reduced their demands. At their talk on the night of the 10th, Stalin, while not admitting that he had given help of any sort to the Chinese Communists stated "categorically," that he would support only the National Government in China and that all the military forces in China must come under the control of the government.[26] Accord came into sight—except in regard to the treatment of the Manchurian ports and railways. The unadjusted differences in this field were deep, being in reality the issue as to whether China or the Soviet Union would be in control. Soong said he could not give in any further. He suggested that he might return to Chungking to consult

suggested that the matter be taken up directly with Moscow. It was on the table awaiting discussion when Soong came to Moscow.

In regard to Outer Mongolia, the phrase "status quo" used in the Yalta Accord could be understood in any one of several ways. The Chinese government throughout its negotiations with the Soviet Union took the position that it meant the formal political status, as defined in Article V of the Soviet-Chinese Agreement of May 31, 1924; in this the Soviet Union recognized Outer Mongolia as an integral part of China. The Soviet Union argued (1) that this had been modified by later statements, and (2) that in actual existing fact, Outer Mongolia was independent.

[25] Harriman's report to the President, July 9, 1945.
[26] As told by Soong to Harriman and reported by Harriman to the President July 11th.

with the Generalissimo. Stalin said he thought it would be better for both to come to an agreement before he left for Potsdam, as he wanted to decide there with President Truman the date when the Soviet Union would enter the war against Japan. The hint did not shake Soong. Finding in their last talk on the night of the 12th that Stalin would not give way, that he insisted that Dairen must be in the Soviet military zone and that the railways be under Soviet control, Soong said that he must seek guidance in Chungking. He would, he told Stalin, be ready to come back to Moscow when Stalin wished. Stalin gave Soong the usual ritual dinner. On the 14th he left for Chungking. Stalin and Harriman, separately, left for Potsdam.

Soong, after one of his first talks with Stalin, had again tried to quiz the American government about the intended meaning of parts of the accord which Roosevelt had signed at Yalta. Byrnes (who had just succeeded Stettinius as Secretary of State) answered through Harriman that both he and the President thought it unwise for the American government to act as interpreter. Having made this disclaimer, the Secretary of State had then gone on to say that he understood that the railways should be jointly owned and operated by the Soviet Union and China, and that while the American government did not wish to share in the control of administration of the port of Dairen, it would expect to have free and equal access to the port as well as to the railways.[27] The Ambassador had also told both the Soviet government and Soong that the American government expected to be consulted before any agreement was finally made.

Just before he left Moscow, Soong asked Harriman to inform the President of his impressions of the outcome of his talks thus far. He felt that the Chinese offer had already met any reasonable interpretation of the Yalta Agreement in regard to the ports and railways and had been more yielding than required in regard to Outer Mongolia. Soong thought that the terms offered by the Soviet government in regard to the Treaty of Friendship were satisfactory. He valued the Soviet promise not to back the Chinese Communists and insurgents in Sinkiang. He was pleased by a promise which Stalin had given him to withdraw Soviet troops quickly from Manchuria after Japanese surrender. Stalin had said that he would rather not have any stipulation in the agreement itself in regard to the time of this withdrawal but that the evacuation would begin within three weeks after the Japanese defeat and, he

[27] Telegram, Byrnes to Harriman, July 4, 1945.

[320]

thought, could be completed within two months, three at the most; and then had said he would put the promise in writing. Soong was also satisfied with the civil affairs arrangement whereby the Chinese government would take over authority from the Soviet forces in Manchuria as they withdrew. Soong said that he hoped that President Truman would at Potsdam try to get the Russians to give ground on the two unsettled matters, the Manchurian ports and railways. In general he gave Harriman the impression that his parting from Stalin was friendly, and that he was pleased with the frankness of the talks and the attitude of the Soviet government.

The President and Byrnes were loath to become involved in the negotiations, though wishful that an agreement would be concluded before the meeting at Potsdam. For there they knew that, together with European questions, they would have to decide upon all the final phases of the defeat of Japan. Plans and arrangements in these fields were being carried forward with great urgency.

CHAPTER 29

Agreements at Potsdam: July 1945

TRUMAN, STALIN, AND CHURCHILL met at Potsdam to deal first of all with the European problems following on the defeat of Germany. But while they were there (July 17th to August 2nd) all the unsettled business cast up in the last phase of the war against Japan was flung upon them. During their fortnight of consultation, the three heads of state and their military staffs were compelled, in addition to the multiple affairs of Europe, to make related decisions about the Japanese surrender, Soviet entry into the war, and the unfinished Sino-Soviet accord. Secretary of War Stimson took station close by to wait for word of the scheduled test of the atomic bomb in New Mexico, so that he could quickly pass on the news and discuss its bearings.

The terms offered Japan had been announced often: unconditional surrender; take it or leave it. The American government had been loath to promise any alleviation of this sentence. It would not accept in advance any restraining conditions upon its right to impose upon Japan any terms it saw fit. But both Roosevelt and Truman had sought to make known that this right would not be used in a spirit of vengeance, that the United States would not oppress the Japanese people or condemn them to prolonged misery.[1] The British had fallen in with the American attitude. The Soviet government had commended it.

The Japanese government in late May and early June had begun to

---

[1] This formula of surrender had been first publicly announced at a joint press conference by Roosevelt and Churchill at Casablanca January 24, 1943. At that time the President had explained that the term "unconditional surrender . . . does not mean the destruction of the population of Germany, Italy or Japan but it does mean the destruction of the philosophies in those countries which are based on conquest and the subjugation of other people." During his visit to Hawaii in July 1944, he had been asked by the press (July 29th) whether "the goal with Japan is still unconditional surrender." His answer was that it was still the goal with everybody, that despite complaints that it was "too tough and too rough" he and Churchill had not modified it. But he had gone on to relate in dialogue the talk that is supposed to have taken place between Grant and Lee which preceded Lee's acceptance of "unconditional surrender" and was followed by Grant's generous recognition of the essential needs of the beaten Confederate states. The dialogue—which historians do not authenticate word by word—was a way of making the point with which Roosevelt concluded his tale. "There you have unconditional surrender. I have given you no new term. We are human beings—normal thinking human beings. That is what we mean by unconditional surrender." On May 8, 1945, Truman in a press conference had repeated this interpretation in substance, concluding with the statement that "unconditional surrender does not mean the extermination or enslavement of the Japanese people."

try to see if there might not be some way of escaping this ultimate capitulation. It had sought to find out through the Soviet Ambassador in Tokyo whether the Soviet Union could be induced to stay out of the Pacific war, and perhaps mediate with Japan, the United States, and Great Britain. Stalin had told Hopkins that he was paying no attention to these Japanese tenders. The American comment had been, that was the right way to deal with them. During June there was much discussion in the high ranks of the American government as to whether our blank demand ought to be filled in. Acting Secretary of State Grew, Secretary of War Stimson, Secretary of the Navy Forrestal, all were in favor of explaining what was meant by "unconditional surrender," with the thought of inducing a response from Japan.[2] But the President thought it wise to wait until he talked with Churchill and Stalin before deciding what could best be said next to the Japanese government. Otherwise the utmost confusion might result.

The Japanese government, on learning of the meeting in prospect of the three heads of state, tried harder to enlist Soviet interest. The Soviet government remained unresponsive. Then, on July 12th, four days before the opening of the Potsdam Conference, the Japanese government had asked Sato, its Ambassador in Moscow, to inform Molotov that the Emperor wished peace and was preparing to send a special envoy to Moscow to arrange it. Prince Konoye, who had been Prime Minister when Japan had flung herself into the war in 1941, was the person in mind for this mission. The radio message containing this instruction to Sato was intercepted and one other passage of it was of confirmatory interest. It read, "Should, however, the United States and Great Britain insist on unconditional surrender . . . there is no other way for Japan but to fight through the war at all hazards. . . ."[3] Sato was

[2] See Grew, *Turbulent Era*, page 1421, *et seq.* The main point under discussion was whether or not to state that the American government would allow the Japanese to keep their imperial institutions if the people so wished.

[3] The text of this and other messages that were sent back and forth between Foreign Minister Togo and Ambassador Sato between July 12th and August 8th were presented as exhibits to the International Military Tribunal for the Far East, Nos. 2696, 2697, 2698, 2699, 2700, 2701, 2702, 2704, and 2705. In the instruction sent to Sato on July 21st to give him further guidance in regard to the Konoye Mission, Togo repeated, "We cannot accept unconditional surrender in any circumstances. It is obvious that, if the war be protracted, more blood will be shed by both sides, yet the Japanese nation will rise as one man against the enemy, if it persistently demands unconditional surrender."

Informative accounts of the months of discussion within the Japanese government and around the Emperor as regards seeking peace terms are given in the Defense Depositions presented by Togo, Secretary of State for Foreign Affairs, and Marquis Kido, Lord Keeper of the Privy Seal, to the International Military Tribunal for the Far East, and in Toshikazu Kase's book, *Journey to the Missouri*.

told that Molotov was too busy to see him, because he and Stalin were getting ready to go to Potsdam. The answer therefore would be delayed, explained Lozovsky, Vice Commissar for Foreign Affairs.

Stalin might well have felt pleased with his position on the eve of his departure for Potsdam. Japan was bidding for Soviet peace and mediation, and no doubt willing to pay for them.[4] The Chinese government was bargaining for protection against Soviet force and influence. The expanding and equipped Soviet armies were along the Manchurian and Mongolian frontiers, ready and able to carry out any command he might give. Thus he could be sure of getting, in one way or another, much if not all of what he wanted out of this Far Eastern segment of war and diplomacy.

As the conference was gathering on July 16th, the first atomic bomb was detonated. The news was flashed to Stimson, who hurried to pass it on. Truman was soberly impressed. Churchill was vocal ". . . Gunpowder . . . trivial. Electricity . . . interesting. This . . . this is the second coming in wroth." But Stalin seemed to evince slight interest in the occurrence. We now know why: for at least a month the Soviet intelligence service had had full knowledge of the bomb and the coming first test.[5]

On the same day, the Combined Chiefs of Staff discussed the question of defining the term "unconditional surrender," but not to a conclusion. The British Chiefs of Staff saw advantages in explaining the term in a way that would not involve the ending of the Imperial institution; then the Emperor would be in a position to order the Japanese forces outside of the home islands to surrender, while otherwise they might fight on alone. The American Chiefs of Staff referred to the possible issuance of an ultimatum which would explain what the term would not mean rather than what it would mean.

During the next week while the heads of state were absorbed in the attempt to adjust their ideas about the settlement of Europe, Far Eastern matters were left for the staff to study. On the 24th the Combined Chiefs of Staff reported to the President and Prime Minister on their overall concept for the prosecution of the war in the Pacific. They still visualized "invading and seizing objectives in the Japanese home islands

----

[4] As expressed by Kase, *ibid.*, page 194, "We did not regard it as impossible for the Soviet Union to sell favors to us by playing the role of an honest broker with the United States and Great Britain."

[5] "Traitor—Klaus Fuchs," by Alan Moorehead, *Saturday Evening Post*, May 31, 1952.

as the main effort."⁶ And they recommended that the common policy should be "to encourage Russian entry into the war against Japan. Provide such aid to her war-making capacity as may be necessary and practicable in connection therewith." But the American Joint Chiefs of Staff had come to recognize that the war might come to a sensationally quick end. In this interval they were sending messages to MacArthur and Nimitz, warning them that it might "prove necessary to take action within the near future on the basis of Japanese capitulation, possibly before Russian entry," and that "coordination of plans for the procedure to be followed in the event of Japanese governmental surrender is now a pressing necessity."⁷

Stalin had again (on the 17th) told Truman that the Soviet Union would enter the war, but only after the agreement with China was completed. The wish to have the Soviet Union in the war had lingered on despite the proof of our power that glowed through Japan's ashes and rubble. As Truman himself later remarked, "At the time [Potsdam] we were anxious for Russian entry into the Japanese war."⁸

In preparation for that event, the American and Soviet Chiefs of Staff (July 24th-26th) worked out a basic agreement to synchronize operations against Japan. G-2, the Military Intelligence Division of the War Department, had, in an impressive report on the Chinese Communist movement submitted on July 5th, concluded that "In order to prevent the separation of Manchuria and North China from China, it is essential that if Soviet Russia participates in the war, China not be divided (like Europe) into American-British and Russian zones of military operations."⁹ How thoroughly this report was read, how carefully the question

⁶ The plans of operation up to and including the first landing on the southernmost of the four main islands of Japan, Kyushu, had been authorized at a White House conference on June 18th. Preparations had gone forward. Then at their session of June 29th the Joint Chiefs had settled upon November 1st as the starting date of this operation.

⁷ Messages, July 21st and 26th, Joint Chiefs of Staff to MacArthur and Nimitz. Ray S. Cline, *Washington Command Post*, pages 348-349.

⁸ Memo, Truman to Byrnes, January 5, 1946, printed in *Mr. President*, by William Hillman, page 123. The memo went on to observe, "Of course we found later we didn't need Russia there and that the Russians have been a headache to us ever since."

On that point, study of the Japanese records, especially the monographs prepared by Japanese military officials under the supervision of SCAP, support the conclusion stated by the United States Bombing Survey in their Summary Report (Pacific war) page 26, ". . . it is the Survey's opinion that certainly prior to 31 December 1945, and in all probability prior to 1 November 1945, Japan would have surrendered even if the atomic bombs had not been dropped, even if Russia had not entered the war, and even if no invasion had been planned or contemplated."

⁹ Report entitled "The Chinese Communist Movement." Published as Part 7A, *Hearings, Institute of Pacific Relations*, page 2305.

was weighed, I do not know. But in any case some division into zones of military *operations*—not necessarily the same as zones of military *occupation*—was inescapable. All forces—the Americans in the Pacific, the Russians from Siberia, the Allies in China—would at the same time be converging on Japan, Manchuria, and Korea. Which force was to do what, and where, and at what line was each to stop? It was essential to assign spheres of military operation, even though it was foreseen that they might have political consequences.

Agreement was reached on an air-sea operational line that was to become effective when the Soviet Union entered the war. This line ran from the interior of Asia into Manchuria roughly in the form of a parabola and down to Busui Tan (Cape Boltina) on the Korean coast, then through the Sea of Japan to a point in the La Perouse Straits approximately midway between the southern tip of Sakhalin Island and the northern tip of Hokkaido.[10] American forces were to operate south, and Soviet forces north of this line. The division meant that part of Southern Manchuria and practically all of Korea, as well as the Japanese home islands, were in the United States zone of operation. Naval and air operations in the Sea of Okhotsk (the southeast side of which is enclosed by the Kurile Islands) were to be coordinated as carried on.

During these same late July days Truman and Byrnes—in consultation with the Joint Chiefs of Staff—decided upon the statement to be addressed to Japan. Its text was read by Churchill, who found no fault. This was one of his last acts at the Potsdam Conference. The election results were announced: Churchill was out, Attlee was in. Both had gone back to London from where two days later Attlee returned to Potsdam with substantially the same opinions on the issues before the conference as Churchill.

During the changeover, the Declaration was cabled out to Chiang Kai-shek. He approved it quickly, with the comment that once again he had not been given a chance to share in the preparation of a document of vital concern to China. Copies were distributed to the press at 7:00 o'clock on the evening of July 26th. Byrnes sent one at the same time by messenger to Molotov. Molotov promptly asked that it not be issued

---

[10] All points inclusive to the United States. The operation boundary line was subject to change by agreement.

This information was sent to MacArthur and Wedemeyer on August 6th, with instruction not to divulge it to the Chinese until Soviet entry into the war. The negotiation of this agreement is briefly discussed in *Fleet Admiral King: A Naval Record*, pages 616-617.

for two or three days. Byrnes was told of Molotov's request only on the morning of the 27th, by which time the whole world knew of the Declaration. Byrnes explained to Molotov that since the Soviet Union was not at war with Japan he had not wished to embarrass it. Molotov had often given this reason for doing or not doing something.

The Potsdam Declaration is well remembered. It stated the terms offered Japan on surrender and clearly defined what was or was not meant by them. The ultimate sentences read, "We call upon the Government of Japan to proclaim now the unconditional surrender of all Japanese armed forces. . . . The alternative for Japan is prompt and utter destruction." With a haste very soon regretted, the Japanese Prime Minister, Suzuki, announced that Japan would ignore the ultimatum. New orders were hurried off to Sato in Moscow—to try again to arrange that Prince Konoye should be received, so that he might seek Soviet mediation to end the war. Stalin told the President the answer would be no.

The formalities for Soviet entry into the war were hurried on. Molotov discussed with Truman and Byrnes the problem of deciding what explanation should be given for its entrance into the war at this time, in the light of the fact that the Soviet Non Aggression Pact with Japan had not expired. Stalin, having a cold, excused himself from this discussion. Molotov wanted the American and British governments to ask the Soviet government to take this action on the ground that Japan had rejected their ultimatum and that Soviet entry would shorten the war and save lives. Neither the Americans nor the British wanted to seem to be seeking a favor. The State Department lawyers who were at Potsdam thought up another reason, which President Truman passed on to Stalin on July 31st. It was that the Soviet Union might cite the Moscow Declaration of October 30, 1943, and certain Articles of the United Nations charter as providing a proper basis for the Soviet action in cooperating, ". . . with other Great Powers now at war with Japan with a view to joint action on behalf of the community of nations in maintaining peace and security."[11] Stalin found the idea good. But, as will be seen, when he got around to it, he wrote a declaration of war which made it seem as though the Soviet Union was doing its solemn duty on request.[12]

Thus when the Potsdam Conference adjourned at midnight August 1st, it was settled that the war against Japan would go on until the

[11] James F. Byrnes, *Speaking Frankly*, page 209.
[12] See Chapter 30.

ultimatum was accepted. The Soviet forces were expected to join the war very soon, directing their assault on the lines set down in the operational agreement reached by the military staffs. But Stalin was still saying that he would not order his troops to move until the agreement with the Chinese government was signed.

State Department officers who were at Potsdam—particularly Dooman and Vincent as well as Harriman—were urging the Secretary of State to take more active heed of the Sino-Soviet talks about this agreement and to intervene in them. The memos that they wrote bluntly expressed the opinion that in some ways the Yalta Accord marked a retreat from policy that the United States had long maintained. They agreed that the promise which Roosevelt had given at Yalta to try to secure Chinese concurrence must be kept. But they advised that the American government should throw its support firmly behind Soong in resisting the Soviet demands which stretched out what had been granted at Yalta. Therefore they proposed that the President and Secretary of State should talk the subject out with Stalin and Molotov; and if they agreed, invite Soong to rush to Berlin to join in the discussions.

Stimson, prompted by Harriman, also (on the 15th) urged the President again to make absolutely sure that the Russians did not block off our trade with Manchuria by their control of the railways, saying that it looked to him as though the Russians were planning to do so. On the next day he went over the same ground with Byrnes. Truman thereupon, on the 17th, just before the formal sessions of the conference, broached the subject to Stalin. Their talk seems to have been brief. The only account of accessible record tells merely that Truman told Stalin that the United States wanted to be sure that Dairen was maintained as an open port, and that Stalin answered that if the Soviet Union controlled the port it would have the status of a free port.[18] But it must

[18] Byrnes, *Speaking Frankly*, page 205.

On this same day and in the days immediately following, State Department officers who were in Potsdam wrote a series of memos advocating that the American government take a more positive part in the Sino-Soviet negotiations. These memos may have been in part prompted by the receipt from Washington of a study of the subject which the State Department had been making—as instructed by Byrnes at Harriman's earlier suggestion.

The ideas of the State Department officers were expressed in four memos. The first of them, dated July 17th, was written by Dooman. The second, dated July 19th, was written by Vincent. These did not express any general view in regard to the underlying meaning of the Yalta Accord but affirmed that in regard to the arrangements for Port Arthur, Dairen, and the Manchurian railways, the American government should firmly insist on strict limitation of Soviet rights, along the lines of Soong's offers. The third memo of the same date, July 19th, was a joint memo from Vincent and Dooman to Assistant Secretary

have gone further than that. For at dinner that evening the President told Stimson that he thought he had clinched the Open Door in Manchuria. So the subject was allowed to rest while the conference went on.

Soong was back in Chungking. Chiang Kai-shek, after talking with him, sent a message on July 20th to Stalin, saying in effect that he trusted Stalin would recognize that China had made the utmost effort to meet Soviet needs and that he could not go beyond what the Chinese people were ready to accept. Through Hurley he sent Truman a copy of this message, saying that he hoped the President would impress this view upon Stalin. But the President either thought that he had done all that needed doing, or felt too deeply engaged in other difficulties with Stalin to get further tangled at that moment with this obscure matter of rights in Manchuria. In any case, his answer of July 23rd to Hurley for Chiang Kai-shek was guarded. It said that the President had asked the Generalissimo to carry out the Yalta Agreement but he was not asking him to exceed it. If, this curt reply continued, Chiang Kai-shek differed with Stalin on the interpretation of that agreement, the President hoped that Soong would be sent back to Moscow to continue his efforts to reach a complete understanding.

A week later, after the ultimatum to Japan had been sent and the United States-Soviet staff agreement on military operations completed, Byrnes was struck by a sense of the importance of having the Sino-Soviet treaty finished quickly. On the 28th he sent off a message to Hurley stating this, and concluding that it was important that Soong should communicate with Stalin, asking a chance to return to Moscow to resume talks.[14]

Soong was by no means eager to return to Moscow. Hurley reported on the 29th to Byrnes in Potsdam that Soong said that when he left Moscow it was clearly understood that Molotov would let him know

---

Dunn which forcefully summed up these views again and repeated the suggestion that Soong be invited to Potsdam. The fourth, on the 23rd, after the receipt of the message from Chiang Kai-shek, was written by Vincent to Dunn, with a copy for Harriman. This proposed that the American government should seek to secure a written understanding in regard to the Sino-Soviet agreements about Manchuria which were under negotiation, for the purpose of reserving the historic American position in the face of potential encroachment. It also stated the belief that the commitment taken by us at Yalta in regard to Manchuria and our undertaking to get China to accept these commitments placed us squarely in a position of responsibility which we could not transfer to the Chinese on the theory that the negotiations were bilateral and that China should get as good terms as it could.

[14] On the same day Byrnes told Forrestal he was most anxious to get the Japanese affair over with before the Russians got in, with particular reference to Dairen and Port Arthur. Once the Russians were in there, he felt, it would not be easy to get them out. *The Forrestal Diaries*, entry, July 28, 1945.

when Stalin returned so he could reach Moscow soon thereafter. He did not want to seem overanxious. In fact he was averse to returning at all; he wanted Wang Shih-chieh to be appointed Foreign Minister and sent to Moscow in his place. Hurley was inclined to think this was because Soong was frightened of his political future. Hurley related that when he saw him the first time after his return from Moscow, Soong had thrown up his hands and said, "I am a broken man. I am personally ill from strain and overwork." And later, "This proposed agreement will be destructive politically to the man responsible for it." Hurley told Chiang Kai-shek that he thought Soong the only man in China other than the Generalissimo himself "with the proper hand to negotiate with Stalin." It was arranged that Soong would return to Moscow, but that Wang Shih-chieh would be appointed Foreign Minister and go along with him. Hurley concluded the report of his talks on this subject by saying that there was every indication that Chiang Kai-shek was anxious to have a just, friendly, and early agreement with the Soviet Union.

During the last days at Potsdam (July 28th to August 2nd), Harriman reverted to the question of the Sino-Soviet negotiations. He wrote a vigorous memo to Byrnes urging that the American government support the Chinese against excessive Soviet demands, and that we secure clear recognition by both the Chinese and Soviet governments of the Open Door in China. In this he wrote out the instructions which he wished to have given him for a talk with Stalin after they both got back to Moscow.

On shipboard on his way home, Byrnes took up with this advice. On August 5th he sent Harriman, who was by then in Moscow, the requested orders. These authorized the Ambassador to tell Stalin that the American government (1) thought that Soong had fairly met the terms of the Yalta Accord and hoped very much that Stalin would not insist on more; (2) asked that no arrangement be made, with particular reference to the inclusion of the port of Dairen in the military zone, which might prejudice our interest. This would be contrary to the Open Door policy and we were opposed to it; and (3) suggested that the Soviet government conclude at once a written agreement with us to be published at the same time as the Sino-Soviet treaty, reaffirming Stalin's verbal assurances (to Hopkins) that the Open Door policy would be observed in Manchuria. The message had one other point of interest: it said that while the American government much preferred to have Dairen a "free port" under the Chinese administration, if necessary it would not object to the creation of an international commission consisting of representatives of the Chinese, Soviet, United States, and possibly the British governments, to supervise the operation of Dairen as a "free port."

Just about then (August 6th) a message came in from Attlee saying that he understood that the Russians were pressing for concessions which were beyond Soong's interpretation of the Yalta Agreement. Since Soong might ask for British support, the Prime Minister said that he would like to act in consonance with us, and so would like to know what guidance the American government had given Soong and what the American government was prepared to do to support the Chinese. Truman answered by sending Attlee the substance of the instruction to Harriman, with the added comment that he was unwilling to give a broader interpretation to the ambiguous reference to the "pre-eminent interests of the Soviet Union" than was clearly intended. Whether or not the British government did concert its injunctions with ours, I do not know. But Harriman, during the last week of Sino-Soviet negotiations that were about to begin, gave help to the Chinese as authorized by Washington. Of his efforts and of the accord that was signed, the story is best told in connection with greater historic events with which they were linked—Soviet entry into the war and the surrender of Japan.

But before telling of these greater events, a brief note should be made of another effort made by the Americans at Potsdam in China's behalf. It was agreed early in the conference that it would be necessary for the Foreign Ministers of the greater powers to meet often to work out the peace settlements. It was proposed that they form a Council of Foreign Ministers. The American government wanted the Foreign Minister of China to be a member of this council. Both Stalin and Churchill thought this unjustified since the council would be dealing mainly with European questions. Truman proposed a compromise: that China should be granted membership with the understanding that it would take part in the work of the council when it was dealing with "problems concerning the East or problems of world wide significance." It was so decided. An invitation was sent to Chiang Kai-shek to appoint someone to speak for China at the first meeting of this council soon to be held in London. He accepted with satisfaction.[15]

[15] But he took occasion to stress his wish to be included in any and all United Nations conferences on Asia.

This action, along with the selection of China as one of the permanent members of the Security Council of the United Nations, was conceived as meaning the full admission of China into the group of governing diplomatic powers. At Potsdam it was expected that this council would prepare the peace treaty with Japan. But the American government concluded that it was not the appropriate body; and it played little or no part in the determination of other Far Eastern questions. As the months passed, China's weakness, due largely to its internal dissensions, further reduced its role. So the elevation of China at Potsdam turned out to be a milestone on a road that went no further.

CHAPTER 30

From Potsdam to V-J Day

To RECALL the rapidity with which the war in the Far East now moved to its great climax:

July 26: the Potsdam Ultimatum

Extract from the Proclamation defining terms for the Japanese Surrender: "The terms of the Cairo Declaration shall be carried out and Japanese sovereignty shall be limited to the islands of Honshu, Hokkaido, Kyushu, Shikoku and such minor islands as we determine. . . .

"We call upon the Government of Japan to proclaim now the unconditional surrender of all Japanese armed forces, and to provide proper and adequate assurances of their good faith in such action. The alternative for Japan is prompt and utter destruction."

August 6: Atomic Bomb on Hiroshima

Extract from Statement by President Truman: "Sixteen hours ago an American airplane dropped one bomb on Hiroshima, an important Japanese Army Base. . . . It is an atomic bomb. . . . The force from which the sun draws its powers has been loosed against those who brought war to the Far East. . . . If they do not now accept our terms they may expect a rain of ruin from the air, the like of which has never been seen on this earth. . . ."

August 8: the Soviet Union Enters into the Pacific War

Extract, Statement to Japanese Government: "The Soviet Government declares that from tomorrow . . . the Soviet Government will consider itself to be at war with Japan."

Extract, message Chiang Kai-shek to Generalissimo Stalin, August 9: "The entire Chinese nation is greatly heartened with the Soviet Union's declaration of war against Japan. . . . It is my firm conviction that the entry of the Soviet Union into the war . . . will hasten the complete collapse of desperate Japan . . . and will bring about the early realization of durable peace in East Asia."

August 9: Atomic Bomb on Nagasaki

Extract, President Truman's address: "Having found the bomb we have used it. . . . We shall continue to use it until we completely destroy Japanese power to make war. Only a Japanese surrender will stop us. . . ."

August 10: Conditional Acceptance by Japan of the Potsdam Ultimatum

Extract, the Imperial Decision: "The Army vigorously advised the necessity of giving decisive battle to the invading enemy on the homeland. . . . But I think that now is the time to bear the unbearable. Recalling Emperor Meiji's feeling when he was confronted by the Triple Intervention, I repress my tears and approve the draft plan."

August 11: Allies' Reply

Extract, Secretary Byrnes' reply to Japanese government: "From the moment of surrender the authority of the Emperor and the Japanese Government to rule the State shall be subject to the Supreme Commander of the Allied Powers, who will take such steps as he deems proper to effectuate the surrender terms."

August 14: Sino-Soviet Agreements Concluded

Extract, Treaty of Friendship and Alliance Between the Republic of China and the U.S.S.R.: "The High Contracting Parties, having regard to the interests of the security and economic development of each of them, agree to work together in close and friendly collaboration after the coming of peace and to act according to the principles of mutual respect for their sovereignty and territorial integrity and of non-interference in the internal affairs of the other contracting party."

August 14: Imperial Rescript Ending the War

Extract, Imperial Rescript: "Should we continue to fight, it would not only result in an ultimate collapse and obliteration of the Japanese nation, but also it would lead to the total extinction of human civilization. Such being the case, how are we to save the millions of our subjects, and atone ourselves before the hallowed spirits of our Imperial ancestors? This is the reason why we have ordered the acceptance of the provisions of the joint declaration of the powers."

September 2: The Formal Surrender Signed at Tokyo Bay

Extract, Instrument of Surrender, Signed by Representatives of the Japanese and governments of the United Nations at war with Japan: "We hereby command all Japanese forces wherever situated and the Japanese people to cease hostilities forthwith. . . ."

The rush of these events forced the American military organization to innovate its measures for dealing with Japan and China in great haste. A variety of "outline" plans to deal with various contingencies had been worked out by the planning staffs; but it appears that no "operational" plan detailing what American forces would do, had up to then been completed or approved. On July 20th, on orders sent from Potsdam, the Joint War Planning Committee had put aside all other business to write a report on the steps ahead in the event of the Japanese collapse or surrender in the immediate future. By the 30th a provisional plan and directive were ready; and they were sent out to MacArthur and Nimitz. These directives left the main tasks of winding up the war in China to Soviet and Chinese forces—aided by American staff, air, and supply units and the American navy. They contemplated a quick entry into Japan on the way toward control over the whole country. In connection with these activities, they provided also for the immediate occupation of several ports on the mainland of China— Shanghai, Chefoo, and Chinwangtao, near the border of Manchuria, and Fusan in Korea. The Joint Chiefs added a note that while they did not want to get involved in a campaign on the mainland of China except in the air, it was thought best to take these ports, and also the northern tip of Formosa, in order to help the Chinese forces recover the country. It will be recalled that a few days before an agreement had been reached between the American and Soviet staffs as regards sea and air spheres of operation.

Wedemeyer was asked on the same day to find out Chiang Kai-shek's ideas in regard to (a) the command of American troops that might land in China, (b) what the mission of such United States forces would be relative to the Generalissimo's forces, and (c) how to provide supplies and air support to enable these forces to mop up the Japanese in China. Chiang Kai-shek answered (a) that he wished all American forces that landed in China to come under Wedemeyer's command, (b) that he wanted Wedemeyer to plan at once to move Chinese government troops into the places which American forces might take and to other key areas. The Chinese government—helped when needed by the U.S. forces—would assume responsibility as soon as possible for the civil affairs in areas occupied by the Americans, to maintain order and relieve suffering. And (c) that the American units avoid as far as possible any cooperation with Communist forces.

The nature of this consultation at this date reflects the fact that neither the American nor Chinese military organizations were really ready and in position to do the job ahead: quickly to take possession of the areas of China held by the Japanese. The time had come which was to test whether the Chinese government could summon up the military means, the energy, and the influence among the Chinese people to take effective control over the vast sphere deeded it at Cairo. This included not only the parts of China which it had governed before the Japanese invasion but also the North where the Communists ruled, the great areas of Manchuria which long had lived apart, and Formosa. The atomic bomb, the precipitous end of the war, threw off balance what plans there were for the gradual return of the Chinese government forces into the liberated areas, and caught the American organizers of the war without an advanced program for action in China. The resultant lag, short as it may have been, was of use to the Communists, even though they too were taken by surprise.

Wedemeyer thought Chiang Kai-shek's ideas sound. In passing them on to Marshall he offered the opinion that it would be unwise to count on having substantial Chinese help in disarming, demobilizing, and deporting the Japanese in China until government troops were in control of communications, ports, and food centers. He recommended that American forces establish themselves in and operate ports and nearby air bases on the coast of China to ease the supply situation and give the needed mobility. He pointed out that shortage of shipping and poor land communications within China—both needed to redeploy Chinese troops into critical areas quickly—made it advisable to plan for large scale air transport operations.

If these measures were taken—the question presented itself squarely —how much resistance, Communist and otherwise, would be met, and when and where? The end of the war was at hand, and there was no peace or unity in China, not even a truce. Both Hurley and Wedemeyer had done their best, within the instructions, to prevent the divisions from becoming more tense and active. Wedemeyer began to worry about the situations which American forces might run into when they landed. What was to be done, for example, if the Communists managed to take over any of the cities or ports before Chinese government or American forces could, and held fast?

This anxiety led Wedemeyer at the end of July to consult Chiang Kai-shek about a revised version of an old proposal: that American officers should be assigned to Communist military units, as they already were to the government units, for the purposes of watching and reporting on their location and employment; that all American officers attached to both sides would report to him (Wedemeyer), thereby enabling him to obtain a true, objective, and non-partisan knowledge of what went on. Then he would keep both Chiang Kai-shek and Mao Tze Tung currently informed of the actions of their own forces. By sharing proved information, he hoped that fighting between the Chinese as well as incidents with the Americans could be avoided. But the proposal came to nothing.

On August 2nd, he issued a reminder to all his local commanders to make sure that they understood American policy—as laid down in his original directive of October 1944: that American resources were not to be used to suppress civil strife except insofar as necessary to protect American lives and property. He had in mind not only the risk of encounters with the Communists in the North but also possible troubles with other resistant elements, as in Yunnan, where the Governor was at odds with General Chen Cheng, head of the government forces in and around Kunming.

On August 10th, the day on which Japan offered to accept the Potsdam ultimatum provided the Imperial institutions were preserved, the War Department sent messages to all American combat theaters and commanders, giving them interim plans and instructions to be executed when Japan stopped fighting. The directive given to Wedemeyer was supplementary to his original one. Together the orders governed the use of American military power in China during the crucial months ahead. The essentials of this directive were:

1. American military assistance was being continued in order to support Chinese military operations essential to the reoccupation by Central Government forces of all areas in China then held by the Japanese, and the placing of such forces in Japan proper, Formosa, and Korea.

2. American forces were being prepared to secure control of key ports and communication points in the China Theater. On landing, these forces were to pass into Wedemeyer's command; and he was to be responsible for coordinating with Chiang Kai-shek the planning and execution of operations in the China Theater.

3. American ground forces were not to become involved in any major land campaign in any part of the China Theater.

4. Wedemeyer was to help the Central Government to transport its troops rapidly to key areas in China and give them such support as was normal to his mission.

5. The American forces were to limit their dealings with Chinese forces and agencies other than those of the Central Government strictly to military requirements.

6. The American forces were authorized, when necessary, and at Wedemeyer's discretion and with Chiang Kai-shek's approval, to act temporarily for Chiang Kai-shek in accepting local surrenders of the Japanese. They were to turn over such points in China that were liberated by them only to agencies and forces accredited by the Central Government in China.

7. All these instructions were to apply only insofar as action in accordance therewith did not impair the basic principle that the American government would not support the Chinese government in civil war.

This general injunction (No. 7 above), it may be surmised, was intended to lessen the chance that the Chinese government, made bold by the American support provided under this directive, would turn its armies against the Communists. But it need hardly be said that this cautionary provision did not make it any easier for Wedemeyer to know just what he could do. In advance of every action entered in pursuance of his defined mission he had to weigh the chance that the Communists might protest, and that it might lead to clashes in which American forces became involved. He soon found it necessary to appeal to Washington for clarification of this feature of his orders, and some loosening of its restraint.

By this directive of August 10th the Chinese government was assured of vital help in the task of regaining control of the country. But the directive did not determine specifically how great or rapid that help would be. MacArthur and Nimitz were ordered to work with Wedemeyer in the preparation of plans for the operations on the China coast. One paragraph of this order bore on the question of how many American troops could be brought into China, and how fast. "The occupation of Japan proper is regarded as the supreme operation and is the first charge on the resources available to the Pacific commander." This meant in effect that American landings in China were to be carried out when and as they could be fitted in with the many other urgent movements of ships and men in the Pacific. To make up his detailed plans to move Chinese troops, Wedemeyer thus had to wait upon the decisions of the Pacific commanders. He also had to wait upon Chiang Kai-shek, who had not yet designated the Chinese forces which were to be moved first.

Wedemeyer did his best to hurry up the program. On August 12th (Chungking time) he sent messages to Marshall, MacArthur, and Nimitz in which he stressed the danger that activities of the Chinese Communists might hinder the attainment of American objectives. Yenan was on that day ignoring the authority of the government and issuing a radio order to the Japanese and its puppet forces to surrender to Communist commanders. Wedemeyer therefore urged that the American landing contingents should arrive in China as soon as possible, on a first priority basis. The Joint Chiefs of Staff took these proposals coolly. When on August 14th they told Wedemeyer to go ahead with his orders, they stated that they could not grant operations in China priority over those in Japan and Korea; that in fact the maximum American force he could expect for some time was two divisions.[1] But all branches of the

[1] Joseph Alsop in his article "The Strange Case of Louis Budenz" in the *Atlantic Monthly* for April 1952, wrote that General MacArthur "refused to lend General Wedemeyer the seven American divisions that might have contained the Communists in Manchuria."

American air force in China were being rapidly expanded, and they got ready to move Chinese troops anywhere.

The tasks ahead were not small: to ensure the surrender of the Japanese located throughout half of China, to secure their weapons, to establish the authority of the government in the large or vital cities, communication points, and ports. And to do these things first—before the Communists interfered and possibly against their armed opposition. These assignments proved far in excess of the capacities of the Chinese civil or military organization to carry out swiftly and well—even with the emergency American aid. But before telling of the contest that ensued for the control of China, it is necessary to take account of other important occurrences of this fortnight before V-J Day.

The Soviet armies were hurrying to be in on the kill. Stalin had not waited, as he had so often said he would, until China concurred in his claimed reward for joining the Allies. On August 8th, at 5:00 p.m. (Moscow time), two days after the bomb dropped at Hiroshima, Molotov abruptly told Sato, the Japanese Ambassador in Moscow, that the Soviet Union was going to enter the war. His declaration was so phrased as to make it appear that the Soviet Union had made this decision on an Allied request after the Japanese rejection of the Potsdam Declaration.[2] This was wholly misleading and needless to say made no reference to the Yalta Accord. In the early dawn of the next morning the Soviet armies entered Manchuria. The Chinese government took almost as much notice as the Japanese. Within five days the Soviet troops had gone far ahead on three fronts. They were well within Northern Manchuria and making wide encircling movements in the direction of South Manchuria. No one could be wholly sure where they would stop, what they would do while in occupation, or how long they would remain.

True, there were picket fences (not stone walls), made or in the making. One of these was the United States-Soviet agreement, already noted, regarding air and sea zones of military operation. This might be made more effective if American troops were landed in South Manchuria at Dairen. Such a step was proposed either at this time or shortly

[2] The Declaration of War referred to the Potsdam ultimatum of July 26th, then went on as follows: "Taking into consideration the refusal of Japan to capitulate the Allies submitted to the Soviet Government a proposal to join the war against Japanese aggression and thus shorten the duration of the war. . . . Loyal to its Allied duty the Soviet Government has accepted the proposal of the Allies and has joined in the declaration of the Allied Powers of July 26th. . . . In view of the above, the Soviet Government declares that from tomorrow . . . the Soviet Government will consider itself at war with Japan."

[339]

afterwards. It was carefully considered, then turned down, whether because it was thought that the necessary troops and shipping would not be available, or because of concern over possible Soviet reaction, is hard to know. Memories differ. Another possible fence was the Sino-Soviet agreement which Soong and Stalin were during these days again arguing out at Moscow.

Then there was also the surrender order in course of preparation. This was General Order No. 1. It was to be issued by the Emperor of Japan in accord with the terms of surrender and by order of General Mac-Arthur, who was to be appointed Supreme Commander for the Allied Powers. Much thought, when writing it, had been given to the situation in China. The basic draft of this General Order No. 1 had been prepared at Washington while the Potsdam Conference was still going on and thereafter was much restudied. The British authorities were consulted about it. On August 13th the President sent messages to Attlee, Stalin, and Chiang Kai-shek, telling each how the surrender was to be directed in his sphere of interest. To Attlee he said that MacArthur would (through Japanese Imperial Headquarters) direct Japanese forces in Southeast Asia and ports of Malaysia to surrender to Admiral Mountbatten and his subordinate commanders. To Stalin he said that Mac-Arthur would direct Japanese forces in the Soviet areas of operation to surrender to the Soviet High Command in the Far East. To Chiang Kai-shek he said that MacArthur would direct all Japanese forces in China other than those opposing the Russians to surrender to the Generalissimo and his subordinate commanders.

Chiang Kai-shek answered that he welcomed this arrangement for China. He added that he was asking General MacArthur explicitly to state in his order that the Japanese were to surrender or to give arms and equipment only to officials of the National Government; and also to state that Japanese Imperial Headquarters and the Japanese commanders in China other than those opposing the Russians would be held strictly accountable for compliance. Both Wedemeyer and Hurley had previously made the same recommendation to Washington. Fears that the Communists might manage to get arms and supplies from the Japanese were confirmed by the broadcast—to which allusion has already been made—by General Chu Teh, claiming full qualifications for demanding and compelling Japanese surrender to Communist forces. The last paragraph of the order issued in this Communist broadcast proclaimed that "Our troops have the right to enter and occupy any city, town or communication center occupied by the enemy or the puppets, carry on military management there to maintain order and appoint a commissioner to look after the administrative affairs of the locality. Those who oppose or obstruct such actions will be treated as traitors."

To pursue the point, General Order No. 1 and suborders, as issued, went far to meet the Generalissimo's wishes. But they did not threaten to punish Japanese commanders who might surrender to Chinese not authorized by the government—perhaps because it was judged unfair; perhaps because it might be construed by some Japanese commanders as sanction to keep on fighting; perhaps because it was believed that the Supreme Commander already had the power to punish violation of his orders. MacArthur gave added weight to his written orders by warning Japanese Imperial Headquarters of the importance we attached to having surrenders made only to those who supported the National Government of China.

General Order No. 1 was put in final form and approved by the President just in time for its use.[3] It was issued on August 15th. Its main pertinent features were:

1. The Japanese Imperial Headquarters were to direct all commanders everywhere to lay down their arms, stay where they were, and surrender unconditionally.

2. The Japanese commanders and all air, ground, and sea forces within China (excluding Manchuria), Formosa, and French Indo-China north of 16° north latitude were to surrender to Generalissimo Chiang Kai-shek.

3. Japanese commanders within Manchuria, Korea, north of the 38° north latitude and Karafuto were to surrender to the commander-in-chief of the Soviet Armed Forces.[4]

4. The above named commanders were stated to be the only representatives of the Allied forces who were authorized to accept surrender of Japanese forces, and all surrenders were to be made only to them or their representatives.

5. The Japanese commanders were to be ordered to disarm their

[3] *Washington Command Post*, page 350. This was true also of the other basic surrender documents—the Instrument of Surrender, the Directive to the Supreme Commander of the Allied Powers, and the Proclamation by the Japanese Emperor ending the war in accordance with the terms of the Potsdam Ultimatum.

[4] The next day, August 16th, Stalin asked Truman to amend this order in two respects: (1) to allow the Soviet forces to receive the surrender on the Kurile Islands, which were in the American zone as defined in General Order No. 1. Truman agreed. (2) To allow the Soviet forces to occupy the northern half of the Japanese island of Hokkaido. The President refused and Stalin was much annoyed.

forces completely and to deliver all weapons and equipment in safe and good condition at such time and at such places as might be prescribed by the Allied commanders indicated above.

General Wedemeyer had been troubled over the provisions that the Japanese in Manchuria were to surrender to the Soviet High Command. He thought it likely that the Chinese Communists in the precincts would either secretly or openly get some of the Japanese arms. In order to lessen the chance of this happening, he had suggested that the Japanese forces in Manchuria might surrender either to the Soviet Russian commanders or to those of the National Government, and to no one else. It is to be doubted whether any such change in language would have had material effect. In any case, the Chinese government was at this time buying protection against this feared chance. The agreements which had been signed the night before in Moscow were thought to assure that the Soviet government would have nothing to do with the Chinese Communists and help the Chinese government to attach Manchuria for itself.

Soong had been in Moscow for some days. The Generalissimo had decided to give in more to the Soviet exactions. He had authorized Soong to grant the Soviet Union a military zone north on the Kwantung Peninsula to the line of the former Russian Czarist lease, but excluding Dairen and the connecting railway. In their first talk (August 7th) Stalin had shown that he was determined to have still more: to get under one guise or another control of the port of Dairen and the ways in and out of it. Thereupon, carrying out his orders from Byrnes, Harriman had objected to Stalin. He had asked the Marshal whether he was willing to give written assurances that the Soviet Union would support the Open Door in Manchuria, and the Marshal had said, "This can be done." Thereupon Harriman had presented to him the text of a draft protocol on the subject to be signed by the American and Soviet governments. Then Stalin had come into the open. He had said that he thought the Yalta Agreement had recognized that Russia should have the "pre-eminent position." This being so, he thought the Soviet Union entitled to insist (a) that the Soviet police should exercise security control over the city and port of Dairen; and that the manager of the port should be Russian under a joint municipal administration; and (b) that Soviet officials should control the whole area on the Kwantung Peninsula included in the Czarist lease, in order to protect the port of Dairen against aggression and sabotage.

Harriman had spoken up vigorously against these claims. He denied that the term "pre-eminent" was intended to support Soviet demands of this scope. He had reminded Stalin that President Truman expected to be consulted before any decisions were made that might affect American interests and policies. In reporting this talk to Washington, Harriman had observed that Stalin complained that the Chinese regarded the Soviet Union as an unwelcome guest and that he was angry at their refusal to accept his terms. Apparently he expected Soviet forces to be regarded as liberators. It should be remembered that just a few hours before Molotov had told the Japanese Ambassador that the Soviet Union was about to enter the war and that the Soviet troops were under order to march into Manchuria the next morning.

From then on, it is probable that it was the American watch over what went on rather than the Chinese power to resist, that induced Stalin to compromise with Soong. Harriman had followed up his oral protest by a written restatement (letter to Molotov on August 9th) of the American conceptions. He had reiterated that the American government (1) thought that if Dairen was made an international free port, the "pre-eminent interests" of the Soviet Union in having access to a warm-water port for commercial traffic would be amply safeguarded, and that therefore neither the port nor its land communications should be within the Soviet military zone, and (2) expected the principles of the Open Door and territorial integrity to be respected. This letter ended with the statement that the President greatly wished that Stalin would not press for further concessions, and felt that in connection with any other points under negotiation which affected American interest or principles toward China he should be consulted.

When shortly thereafter Soong told him that he might give in further in regard to Dairen, Harriman tried to ward off later reproach. He said he wanted it understood that the United States government thought the proposals which the Chinese government had made complied with the Yalta Accord; and that if the Chinese government should grant the Soviet Union larger rights, it was only because of the value it attached to Soviet support in other directions. Soong answered that he understood perfectly.

Harriman's reports during the teeming last days of the negotiations (August 11 to 14th) traced the wearing down of Soong's resistance. In return for a promise that the Soviet Union would not exercise in time of peace military authority in the city, port, or connecting railways, Soong agreed that Dairen might be within the Soviet military zone.

He gave in somewhat more as regards details of the management of the Manchurian railways. He accepted after long argument wording he knew to be not as clear and conclusive as it might be in the Soviet pledge to support the National Government and withhold all aid from dissident elements. The reason he gave Harriman was that, "It was after all a matter of good faith." But it may be wondered whether his consent was not influenced by the thought which Stalin put into words at the end of their talk on the 10th: that the Chinese government had better come to an agreement quickly or the Communists would get into Manchuria. The Soviet armies were traveling fast toward Southern Manchuria and China.

Soong's compromises disturbed the State Department. Byrnes sent word to Harriman that he thought the language of the proposed Soviet promise to refrain from helping dissident elements in China and to support the National Government ought to be so explicit that there could be no future misunderstanding. He also said that in his opinion Soong should insist on clear wording of the arrangement in regard to Dairen, to be sure that the Soviet Union would not claim the right to exercise military control during peacetime. He said protest should be made against Stalin's demand for joint ownership of port facilities in Dairen. Harriman at once (on the 12th) wrote out these points in support of the Chinese position in another letter to Molotov, and gave a copy of his letter to Soong. By such injections of its opinions the American government kept trying to ensure that any accord that was signed would conform to its view of what was conceived at Yalta. But it did not promise help if the Chinese stood out to the end and there was no agreement. And it was not willing or prepared to land American forces in Manchuria to hold the disputed places.

The next night, late, on the eve of the Japanese surrender, Stalin and Soong settled all remaining points of difference. On the 14th, while the news of the ending of the war spread, the accords were signed. The Foreign Minister, Wang Shih-chieh, signed for China; Molotov, for the Soviet Union. Almost at once Soong left for Washington. Molotov was at the airfield with a guard of honor to see him off.

Harriman, on informing Washington of this settlement, reported that Soong had told him that he was encouraged; that he thought Stalin had accepted the basic principles for which he, Soong, had stood up; and that he believed that Stalin would live up to the accord. Harriman discussed the accord with Molotov also on the day it was signed. He asked Molotov about prospective relations between the Chinese government and the

Chinese Communists. Molotov's answer was hard to figure out. Harriman also reminded Molotov of the President's wish for a written statement confirming the Soviet intent to observe the Open Door. Molotov demurred; Stalin, he said, saw no need for it since the agreement in itself made so clear that the Open Door would be maintained. Harriman reemphasized the President's wish for a statement that could be published, and suggested that the American and Soviet governments exchange notes reaffirming Stalin's verbal assurances. In reporting to Washington on this talk, the Ambassador remarked that he doubted whether the Soviet government would accede to this idea unless strongly pressed.

The Far Eastern watchers in the State Department continued to be bothered by the chance that the Sino-Soviet agreements would in effect traverse the principles of the Open Door and the integrity of China. But it was decided to wait until Soong got to Washington before taking up these matters again. Other more sensational events in the Far East were commanding attention.

The accord between the Chinese and Soviet governments was expressed in a connected group of nine detailed documents.[5] Events have since washed away the interest attaching to most of these details. But a few main passages are instructive to any judgment of the attitude and behavior of the Soviet and Chinese governments as time went on.

First, as bearing upon the way in which the Soviet Union dealt with the Chinese government and the Chinese Communists: Article V of the Treaty of Friendship and Alliance and Paragraph 1 of the note signed by Molotov relating to this Treaty:

The High Contracting Parties, having regard to the interests of the security and economic development of each of them, agree to work together in close and friendly collaboration after the coming of peace and to act according to the principles of mutual respect for their sovereignty and territorial integrity

[5] They were:
1. Treaty of Friendship and Alliance
2. Notes exchanged relating to this Treaty
3. Notes exchanged relating to Outer Mongolia
4. Agreement concerning Dairen
5. A supplement to this Agreement about Dairen
6. Agreement on Port Arthur
7. Appendix to this Agreement on Port Arthur
8. Agreement on Relations between the Chinese Administration and the Commander-in-Chief of the Soviet forces after entry into the "Three Eastern Provinces."
9. Agreement on the Manchurian railroads
The text of all are printed in *United States Relations with China*, pages 585-596.

and of non-interference in the internal affairs of the other contracting party.[6]

In accordance with the spirit of the aforementioned Treaty, and in order to put into effect its aims and purposes, the Government of the U.S.S.R. agrees to render to China moral support and aid in military supplies and other material resources, such support and aid to be entirely given to the National Government as the central government of China.[7]

Second, as bearing on the attempts of the Chinese government to reoccupy Manchuria:

In the course of conversations regarding Dairen and Port Arthur and regarding the joint operation of the Chinese Changchun Railway, the Government of the U.S.S.R. regarded the Three Eastern Provinces as part of China and reaffirmed its respect for China's full sovereignty over the Three Eastern Provinces and recognized their territorial and administrative integrity.[8]

1. After the Soviet troops enter the "Three Eastern Provinces" of China as a result of military operations, the supreme authority and responsibility in all matters relating to the prosecution of the war will be vested, in the zone of operations for the time required for the operations, in the Commander-in-Chief of the Soviet forces.

2. A Chinese National Government representative and staff will be appointed for the recovered territory, whose duties will be:

(a) to establish and direct, in accordance with the laws of China, an administration for the territory cleared of the enemy.

(b) to establish the cooperation between the Chinese armed forces, both regular and irregular, and the Soviet forces in recovered territory.

(c) to ensure the active cooperation of the Chinese administration with the Commander-in-Chief of the Soviet forces and, specifically to give the local authorities directions to this effect, being guided by the requirements and wishes of the Commander-in-Chief of the Soviet forces.

3. To ensure contact between the Commander-in-Chief of the Soviet forces and the Chinese National Government representative a Chinese military mission will be appointed to the Commander-in-Chief of the Soviet forces.

4. In the zones under the supreme authority of the Commander-in-Chief of the Soviet forces, the Chinese National Government administration for the recovered territory will maintain contact with the Commander-in-Chief of the Soviet forces through the Chinese National Government representative.

5. As soon as any part of the liberated territory ceases to be a zone of immediate military operations, the Chinese National Government will assume full authority in the direction of public affairs and will render the Commander-in-Chief of the Soviet forces every assistance and support through its civil and military bodies.[9]

[6] Article V of the Treaty of Friendship and Alliance.

[7] Paragraph 1, note signed by Molotov relating to this Treaty.

[8] Paragraph 2 of the note signed by Molotov relating to the Treaty of Friendship and Alliance.

[9] Paragraphs 1-5 of the Agreement Regarding Relations Between the Chinese Admin-

Now these studied and measured provisions seem empty. But at the time all countries concerned thought that they would work advantageously not only for China but for the whole system of Allied relationships.

Soong's first appraisal—as already remarked—was that they were satisfactory. The Soviet press reported him as saying, at the airdrome before taking flight from Moscow, "I may say the sincerity shown by Generalissimo Stalin and Mr. Molotov during these conversations inspires me with confidence in the stability of Sino-Soviet relations."[10] Chiang Kai-shek told Hurley that he was "generally satisfied."[11] He repeated this opinion when he signed the accords on August 24th. A few days later, when talking with the President, Madame Chiang Kai-shek said the same thing, and thanked the President for the help which the American government had given. The Soviet officials and press treated the accord as another proof of the Soviet wish for peace, friendship, and justice. The American government said little, and that in a tone of lofty distance. On August 27th, Byrnes spoke to the press of the agreement as "an important step forward in the relations between China and the Soviet Union," adding that the American government welcomed it as a "practical example of the continuing unity and mutual helpfulness which should characterize the actions of members of the United Nations in peace as well as in war." American opinion agreed. Prevailing sentiment was in accord with the lead editorial in the *New York Times* on the Russo-Chinese pact, which began, "A victory for peace as great as any scored on the battlefield has been won by Russian and Chinese statesmanship," and ended ". . . it is one of the virtues of the Russo-Chinese agreements that they are based on reality and mutual interest instead of abstract theory, and it is this element which makes them the great contribution toward peace that they so plainly are."[12]

The State Department and White House were hopeful but not thor-

---

istration and the Commander-in-Chief of the Soviet Forces After the Entry of Soviet Troops Into the "Three Eastern Provinces" of China During the Present Joint Military Operations Against Japan.

[10] Telegram, American Embassy Moscow, to State Department, August 17, 1945.

[11] Hurley regarded the agreement as a vindication of his predictions. He reported to the State Department with satisfaction that the Generalissimo now "admitted" that these accords proved that the Soviet government really did intend to support the National Government and to help unify Chinese armed forces and support a unified democratic government. He remained of this opinion as late as December 1945. See his testimony before the Senate Foreign Relations Committee, December 1945.

[12] *New York Times*, August 28, 1945. It may be in order to note the fact that the news reporting in this paper on Far Eastern matters and from Far Eastern places during this momentous and crowded month of August 1945 was superbly informative and accurate.

oughly convinced. If this agreement worked well, it would dissolve several anxieties that weighed upon them: it would avert friction between China and the Soviet Union, allowing the work of restoring peace and order in the Far East to go on smoothly; and it would lessen the danger that the Chinese Communists would keep China divided and at war. But among the watchful ranks of the State Department some doubt lingered as to whether it would work out that way.

The reasons for mistrust were ably expounded in a message which the American Embassy at Moscow sent to the State Department on September 4th. Its cautionary comments, the Embassy explained, were provoked by the unrestrained praise in the American press, which was based on misconceptions. Some of the main points in this contemporary appraisal should be kept alive in the record.

1. The Soviet government, this report began by making clear, did not need the pact to get any of the immediate advantages which the Red Army was gaining. All these, including the military occupation of Manchuria and the Liaotung Peninsula, could and would have been achieved, pact or no pact. But the pact did give legality to acts and situations which otherwise might have led to disputes and complaints against the Soviet Union.

2. Nothing in the internal regime of Outer Mongolia, the report continued, would be changed because of the recognition of independence. But it would eliminate a possible source of future Chinese irredentism. Further, it might make the area more useful as a base from which to bring other adjacent territories under Soviet influence.

3. There should be no illusions, the Embassy warned, regarding the effect of the pact on Manchuria. The willingness of the Soviet government to admit the Chinese government to the control of civil affairs in Manchuria and to evacuate Soviet forces did reflect mature Soviet statesmanship. But the initial Soviet position as the occupation power with greater proximity, and the far greater scope and discipline of Soviet power, should make it easy for the Soviet government to remain master of the situation—in all essential respects—after its forces were evacuated. It was tacitly understood, the Embassy thought, by both the Chinese and the Russian negotiators of the pact that the Chinese officials in Manchuria would have to be amenable in the main to Soviet influence. The Communist forces from Yenan, the Embassy noted, had already been ordered by their commanders to enter Manchuria and accept the Japanese surrender there in cooperation with the Red armies. The Soviet authorities in Manchuria and other elements friendly to the

Soviet Union might be expected to encourage the use of these Communist trained forces so that they would play a prominent part in both the civil and military administration of Manchuria after the Red Army left.

4. Continuing, the Embassy observed that the promise given by the Soviet government that it would support the Chinese government and not interfere in Chinese internal affairs merely reaffirmed the state of affairs in existence for some years. It was probable that if the Kremlin exerted control over Yenan it was through party channels and not through exposed government channels. If it wanted to exert control in the future, it would be by the same route. Thus, the Embassy concluded, while the Soviet signature of the pact lessened the chance that the Chinese Communists would be able to bargain with the Chinese government on the basis of implied Soviet military support, at the same time its acceptance might (a) disarm critics by dispelling mistrust of Soviet intentions in China, (b) remove any excuse for a combined Chinese-American crusade against Yenan as the spearhead of Soviet penetration of China, (c) appear to place the policy of the Soviet government in China on a high, disinterested plane while the Communist Party in the Soviet Union through its own agencies could continue to give quiet but effective support to Yenan's program of democratization and exert political pressure on Chungking to compromise with Yenan.[13]

If the State Department was impressed by the mistrustful forecasts which came in from Moscow, no way was found of testing in advance whether they were right or wrong. But it had—even before then—resumed the effort to safeguard the historic principle of the Open Door in China. It had sought to eliminate any sound basis for criticism by getting both Stalin and Chiang Kai-shek to declare publicly and plainly —and for an American audience—that they were going to see that the door in China and Manchuria was kept open. But it appeared that the government had waited too long for the purpose.

On August 22nd, shortly before the accords were signed by Chiang Kai-shek and published, Byrnes had informed Harriman that the President wanted him to see Stalin at once if he could, or Molotov if Stalin was not to be seen. He was to urge that oral assurances were not enough to satisfy American public opinion; written ones, in plain words, were needed. Byrnes had added that he thought our wishes would be best

[13] Paraphrase of this cable is printed in *United States Relations with China*, pages 122-123, incorrectly dated September 10th.

met if the Chinese and Soviet governments made a joint statement, affirming their devotion to the Open Door, at the same time that they published the agreements.[14] The Chinese government was known to be willing to join in such a statement.

Harriman spoke to Stalin, who agreed to the issuance of some statement. But he proposed that, instead of a joint statement, the Soviet government should issue its own and the Chinese government do the same. He offered to let Harriman see in advance a draft of the Soviet statement, and said that he would coordinate it with the one to be issued in Chungking. Apparently the Soviet Foreign Office then asked the Chinese Ambassador in Moscow to let it read the text of the statement which the Chinese government was going to issue. The Ambassador consulted Chungking and was told that it was not yet ready, and that the matter was being referred to the Chinese Foreign Minister, who was by then, along with Byrnes and Molotov, in London at the meeting of the Council of Foreign Ministers.[15] While at London, Harriman reminded Byrnes of the subject. The Secretary of State apparently never got around to discussing it, perhaps because the conference came to an unexpectedly quick end.

Hurley had in the meanwhile (on September 6th) also reverted to the subject of the joint statement. In a message to the State Department he said that he was now of the opinion that the ratification of the Sino-Soviet agreement had accomplished the purpose, but he asked whether it was desired that he should take it up with the Chinese government. The inquiry was sent to the files with the notation "no action to be taken at this time." Perhaps because Hurley's opinion was thought to be correct. Perhaps because the publication of the Sino-Soviet agreement had provoked no alarm in the United States. Perhaps because the Chinese government seemed in no hurry. In any case, the project was allowed to lapse.

Within the State Department at this time important changes had been occurring among those directly concerned with Far Eastern affairs. Joseph C. Grew resigned as Under-Secretary. Dean G. Acheson, who had been one of the Assistant Secretaries of State since 1941 and who had resigned, was recalled to take his place on August 16th. During the

---

[14] This instruction is published in *ibid.*, pages 118-119.

[15] This information was transmitted by Harriman to the State Department on September 12th from Frankfort, Germany. Harriman was waiting to be invited to join Byrnes at the London Conference, and the Chinese Ambassador was on his way to that conference when they met.

frequent intervals when Byrnes was abroad during the rest of 1945, Acheson was in active charge of the State Department, in close working relations with the President. John Carter Vincent was advanced from Chief of the China Affairs Division to Director of the Office of Far Eastern Affairs. In that post, and because of his close touch with the Chinese situation, he became the chief producing scribe on policy toward China.

PART THREE

From the Surrender of Japan to the Marshall Mission

CHAPTER 31

The Struggle for Control of China

THE Germans were defeated; Hitler and the evil that belched out of him were dead; the Japanese had given up. The American nation relaxed and began to turn to the future of its ordinary affairs. During the weeks after V-J Day, the press and radio told by stories and pictures of the entry of our soldiers into Tokyo and the ceremonies of surrender on the *U.S.S. Missouri* anchored in Tokyo Bay. Like corn after rain, the question sprouted—how soon will our fighting men be back home? Plans for great movements of forces from Europe to the Far East were hurriedly canceled. Orders were issued, as fast as they could be written, to disperse the vast expeditionary force we had been collecting to invade Japan.

Few gave thought to the situation in China, which might so greatly affect the value of the victory that was being hailed. Officials were left to worry about it. The harder they looked, the clearer it became that the defeat of Japan did not mean the end of trouble either for China or the United States.

The state of China, as summed up in the flow of reports to Washington, was poor in every respect.[1] Trade with the outside world was gone. Inflation was extreme; students, officials, soldiers were finding it very hard to live. Ninety per cent of China's railways were out of operation. The rolling stock had been smashed and burned, tunnels and bridges knocked down. Almost all of the river shipping on which China had so greatly depended had been destroyed or stranded. In most areas the roads were very bad and trucks few. The only practical rapid means of transport left for Chinese armies, civilians, and products were air and coastal shipping. The rural economy was suffering from eight years of neglect and destruction. In many places there were shortages of farm labor, livestock, fertilizers, and tools, which reduced the production and supply of the main crops such as rice and cotton.

There were in China proper more than one million Japanese soldiers, and almost as many in Manchuria; about six hundred thousand puppet troops scattered in various parts of China and another three hundred

---

[1] An interesting review of the situation in China at the time of the surrender of Japan as seen by the Chinese government is in a memorandum which it gave General Wedemeyer in 1947. *United States Relations with China*, pages 817-822.

and fifty thousand in Manchuria; and Soviet forces estimated at about seven hundred thousand were being deployed in various parts of Manchuria. There were dissident movements in some provinces. It was not sure that some of the local governors and military chiefs would stand by the Central Government. Finally, there were the Communists. They had a well-organized and determined regular army which some estimates put as high as half a million men, and even larger guerrilla forces and local defense troops. These Communist units were dispersed widely through central, north, and even coastal China.

The government was confronted with multiple new tasks. There were armies to be moved, supplies to be gotten and transported, new zones of command to be organized. There were civil governments to be established in scores of cities and towns. These operations had to be arranged, financed, and executed quickly, or control of many parts of China would fall to local groups or to the armed Communist enemy.

The government was not in as good a position as had been hoped and planned. It had been thought that before these tasks pressed, most of the thirty-six government divisions sponsored by the United States would be well trained and equipped and the rest partly so. But this goal had not been achieved. It had been expected that the main armies would have moved toward the north and the coast and be close to the large cities and ports, from which positions they could move toward Manchuria. But when the fighting ended they were still mostly in the distant southwestern provinces. It had also been hoped that trucks to carry troops and supplies would have been brought over the Burma Road and through the recaptured ports in the Canton-Hong Kong area. But the actual conveyance over the Burma Road was still small and difficult, and no ports had yet been opened. The time needed to take quick advantage of victory had been foreshortened—in New Mexico and Moscow.

The Soviet entry into the war, the portended end of the war, the Japanese surrender, the imminent arrival of American forces—these set all elements in China in excited motion. The Chinese government in a great flurry began to order its troops and officials toward the areas to be taken over from the Japanese. Wedemeyer stood by, advised on plans, got the American air force ready to move the government troops, and awaited the arrival of new American contingents at the ports. The Communists, without waiting for official notice of the Japanese surrender, set about trying to get control of as much of China as they could.

On August 10th Chu Teh, Commanding General of the Communist forces, announced that Japan had surrendered unconditionally—which was not then true. He proceeded to declare that on the basis of the Potsdam Declaration any anti-Japanese armed force in the liberated areas could order the Japanese and puppet troops to surrender and lay down their arms, under threat of destruction. The American mission in Yenan reported that General Chu Teh was suiting his action to his words. He ordered all Communist army units to advance against Japanese troops at all points. "Our troops," one passage in his order read, "have the right to enter and occupy any city, town and communication center occupied by the enemy or the puppets, to carry on military management there to maintain order, and appoint a commissioner to look after the administrative affairs of the locality. Those who oppose or obstruct such actions will be treated as traitors."

Chiang Kai-shek at once denounced this as "an abrupt and illegal action." On the 12th he issued an order to General Chu Teh forbidding his forces to take any independent action against the Japanese, and demanding that they remain where they were and await orders from Chungking.

In another broadcast over the Communist radio of Yenan, Chiang Kai-shek was denounced as a "Fascist chieftain" and he and his regime accused of regarding ". . . the Japanese and puppets as dearer than their own countrymen and their own countrymen more hateful than Japanese and the puppets." It asked, "Can there be any doubts that once the war ends the danger of civil war will become a grave reality?" And concluded, "We want to announce to our three great Allies, the people of China and the world that the Chungking High Command cannot represent the Chinese people and the Chinese troops which really oppose the Japanese. The Chinese people demand that anti-Japanese troops in liberated China under Commander-in-Chief Chu Teh have the right to send their representatives directly to participate in accepting a Japanese surrender by the Allies."[2] The American observers in Yenan thought that the Communists expected to lose the Shanghai area, and that their hopes were pinned on North China and Manchuria.

The official announcement of the Japanese surrender was heard in Yenan at about the same hour on August 15th (Yenan time) as the news that the Soviet government had signed an accord with the hated Chungking regime. The Communists held a victory celebration. But the Amer-

[2] The text of the broadcast as recorded by the Federal Communications Commission is printed in the *New York Times*, August 14, 1945.

ican observers in Yenan thought it to be a last-minute effort and without spirit. They had the further impression that the Sino-Soviet pact left the local Communists hurt and bewildered. But they advised that despite the shock of this pact, the Communists would fight on for the control of China rather than accept the arrangements which Chiang Kai-shek was offering them. Colonel Yeaton, the head of the Observers Mission, hurried to General Wedemeyer an estimate of Communist military and political capabilities in North China. Its summary was: "The Communist army does not possess strength enough militarily to directly oppose the Kuomintang armies in position warfare; but over a long period of time as an occupying force the Kuomintang cannot hold out even with United States help."

On August 16th General Chu Teh, calling himself Commander-in-Chief of the anti-Japanese forces in the China Liberated Areas, Headquarters Yenan, placed his case before the American, British, and Soviet governments. He sent identical notes to their embassies in Chungking, giving glowing versions of what the Communists had done to win the war. The notes claimed that the Communists, in contrast to the Kuomintang habit of waiting for victory with folded arms, had liberated major areas in nineteen provinces of China. They defended the Communist record in negotiations for political and military unification and blamed the Kuomintang for failure. They challenged the right of the government and its high command to represent the broad Chinese masses or the armed forces in the liberated areas, and asserted that only the "peoples armed forces" under the control of Yenan had the title and the quality to accept Japanese surrender. Yenan in these notes set itself up as a rival government to that in Chungking. It demanded the right not only to accept the surrender of the Japanese, but also to participate in the formalities of the surrender of Japan, in the control of Japan, and in the peace conference with Japan. These claims were accompanied by requests that the American government at once cease to give Lend-Lease aid to the Chungking government and refuse to help it in any way if civil war occurred in China.[3]

Wedemeyer sent on Chu Teh's argumentative brief to Washington. His following comments mirrored the disjointed situation that he faced.

[3] Another report from Colonel Yeaton on August 15th, based on talks with General Chu Teh and Chou En-lai, indicates that the Communists wanted the United States to stop Lend-Lease at once, to take back all the material already given to the Kuomintang in the event that fighting occurred between the Kuomintang and Communist forces, and to abstain from helping the Kuomintang forces from occupying the cities in the rear of the Communist lines in north and central China, especially in regard to the transport of Kuomintang troops by sea and air to Nanking, Shanghai, and other centers.

They added up to a judgment that Chu Teh's proposals should be rejected and Chiang Kai-shek's leadership favored. But he saw ahead—unless some move of the Great Powers prevented it—a civil war. Thus, he said, while carrying out the missions entrusted to him he might inadvertently afford direct U.S. assistance to the Central Government in subduing Communist armed forces. In this dilemma and in the absence of specific guidance, he was continuing to give full support, including air-lift, to the Chinese government, but also instructing U.S. liaison personnel to withdraw from the vicinity of clashes between Chinese forces as quickly as practicable, using force only to protect themselves and the U.S. property in their possession. The War Department allowed him to follow this course, perhaps.

During these same few days Washington tried in several ways to strengthen the hedge against expansion of Communist strength. Marshall (on the 17th) advised MacArthur that deep anxiety was being felt over the chance that the schism in China would be made worse by surrender of Japanese armed forces to the Communists. The State Department thought, Marshall informed him, that when he, MacArthur, talked to the Japanese about repatriation, he ought to make it clear that the clause in the Potsdam Declaration which dealt with the return of Japanese armed forces to their peaceful occupations applied only to those who surrendered themselves and their arms to Chiang Kai-shek and his subordinates. The State-War-Navy Coordinating Committee (SWNCC) drew up an answer to Chu Teh's note which Wedemeyer transmitted to Yenan. This said in substance that the United States, the United Kingdom, and the Soviet Union had agreed that Chiang Kai-shek, as Allied Commander-in-Chief in the China Theater, should receive the surrender of Japanese armed forces in China, and the American government hoped that the Communists would cooperate with him to the full.

The State Department wanted to follow this up by action which might impress the Communists more. It prepared the text for a possible public statement which might be issued with the concurrence of the British, Soviet, and Chinese governments. It was to confirm that all four powers were behind General Order No. 1, by the terms of which the Japanese in China were to surrender only to Chiang Kai-shek, as Allied Commander-in-Chief; and it was to state their opinion that the issue raised by the Communists was not conducive to the attainment of a unified and democratic China. Byrnes instructed Ambassador Winant in London to consult Bevin, and Ambassador Harriman in Moscow to consult Molotov. Bevin—with some revisions of language that reduced its force—said it would be all right with the British government. Molotov said that the Soviet government had no observations to make. Byrnes decided to give up the idea, on the ground that the publication of the texts of the Sino-Soviet accords on August 24th ended the need for it.[4]

After the Japanese surrender, it was possible to believe that diplomacy might manage to confine the Chinese Communists. The Soviet government had agreed—by any usual interpretation of the words of its treaty with the Chinese government—to refrain from supporting or helping its Chinese kin. The American government was extending its help to the Generalissimo in the struggle to get control of China and urging the Communists to cooperate with him.

Hurley was confident that the Communists would come to find their cause better served by reaching an agreement with the government. The chance for which he had been waiting he thought at hand, and he had moved with boldness to use it. Immediately upon the completion of the Sino-Soviet accord and the issuance of General Order No. 1, he had urged Chiang Kai-shek to invite Mao Tze Tung to Chungking. Chiang Kai-shek had agreed. An invitation had been sent off at once on August 16th, the day on which General Chu Teh presented to the Allied governments the Communist claim of the right to share fully in the acceptance of Japanese surrender and in the settlements to follow. The Generalissimo's message to Yenan had stated: "We have many international and internal problems awaiting settlement. . . . Those involve our national welfare. Please do not delay coming here." Mao Tze Tung had followed up Chu Teh's demanding note to the Allies by a refusal to accept Chiang Kai-shek's appeal. Hurley had advised the Generalissimo not to heed these answers, and so show that he could lead the nation well and generously in peace as in war. When a report came to his ear that it was being said in Yenan that the Chungking government was declining to guarantee the safety of Mao Tze Tung, Hurley had at once sent word to Mao that he was willing to fly up to Yenan, then fly back to Chungking in the same plane with the Communist leaders, and be responsible for their lives while in Chungking.

Mao Tze Tung had briefly hesitated. He had said he would send Chou En-lai, and then follow himself if the first consultations gave enough reason. Chiang Kai-shek had answered that he would be glad

<hr />

[4] Telegrams, August 23, 1945, Byrnes to Winant and Harriman; August 24th, Winant to Byrnes; August 27th, Harriman to Byrnes; and August 28th, Byrnes to Winant.

to receive Chou En-lai, but he hoped that Mao would decide to come along. Mao then said he would come. He had notified the Generalissimo that he would welcome Hurley's visit and that both he and Chou En-lai would return with Hurley to Chungking to confer on all the important issues: on the questions which were leading to civil war in China. "Your younger brother," his message to Chiang Kai-shek ended, "is preparing to come in the immediate future." It may well be that his change of mind was caused, first, by the American answer to his demand for the the right to accept Japanese surrender which was received while he was wavering; and, second, by the publication of the full terms of the Sino-Soviet accords on August 24th. Chiang Kai-shek and Mao Tze Tung had not been in each other's presence since 1927, just before the great division within the Kuomintang.

Just before leaving Chungking for Yenan as mediating guardian, Hurley was told by Colonel Yeaton what he should expect to learn. This did not conform to the past run of Hurley's notions. Yeaton said that the Communists in Yenan really felt that Chiang Kai-shek was knocking at their door and that the world was looking to them to save the peace; they were interpreting Chiang Kai-shek's and Hurley's invitation to mean that both the Chinese and American governments needed them. They were out after a chance within a coalition government of getting control of China. But still Yeaton thought it might be possible to work out a transient arrangement under which the control of China would be loosely divided, by regions, among the government forces, the Communist forces, and local warlords, all to cooperate under some loose central administration.

Hurley spent only a day in Yenan. His visit was marked by personal friendliness and seemed to augur well. On August 28th he flew back to Chungking with Mao Tze Tung. The Communist leader stayed in the Chinese capital about a month, arguing the Communist cause. While he was there, American planes and ships were moving government troops and officials into the vital ports and cities of east and central China; and government and Communist forces were engaged in frantic skirmishes over all the provinces of North China.

The talks between the government and Communists that ensued during the last of August and first half of September were friendlier than the previous ones. The government offered more place and chance to the Communists, and the Communists seemed less arrogant and unyielding. Hurley led the talks along. He urged both sides to try to agree on essential principles and avoid quarrels over small points of position. He would not allow them to conclude that they could not agree; and whenever they seemed about to do so, got one side or the other to make a new offer. He firmly believed that in the end both sides would come to see that they could not have their full way. For Chiang Kai-shek was being told clearly by the American government that he could not count on unqualified and unlimited future aid (as will be told more fully), while the Chinese Communists were faced by the provision in the Sino-Soviet treaty that Moscow would give them no support.

Hurley was eager to return to the United States for medical care and for guidance. But when both sides asked him to postpone his departure from September 18th to the 22nd, he did so, thinking that a little more work might bring agreement into sight. The report that he sent off to Washington just before he left for the airfield concluded, "The spirit shown by the negotiators is good, the rapprochement between the two leading parties of China seems to be progressing, and the discussion and rumors of civil war recede as the conference continues."[5] This view of the situation may be regarded as evidence of the vitality of Hurley's purposeful effort. In reality the only common ground reached during these talks was the wide one where general avowals may roam without getting in each other's way. The government and the Communists were still far apart as regards the actual terms of cooperation, of adjustment of political and military power.

The way in which the situation in the provinces was developing gave little reason for thinking that the struggle was in suspense and peace pending. During September and October American transport planes moved three large armies to key sectors of east and north China.[6] American Marines (the 3rd Amphibious Corps)—about fifty thousand of them—were landed and secured ports and airfields at Tsingtao, Tientsin,

[5] Hurley telegram, September 22, 1945. The main portions of this report are printed in *United States Relations with China*, pages 105-107. An omitted sentence reads, "I pointed out [to the negotiators] that an attempt to agree on all the details of government and reorganization of troops in advance would in all probability lead to interminable debate."

[6] The Shanghai-Nanking sector was given first priority. The Chinese 94th Army (some 35,000 men) was lifted from Liuchow to Shanghai, some nine hundred miles, by C-54s based on Bengal in India, some fourteen hundred miles from Liuchow, which had to carry the fuel for the full round trip, forty-six hundred miles over the Hump. The Chinese 6th Army (some forty thousand men, veterans of the Burma campaign) were flown by C-46s from Chi-chiang to Nanking, some eight hundred miles. Other forces were flown from Hankow and Shanghai to Peiping. These movements were completed in October. Statement by General Wedemeyer at News Conference, October 22, 1945, Washington.

Peiping, and Chinwangtao. It was planned to evacuate most of the Japanese through these ports, and deemed essential that they be strongly held, so that the deportation should be orderly. In addition, small detachments were protecting the railroad between Tangku and Chinwangtao, and coal mines and bridges at Tanshan. Thus helped, the government forces took over the large cities and ports of central and eastern China. In the Shanghai-Nanking region and most other areas south of the Yangtze, they met almost no Communist or local opposition; they were able to secure the surrender of the great majority of the Japanese troops in these regions, along with their arms and reserve stocks.

But at the same time a jagged Communist barrier was being extended in length and depth across much of North China and the routes to Manchuria. In great number and good order Communist units went far and wide. The countryside around Tientsin and Peiping, and the coastal areas in Shantung north up to the Great Wall, were alive with them. They avoided pitched battles, but blocked roads, cut railways, and did their utmost to arouse opposition to government forces among the local people. They might well have gained control of some large cities and railways had they not been guarded by the Japanese—in accordance with General Order No. 1—until government or American troops arrived. In the main the Japanese evaded or resisted their demands for surrender, but still the Communists managed to get a substantial amount of arms, ammunition, and supplies from the Japanese and puppet forces. October found them concentrated in strength north and west of Peiping in a triangle Peiping-Kalgan-Tatung, active in the provinces of Shansi, Hopei, Honan, Chahar, and Shantung, while smaller forces were on their way farther north into Jehol and toward Manchuria. Of their intention of going wherever they could, those moving Communist units made no secret.

This threatening contest in the provinces was the contrasting background of the talks that had continued in Chungking. On their termination in the middle of October, the government and the Communists issued a joint summary of their conversations. This summary conveyed to the hopeful the same impression as the report which Hurley had made on leaving China for home three weeks before—that the internal division of China might still be settled by peaceful means.[7] It stated

---

[7] This joint statement of October 11, 1945, is printed in *United States Relations with China*, pages 577-581.

that agreement had been reached on two of the three most contested matters, to wit: (a) the methods and terms of military unification, (b) the steps through which and the principles on which a constitutional and democratic form of government were to be established. Even the unsettled difference in regard to the third of the most disputed issues— political control of the areas which the Communists claimed by right of liberation—was so treated as to induce the belief that the two sides were not far apart. The whole had a tone of good-tempered moderation, which seemed corroborated by what each privately was saying to the Embassy.[8]

But Walter S. Robertson, who was in charge of the Embassy in Hurley's absence, advised the State Department not to take this statement of progress toward agreement too literally, even though both sides said it was so. His glum advance comment, based on his talks with them, ended with the judgment, that "While the joint statement will probably emphasize points of agreement and infer that negotiations are progressing satisfactorily, we are of the opinion that the two sides are far apart on the basic question of the political control of the liberated areas now dominated by the Communists."[9] Even so, the State and War Departments and the White House regarded it as the first genuine measure of progress toward a settlement by peaceful means of the internal struggle in China. As Acheson, who at the time was Under-Secretary of State, has since observed, it marked out "the basis for the efforts which General Marshall later took on."[10]

The American government was, of course, eager to believe that its policies toward China were proving correct and effective. The gravity of the problems that would have to be faced if they failed and internal struggle continued, was becoming all too plain. The Chinese government was already asking for greater and more prolonged help in the uncompleted tasks of disarming the Japanese and taking control over North China and Manchuria. If we refused these requests, the Chinese government would probably not be able to do either, and China would remain divided and close to if not in a state of civil war. No one could be sure that even if we gave what was being presently asked, that would be the end, that we might not be dragged deeper into the Chinese disorder.

[8] Telegrams, October 2nd and October 8th, from American Embassy in Chungking to the State Department to be passed on to Hurley.
[9] Telegram, October 8, 1945, from Chungking.
[10] *Joint Committee on the Military Situation in the Far East*, page 1844.

Each extension of our activities increased the chance that we might get involved in irregular warfare against the Chinese Communists. The signals of trouble ahead were up. Wedemeyer was taking pains with the planning of the movement of Chinese government forces. He would not execute operations which he deemed for the direct purpose of striking against the Communists.[11] He was also careful to see that the Americans under his command kept out, as far as they could, of situations where there were, or might be, clashes. By these rules Americans in uniform managed to transport the government troops, to supply them, and to maintain liaison with them with little trouble. The Communist forces in the field were careful to avoid fights with them. But the Communist leaders in Yenan—Mao Tze Tung, Chou En-lai, General Chu Teh—all complained about the way in which we were enabling the government to spread its authority.

Also, one important movement of American Marines was canceled because of the risk that it might bring about a fight. It had been planned to land a detachment at Chefoo, a seaport on the northern coast of Shantung. This port was only sixty-five sea miles from Dairen. Under our control it would be a good point from which government troops might be ferried into Manchuria. Under the Communist control it might serve similarly well as a point from which the Communists could move forces either into Manchuria or south into Shantung, where they might surround the American Marines at Tientsin. American military headquarters decided to send the cruiser *U.S.S. Louisville* and several destroyers to land Marines and take over the port. Advance news of this intended movement reached Yenan. On September 27th, General Chu Teh sent word to General Wedemeyer that if American forces made this and other nearby landings, the Communist 8th Route Army would find it hard to tell what their purposes were, since that army was in complete control of this area and there were no Japanese nearby. Thus, Chu Teh's message continued, if the Americans went ahead without agreement with the 8th Route Army, the Chinese would think that

[11] Wedemeyer had explained to the War Department, as noted earlier in this chapter, the problem he faced in carrying out his assigned missions effectively without infringing on the injunction that he was not to support the Chinese government in civil war or become involved in actual fighting except to protect American lives or vital American property. He had specified the course he intended to follow—along the lines already indicated. This intent was reviewed by the Joint Chiefs of Staff and SWNCC and discussed with Secretary Byrnes. All concurred in approving the careful course which he marked out. The problem of decision recurred; as when later Chiang Kai-shek asked him to move government forces to Tangku where there were no Japanese, but where there were dissidents. He refused and the War Department upheld the decision.

the United States was interfering in Chinese internal politics. On October 4th, an American colonel went ashore and asked the Communists to leave the port. On the 7th, General Chu Teh sent second word to American military headquarters in China that this surprised him greatly for reasons he had already given. He said that he thought that the American demand was unnecessary; therefore he asked the Americans not to land at Chefoo; but if they went ahead anyhow without an advance agreement with Communist headquarters and trouble resulted the full responsibility would rest upon the United States. He broadcast the same message over the radio.

The American naval vessels that were carrying the Marines were already off the port of Chefoo. Admiral Barbey, who was in command of the naval force, and General Rockey, who was in charge of the Marine units, both confirmed the fact to American military headquarters that there were no Japanese troops in the region and no apparent reason for American entry. They therefore recommended that the landing not be made. American military headquarters concurred. Chiang Kai-shek was duly consulted. When Admiral Barbey was asked by press correspondents to explain the decision, he answered, "Chefoo was in control of the 8th Route Army. The city is well policed and there are no disorders. As there are no Japanese and no prisoners of war and no American internees there is no military reason for landing United States troops at this time. I so reported and recommended the above, the General Kellar Rockey U.S.M.C. concurring. The recommendation has been approved."[12]

Some of the American ships remained in the harbor of Chefoo to watch what went on. As epilogue, it may be noted that an active traffic was taking place between the Chinese Communists in Chefoo and the Russians in Dairen, and between the Communists in Chefoo and those in Hulutao and Yingkow, ports on the Manchurian coast which the occupying Soviet authorities were refusing to allow Chinese government troops to enter.

The episode illustrated the trouble into which American forces might run if and as they extended their operations into those areas of North China and Manchuria where the Communist forces were in strength. The landings might not be contested, but the surrounding Communist opposition would be stubborn, skilled in scattering through the countryside and in conducting guerrilla warfare against supplies, communica-

[12] Moorad, *The Lost Peace*, page 90.

tions, and outposts. The Communists did not, if they could help it, yield a district once and for all and let it return to rest.

Such, then, was the uneven and contrasting view of the Chinese scene which shaped itself during the two months after V-J Day: a joint affirmation by the government and Communists that they were moving toward a settlement by peaceful means; a confirmed knowledge that if peaceful means failed, the United States would be forced to make a hard choice between allowing China to go its own way or accepting substantial burdens and nasty risks. All planning was further complicated by the fact that the disarmament of the Japanese in North China was not complete, and the business of securing control over Manchuria was hardly begun. Both Hurley and Wedemeyer had been asked by Chiang Kai-shek to go to Washington, the better to explain to the President and the Chiefs of Staff his situation, his efforts, and his needs. They had arrived at the end of September while the government was in great perplexity over the further steps in its policy of aid for the Chinese government.

CHAPTER 3 2

How Much Aid for China After the War?

THE authorities in Washington were not, in fact, ready to tell anyone—Hurley, Wedemeyer or Chiang Kai-shek—what we proposed to do from then on in the way of aid and support of the Chinese government. They were puzzling about both the immediate and later phases of the problem. The two connected questions before them were: (1) Could the American government soon end the direct help of the kind being given to the Generalissimo's forces? That had been conceived as temporary, as a phase of the completion of the defeat of Japan which would be ended when the Japanese in China were disarmed and evacuated. (2) What assistance should be given Chiang Kai-shek for the improvement of his own armed forces, upon which the military tasks faced by the government would permanently devolve?

It will be recalled that in May the American government had postponed decision regarding future military assistance for the Chinese government.[1] The question had been brought forward again at the time of the Japanese surrender in August but had not been settled; and it was kept in suspense while the American forces proceeded with the first post-surrender program. What had occurred must be briefly related.

On August 11th, after Chiang Kai-shek had read over and approved the terms of acceptance of the Japanese surrender, he had asked about the prospects for future aid. Both Hurley and Wedemeyer had reported to Washington the Generalissimo's urgent interest and large ideas. Wedemeyer said that he had often told Chiang Kai-shek that when the war ended new arrangements would have to be made to get supplies from the United States, whether Lend-Lease or otherwise. But he said that Chiang Kai-shek harked back to what he regarded as a promise made by Roosevelt at Cairo to equip ninety Chinese divisions as a peacetime army and was asking that we make good on it. Hurley's message had been to the same effect as Wedemeyer's. He too said that he had told Chiang Kai-shek that as far as he knew Lend-Lease would end on V-J Day.

The general Lend-Lease program had been terminated as abruptly as the war. But an exception had been made for the support of Chinese military operations deemed essential to the reoccupation of all areas in the China Theater held by the Japanese, and the placing of Chinese

[1] See Chapter 27.

occupation forces in Japan proper, Formosa, and Korea.[2] This would, it had been thought, take care of the immediate needs. But Chiang Kai-shek was thinking beyond that. Through both Wedemeyer and Hurley he had continued to ask for equipment for a very large permanent ground force and a substantial air force. His idea was to have these forces use American tactics and technique as well as weapons. Therefore, to advise and assist, he had also wanted the American government to maintain a permanent military mission in China. He wished Wedemeyer to head this mission.[3]

The War Department had thought that political rather than military reckoning ought to govern the decision on these requests. Perturbed by the unsettled prospect in China, it had urgently asked for guidance. Assistant Secretary of War McCloy on September 1st had passed on to the SWNCC a memo from the Acting Deputy Chief of Staff which stressed the need for quick answers. The memo recounted that through military Lend-Lease we had been equipping and training what was to be the Chinese army program of thirty-nine divisions and a small Chinese air force.[4] About one-third of the necessary equipment for the army program, it summed up, had already been given to the Chinese government; about one-third was in the India-Burma and China Theaters, but not yet turned over to the Chinese government; about one-fifth was on its way to China; and the rest was in the United States.[5] Little

[2] That had been decided on August 17th at a White House conference attended by the President, Byrnes, Leahy, Stimson, Crowley, and Snyder. The form and terms of the exception for China were worked out by the Joint Chiefs of Staff in a memo for the President. On September 5th the President issued another directive based on this memo which provided for the continuance for six months of certain kinds of Lend-Lease aid for China for these purposes. Under this exception the American government after V-J Day: (1) transported Chinese forces by air and sea, (2) continued to transfer the Lend-Lease equipment and supplies that were already in China and also released to China some supplies and equipment left in the India-Burma Theater, (3) turned over many airplanes, particularly transport planes, to the Chinese air force, (4) turned over large stocks of American ammunition in West China.

[3] Chiang Kai-shek's ideas are fully reported in Hurley's telegram of September 2, 1945 to the State Department.

[4] The accepted program at this time was to equip the thirty divisions in the Y force which Stilwell had organized, plus ten per cent of the equipment needed for a second thirty divisions, plus the divisions which had been fighting in Burma, plus one special division to be recruited from university students. The program contemplated that most of the needed small arms and small arms ammunition would be supplied by the Chinese, and that the United States would provide the ordnance, heavy howitzers, anti-tank guns, etc.

[5] By November 30th, three months later, between eighty-five and ninety per cent of the equipment to be transferred under this program to the Chinese government was in the China Theater, but some of it had not yet been turned over to the Chinese government. Memo, Freeman, China Affairs Division of the State Department, talk with Colonel J. R. Crume.

had yet been done, the statement continued, to restore the Chinese air force. But the commanding general of the American army air force had a recently prepared plan for the purpose which could be carried out cheaply and quickly from the American surplus.

The State Department member on SWNCC had called Secretary Byrnes' attention to the wish of the War Department for a prompt decision so that there would be no hiatus in whatever program was to be executed. Byrnes had hastened to send his recommendations to the President. He had advised that we should try to meet Chiang Kai-shek's desires as far as possible. He had referred to Soong's repetition of Chiang Kai-shek's request that we should complete our commitment to equip ninety (or even a hundred) Chinese divisions. In that regard, Byrnes had advised Truman that Hopkins affirmed that Roosevelt had made "some such commitment" at Cairo, but that it was vague and loose and that it was hard to believe that either Roosevelt or Chiang Kai-shek thought of the program as separate from the fight against Japan, which was now over. Byrnes had suggested some ways in which we might complete the equipment of the thirty-nine divisions. He had left to the defense departments the question of whether or not a permanent military mission was to be established in China. Marshall had favored it. He had so informed Wedemeyer on September 4th, explaining that his thought was to end American operational activities in the China Theater as soon as feasible, but not to inactivate that theater until the mission was well established and there was a smooth transition.

By the 7th of September, discussion between departments had gone far enough to give the President a basis for a preliminary answer to Soong. The President had told him that though the question of furnishing an American military advisory group was still under study by SWNCC, he could definitely say that the personnel could and would be furnished for the purpose; but Soong had been asked to consider whether it might not be better if those Americans who served on the advisory group should not be released by the American government and enlisted under the Chinese government. The President had seen no reason why Wedemeyer might not head this group as Chiang Kai-shek wished. In regard to the request that the United States equip additional Chinese divisions, the President had said that a careful search of the records had not disclosed anything relative to the promise which Chiang Kai-shek said had been made at Cairo.[6] Soong had asked whether the

[6] There was, as far as I know, no official record of the commitment. But, as has already been told, both Hopkins and Marshall understood from the President that he had agreed

President had consulted Harry Hopkins. The President said that he had, but had promised to talk with him again. He had gone on to remark that now that the war was ended some of his powers had lapsed and that he had to consider the views of Congress. The President had ended by saying that he would try to expedite more conclusive answers on these matters. Soong had answered that he would postpone his departure in order to await them.[7]

A report of this talk had been sent through Hurley to the Generalissimo. A few days later Chiang Kai-shek had explained his ideas further to Wedemeyer. He argued that China needed a great number of divisions because the size of the soldiers was smaller than American, and the size of the divisions was much smaller, and that communications with the vast area to be defended were so poor. Thus he had asked Wedemeyer to tell Marshall that he thought China should have ninety divisions. Thirty of these ought to be trained, organized, and equipped comparably to American divisions; they would deal with possible attacks against China. The other sixty ought to be trained, organized, and equipped comparably with the Chinese divisions sponsored by the United States; these would maintain political stability.

Here was the same familiar split between American military judgment and the Generalissimo's conception of his needs. The War Department was convinced that the Chinese government would be better with a good and well-equipped small army which it could afford than with a big, poor, half-starved army. The Chinese government clung to the wish for a great force to be maintained in all regions of China to meet local situations and hold them under control.

By September 13th SWNCC had formulated more certain answers for the Generalissimo. The Secretaries of War and Navy had approved them and Acting Secretary Acheson passed them on to the President, along with the text of a statement which, it was suggested, the President might make to Soong. This the President had followed word for word in his next talk with Soong on the 14th.[8] He had told Soong that the United States was prepared to help China to develop armed forces of a moderate size for the maintenance of internal peace and security and the assumption of control over the liberated areas of China, including Manchuria and Formosa. The exact amount of assistance was to be

---

in a vague way that we would equip up to ninety divisions, but had left open the question of when this should be done.

[7] This summary of the Soong-Truman talk of September 7th is taken from a memo of Acting Secretary Acheson, who was present at this talk.

[8] *United States Relations with China*, page 939.

decided in further conferences between the two governments. At the moment, it was thought practicable, subject to suitable mutual arrangements, to provide equipment and supplies to complete the thirty-nine division program for the ground forces, to furnish certain naval craft, particularly those suitable for coastal and river operations, and to equip an air force of commensurate size. What more, if any, could be done, would be settled after further talk with General Wedemeyer and further analysis by the Joint Chiefs of Staff. The President had confirmed his approval of the military advisory group. But he said that it would be easier to define its size and composition and functions later. Finally, the President had explained that this program was subject to one general condition. As expressed in the memo from which the President talked to Soong, "Having in mind statements by the Generalissimo that China's internal political difficulties will be settled by political methods, it should be clearly understood that military assistance furnished by the United States would not be diverted for use in fratricidal warfare or to support undemocratic administration."

Once more the student is left to wonder whether it was seen that this condition might restrict effective execution of the whole program. Clashes were occurring in China even then which might be called "fratricidal warfare." The existing administration in China was admittedly "undemocratic." Was it intended, then, that the statement be taken to mean that the American government would not go forward with the program if the Chinese government found itself fighting the Communists? Or if no agreement was reached with the Communists for the reconstitution of the government? It may be hazarded that this condition was not intended to have such full and definitive meaning, that the meaning was to be read from the verb "diverted." It should be considered with reference to the effort which Hurley was making at this very time to bring the two sides together and avert civil war. It will be remembered that during the first weeks of September it seemed—to Hurley at least—as though the decision by the Chinese might be sent either way by our touch. The talkers in Chungking seemed to be coming closer to accord, while the opposing forces in the provinces seemed to be nearer war than ever before.

To venture an interpretation: the American government was trying by this conditioned promise of help to embolden Chiang Kai-shek to risk his own fate and that of his party in a gamble for internal peace and unity. But at the same time it wanted to avert the chance that with this help in sight he might cease trying to settle his quarrel with the

Communists by peaceful means, and attack them. The only way perceived out of the Chinese dilemma was by the establishment of a constitutional democracy in which all factions would take their place. Was this for China, considering the condition of the people and the depth of division, a real possibility almost in reach? Or was it only a mirage? Perhaps the answer is to be found in the lexicon of work-a-day practical politics; in that book any arrangement for governing China on which the opposed parties agreed could be regarded as "democratic," or progress toward democracy.

In any case, Chiang Kai-shek seems to have taken the answer calmly as he went on with his discussions with Mao Tze Tung in Chungking. After all the American government was currently making it possible for him to extend his control over central and east China.

SWNCC and the Joint Chiefs of Staff had gone on with their discussion of this program which was to come into effect as the American forces sent to China as part of the war effort were withdrawn. While their talk had proceeded through September, the American military organization was reaching the conclusion that they could be taken out of China within a few months; that the tasks which had been assigned to them in the August 10th directive would by then be completed. The presumption spread that although there were still large numbers of armed Japanese in China, this phase of American aid and action would soon be ended unless new tasks were assigned.

As summarized by General Stratemeyer (in charge while Wedemeyer was in Washington) in a report of October 4th, all assigned tasks would be completed by the end of the year; and thus, unless the War Department extended the scope of the present mission and gave the China Theater extra jobs to do, or gave new orders to United States forces to remain in China for occupation purposes, it seemed that our troops should be sent home as soon as possible, once their jobs were done. To retain personnel in the theater, Stratemeyer thought, after their work had been completed would hurt their morale. Later, after Wedemeyer had returned to China, he confirmed this estimate, stating that unless new tasks were assigned, and if shipping was provided to take American troops away, the Chinese theater of war could be deactivated as of December 15th.[9]

[9] There were at the beginning of September about 60,000 American troops in the China Theater, apart from the Marines. During that month some 16,000 were returned under the War Department demobilization policy. It was currently planned to return about twenty per cent of the remaining strength in each of the following months through December. Statement by General Wedemeyer at a news conference, October 22, 1945, Washington, D.C.

The mission of the Marines, as originally defined, was also taken to be near completion. As stated in the original orders to the commanding officer, it was to seize and hold the Tientsin, Tsingtao and Chefoo areas, and such intermediate and adjacent areas as he might deem necessary for the security of his forces; and to disarm the Japanese in these areas and hold them pending the arrival of adequate government forces.

The Japanese in these places had been disarmed. Government forces, it was judged, were available to take over the task of maintaining security. Thus the mission was regarded as nearing its end. There were other good uses for these divisions of Marines. The Secretary of State was uneasy at their continued presence in China. The Chinese Communists were assailing their activities as favoring the government side. On this score they were accusing us of not being impartial in our mediation efforts around which the State Department was seeking to shape our policy. Further, it was feared, and with reason, that if the Marines prolonged their stay in China, the Soviet Union might use that fact as pretext or cause for keeping its forces in Manchuria.

On October 20th the Joint Chiefs of Staff asked American military headquarters in China to recommend a schedule of withdrawal for the Marines. The answer was that unless their mission as originally conceived was changed, the transfer could start November 15th; for it was expected that by then the Chinese government would have occupied the areas held by the Marines; and if they stayed on they would surely get involved in the civil war. While waiting for final word from Washington, military planning in China went along on the supposition that the mission of the Marines would be adjudged at an end and they would soon be ordered home.

While these lines of withdrawal were being sketched out, the State, War, and Navy Departments, through SWNCC, had gone on with their discussions about the continuation of aid to the Chinese government for building up its own armed forces. Under the guidance of the State Department member, the proposal submitted by this Committee would have subordinated the program for military aid to the satisfaction of our political ideas.[10] But the Joint Chiefs of Staff had thought these conditions to be at the same time both tenuous and too rigid. In the report that was finally adopted by SWNCC on October 22nd the statement of political aims and conditions was smudged. The pertinent para-

[10] Report submitted by SWNCC to the Joint Chiefs of Staff, September 26, 1945.

graphs, set down to guide the execution of the approved program of future military aid for the Chinese read as follows:

6. The achievement of these objectives in China requires a friendly, unified, independent nation with a stable government resting, insofar as practicable, on the freely expressed support of the Chinese people.

7. . . . The following should be established as policies of the United States:

(a) To support and assist the national government of China in development along lines which are compatible with our basic objectives in the Far East.

(b) To assist and advise China in the development of modern armed forces, ground, sea and air, for the following purposes only:

1) Maintenance of internal peace and security in China including the liberated areas of Manchuria and Formosa, and

2) The fulfillment of those obligations which may devolve upon China in the occupation of Korea and Japan.

(c) To discontinue our assistance to the development of Chinese armed forces, upon due notice to the Chinese Government if at any time it is established to the satisfaction of the United States Government that the Chinese armed forces are being used in support of an administration not in conformity with the general policies of the United States, to engage in fratricidal war, or to afford a threat of aggression.

8. The extent to which political stability is being achieved in China under a unified, fully representative government is regarded by the U.S. as a basic consideration which will at all times govern the furnishing of economic, military, or other assistance to that nation. . . ."[11]

The Joint Chiefs of Staff were completing their studies of the size and nature of the action that would fill this bill. They submitted a proposal for the military advisory group and asked that the State Department proceed to negotiate an agreement with the Chinese government for its establishment. They also prepared a program for the provision of equipment in accordance with this report. But questions were being raised in regard to both, and neither was in reality determined.

Summarily, then, the military program for China which the American government conceived between V-J Day and the latter part of October looked toward:

1. The termination of direct American military activity in China and of help in transport and supply of government forces.

2. The deactivation of the China Theater of War.

3. The return of the Marines to the United States.

4. The provision of means whereby the Chinese could have thirty-

---

[11] This is SWNCC 83/6.

nine well-supplied and equipped ground divisions, a small navy suited to its local needs, and an air force of some size. But this was conditional upon the satisfaction of several vaguely defined political conditions, still to be construed.[12]

5. Enabling the Chinese government to recruit and organize an American military advisory group which would help to train the Chinese forces in the use of this equipment and suitable tactics. But the size and functions of this was still under discussion.

But around the middle of October the State, War, and Navy Departments, which had so tediously put this program together, began to wonder whether it should not be revised or discarded. All three suffered sudden doubts about this line of conduct. Reluctantly they turned to face the fact that if it was carried through on schedule, China might fall apart and be lost to us.

When Wedemeyer left Washington at the end of October, he asked whether and when his current mission would end. He was told that the answers would follow him. On November 1st the War Department informed him that neither it nor the Joint Chiefs of Staff had as yet set a definite date for the inactivation of the China Theater. Two days later it quizzed him as to the ability of the Chinese government to maintain control of the areas guarded by the Marines, and as to what would follow on their withdrawal. Thus began a searching reexamination, which went on through November, of all previous plans in regard to China. This resurvey was thrust upon the authorities in Washington by the ominous trend in the situations in North China, the border region of Sinkiang, and Manchuria. Those must be retraced in order to understand the crisis of decision that lay ahead.

[12] Particularly the paragraph quoted in the President's statement to Soong on September 14th and Paragraph 7(c) of the SWNCC Report of October 22nd, also quoted.

CHAPTER 33

The Darkening Prospect

THROUGHOUT North China the situation was out of hand. As tersely summed up by the military attaché, "The fighting is becoming more bitter and larger numbers of men are being involved."[1] The Communists, through guerrilla and local units as well as regular forces, were securely established in the area east and north of Peiping, in the Shansi-Hopei-Chahar border region around Kalgan, and various points in Shantung and other land approaches to Manchuria. They dominated some sections of the railroad north from Peiping. They usually gave way or scattered before strong government forces. But they were confident that they would enlarge and strengthen their control throughout these northern regions and over Manchuria. For many of the Chinese living in the areas entered by the Communists accepted or joined them. In contrast to their own growth and vitality, they were sure that the government strength would soon decline. They were relying on their opinion that the morale of most of the government troops was low; that the soldiers were tired of war; that they were longing for the southern country from which most of them had come; that they would find the cold northern weather unpleasant and the northern grain diet disagreeable; and that the country over which they would have to fight was unfamiliar. Further, they counted on their power to interrupt the long lines of communication on which the government forces had to rely. This opinion was supported by defections of government armies and commanders in some engagements.[2]

It is probable that the Communists were regaining assurance that the Soviet Union was not going to be indifferent to them. There was regular liaison by November between the Soviet Union and Yenan. Communications went to and from Moscow by coded messages sent through the Yenan radio station and relayed into the Soviet net at some point in Manchuria. Numerous contacts were made in the field between the Soviet and Chinese Communist forces in Hopei and Chahar; and either then or later Soviet missions were flown into Yenan to discuss the future plans of the Red Army in Manchuria and to coordinate with the Chinese

---

[1] Telegram, November 11th from Chungking.

[2] As in Northern Honan, where two government armies quit and their generals went over to the Communists. Report of military attaché for week ending November 17th, 1945. Telegram, November 18th from American Embassy, Chungking.

Communist army. Soviet representatives attended the meetings of the Politburo of the Chinese Communist Party in Yenan. Some of the Communist troops were being equipped with weapons taken from the Japanese, either by the Communists or the Soviet forces.[3]

This barrier of Communist resistance in North China had proved itself strong enough to compel both Chiang Kai-shek and the American military representatives in China to conclude that the government forces which had been transported north would not be enough. Chiang Kai-shek began to ask us to move several more of his armies by air and sea to North China, and also to keep the Marines in place. The first of a series of such requests was made on November 5th, when he asked Wedemeyer to change the schedule and routes of American ships and Chinese troop movements. Wedemeyer felt compelled under his orders to refuse. He answered that these proposals exceeded the original plans for Chinese troop movements as worked out in August by the Chinese-American General Staff. The trouble was being caused, he observed, not by the Japanese but by dissident Chinese, and it was not within the scope of his mission to use shipping to move troops to fight a civil war.

Wedemeyer's answer was confirmed by Washington pending further instructions. But by then, back in Washington, a review was underway of the plans and orders in force. Worried doubts were spreading as to whether we could end the program of support as contemplated; whether we were willing to leave this situation in North and Northeast China to the fortunes of a chaotic civil war. The outcome of that, all agreed, would be bad in one way or another—either exhaustion of all China, or its division into two or more parts, or possibly even Communist domination of the whole country. Such thoughts as these marched up against the surging wish of the American people to disband their wartime armies and to free themselves from their wartime engagements.

Trouble had also occurred in the vast interior province of Sinkiang, next to Mongolia and Siberia. In the note which Molotov had written in August to the Chinese Foreign Minister in connection with the Treaty of Friendship, it had been said, "As for the recent developments in

[3] Many items of information on these points are contained in the reports of the military attaché and of the Observer Mission in Yenan. However, some of the items were said to be merely rumors, some to be second- or third-hand, some as having been passed on by the Japanese government; some were clearly proved, others not. The most extensive review of the contact during this period and thereafter between the Chinese Communist regime and the Soviet Union which I have seen is a report submitted in May 1946 by Colonel Ivan T. Yeaton for the period from July 1945 to April 1946 during which he was commanding officer of the United States Observer Group in Yenan.

Sinkiang the Soviet Government confirms that . . . it has no intention of interfering in the internal affairs of China."[4] But the vow had not brought tranquillity.

Revolts had broken out again in August-September. And again the rebels, mainly Moslem tribesmen, had pronounced a revolution: their appeal was for race equality, a native army, the end of Chinese domination, the return of local government to natives, and the restoration of trade with the Soviet Union. And again the local Chinese officials were of the opinion that the revolt was just a conspiracy incited by Soviet agents and armed by the Kazak kinsmen living across the border in Soviet territory.

For a brief time in September the State Department had thought of offering to mediate to get the facts and issues defined. But then it had learned that the Chinese government had appealed to the Soviet government to use its good offices. Moscow had then appeared to make a real effort to calm the situation. The rebels had wanted to be treated as equals—as representatives of "The East Turkestan Republic"—which implied recognition of their independence of Chungking. But Moscow had told them that it would not recognize their regime and advised moderation. The Chinese government seemed ready to grant a substantial measure of autonomy and correct the faults of administration. By November the situation had quieted down, but the rebellious groups were not reconciled to Chungking. The Chinese government had cause to wonder from day to day what might happen next in this distant area in the west, as it struggled for control in North China and Manchuria in the east.[5]

The situation in Manchuria was also becoming more and more confused. The hope that the Sino-Soviet accord made a firm road for the extension of official authority over Manchuria was being destroyed by doubt. The value of that agreement was marked down after the first attempts made by the American navy to move Chinese government forces to Manchuria. What had been happening in this region since the Japanese surrender makes a tale of great interest.

The spread of Soviet forces through Manchuria had been swift and extensive. The Emperor's surrender order of August 15th had been ignored; General Antonov, the Chief of Staff, had directed his forces

[4] *United States Relations with China*, page 587.

[5] This is a most condensed sketch of the rebellion in Sinkiang and the efforts to deal with it, as reported to Washington by Angus Ward, the American Consul in the capital of Sinkiang, via the American Embassy in Chungking during September and October.

to continue their offensive operations until all the Japanese troops had laid down their arms.[6] Detachments had been sent to occupy the main cities, Harbin, Kirin, Changchun, Mukden, Dairen, and Port Arthur. When the Soviet armies stopped their march, they were over all parts of the "Three Eastern Provinces'" known as Manchuria. They were also some distance within the adjoining Chinese provinces of Jehol and Chahar, entering junction towns of Chihfeng (in North Jehol) and Tolun (on the Jehol-Chahar frontier) which would be important in the contest between the government and the Communists. Units had also wandered down to Shanhaikwan (a port in Northern Hopei) and Kupeikow (a city on the Jehol-Hopei border north of Peiping) along the Great Wall.[7] On August 27th Stalin had told Harriman that Chiang Kai-shek had feared that the Red Army would advance to Kalgan (province of Chahar) and Peiping and unite with the Chinese Communists in those areas. But he explained that he had reassured Chiang Kai-shek that he did not want to occupy these areas, and he would not. Another remark made by Stalin to Harriman in this talk took on more interest in a later light. He had said that the Russian army had not as yet found any Communist guerrilla units in Manchuria and that they had not yet contacted Chinese Communists anywhere.

The advance of the Soviet forces into Manchuria had been reported in the Soviet press with great pride. Many stories told of the delight of the natives at being freed of Japanese control by the Red Army. Readers of *Pravda* on August 22nd learned for example that the "proprietor of the Jap hotel [in Harbin] offered the Soviet soldiers Havana cigars which were refused"; and readers of other papers that "Chinese in wide brimmed hats and shabby clothes welcome our men with joy. Women bring water to our weary men. An old man with a portrait of Stalin on his breast bows low to those who have liberated his country from the Japanese yoke."[8] The American Embassy in Moscow had noted

---

[6] *New York Times*, August 16, 1945. The Japanese government urgently requested General MacArthur to take steps to end the Soviet offensive, saying that the Japanese forces in Manchuria were having great trouble in obeying orders to cease hostilities because the Soviet troops were still attacking. *Ibid.*, August 17th.

[7] The province of Jehol had been administered by the Japanese as part of Manchukuo. There seems to have been no military agreement between the Soviet and Chinese governments as to exactly where the Soviet sphere of military operations should end. The Japanese commander in North China, General Takamori on August 25th sent messages to General Wedemeyer and Generalissimo Chiang Kai-shek that Soviet forces were beginning to advance south of Kupeikow into North China and attempting to disarm Japanese forces in the area, and that he was rejecting their demands for surrender and delivery of arms. The matter was settled informally between the Soviet and Chinese military.

[8] *New York Times*, August 18, 1945.

that these stories did not bother to mention the fact that the Soviet Union had recognized Chinese sovereignty over Manchuria.[9]

Very soon after Russian forces entered a district, new "democratic unions" of various types had been formed and assumed control of the local government. The history and tendencies of these local groups were varied. Some were local resistance forces which had been fighting the Japanese in an underground way; these had linked up loosely with an anti-Japanese volunteer army which had been operating in the mountain regions of eastern Manchuria. The Russians were encouraging and supervising this work of political resurgence in Manchuria.[10] Our Embassy at Moscow foresaw the chance that these groups might combine with Communist elements that were on the move toward Manchuria, and that Yenan would absorb them into provincial Communist regimes.

Such portents had stirred queries about the value of the agreements with the Soviet government which bore upon the restoration of Chinese control over Manchuria and the evacuation of the Soviet forces. The Chungking government had realized, as Soong had remarked to Harriman, that the agreements would be worth no more than Soviet good faith. But still it had counted on the accords to ease and guard its way into Manchuria. It had regarded them as a Soviet promise to facilitate the entry of government forces into the Three Eastern Provinces, to retain captured Japanese weapons until these forces could take them over, to prevent unfriendly groups from assuming control, and to assist agents of the Chinese government to set up administrations in each section of Manchuria as it was cleared of Japanese.[11]

[9] Telegram from Harriman, August 23, 1945.

[10] Telegram from Harriman, September 6, 1945, giving substance of Tass dispatch from Manchuria published in the *Red Fleet* of September 6th. Harriman noted that this was the first time that the Soviet press had revealed these activities.

[11] These expectations were current in Chinese official circles although the actual language of the August agreements did not define in a specific and positive way what the Soviet obligation was in these matters. In this connection, another contemporary opinion is of interest. On October 31st, 1945, Ambassador Winant in London reported on his talk with the British Foreign Office on this topic in paraphrase as follows: The Foreign Office is not sure that the Sino-Soviet Treaty is having the beneficial effects at first expected. They consider disturbing reports that Soviet permission had been given to units of the 8th Route Army to march into Mukden and other cities. It is apparently the contention of the Soviets that the 8th Route Army can be considered to be Chinese government troops within the meaning of the Sino-Soviet Treaty; technically, this argument may be correct but Foreign Office says that no one outside of Moscow seems to have given this interpretation of the treaty before.

The Soviet government later summarily denied the Chinese interpretation of the accord. As argued by Malik during the debate in the General Assembly of the United Nations on January 26, 1952, "Under the Yalta Agreement the U.S.S.R. had under-

In August Stalin had also assured Soong in Moscow that the Soviet forces would begin to withdraw from Manchuria within three weeks after the Japanese surrender, and be entirely out within three months.[12] He had told Harriman on August 27th that he expected the Chinese government to send its troops into Manchuria and take over from the Russians. Harriman had speeded this remark to Hurley, who had passed it along to Chiang Kai-shek. The Chinese government, after consultation with Wedemeyer's headquarters, had started to make plans to move troops into Manchuria. It was seized with a need for haste, for by September the Communists had begun to seep into Manchuria. Some were moving east by land through Inner Mongolia and Jehol, where they were joined by other Communist units, enlisted or conscripted. Others were coming north by boat and junk from Shantung.

As early as September 10th Soong had presented to Acheson, who was Acting Secretary while Byrnes was in London, a request from Chiang Kai-shek to the President that the United States provide vessels to transport his troops from Canton to Dairen. The Generalissimo had stressed the urgency of getting them into position in Manchuria before the Russians left. Soong had made the point that according to existing plans the ships needed to move them into Manchuria would not be available until December. This would be too late, he explained, since if government troops were not on the spot when the Russians got out, Chinese Communist troops would be likely to move into the vacated areas.[13] Acheson had asked Soong if it was not possible to move them overland. Soong had said this could not be done because of the conditions on the railroads.

Acheson had consulted the President. The President had referred the matter at once to the Joint Chiefs of Staff, who had immediately asked Wedemeyer to submit recommendations as to what American shipping would be needed to move Chinese forces to Manchuria. Wedemeyer had submitted a schedule for carrying them to Manchurian seaports. The Joint Chiefs had approved this schedule, reaffirming that it was our policy to help the Chinese government establish its troops in liberated

---

taken the obligation to aid China in its liberation from the Japanese yoke. No obligations had been undertaken by the U.S.S.R. to aid the Kuomintang Government in China's internal strife."

[12] This was evidenced by the minutes initialed on August 14th and published along with the agreement.

[13] It may be noted that the first units of the Communist 8th Route Army were being seen on the streets of Mukden by September 10th. These wore armbands with inscriptions in both Chinese and Russian. The Chinese characters read "8th Route Army." Military attaché's report, September 24, 1945.

areas, particularly Manchuria, as rapidly as practicable. The President thereupon on September 18th had instructed Acheson to give an answer to Soong based on this decision: to the effect that the commanders of the American army and navy forces in the Western Pacific were being ordered to take Chinese troops to Manchuria on dates and to ports as would be specified by Wedemeyer to Chiang Kai-shek; and that the Joint Chiefs of Staff fully expected adequate American shipping to be available as soon as the Chinese government troops were ready to embark for Manchuria. Acheson had so advised Soong.

But it had taken some weeks to arrange the actual movement. The Chinese armies named for Manchuria had first to be moved from the interior to points of embarkation. The landing vessels—type of assault shipping—had to be assembled and sent down to the loading ports. The Chinese government planned to send trucks along with some of its troops to carry them overland from the ports. Others were to be moved into the interior by rail.

The Generalissimo, meanwhile, had appointed General Hsiung Shih-hui to deal with the Soviet command in Manchuria and to direct the preparation for assumption of government control throughout the Three Provinces. General Hsiung had sought out General Malinovsky, the commander of the Soviet forces in Manchuria. They had arranged, in conformity with Stalin's promise, that the Soviet troops were to be withdrawn gradually from the south to the north; they were to start their egress in the middle of October, a few weeks later than the original plan, and by the end of November all were to be back in the Soviet Union.

The first expedition of Chinese troops destined for Manchuria had made ready to leave in time to reach Dairen as soon as the Soviet forces withdrew from that port. On American advice, General Malinovsky had been given advance notice of its coming. The Soviet response had been quick and disturbing. On October 6th the Soviet Ambassador in Chungking had told the Chinese Foreign Minister that the Soviet government objected to the landing of Chinese troops at Dairen. The reason given was that by treaty Dairen had been denominated a commercial port which was to be used only for trade purposes, and the Soviet government did not want to see the treaty violated. This was a perversion of the agreement. Certainly when the Chinese refused to allow Dairen to be included in the Soviet military zone in peacetime they had not thought they were debarring themselves from the use of the port to reenter Manchuria. There is no single clause in the Soong-Stalin talks about Dairen to give plausibility to the Soviet position. The Chinese government had disputed this interpretation of the treaty with both the Soviet Ambassador at Chungking and the Soviet commander in Manchuria. The Chinese Foreign Minister had pointed out that the treaty recognized Chinese sovereignty over Manchuria and therefore it was proper for China to send troops through the port. He had tried to ease the way toward consent by emphasizing that the Chinese troops would not remain in Dairen but would move on in order to take over the areas which—in agreement with the Chinese government—the Red forces were beginning to evacuate.

The American government had been kept informed of these Russian refusals and their twisted justifications.[14] It had not spoken up for the Chinese request to enter the port of Dairen. Nor had it protested against the Soviet denial. In its view, the taking over of Manchuria from the Russians by the Chinese was a problem to be solved between those two governments. Thus the whole responsibility for keeping the Soviet government informed and for working out landing arrangements was left to the Chinese themselves. In carrying out its accepted part of the task—which was to land Chinese troops at the Manchurian ports—the American authorities refused to take the risk of having Americans mixed up in engagements with either Soviet troops or the Chinese Communists.

On October 19th General Stratemeyer (in charge while Wedemeyer was in Washington) had informed Chiang Kai-shek that if no agreement was reached very soon with the Soviet government about a landing at Dairen, the American navy proposed to disembark the expedition at Chinwangtao instead; this was the Chinese port nearest to Manchuria which could handle heavy shipping. The navy did not want to have its ships, jam-packed with Chinese soldiers, kept floating at sea for a long time. General Malinovsky had again informed General Hsiung that he did not have authority to allow a landing at Dairen. But he had gone on to say that the Soviet government would not oppose landings at other ports of Manchuria—Hulutao, Yingkow and Antung; that in fact the Soviet government was even willing to provide some vehicles needed to move the Chinese troops from these ports. Rather than prolong the delay in starting his troops to Manchuria, the Generalissimo gave up the idea of landing at Dairen. He asked the American navy to take them to Hulutao instead, and the navy agreed to do so. The Chinese government had on October 25th told the Soviet Ambassador in Chungking of the change

[14] The State Department's sources of information were the Chinese Foreign Office through our Embassy in Chungking and the Chinese Ambassador in Moscow through Harriman. The War Department had been kept advised by various reports from American military headquarters in Chungking and the commander of the 7th Fleet, Admiral Kinkaid.

of plans, and had asked him to transmit this information to Malinovsky. But when the American ships entered the harbor at Hulutao they had found the 4th Chinese Communist Route Army in control of the port. On the 27th Admiral Barbey, in charge, had made contact with the local commanding officer of the Communists. This official declared that he would resist entry of the Chinese government troops. Following a conference the next day between Admirals Barbey and Kincaid, Chiang Kai-shek had been told that it had been decided to land the troops that were afloat at Chinwangtao as the best possible solution under the circumstances.

But Chiang Kai-shek had continued to want to have them land at Hulutao. Therefore he proceeded to try to clear away the obstacles. The Soviet government was then saying it did not have enough forces at that spot to guarantee a safe landing there, but would do so at Yingkow. This was judged unsatisfactory since, in the words of the later memo in which the Chinese Foreign Office reviewed these episodes, "As Yingkow harbor facilities are not adequate for large troop transports it was felt necessary to land troops at Hulutao in order to have sufficient Chinese forces there in time to take over the evacuated territories when the Soviet forces pulled out."[15] On the 30th the Soviet Ambassador in Chungking had been asked to have Malinovsky protect the Chinese landings at Hulutao as well as Yingkow. But—the matter is obscure—whether another refusal was received or whether the Chinese government was afraid of further delay, the project to land at Hulutao was given up.

The American naval task force carrying the Chinese troops had gone on to Yingkow. On arrival at that port, American naval officers had gone ashore with a view to conferring with Soviet officers. Again they found, as at Hulutao, that the Chinese Communists were already there. They were digging trenches and building barricades near the landing points. Admiral Barbey, obedient to his orders, did not try to force the situation. He left it to the commander of the Chinese to negotiate with the Russians, to have the Russians make good on their promise of an unopposed landing.

Hsiung had discussed the situation again with Malinovsky. He asked why, since the Soviets had said there would be no trouble in landing

---

[15] Most of this account of the dealings between the Chinese and Soviet governments about landings in Manchuria is derived from this long memorandum on the subject, the first of a series, given to the American Embassy at Chungking. Robertson, who remained in charge of the Embassy while Hurley was in the United States, radioed the Chinese memo to the State Department on November 16th.

troops in Yingkow, there were now a large number of Communist troops around the port. Malinovsky had another story. He said that the guarantee of safety was no longer in force.[16] The Communist troops, he stressed, did not get into Yingkow from areas controlled by the Soviet forces but had come from the south, from China. He added that it was a large force and that it could not be stopped unless Soviet troops who had already evacuated the port were called back again, and this would cause a postponement of the general Soviet withdrawal. He suggested that the commander of the government troops should talk the situation over with the commanders of the Communist 8th Route Army. Hsiung said that was not possible. He asked what the Soviet army would do if trouble arose. Malinovsky's answer was that it would not interfere in Chinese local affairs. General Hsiung, before quitting this interview, remarked that if the Chinese government found it impossible to take over Manchuria on the schedule agreed on with the Soviet government, the responsibility would be on the Soviets. The Russian Marshal flared up and answered that he would report the whole situation to Moscow.

The American ships, the 7th Amphibious Force, had stayed in the port of Yingkow. No Russian representatives appeared to straighten out the situation. Instead, Communist guards refused to allow anyone ashore. The Deputy Mayor, speaking from the docks, said that the Communist troops would resist any effort to land in the Yingkow area. Admiral Barbey concluded that any attempt to land would endanger American lives and violate our policy of not interfering in civil strife. Therefore he carried out the decision to land at Chinwangtao. From there the Chinese forces could start a long march overland through the Shanhaikwan defile into Manchuria.

In one of the talks Hsiung had with Malinovsky (that of November 5th), the Russian had said that it would be all right if Chinese troops were carried *by air* to focal points *within* Manchuria, particularly Mukden and Changchun. Such an operation, he agreed, might be begun five days after the Soviet troops withdrew from these places, and he promised to give the Chinese government ten days notice of withdrawal. Chiang Kai-shek now asked us to transport Chinese troops in American planes piloted by Americans, not only to the borders of Manchuria but to

[16] K. C. Wu, the Minister of Information, told the American Embassy in Chungking that the Soviet guarantee of a safe landing at Yingkow was for the period November 5th-10th, but that when the government troops arrived in this port on November 7th the Soviet forces were gone and the Chinese Communists in control. Telegram, American Embassy, Chungking to State Department, November 10, 1945.

points within Manchuria. This request was underscored by pointing out how little time remained.

According to the agreement then in effect between the Soviet Union and the Chinese government, Soviet troops were scheduled to be entirely out of Manchuria by December 3rd, leaving all three provinces wide open to the inflowing Communist forces. Unable to foretell when if ever the troops he was trying to move toward Manchuria by foot and rail would get there, unable to send them in by sea, and unsure as to whether the American government would agree to fly them in, Chiang Kai-shek accepted a Soviet offer of more time. It was arranged that the schedule of evacuation should be postponed a month—that the Soviet forces should not quit Manchuria until January 3, 1946.

During this same period the mission which the Chinese government had sent to Changchun to lay the ground work for the civil government of Manchuria was demoralized and routed. Two large groups of officials had been flown there early in October. The civilian section included the men selected by Chiang Kai-shek to be mayors for Dairen and Harbin, provincial governors, commissioners of public health, education and police. There were about five hundred in all.

At first General Malinovsky and his staff had been cordial and helpful. A new local government had been formed which was friendly to the mission. General Hsiung began to recruit in the neighborhood a police and military guard. Gradually his staff had found it hard to do so, and got the impression that the people thereabout had been warned not to enter into his service. During October and in early November Communist elements had gradually moved toward Changchun. Without Soviet interference they surrounded the mission headquarters and staff. Overnight the local government changed. The new government was hostile to the mission, and harassed it in such ways as turning off the light and water supply. General Hsiung complained to the Soviet commanders, but nothing was done to protect them.

Then some thousands of Communist troops entered the city while others concentrated near the Changchun airfield. Alarmed, Chiang Kai-shek sent a message to Stalin, asking him to receive a special representative. The Soviet Foreign Office sent back word that Stalin was not in Moscow, and that the Generalissimo's message would be held till he returned. Fearful that the mission would be captured, and having no word from Stalin, Chiang Kai-shek decided to withdraw it. Hsiung advised Malinovsky that this was being done, adding that the Soviet government was to blame. Malinovsky answered only that he was sorry. Presently, after the mission had left, Stalin sent word that he would receive the Generalissimo's representative in December.

These Soviet refusals to enable Chinese government troops safely to enter Manchuria through convenient ports made the whole attempt of the Chinese government to secure control of Manchuria more onerous and dangerous. The denial tired out essential military units at sea and used up supplies. It compelled the government forces to struggle wearily overland by foot or railroad over routes in which they were harassed by Communist guerrillas and delayed by destruction of the railroads. The consequent delay gave time for the Chinese Communist forces to move far into Manchuria, and to acquire Japanese weapons from stocks left about by the Soviet forces. It also allowed them to set up propaganda and recruiting offices and local governments. There were not many weeks lost—roughly four or five—but they were vital, and made a great difference in the contest for control of Manchuria.

Thus, in the middle of November—three months after V-J Day—a hard crisis of disappointment regarding the whole Chinese situation was at hand. The Chinese government was confronted with facts which wiped out its hopes of quickly emerging as the accepted government of a whole and peaceful China. As the cold winds of winter began to blow from the north, China seemed to be falling apart. Even in the regions and the cities where the Chinese government had established itself, there was trouble. The tasks of restoring orderly and decent living conditions and then creating a competent government organization were not being well carried out. Too many of the officials appointed by Chungking were unsuitable, incompetent, or corrupt. The masses of the Chinese people within the area of government control were discouraged and unresponsive. Despite American help, government forces had been unable to secure firm control of large sections of north and north coastal China; hundreds of thousands of Japanese remained still armed in these regions; Communist groups, guerrilla groups, local resistance groups, were overrunning many sections; and the means for taking over Manchuria from the Russians were lacking.

This somber state of affairs, portrayed in full by both American Military Headquarters and the American Embassy, was studied by the already disturbed officials in Washington who were directing our China policy. The State, War, and Navy Departments became really alarmed. The situation seemed to presage the failure of both our expectations and our plans. It began to seem likely that unless new measures were taken, our effort to bring about a settlement by peaceful means would fail; that the whole conception which had been in the American mind since the Moscow and Cairo conferences of a unified and friendly China as one among the great powers, would turn out to have been an illusion. In sum, the course of events sharply produced the question of whether, if the American government clung to its scheduled plans to end direct support of the Chinese government and to withdraw from that theater, our whole great effort there would subside in dangerous failure.

These disturbing perceptions governed the urgent reexamination of policies and decisions which was already underway. Were we to continue our posture of impartiality and caution? If not, what actions were required; and which would be accepted by the American people, when their strongest urge was to bring American fighting forces home? And if we reversed our course, might we not be deeply dragged into China's internal fight and fail in the end anyway? The circle of anxiety was neatly rounded by McCloy, who had just returned from China, in a meeting with the three Secretaries on November 6th. "The Kuomintang must have our support to be able to cope with the situation. If the Russians, however, decide to give active support to the Chinese Communists, then we are in a real mess."[17] Among these bruising questions the government tried hard to find some route by which it might rescue our policy from failure and China from misery.

But before telling of the efforts to find that route, a quick glance must be taken at one other connected element in the situation with which the government was confronted.

[17] Memo of meeting: Byrnes, Patterson, Forrestal, McCloy, Matthews, and Gates, November 6, 1945.

CHAPTER 34

Contemporaneous Trouble about Japan

WASHINGTON was at the same time having trouble with Moscow over the system for conducting the occupation of Japan. The Soviet government was sulking over the issue and might show its ill will in China. To understand why, we must pause and glance back at what had been happening in this adjacent sector of Far Eastern diplomacy.

The Soviet government had yielded to the American wish that an American supreme commander should accept the formal surrender of Japan for all the Allies.[1] On September 2nd MacArthur, watched by the decorated men of the other powers who had fought Japan, had carried off the ceremony. Soon thereafter Byrnes, having had four weeks in Washington after his return from Potsdam, had set off on his next bout of peace-making. He left for London on the *Queen Elizabeth* to participate in the first meeting of the Council of Foreign Ministers. The problem of how the control of Japan was to be exercised awaited them.

MacArthur had moved to put into effect the conditions of surrender agreed at Potsdam. But there was no accord among the Allies as to how the next steps in the making of policy for Japan were to be taken, or how the control of the occupation was to be shared. The American government had proposed in August that there should be created for the guidance of occupation policy a Far Eastern Advisory Commission (FEAC).[2] This Commission was to be made up of the four major Allies (one of which was China) and such other of the United Nations as were located or had territories in the Far East. The Commission was to have the duty of recommending policies and methods for the fulfillment of the Potsdam surrender terms. It was not to be authorized to give advice on military activities. Its headquarters was to be in Washington.

The Soviet government had at first seemed to think this kind of arrangement all right. But the British government had demurred because the FEAC was to have only advisory powers and because India was not included.[3] Australia and New Zealand had also wanted a more active

---

[1] When Harriman on the night of August 11th gave Molotov a message to this effect, Molotov answered with a memo which agreed, but asked consideration for the proposal that a Soviet supreme commander should also participate. Harriman rejected the answer, as a "conditional" acceptance. Molotov consulted Stalin, who said it was "unconditional," and the language of the Soviet reply was changed accordingly.

[2] Later called the Far Eastern Commission.

[3] The main points of the discussion between the American and British governments at this stage are stated in: communication from President Truman to Prime Minister

part. Then it had appeared in the very first meeting of the Foreign Ministers on September 11th that the Soviet Union, on the grounds that the situation had changed, was no longer willing to agree to go forward. Molotov, in session after session, had grumbled over the way in which the conditions of surrender were being carried out. He had averred that the Japanese were not being taken prisoners of war and were being left to disarm themselves—which practices he thought dangerous. Further, he had complained that MacArthur was acting without consulting anyone. The orders under which MacArthur was operating up to then had been drawn up by the American government, based on its views of the surrender terms agreed on at Potsdam.

Byrnes had denied the fairness of all of Molotov's charges. But his main answer had been that once the Advisory Commission was created, there would be a joint determination of occupation policies, and the Soviet Union would have a full chance to express its wishes. A full chance, yes, Molotov in substance had said, but only as one of several and only as an equal among the several. What Molotov then had wanted was a system under which the four main Allies would jointly decide and execute all elements of Allied policy in regard to Japan—a control council. Garrison duties within Japan were to be similarly shared. Further, this control council, he had argued, should be operated under the rule of unanimity, which meant that it could not work at all unless the Soviet Union was pleased.

In this whole realm of dispute, the American government had stood firm. It had been willing to take full counsel about occupation policy and to seek agreement. But it had not been willing in case of dispute to yield the ultimate right and power to shape and direct policy; and it had remained determined not to allow the Soviet government a position from which it could either rule or ruin ("treat or tricks," as the children say on Halloween night). The British Cabinet having been persuaded to agree to the American proposal, Byrnes at London had refused to give way. On the last day of the meeting of the Foreign Ministers, Molotov had formally notified him that the Soviet government would not agree to the establishment of such an Advisory Commission until the question of the control council was settled. On his return to Wash-

Attlee, August 11th; aide-memoire, British Embassy in Washington to State Department on August 20th; State Department aide-memoire to British Embassy, August 23rd; memo, Dunn to Secretary of State, August 30th; and aide-memoire, British Embassy, August 30th; oral communication, Sir George Sansom to Ballantine, September 4th.

ington Byrnes had none the less proceeded to issue the invitations for the first meeting of the Advisory Commission.[4]

During this conference at London, Byrnes and Bevin had been at odds with Molotov over another question—whether or not China would be allowed to take part in the making of the European peace treaties. The understanding that had been made at Potsdam about this turned out to be both confusing and murky. Since Byrnes had failed to sway Molotov, both Truman and Attlee had appealed to Stalin. They asked that China be allowed at least to be present in the final peace conference discussions. But Stalin had maintained that this would be neither just nor sensible. The London meeting of the Council of Foreign Ministers had broken up over this issue on October 2nd.

If the President and Secretary of State feared that their firm stand on Japan might influence the Soviet treatment of China, they had not allowed the fear to sway them. On October 18th, however, Harriman had sent a reflective warning. He thought that Stalin would continue to argue that after inviting the Soviet Union to come into the war we were now excluding it from appropriate and fair consideration as regards Japan after defeat. In the event that the impasse continued, Harriman thought that the Soviets would pursue a unilateral policy in those other areas which they dominated. He had reminded Byrnes that Stalin had told Soong, when he was in Moscow, that China as well as the Soviet Union should realize that the United States might take a "weak" course toward Japan; that in time its interest would lapse, in contrast to the more lasting interest of China and Russia to eliminate Japan as a threat in the future.

But Byrnes had attributed the stubborn ill will which the Soviet Union had shown at the London meeting primarily to its concern over the European peace treaties.[5] On this supposition he had advised President

[4] Statement of September 29, 1945, State Department Bulletin, October 7, 1945. However, its Terms of Reference, not published, were subject to further discussion. The American government had trouble with the British government about these, as well as with the Soviet government. Bevin, under orders from the War Cabinet, wanted a revision, whereby any directive on nonmilitary matters to be issued by MacArthur would have to have prior approval of a majority of this Far Eastern Advisory Commission, including two of the powers parties to the Potsdam Declaration (the United States, Great Britain, the Soviet Union, and China). Byrnes rejected it. A compromise arrangement in which American wishes prevailed was presently worked out. Telegrams, Byrnes (in London) to Acheson, October 1, 1945; Byrnes (in Washington) to American Embassy, London, October 22, 1945; memo, October 24, 1945, by Vincent of talk with Sir George Sansom of the British Embassy, Washington.
[5] See Byrnes's book, *Speaking Frankly*, pages 213-218.

Truman to try once again to reach an amicable understanding about them with Stalin. The British Foreign Secretary, Bevin, though not enthusiastic, had agreed to join in the effort. The President thereupon had sent a placating letter for Harriman to present to the Marshal. Stalin was on vacation. But he invited Harriman down to see him at his dacha at Sochi on the Caucasian coast.

After reading Truman's message carefully, Stalin had looked up and his first words were, "The Japanese question is not touched upon here." Harriman had answered (this was October 24th) that the question was being reviewed in Washington.[6] He had then gone on to explain the thinking of the President and his advisers. The point he tried to keep to the fore was that Byrnes was willing to go over all aspects of the problem again if Stalin sent a representative to the first scheduled meeting of the Advisory Commission in Washington. Stalin's comment had been merely to the effect that under such an arrangement as Harriman said the President had in mind, it might be more logical if countries other than the United States did not send troops into Japan. If they did, certainly the effect would be to restrict MacArthur's powers.[7]

On the next day Stalin had been less genial. He had stated that he had the impression that the American government had avoided the chance to settle the matter by direct talk; that it was dragging it out, as shown by Byrnes's refusal to discuss it in London. Further, he had continued, the Soviet government could not accept responsibility for MacArthur's actions in Japan since it was neither informed nor consulted. Almost sullenly he had referred to his decision to recall the Soviet representative in Tokyo, General Derevyenko, for this reason. In fact, Stalin's accusation mounted. "The Soviet Union was being treated like an American satellite in the Pacific—a role it could not accept." It would be more honest, he had remarked, if the Soviet Union were to quit Japan than to remain there "like a piece of furniture." Over Harriman's protesting interruptions he had railed on, asking why the Japanese press and radio were allowed to denounce the Soviet Union and why the Japanese commanders were not arrested.[8]

[6] Under-Secretary Acheson on October 23rd had a long Telecon conference with Assistant Secretary of War McCloy and General Marshall, who were in Tokyo, reviewing the problem with General MacArthur. The essence of MacArthur's position was (1) that there should be no form of Council in Tokyo with "executive authority independent of or coextensive with his," (2) that he was willing to work closely with an Allied group of political and military advisers.

[7] This talk between Stalin and Harriman on October 24th was long and comprehensive. I have given only condensed bits of the points concerned with Japan, as recorded in memo by Edward Page.

[8] A possible clue to the reason for Stalin's anger is suggested in another passage of

Byrnes has since recorded that it was only on getting Harriman's report on these talks with Stalin that he realized that the Soviet government was really angry about Japan.[9] He had thought it just as well on the whole, if not for the best, that the entire occupation should be left to the Americans. But MacArthur had wanted the other foreign contingents; without them he had reckoned that another hundred thousand Americans would be needed. No one was sure where they were to come from. The pace of demobilization was speeding up and voluntary recruiting was small. The War Department also was upset at the threat to United States plans for the occupation forces, the strength of the army and demobilization.[10] Secretary of War Patterson suggested that British, Chinese, and Australian troops might take part even though the Russians refused. But this worried Byrnes as making for two worlds and preparing the way to another war.[11] Soviet Russia could, Byrnes was aware, greatly disturb the situation in China, Manchuria, and Korea if it chose. The British government was afraid that it might do so in compensation for being without a part in the control of Japan.[12]

So was the Chinese government, when it learned that the Soviet government was not going to take its place in the first meeting of the FEAC. In a call on Under-Secretary of State Acheson on October 29th, the Chinese Ambassador proposed that at the first meeting he should make a motion expressing regret at the absence of the Soviet Union, and suggest that the meeting adjourn for a week to give a chance for the Soviet Union to reconsider. When the FEAC met, the motion was made and the adjournment was taken—but with no result. Despite further exchanges of messages during November between Byrnes and

---

Page's memo. This states, "Stalin said that the Soviet had maintained twenty to forty divisions on the Manchurian frontier and had sent seventy divisions against Japan. 'Furthermore, it had been ready to help the United States by landing troops on the Japanese islands. This offer had been rejected.'" To this point in the memo Page appended a footnote of his own, "When Stalin made this remark it was quite obvious from his tone of voice and from the expression on his face that he was still very irked at our refusal to permit Soviet troops to land at Hokkaido."

[9] Byrnes, *Speaking Frankly*, pages 213-218.

[10] Memo Assistant Secretary of War McCloy to Under-Secretary of State Acheson, November 15, 1945.

[11] He told the Secretaries of War and Navy at their meetings on October 30th and November 6th that since Stalin did not wish to place a Russian force under MacArthur's command it might be better not to request forces from the other Allies. He had the impression that the Soviet government believed the rest of the world was ganging up on it, and considered it most important for future peace to try to work in cooperation with them. Memos, meetings of the three Secretaries, October 30th and November 6th, and *Forrestal Diaries*, pages 106-107.

[12] Memo, Vincent talk with Sir George Sansom of the British Embassy, Washington, October 24, 1945.

Molotov and despite Harriman's utmost efforts at persuasion, the Soviet government had clung to the essentials of its demands.[13]

The dispute remained unbridged. Whether or not it was influencing or might influence Soviet actions in or toward Manchuria and North China was not to be known. But it was an extra crease in the darkening prospect which the American government faced during the crisis of decision in China policy.

[13] The essence of these was clearly expressed in an amendment regarding the operation of a Four Power Council which was also being discussed, set forth in a memo which on November 5th Molotov gave Harriman:

"Three. He [The Supreme Commander] will consult and advise with the [Four Power] Council upon orders involving questions of principle in advance of their issuance. If there is disagreement on the part of one of the members of the council with the Supreme Commander (or his deputy) on questions of principle . . . the decision of the Supreme Commander on these questions shall be withheld from execution until agreement on these questions has been reached between Governments or in the Far Eastern Commission."

Harriman's interpretation of the meaning of the Soviet proposal is convincing, "By the amendments . . . Molotov, however, seeks to obtain complete veto of all policies and interpretation of these policies to tie our hands in such a way that the functioning of control of Japan would be impossible without Soviet approval." Telegram, November 6, 1945, Harriman to Byrnes.

Crisis of Decision: Toward New Policy

THE Joint Chiefs of Staff were by this time impressed by the seriousness of the crisis. They turned more incisively to the question of whether the formulated orders for the China Theater should be carried out or changed. On the 10th of November they urgently asked the Departments of State, War, and Navy for guidance as to whether (1) American policy called for a continuation of American military aid to China until the situation in North China and Manchuria was reasonably stabilized, (2) the Marines should be withdrawn from China beginning November 15th as planned, or kept there until the situation was clearer. They had concluded, and so advised the Secretary of State, that in any case they thought it best not to close out the China Theater until the Military Advisory Group was established.

The War and Navy Departments tried to extract the answers to these queries from the State Department. They pointed out that the original and accepted intent of our military aid to the Chinese government was to enable it to occupy areas held by the Japanese, and that the plans had been measured to that end; but it now appeared "that the major immediate task of these forces will be to insure that the control of the liberated areas is secured by the National Government and is not usurped by the Communists, and the [Chinese] forces already moved are being utilized accordingly."[1] Hence they thought that the decision would depend on a judgment of political aims and consequences. The State Department writhed with uncertainty as it grappled with it.

As recounted, Wedemeyer had been quizzed about the plans and positions of the Chinese forces, and on the role being played by the Marines and the effects of withdrawal. On the 14th his preliminary answer arrived. This in substance informed Washington that:

1. The Marine forces had most carefully observed their assigned mission of occupying key areas in North China; and their presence was a deterrent to major disorders.

2. The four armies which the Chinese government had in the general area of Peiping-Tientsin-Taku-Chinwangtao ought to be enough to occupy at once the key positions held by the Marines and to control the

[1] Extract from memo, State Department member of SWNCC to Secretary of State Byrnes, November 13, 1945.

limited areas originally marked out for them; and if these armies were used to take over from them the Marines could soon be relieved.

3. Should the Generalissimo try to expand the area under his control with his present forces, particularly into Manchuria, the Marines would be needed indefinitely to hold the sections they were in.

4. The Communists were strongly disputing the North China area and threatening all lines of communication. There was local sympathy for them in many points.

5. The Chinese government was completely unprepared for the occupation of Manchuria against Communist opposition.

6. Although the Soviet forces in Manchuria were making an outward show of cooperating with Chiang Kai-shek's representatives, they appeared rather to be creating conditions which favored the attempt of the Chinese Communists to acquire exposed areas in the north and in Manchuria, and preventing the Chinese Central Government from recovering them.

Wedemeyer reported that—in the light of these facts—American military headquarters had advised Chiang Kai-shek that he should strive, as immediate objectives, to consolidate his control of the area south of the Great Wall and north of the Yangtze, making the overland lines of communication in that area safe before sending his forces into Manchuria.[2]

Within the State Department there was a great turmoil of argument. Both the dangers of doing little and the costs and dangers of doing much were visualized in the papers written within the Office of Far Eastern Affairs of the Department.[3] Baffled but not beaten, it took up again its pursuit of the unattainable—a lasting solution of China's internal struggle by peaceful political means. Under its guidance, the

[2] Reference is made to this answer in *United States Relations with China*, page 131. The revision in Wedemeyer's judgment since V-J Day may be illustrated by an answer which he had given less than three months before at a press conference on August 30, 1945, in response to a question about the Communist situation around Shanghai. "I don't think it should affect it. I do not believe the Communists are strong either in number or effort anywhere in China. I have said that many times before. They haven't the equipment, and they haven't had the training, and about their numbers, I think that has been overestimated, but I could be wrong about that, however, those are just my views. Regardless of their number or equipment, I do not anticipate any difficulty with the Communists."

[3] The most effective presentation of the reasons for continuing and extending aid to the Chinese government was a memo prepared by Everett F. Drumright, Chief of the China Division, which Vincent forwarded to the Under-Secretary and Secretary of State as a well-thought-out and well-written statement of the thesis that, "We should above all afford to the Chinese Government the necessary assistance in recovering all lost territory and especially Manchuria."

State Department groped for a course that would concurrently (a) give the Chinese government more time and chance, and (b) provide more urgent incentive to both of the opposed sides to reach a peaceful settlement. In their last public comment—the statement about their negotiations which they had jointly made on October 11th—the two opponents had, it will be remembered, reaffirmed that they still wished for such a solution rather than a finish fight. Could we not—by use of our power to give or deny help to either one or both—cause them to suit their actions to their words and compromise? This was the train of purpose that ended in the directive given to General Marshall when he was sent to China a month later.

Before the questions raised by Wedemeyer's reply of the 14th were fully analyzed, another message came in from Chungking telling that the Marines had been involved in a nasty incident with the Communists on the Chinwangtao railroad. To Wedemeyer this was a sign of further trouble ahead if the Marines remained. Since his orders cautioned him not to get involved in civil war and since it was almost sure that he would get involved in other such incidents if the Marines stayed, he recommended their withdrawal at once.

As a temporary guide for Wedemeyer, who did not know whether or not to start this withdrawal, an answer was hurried out on the 19th by the War Department, and supplemented the next day. Wedemeyer was told that the Secretary of State was developing an approach to the situation which would soon be checked with the President. This approach called for the retention of the Marines in North China for the time being in order to complete the disarmament and evacuation of the Japanese in that area. The Secretary of State, the message to Wedemeyer went on, particularly wanted his opinion as to whether the Chinese government forces would be able to clear the Japanese out of North China and Manchuria without further American aid; and also his appraisal of the military consequences of either retaining or withdrawing the Marines. This request for information seems to evidence a wish to postpone decision, possibly also a wish to try to define the problem as a military rather than a political one.[4]

[4] A reference is made to this radio message of November 19th to Wedemeyer in the *Forrestal Diaries*, page 109, along with the following editorial comment: "The Chinese Communist armies under Mao Tze Tung were at that time less well organized and far less well armed than they were later to become. But the State Department, impressed by the backwardness, corruption and unpopularity of the Nationalists under Chiang Kai-shek, convinced that Mao's Communists represented an important popular movement and that the United States could not openly combat it without suffering disastrously from the charge of 'imperialist meddling,' wished to stay clear of the struggle between

The Secretaries of State, War, and Navy met again on the 20th. But their talk that morning did not settle anything. All were alert to the points emphasized by Secretary of War Patterson: that if we got out of China while substantial numbers of Japanese remained in Manchuria it would be inconsistent with our policy in Asia, namely, to get the Japanese home; and that would invite a vacuum of anarchy in Manchuria into which either the Russians or Japanese would flow, the Russians first. Both Forrestal and Patterson thought that the peril of keeping the Marines in China was not really great. They were inclined to welcome rather than regret the fact that their presence was a help to Chiang Kai-shek and that their continued presence would be a continued help to him. But all were also aware that under the demobilization plans then being put into effect, total American forces available for service abroad would be too small for the many assignments in Europe and the Pacific for which they might be needed. This whole discussion seems to have been shadowed by what is aptly termed in the *Forrestal Diaries* the "swift evisceration of our armed strength."

After taking note of the inquiries that had been addressed to Wedemeyer the day before, it was agreed that the Secretaries of War and Navy should prepare a statement of their views on the military aspects of the situation in China as further guidance for the Secretary of State. Each of the three Cabinet officers was trying to get the answers from the others, or at least be able to base his decision on the authority of the others.

While Patterson and Forrestal were working over this statement for Byrnes, Wedemeyer, in a series of long messages, answered the queries which had been put to him.[5] These still stand in the record as

Chiang and Mao. This telegram clearly recognized the difficulty: even to help Chiang get the Japanese out would 'result in some collateral aid or prestige in favor of the National government vis-à-vis the Communists,' yet 'conversely withdrawal now' of American troops 'may mean substantial frustration of a policy we have long supported which contemplated unifying China under Chinese National forces. . . .' The State Department's answer at that moment was that the United States would transport no more Chinese Nationalist troops to Manchuria and 'will not support the National government vis-à-vis the Communists except insofar as necessary to get the Japanese disarmed and out of China'; but its weakness seems to have been apparent from the urgent concluding demand upon Wedemeyer to give his views."

[5] On the 20th (Chungking time) before he had received the latest request for information and advice which was made of him (November 19th-20th, Washington time) Wedemeyer sent the War Department a résumé of the situation in China and the circumstances affecting the presence of American forces. Then, in response to Washington's queries of November 19th, he sent two other long messages: the first, on November 23rd, dealing mainly with the question of whether the Chinese government forces would be able to clear the Japanese out of North China and Manchuria without further American

an interesting estimate of the dilemma faced by the Chinese and American governments at this juncture of decision.

In sum, Wedemeyer had the impression that the task faced by Chiang Kai-shek of bringing about stability and democracy in China was beyond his powers, as he thought they would be beyond those of any one man. For, among many reasons, the Generalissimo lacked able, honest advisers and assistants; he was surrounded by selfish and unscrupulous men; he was loyal to war lords and officials who had helped him in the past but who were now exploiting their position to enrich themselves and their families (only South Chinese had been appointed as governors and mayors in North China). Such was the general situation as Wedemeyer saw it.

To the first of the direct questions asked him by Washington—would the Chinese government be able to clear the Japanese out of North China without further American aid—Wedemeyer answered that it would not. The Chinese government, he reported, exercised a modicum of control in the area from the Yellow River south. He thought that the Generalissimo would be able to stabilize the situation in that area, provided he used the help of foreign administrators and technicians, and made thorough reforms through honest and competent officials. But in most of the region north of the Yangtze to the Great Wall, Wedemeyer went on, Chiang Kai-shek's authority was being effectively challenged by the Communists. He thought it doubtful whether the Chinese government had enough force to gain and retain control of North China at least for many months, possibly years.[6] Even if, Wedemeyer con-

---

aid; the second, on November 26th, dealing mainly with the prospect and consequences of leaving the Marines in China or taking them away, and defining the alternative courses of action which he thought open to the American government.

[6] An interesting report on this subject was written by Lieut. Kohi Ariyoshi, Lieutenant of AUS, of the Yenan Observer Group, at the request of the commanding general of the Chinese Theater. Lieut. Ariyoshi had been sent by his command officer, Col. Yeaton, on a tour of the area in North China disputed between the government and Communist forces. His report, which was forwarded on to Washington on November 27th, stated that the troops which the Generalissimo was now using against the Communists were not wholly loyal to him. Most of them were forcibly impressed into the army. They were in strange territory and would be susceptible to Communist propaganda. Soon, the report continued, the Generalissimo would have the thirty-nine American-trained and American-equipped divisions. But they were not trained for the Communist type of guerrilla warfare, and even if they were all used they were not likely to be able to take charge at once of the Communists, the defectors, war lords, and other enemies. It was easy, the report observed, to underestimate Communist strength because most of it was intangible. It was a combined defense army, local, guerrilla, self-defense corps, youth corps, and so forth—a combination which had shown its effectiveness against the Japanese. It would be able to blockade the cities held by the government forces and cut their communications.

tinued, he acceded to the request which the Generalissimo was making of him to move five more armies to North China, he did not think that the government forces would be strong enough both to defeat the Communists and disarm the Japanese in that area. Certainly, in his opinion, the government did not have enough force concurrently to win control of North China and launch a military and political campaign to recover Manchuria. In this connection, Wedemeyer again reported that he was advising Chiang Kai-shek to concentrate his efforts on securing control south of the Great Wall and executing political and social reforms. He had refused a recent request of the Generalissimo to provide air transport to move two armies to Manchuria. The refusal was in accord with his orders. But, apart from that, Wedemeyer thought that the action would have been ill-advised at the time; and he remarked that the Chinese did not appreciate the supply and security difficulties they would face. The unprotected countryside in Manchuria was broad, and the winters very cold and long.

Answering another of the questions put to him—the military results of retaining the Marines in North China or withdrawing them—Wedemeyer predicted that if they were kept in China they would become involved in fighting. His orders warned him to avoid that, but it would be impossible.[7] Therefore he recommended: either that all United States forces in the China Theater, including the Marines, be withdrawn as soon as possible; or that his directives be changed so as to justify the retention and use of the Marines.

To these estimates he appended some views on the broad strategic aspects of the Chinese situation. He said that there were indications of Russian actions in Korea, Manchuria, Outer and Inner Mongolia, and in the North and Northwestern Chinese provinces of Jehol, Chahar, and Sinkiang. These appeared to form a pattern of effort to create a buffer area in the Far East in which the Soviet Union would have the initiative and paramount influence. But he stated it to be his considered opinion that the Soviet Union was not prepared successfully to carry out this aggressive policy, using the buffer area as the springboard for penetration and territorial expansion; and that it was more logical to assume that Soviet policy would follow a strategically defensive line.

[7] Wedemeyer explained later the nimble tactics he used to execute his mission and still avoid direct intervention and trouble. They amounted in sum to this: he was not allowed under his directives to pick up the Chinese National Army at place A and move to place B to aid in recovering an area from the Chinese Communists or use aircraft for that purpose; but inherent in his instructions to recover territory from the Japanese, he did that, moved them into vacant areas, which caused some friction with the Communists. *Joint Committee on Military Situation in the Far East*, page 2462.

Three essential points which he asked the War Department to help him make clear to the State Department and the President were: that it was impossible to unify China and Manchuria with American assistance without becoming involved in the civil war; that it was impossible to aid the Chinese government in the repatriation of the Japanese left in North China and Manchuria without involving the American forces in civil war; that it was impossible to do either of these things—that is, to effectively help in the unification of China and Manchuria and repatriation of all the Japanese—unless the United States and the other Allied nations provided forces and shipping resources "far beyond those now available or contemplated in the area." Whatever the decision, he concluded, it was essential that his orders be clarified, for it would be impossible for him to carry out the conflicting duties currently imposed upon him.

Wedemeyer's estimates of the situation in China were closely matched by incoming reports of other American observers there. Stevens, the State Department representative at Peiping, wholly confirmed the range of confused fighting in the north—not only between the government and Communists, but also with and among local governors, politicians, commanders, guerrillas, and bandits. Robertson, in charge of the Embassy at Chungking, sent on word of what Admiral Barbey was recommending to the Secretary of the Navy: that in view of the government weakness we should use every possible pressure on both sides to get them into a working agreement, even if that involved giving Mao Tze Tung the complete political and military control he was demanding in the provinces which the Communists dominated. This would at least give a breathing spell during which the Japanese could be evacuated and an attempt made to work out a solution with the Soviet Union. Robertson added the comment that even if Chiang Kai-shek should accede to this, it was doubtful whether Mao Tze Tung, with time running in his favor and covert Soviet support, would settle on those terms. These reports from China did not make the task of the officials in Washington any brighter. In whatever way they were read, and whichever course was chosen, trouble was in sight.

While the reports were being studied, and while the War and Navy Departments were still piecing together the memo which the Secretary of State had asked of them, Chiang Kai-shek radioed the President. This was an urgent appeal from Wedemeyer's answer that under his present instructions and with the means available to him, he could not comply with the Generalissimo's request to move five more Chinese armies by sea to North China. The message stated that due to Soviet connivance with the Chinese Communists a situation had been created making it essential to send at once effective and loyal troops into the Northern Provinces of Shantung, Hopei, Chahar, Suiyuan, and Jehol in order to accept the Japanese surrender and repatriate them. He added that he intended to withdraw the mission he had sent to Manchuria previously and also to postpone entrance there until law and order had been established in North China and the Japanese cleared out. This message remained unanswered until it was finally decided whether or not we were going to clear out of China as previously planned or go in more deeply.[8]

By the 24th of November the Secretaries of War and Navy had drawn up and signed their joint memo to the Secretary of State. But it probably did not find its way to him until the evening of the 26th. The editorial comment made about this report in the *Forrestal Diaries* is justified. "The document was not—one must admit in retrospect—a model of either clarity, conciseness or decision. It was very long; it already showed the symptoms of that 'on-the-one-hand—on-the-other-hand' disease which was to blight so many documents on Chinese policy in the ensuing years, and it skillfully handed the fundamental issue—which the State Department had passed to Wedemeyer, which Wedemeyer had returned to Washington—back to the State Department."[9]

Out of this convoluted review of the problem it seems useful now only to note a few items. The memo advised that Wedemeyer's pessimistic impression of the ability of the Chinese government to secure control of North China and Manchuria should not be accepted as a basis for American policy without much further thought as to what other steps it might be practicable for the United States to take. It took

---

[8] This message was sent through the American Embassy in Chungking to the State Department on November 23rd (Chungking time). The date stamps on the face of the action copy indicates that it was first sent to the Office of the Secretary of State. Then on November 27th it was sent on to the Office of Far Easern Affairs, where it apparently came to rest. Not having received an answer, on December 11th (by which time Marshall's instructions were virtually complete) Chiang Kai-shek anxiously requested a decision. The next day, the 12th, Leahy asked Under-Secretary Acheson whether or not it had been answered. Acheson told Leahy that the State Department had not sent an answer, and that he did not know of any that had been sent through the White House. He suggested that in view of the way in which the situation had changed since the message was sent, and the fact that Marshall was just about to leave for China, we might answer that Marshall would soon arrive with full authority to discuss the questions raised by the Generalissimo's message. This was done.

[9] *Forrestal Diaries*, page 111.

cognizance of the fact which Wedemeyer had so underlined, that his present orders were indeterminate and conflicting; and that the Joint Chiefs of Staff should amend them to provide for the continuation of American forces in China for the time being, and for help to the Chinese in getting the Japanese out of North China; and of the fact that such action would probably involve at least incidental aid to the National Government in its fight against the Communists. But this was all left subject to final decision on general policy on which they felt State Department guidance essential. For the main import of the memo's wandering observations was that, after all, policy should be decided primarily by weighing American political wishes rather than by immediate military necessity.

This report was before the three Cabinet officers when they met again on the 27th. This was a perplexed meeting, attended by various aides, including Acheson and Lovett. No new light was thrown on the problem in what seems to have been an unsystematic discussion. Thought in the State Department was by then beginning to center on the idea of openly using a regulated system of rewards and punishments to induce or compel the two sides to come together.[10] Toward the end of the meeting Acheson summed up the main elements of a program which was then being shaped up in the State Department. The American government was (1) to keep the Marines in China for the time being; (2) to determine the possibility and to prepare for the movement of other Chinese armies by water north and for their support (presumably, though it is not clear in the record, this meant not only to North China ports but also to or for Manchuria); (3) to seek to arrange a truce in the disputed areas when the Japanese were moved out; (4) to continue to try to bring about a political settlement under Chiang Kai-shek with Communist participation, with pressure on Chiang Kai-shek to be pliable in this matter. These ideas appeared to be well received by the Cabinet group. There was also much discussion as to whether to tell the Soviet government what the American government intended to do and line it up with our policy. But Byrnes was perplexed as to just what to ask of the Soviet: whether to ask it to stay in Manchuria until the Chinese government took over, or to get out, or just what. The others could not tell him.

Before these elements of policy were further defined, there was new

---

[10] *Forrestal Diaries*, page 123. This was the favored approach in an important memo which Vincent had written on the 19th entitled "Our Military Position in China." This memo had been read aloud by Byrnes at the meeting of the Secretaries of State, War and Navy on November 20th.

excitement. Hurley had been in and about Washington, awaiting the outcome of the discussion among the decision-makers. As this meeting of the 27th broke up, Byrnes remarked that if it was possible to work out a program along the lines sketched, Hurley could take it back to Chungking for urgent presentation. Secretary of War Patterson asked whether it might not be useful to have him stop at Moscow on his way. Byrnes answered that he thought it better that Hurley get back to China just as soon as the program was settled. A few minutes later, as he was leaving to lunch at the White House, the Secretary of State was told that the ticker carried the news that Hurley had resigned and issued a statement of crashing criticism.

CHAPTER 36

The Hurley Resignation

HURLEY had carried to Washington a letter from Chiang Kai-shek in praise of his work in China and asking that he return. But he was not eager to do so. He felt ill and badly used. Just as he was leaving China, another one of those nagging incidents had occurred to refresh his belief that American policy was being run by the group he thought were trying to oust him. The *News Bulletin* of the United States Information Service (Shanghai Branch) of September 19th had carried a report that he was about to resign; that officially it would be explained that he wanted and needed a rest, but that his real reason would be his dissatisfaction with the China Affairs section of the State Department. This was a roughly true report of his state of mind. But its publication in an official sheet seemed to him to be for purpose: to humiliate him and reduce his influence in China. Presently it turned out that these speculations originated in the United States, not in the Embassy at Chungking.

Then, soon after his return to Washington, he had been rebuffed in his efforts to prevent certain Foreign Service officers who he felt were hostile to the Chinese government from serving in Japan. Noting press reports that George Atcheson and John Service were to be members of a political advisory board under MacArthur to determine American policy in Japan, Chiang Kai-shek had sent a protest to the President.[1] In this he said that the appointments were being interpreted as proof of American sympathy or support for the Chinese Communists, and were making the Communists more obdurate. The State Department, with the approval of the President, had turned the Generalissimo's protest aside with the answer, made on September 25th, that Atcheson and Service would be stationed in Tokyo; that they would deal only with

[1] Substantial extracts from the Generalissimo's memo were introduced by Hurley in his testimony before *Joint Committee on Military Situation in the Far East*, pages 2923-2924.

Atcheson, who had been senior officer in the Chungking Embassy under Hurley, had been withdrawn at Hurley's request on April 9th, 1944. He had then served temporarily as Special Assistant to the Head of the Office of Far Eastern Affairs. Early in September he had been assigned to Tokyo to act as political adviser to General MacArthur.

Service had been transferred out of China at Hurley's request after his last trip to Yenan in the spring. He was brought back to the United States with the thought that he would soon be sent to a new foreign post. He had been temporarily assigned to the personnel section of the Foreign Service and while in that job he had become involved in the *Amerasia* affair.

matters directly connected with the surrender and occupation of Japan; and that they would not go to China. Hurley had taken this episode as proof that the officers who he thought were destroying our Chinese policy still retained influence.

When Hurley talked with Under-Secretary Acheson on September 27th and Byrnes early in October, just after the Secretary's return from London, he had told them he wanted to resign. To both he had spoken as though he thought the time was suitable. The two sides in China were, in his view of the situation, coming together; and Stalin had agreed to support Chiang Kai-shek. These promising trends could be brought to fruition, he had said, but the job would be a tremendous one needing a younger and fresher man. Byrnes had persuaded him to take needed rest and reconsider. Hurley had consented. While he was resting and reflecting during October, the incoming reports from China had given conflicting versions of the chances for a negotiated settlement of the raging quarrel between the government and the Communists. The Joint Statement of October 11th remained as the basis of belief for those who wanted to stay on the cheerful plane. But since, as these pages have told, the prospect in the provinces had darkened and the avowals made in that statement were turning out to be paper-thin, Walter Robertson had been depressed enough by what was taking place to let the State Department and Hurley know on November 4th that he thought the situation "almost hopeless."[2] He had Hurley's trust and respect. It may be surmised—but it is only surmise—that this comment and similar incoming reports of deep dissension between the two sides gave Hurley to think.

Hurley had kept in touch with Secretary Byrnes and the President during November. At least twice again he had tried to resign and was dissuaded. Each time he had dwelt on his troubles with the Foreign

[2] The Communist representative in Chungking, Wang Ping Nan, had called upon Robertson and told him that the "news is very bad," repeated all the familiar charges of Kuomintang aggression, and while he said that current talks might be continued *pro forma*, he appeared to have no hope that anything would be accomplished. Telegram, American Embassy, Chungking, to State Department, October 31, 1945. A few days later K. C. Wu, the Minister of Information in the Chinese government, told Robertson that the Communists obviously did not want to come to agreement with the government, and thought that the Russians were behind the whole situation. They were demanding, he had said, that the government withdraw all its troops from "advance occupied areas and the railways." The Communist broadcasts from Yenan, Robertson also reported, were taking the line that the United States was responsible first of all for the civil war, and to blame for it, and were focusing their attacks on Wedemeyer, alleging that his press statement differed from Truman's. Telegram, American Embassy, Chungking. November 10, 1945. A paraphrase of this message was sent to Hurley on the 18th. These telegrams are referred to in *United States Relations with China*, pages 109-111.

Service officials and each time he had been told that these were matters of the past and to forget them. Both the President and the Secretary of State had promised that they would remove any official who interfered with his policy and administration. Hurley had professed to be reassured, but he was not.

On the morning of November 26th he brought in an envelope to Byrnes which contained a letter of resignation. Again Byrnes refused it, saying he would not pass it on to the President.[3] The Secretary asked him to read some recent reports from China and give him an opinion of them. He outlined for Hurley the policies he had in mind for China. These presumably were still only in provisional and loose form; Byrnes was waiting to talk them over the next day with Patterson and Forrestal. That afternoon, after giving the requested opinion, Hurley said he would return to China almost at once—right after he delivered a promised speech at the National Press Club on the 28th, which was two days off. The Ambassador asked the Secretary to write down the statement of American policy which he had outlined. Byrnes said there "is no change; there has been no change in policy, but if you wish it, I will."

On the next morning, the 27th, the three Secretaries pieced together the main elements of an emergency program. This, while continuing to sustain Chiang Kai-shek's position, looked toward an even more strenuous attempt than ever to bring about a settlement with the Communists. Since American policy was centered on the purpose of preventing civil war in China or a divided China, the task that lay ahead of Hurley was vital. And since each day seemed to be bringing civil war nearer, there was no time to be lost. Hurley had said he would be leaving for China the next day. Byrnes, at the end of their discussion, told his colleagues that if the program on which they seemed to be in accord could be put in shape quickly, Hurley could take it with him to Chungking. But Hurley was on his way back to New Mexico.

Hurley has since referred to incidents which led him to his abrupt decision. Stories that had appeared in the *Daily Worker* and the *Chicago Sun* seemed to him to contain information that could be obtained no-

---

[3] This interpretative account of the Hurley resignation and the reasons therefore is based on varied sources, among which the main ones are Hurley's letter of resignation of November 26th, printed in *United States Relations with China*, pages 581-584; testimony of Secretary Byrnes and Ambassador Hurley before the Senate Foreign Relations Committee on December 5, 6, 7, and 10, 1945; Hurley's testimony before *Joint Committee on Military Situation in the Far East*; the *Hurley Papers*; and several private memos.

where else except from the State Department.[4] Then a Congressman, DeLacy, made a speech in the House of Representatives on the afternoon of the 26th, right after Hurley's last talk with Byrnes. This speech criticized both Hurley and the Generalissimo. The informed reader could detect that the author had special and unpublished information. Hurley, reading the speech in the evening paper, took it as another proof that his secret reports to the State Department were being passed on to the Communists.[5] The purpose was, he thought, to diminish his influence in China and to disturb his relations with Chiang Kai-shek by making him appear as a critic of the government. A report he had heard rang angrily in his memory; this attributed to Byrnes the remark ". . . that the war was over and they were going to give my [Hurley's] job to a deserving Democrat."

But the above may be regarded only as incidents and not the causes of his resignation. Certain it was that he felt insecure about his mission; mistrustful of Foreign Service officers who, he thought, were bent on defeating his effort; and disturbed by the belief that the American government in its eagerness for unity was indifferent to the fate of the Kuomintang regime. In addition to such reasons for being troubled over the assignment—though no statement of Hurley's refers to it—there may have been a perception that the job of bringing about a unified, free, and democratic China was no further along than when he left China. The Political Consultative Conference which the Generalissimo had convoked for November 20th had not met as scheduled; the Communists had failed to name their delegates.[6] Chou En-lai had forthwith gone back to Yenan. Hurley's conviction that after the Soviet government had signed an agreement with the Chinese government, the Chinese Communists would quickly come to terms, was being assailed by events.

Hurley's letter of resignation so twirls about that it is hard to locate its center.[7] It did not admit failure; it diffused blame. It did not attempt

[4] Hurley testimony, *Joint Committee on Military Situation in the Far East*, pages 2936-2937. He also told the Committee that he realized later that the published information which aroused him was taken or stolen from the State Department via the *Amerasia* route, and not passed out by those he suspected.

[5] The speech by Congressman DeLacy, *The Congressional Record*, House of Representatives, November 26th, pages 10993-10995, was a vigorous attack on Hurley, leading to the accusation, "Step by step Ambassador Hurley's reversals of the Roosevelt-Gauss policy in China have made the present civil war unavoidable. He and General Wedemeyer have now committed us to armed intervention."

[6] *United States Relations with China*, page 111.

[7] *Ibid.*, pages 581-584.

to tell of the existing situation in China and trace its conclusions to formative facts. The dissatisfied Ambassador seems in one twist to attribute American difficulties in China to the activities of the professional diplomats in the Embassy and State Department who opposed our policy as he understood it. In another twist he seems to conclude that this policy was confused and divided, simultaneously supporting imperialism and Communism. Some of his comments seem to be a plea for isolation or neutrality, as for example the statement that "The weakness of American policy has backed us into two world wars . . . there is a third world war in the making. In diplomacy we are permitting ourselves to be sucked into a power bloc on the side of colonial imperialism against Communist imperialism. I am opposed to both."

Hurley seems to have thought, if the message which he had sent Byrnes a while back remained a valid guide, that Chiang Kai-shek had even more pronounced views of the same kind about the attitude of the various other great powers to China. He had reported that Chiang Kai-shek had told him that the British, French, and Dutch governments were trying to create a situation, especially in Peking and Shanghai, that would give them an excuse for landing imperialist forces in China; and that the Generalissimo was, moreover, of the opinion that the "imperialists" were actually cooperating with the Chinese Communists, while the American and Soviet governments were cooperating with the National Government of China.[8] This diagnosis of the situation is just as perplexing now as when it was given. Hurley did not seem to think—or if he did, he did not acknowledge it—that Soviet conduct in Manchuria and the response of the Chinese Communists were different than he had hoped; and he did still seem to think that the Chinese Communists were not a true and tried segment of the international Communist movement.[9] He seemed, in contrast, to think that the British in China were

[8] Telegram, Hurley to State Department, September 1, 1945.
[9] Thus in his testimony before the Senate Foreign Relations Committee on December 6th, ten days after his resignation, he said ". . . Please distinguish between them [the Chinese Communists] and the Union of Soviet Socialist Republics, because they are different, and all of this time Marshal Stalin and Commissar Molotov had been telling me, and throughout the entire period of the vicissitudes through which we passed so far as I know they have kept their word to me, that, as I stated yesterday, Russia—and this is my own analysis; it is not a quotation—does not recognize the Chinese armed Communist Party as Communists at all. Russia is not supporting the Chinese Communist Party. Russia does not desire civil war in China. Russia does not desire the division of China and the setting up of two governments. Russia desires closer and more harmonious relations with China.

"Since these conversations with Mr. Molotov and Generalissimo Stalin, Russia has concluded with China the Sino-Soviet Pact and each has exchanged letters solemnizing every one of these agreements. I have read that the Soviet has transgressed certain matters

encouraging the Communists and working solely for their own ends. General Sir Carton de Wiart, Churchill's special representative to Chiang Kai-shek, by his own account felt critical of Hurley for deferring to the Communists. De Wiart was refusing their invitations to visit Yenan, and telling the Generalissimo that he thought that ". . . there was only one answer to the Communists and that was defeat. To me the right time for negotiations is after a victory when, backed by force, words seem to attain a meaning not so well understood before."[10] The two men whom the American and British governments had attached to Chiang Kai-shek were not helping each other's work—though both were against the Communists and had favor in Chiang Kai-shek's eyes for that reason.

In short, it is hard to trace any coherent dividing line between what Hurley thought should be done about China and what the government was planning to do. Luckily there is no imperative need to try to penetrate further the tempest of smoke in which his letter of resignation left the question.

Reflection on Hurley's experience in China suggests the conclusion that, though never so stated, Hurley's resentment reached higher and farther than the professional officers whom he named. His accusations were directed against individual career officials on the score of their individual activity. It is easy to think that in restating them when he resigned, he was also expressing his mistrust or disagreement with the more powerful officials who listened to them—the President, Byrnes, Acheson.[11]

Secretary Byrnes at once asked the Legal Adviser of the State Department to investigate—in the light of national security—whether any of the Foreign Service officers named by Hurley had ever, as accused (a) communicated to the Chinese Communists information regarding Allied military plans for landings or operations in China, (b) told the Chinese Communists that Hurley's efforts to prevent the collapse of the National Government did not really represent the policy of the American govern-

---

that involve the territorial integrity and the independent sovereignty of China, but frankly I have no evidence that would convince me that that is true. I believe that the United States and Russia are still together on policy in China."

[10] *Happy Odyssey*, General Sir Adrian Carton de Wiart, 1950, page 271.

[11] Hurley said as much in his testimony before the *Joint Committee on the Military Situation in the Far East*, pages 2936-2937, where he remarked that he had come to think that he was wrong in including President Truman in the conspiracy against him, and owed him an apology.

ment, (c) advised the Communists to decline military unification unless they were given control, (d) were otherwise disloyal to the government of the United States. The Legal Adviser took no testimony and did not go beyond the easily available records. He found no evidence to support Hurley's charges.[12] He was not asked to and he did not try to explore the realm of difference of judgment in regard to policy between Hurley and these officers. Nor did he venture any judgment as to whether—outside of these precise and formal accusations—some of the career officials had not freely made known their opposition to Hurley and worked against him.

Hurley's resignation did not affect the determination of American policy toward China. But it sped up its completion. Perhaps it also caused the government to make fuller public explanation of that policy than it otherwise would have made. It upset the Secretary of State and angered the President. There was some anxiety over its possible effect on American opinion, and greater anxiety over its possible effect on the situation in China. The President hurried to prevent both.

General George C. Marshall had only a few months before retired as Chief of Staff with the utmost honor. The President asked him to assume the hard and ungrateful job of trying to resolve the situation in China, and thus preserve the results for which we had fought so hard and long in the Pacific. Marshall accepted at once. The wish to have him leave as soon as possible for China brought about quick definition of the decisions that had been in the making.

[12] Byrnes's instruction for this investigation was issued on December 7th, 1945, immediately after Hurley's statement of his detailed charges to the Senate Committee on Foreign Relations. The report of the Legal Adviser was made on March 1, 1946.

CHAPTER 37

Marshall Is Instructed

GENERAL MARSHALL was able to give only broken thought to the guiding directive for his assignment in China. For just then he was testifying before a Committee of Congress about another historic event in which he had been a leading figure—the attack on Pearl Harbor. But a group in and about the War Department went into the subject with and for him.[1]

On November 28th or 29th Marshall talked over his mission with Byrnes. The Secretary of State gave him a short written memo of the course which the State Department had in mind. This followed along the line which Byrnes and Acheson had explained at the end of the meeting with the Secretaries of War and Navy two or three days previously just before Hurley resigned. The attitudes and proposals within the two pages of this memo correspond in large degree to the policy which was followed.[2]

By November 30th the Joint Chiefs of Staff, deeming enough progress toward decision had been made, went on to inform the Far Eastern commanders of the plans in mind to transport more Chinese troops to North China and Manchuria—with the caution that the orders had not yet been approved.[3] The Commanders were asked for their comments. On receipt of this inquiry, General Wedemeyer and Admiral Raymond T. Spruance, Commander-in-Chief of the Naval Forces in the Pacific, flew to Tokyo to confer with General MacArthur.

But Marshall and the group working for him were not satisfied with

[1] These included Generals Hull, Handy, and Craig. Marshall was also aided by a member of *Time-Life* staff, James Shepley, who had done similar work for him when he was Chief of Staff.

[2] John Carter Vincent subsequently testified that he drafted this brief memo in haste, and that he drew largely upon a longer one that he had prepared some weeks before. By his account this earlier memo had specified the four alternative courses open to the American government; the Secretaries of State and War and the President had chosen between the alternatives that course of action which he wrote up in the later brief memo. *Hearings: Institute of Pacific Relations*, pages 1711-1712.

Vincent was under the impression that he had written this first longer memo in late October or early November. If his memory of the date is correct, the memo in question has not come to hand in the State Department files. But, as already noted, the records contain a substantial memo by Vincent dated November 19th, entitled "Our Military Position in China." This summarized four principal courses of action which the American government might take, the conceived advantages and disadvantages of each, and the steps which would be needed to give effect to each.

[3] This message is printed in *Joint Committee on Military Situation in the Far East*, pages 2354-2355.

the short statement of policy which Byrnes had given him. Marshall thought it not sufficiently plain to be understood by the public, easily misinterpreted, and not definite enough to form a sure base for a directive to Wedemeyer. Therefore the Marshall group rewrote it. Marshall, on November 30th, sent the revised version to Admiral Leahy, from whom it found its way to the State Department. Further talk ensued, resulting in a second revised set of papers which the State Department passed back to Marshall. Except for a few minor changes made in subsequent conference, these became the final set of instructions.

The two most difficult points of difference which had to be adjusted in this week of talk would seem to have been:

1. Should we transport Chinese government troops into North China at once—that is, without waiting to see whether a military truce and political accord were effected? Or, as proposed by the State Department, should we defer decision while Marshall tried to arrange such a truce and accord, and not engage in the operation if the action would prejudice these objectives?[4] This State Department formula, unless clarified, would have left the whole decision in foggy suspense. The Generalissimo would have been without any definite basis for calculating the troops available to him. In the final outcome the decision as to whether or not, and when, to move troops into North China was in effect left to Marshall.[5]

2. The gnarl in his directives which was bothering Wedemeyer so much: the injunction that while the American forces in China were carrying out assigned tasks they must not support the Chinese government in civil war or interfere in Chinese politics. Marshall wanted it clearly understood that the American representatives in China could not test every action they took by whether or not it might have some indirect influence on the Chinese internal situation. They ought not, he argued, be put in a position where they were expected to do so. The State Depart-

---

[4] On December 5th Vincent sent Acheson a memo in which he observed that it was disconcerting that in the telegram which the Joint Chiefs had sent Wedemeyer (and the other Pacific commanders) on November 30th it had given too little heed to the arrangements for a cessation of hostilities and convocation of a national conference. He informed Acheson that he had told the War Department that the State Department considered it illogical to arrange for a cessation of hostilities and at the same time assist the National Government in introducing more troops into North China, and that the State Department was therefore inserting in the Marshall redraft of the Policy Statement a phrase to the effect that "National Government troops will not be transported by the United States into areas, such as North China, when their introduction would prejudice the objectives of the military truce and the political negotiations." This was written into the redraft of Marshall's draft of the directive, which on December 8th the State Department submitted to Marshall.

[5] See final paragraphs of memo from Byrnes to the War Department, December 9, 1945, quoted in part on pages 420-421.

ment spokesmen wanted to insure that such incidental effect would be minimized. The final instruction provided that United States support of the Chinese government should not extend to military intervention to influence the course of any Chinese internal strife; and that incidental effects of our assistance to the Chinese government should be avoided as far as possible.[6] But it was left up to Marshall to decide how far they could be avoided, as the Americans carried out movements of Chinese forces and the Marines held their positions.

But in telling of the evolution of the discussion on these two points I have leaped ahead of the rest of this account of the making of Marshall's directive. While—between November 28th and December 9th—Byrnes and Marshall (the State Department and the group working for Marshall) were seeking to fix upon their policy firmly, the incoming news from China encouraged the belief that the general approach in mind would be effective.

In the political realm, the Communists, reversing their refusal, agreed on December 1st to send five of their principal leaders to Chungking to participate in the discussions of the Political Consultative Conference which Chiang Kai-shek had summoned to meet on December 10th. Among these were to be Chou En-lai and his wife. In telling the Embassy of this, the Chief Communist agent in Chungking, Wang Pin Nan, remarked that their forces were not opposed to the movement of government troops into Manchuria; and made much of their wish for cordial relations with the United States.[7] This quickened hope that it would be possible to arrange a truce, to be followed by a general accord on political and military unification.

In the military realm the news was also better. Chinese government troops advanced by rail north from Shanhaikwan to Chinchow, and captured the port of Hulutao against slight resistance. By December 7th they were reported to be within twenty miles of Mukden, and expected to enter the city peacefully very soon.[8] The Communists seemed to be avoiding battle. The reason is not easy to identify. Perhaps the Soviet commanders were restraining the Chinese Communists. Perhaps the announcement of Marshall's appointment caused them to pause. Perhaps some word reached them, seeping out of Chinese sources (who were being

[6] The paragraph in the Statement of Policy given to Marshall which dealt with this point is omitted from the public Statement of United States Policy toward China given out by President Truman on December 15th and printed in *ibid.*, pages 607-609.

[7] Telegram, American Embassy, Chungking, to State Department, December 3, 1945.

[8] United Press Dispatch from Chungking, December 7, 1945.

kept informed by Wedemeyer), that the American government was in the course of deciding whether or not greatly to increase its support of the Chinese government. Perhaps Wedemeyer's recent appraisal of the strength of the Communist forces in or near Manchuria at this time was wrong. According to a report from the Commander of the 7th Fleet, which the Navy passed on to the State Department, the Communists found in Manchuria were disorganized and poorly indoctrinated.[9]

Whatever the explanation, Chiang Kai-shek had the impression that the Communists wanted to play for time. His own plans and hopes, as interpreted by both Wedemeyer and the Embassy, seemed to be swinging along with two possibilities. The first was that the American government would conclude after all that it was essential to give him the help he had asked to place and keep large forces in Manchuria. The second was that the Soviet government would also aid him in accord with those promises which the Generalissimo thought were in the agreements signed in August; he was hoping that the American and British would induce the Soviet government to do so at the next meeting of the Foreign Ministers in Moscow. In the meantime—as he later told Marshall—he was careful not to take any step which might imperil the chances of an amicable adjustment with the Soviets and a settlement by peaceful means with the Chinese Communists.

But his caution was weaker than his eagerness to take control of Manchuria. Briefly, he seems to have intended to postpone his attempt to do so until law and order were established in North China—as he had told the President on November 23rd. But he changed his mind. Perhaps this was because his advancing columns were not meeting serious opposition. Perhaps it was because the Soviet Ambassador in Chungking had informed him that the Soviet government was prepared to guarantee a safe landing for government troops at the airfields of Changchun and Mukden.[10] He consulted Wedemeyer in regard to moving a limited number of government troops to these cities. Wedemeyer's answer was reserved; he explained that he was not yet in a position to give any firm promise in regard to American policy. But he said that he had the sense that the American government would increase its help, particularly in regard to moving Chinese forces and equipment to the North. In which case, he added, his judgment would be that these additional forces should be used first of all south of the Great Wall, to make sure of his control

[9] Situation Report, Hulutao and Mukden. Commander of the 7th Fleet, CINCPAC, December 4, 1945.
[10] Memo, talk Chinese Ambassador Wei Tao-ming, Acheson, and Vincent, December 1, 1945.

in that region and to stabilize the political, economic, and military situation there before deploying resources in Manchuria. But, he continued, if the Soviet Union cooperated as promised, it might be possible to move another army into Manchuria, using the port of Hulutao.

In sum, during the days when the directive for Marshall was being formulated, the policy of the Chinese government was one of asking and of waiting. Wedemeyer was advising Chiang Kai-shek to be careful; to make sure of his position in most of China before risking his forces in an immediate effort to secure control of the whole, including Manchuria. But the conferees at Washington were impressed by the need of getting government troops quickly into Manchuria to stabilize the area.

The answer of the Far Eastern Commanders (MacArthur, Wedemeyer, Spruance) to the inquiry that had been sent November 30th by the Joint Chiefs arrived in Washington on December 7th.[11] This set out a plan and program for (a) transporting six more Chinese armies, and the necessary supplies for these armies, to North China and Manchuria, (b) repatriating five hundred thousand Japanese a month from the ports of China. In sending it on, the authors considered that they were advising on the best available ways and means of executing a policy, not making one. However, a paragraph at the end entered into the realm of policy making: "It is suggested that the U.S. assistance to China, as outlined above, be made available as a basis of negotiation by the American Ambassador to bring together and effect a compromise between the major opposing groups in order to promote a unified, democratic China." This, by ordinary reading, would seem to be in accord with the tactics which Washington by then had just about decided to pursue.[12]

The Joint Chiefs of Staff thought that the plan submitted by the Far Eastern Commanders was satisfactory as a way of carrying into effect the purposes projected; and the President approved it at once.

[11] It is published in *Joint Committee on Military Situation in the Far East*, pages 2247-2248.

[12] This suggestion can, however, be interpreted in at least two ways: as meaning that since our power to give or to refuse help could affect the relative strength of the government and the Communists, we should employ it in whatever ways would cause the two sides to prefer a compromise to its prospects if the struggle continued; or, alternatively, as meaning only that we should use the further help we intended to give Chiang Kai-shek as a potential to strengthen him in his negotiations with the Communists.

It appears to have been concurred in rather hastily by the three Pacific commanders. It may well be that they did not all have the same understanding of it. Each of the three made separate later denials of any intention to favor an attempt to force a "coalition." They were seeking some other unspecified kind of unifying arrangement. MacArthur explained his understanding to *Joint Committee on Military Situation in the Far East*, page 2249. Wedemeyer gave his, *ibid.*, pages 2462-2463. Spruance issued a statement published in the *New York Times*, June 12, 1951.

Thereupon, on Sunday morning, December 9th, Byrnes, Marshall, with their advisers (Acheson, Vincent, and General Hull), met to talk through the policies which Marshall was to follow in China. Some of Marshall's advisers, particularly General Hull, may still have had reservations in regard to the last draft in hand (the revised one which Byrnes had sent to Marshall the afternoon before), thinking it contained opposites which would continue to cause American policy in China to be vague and indecisive.[13] But study of notes made of this discussion on the morning of the 9th, and of the later textual history of the instructions, leaves the impression that by this time there was a real meeting of minds and intentions between the top makers of our policy. After the basic papers had been read aloud, Byrnes stressed his view that it was essential to the United States to have a strong unified China; that otherwise the Russians could be expected to take control of Manchuria and maintain a dominant influence in North China. He explained that the central idea of the program was to put enough weapons in Marshall's hand to induce the government and Communists to get together. Marshall was still perplexed as to how he was expected to use these weapons. He asked what he should do if the Communists agreed to concessions which appeared acceptable while the government refused to give ground. Byrnes told him to tell the government that we were going to withhold the aid we were ready to give it, and that we would have to deal directly with the Communists insofar as the evacuation of Japanese from North China was concerned. The Secretary, it will be observed, changed his answer on this point two days later. And what, Marshall went on to ask, if the Communists refused to make concessions? Byrnes told him then to give full support to the Chinese government and move its armies into North China as requested.[14]

The meeting ended with the sense that a decision had been reached and that the job of formulating policy was all but completed. There remained only the task of casting this in the form of a directive from the President to Marshall, and the editing. Byrnes and Marshall then on the afternoon of the 11th went over once again with the President and Leahy at the White House all the elements of the policy which Marshall was to pursue. Marshall reviewed his understanding of the guidance given him about the course to be followed in the realm left to his discretion; particularly as to whether and when to move more government troops to North China. He was—he summed up—to try to

[13] Memo, General Hull to Marshall, December 8, 1945.
[14] Memo, General Hull, December 10, 1945, written for the record.

induce both sides to make reasonable concessions toward a truce and the development of a broad representative Chinese government. If the Communists refused to do so, he was authorized to transport government troops into the region. But if the Generalissimo refused to do so—and the difference was explicitly stated—he was not to be abandoned. Rather than accept the tragic consequences of a divided China and a probable Russian resumption of power in Manchuria, we would continue anyhow to back Chiang Kai-shek to the extent of assisting him to move troops into North China in order to complete the evacuation of the Japanese. Both the President and Byrnes now concurred.[15]

The two main papers, then ready, were approved by the President. The letter of instruction from the President to Marshall to which these were to be appended was still in the hands of the draftsmen in the State Department.[16] It was completed within the next few days. On the morning of the 14th Marshall and Acting Secretary of State Acheson went over to the White House for a final talk. The President asked Marshall if

[15] Notes by General Marshall on meeting with the President, Byrnes, and Leahy, 3:30 p.m., December 11th.

Extract from these notes, "Finally, General Marshall stated that if the Generalissimo, in his [Marshall's] opinion, failed to make reasonable concessions, and this resulted in the breakdown in the efforts to secure a political unification, and the United States abandoned continued support of the Generalissimo, there would follow the tragic consequences of a divided China and of a probable Russian reassumption of power in Manchuria, the combined effect of this resulting in the defeat or loss of the major purpose of our war in the Pacific. Under these circumstances, General Marshall inquired whether or not it was intended for him, in that unfortunate eventuality, to go ahead and assist the Generalissimo in the movement of troops into North China. This would mean that the Government would have to swallow its pride and much of its policy in doing so.

"The President and Mr. Byrnes concurred in this view of the matter; that is, that we would have to back the Generalissimo to the extent of assisting him to move his troops into North China in order that the evacuation of the Japanese might be completed."

[16] The formulation of policy had been, up to the December 9th meeting, expressed in two papers—a Statement of Policy and a Memo to be sent by Byrnes to the War Department. During the next several days the State Department composed a letter from the President to Marshall as Special Representative of the President in China, as a Directive to which these two papers were attached. Marshall was told to regard them as part of the letter. The public Statement issued by the President on December 15th was based on the Statement of Policy.

The President's letter, the memo from Byrnes to the War Department, and the Public Statement are published in *United States Relations with China*, pages 605-609. The Statement of Policy is not published—a footnote (page 605) explaining "not printed; it did not differ substantially from the final text." This notation is in a sense misleading, for the Press Release was not really a final text of the Statement of Policy. The divergence between the two is mainly in omissions from the unpublished Statement of Policy; and they can be explained by a wish not to reveal too openly to the Chinese factions what tactics Marshall was going to pursue.

For a full knowledge of the policy visualized, account should also be taken of the message sent on December 13th and the directive sent on December 14th, by the Joint Chiefs of Staff to General Wedemeyer, General MacArthur, and Admiral Spruance in regard to operations in China.

the letter and enclosures were satisfactory to him. Marshall said they were. He repeated his understanding that one phase of his directive was not in writing, to wit: that in the event that he was unable to secure a reasonable response from the Generalissimo it would still be necessary for the American government to continue to back the National Government of the Republic of China within the terms of the announced policy. The President again confirmed that this was correct, and so did Acheson. That afternoon the President sent this packet of instructions over to Marshall while he was in Acheson's office. On the next day the President issued his public statement of United States policy in China. The Marshall mission was launched.

The program which the American government adopted may be briefly summarized and analyzed.

Its main aims were two:

To develop a united and democratic China.

To assure that the Chinese government would be able to extend its sovereignty over Manchuria, as confirmed at the Cairo Conference and in the Yalta Agreement and the Sino-Soviet accord.

The main steps which Marshall was to seek to realize were:

To effect a truce, particularly in North China; and

Concurrently, to have the Chinese government call a national conference of representatives of the major political elements to bring about the unification.

The range of measures—immediate and potential—to be used in this essay in persuasion were:

1. The Marines were to be kept in North China, with the avowed purpose of completing the disarmament and evacuation of the Japanese.

2. We would assist the Chinese government at once in transporting troops and needed supplies to Manchurian ports; that is, without waiting to measure the response to the effort to bring about unity.

3. Arrangements were to be promptly perfected for transporting other Chinese forces into North China. But the Chinese government was not to be told of these arrangements and no more Chinese government troops were to be moved into North China pending Marshall's effort to arrange a truce and political conference. They were to be executed only when General Marshall determined either:

(a) "That the movement of Chinese troops to North China can be carried out consistently with his negotiations" or

(b) "That the negotiations between the Chinese groups have failed or show no prospect of success and that the circumstances are such as to make the movement necessary to effectuate the surrender terms and to secure the long-term interests of the United States in the maintenance of international peace."

Marshall, it was understood, would employ this discretionary power in such ways as would induce or compel concessions by the government, by the Communists, and by the other factions. And by unwritten agreement the Chinese government was not to be abandoned, i.e., left entirely without help, no matter how the effort to bring about a peaceful settlement fared.[17]

4. A promise of American loans, economic technical assistance, and military aid (the United States Military Advisory Group). But all Chinese leaders, including Chiang Kai-shek, were to be told frankly, ". . . that a China disunited and torn by civil strife could not be considered realistically as a proper place for American assistance along [these] lines. . . ."

There is cause to remark upon two features of this program, not before so clearly defined.

The plans as regards movement and supply of government troops differed from those which Wedemeyer had been recommending to Chiang Kai-shek. He had been advising that the prudent course in the instant situation within China was to use all available government resources to improve its control south of the Great Wall, and to improve conditions in that region. In contrast, the course sanctioned by the American government contemplated a quick advance into Manchuria, and, subject to Marshall's finding, into North China. Chiang Kai-shek had been pleading with the President to do both. His requests gained attention in part because of the risks of the course which Wedemeyer had felt compelled to advise—in recognition of the hard facts before him. That might have meant that Soviet forces would prolong their occupation of Manchuria; it would have left both Manchuria and North China open to Communist initiatives; it might have left the several hundreds of thousands of Japanese still in North China in a position where they would be forced to surrender to, and turn their arms over to, the Communists. Wedemeyer's advice, it should be remembered, was originally based on the expectation that the Marines would be withdrawn and the China Theater terminated. In December it was decided not only to

[17] Meanwhile the completion of the thirty-nine division program was deferred pending Marshall's recommendation as to the future needs of the government forces.

postpone these actions, but also to provide greater means of transport and supply for the government forces. This switch affected the estimate of military possibilities.

In regard to the attainment of unity, Washington still had only a formula. None of the main participants in decision seems to have had a firmly fixed idea as to the form of democratic government which might emerge in China. That was to be left to the Chinese themselves to work out. Marshall's instructions did not debar some kind of coalition, transient or prolonged. But their emphasis and accent were on the attainment of a constitutional, popularly controlled form of government of the type familiar to the West, within which the several parties, the Kuomintang, the Communists, and others would carry on their struggle by legal means. This meant, in effect, that the policy and project were based on the hope that the two sides could (not only could, but would if shown how) live together, abiding by the same rules of law and political behavior. Or to state the matter in another way, on the idea that the differences in the interests and purposes between the factions could be reduced to the dimensions manageable under a democratic form of government; that they would trust each other enough to allow democratic processes to work; and that each would be willing to let the others live if it was let live.[18]

It will not be forgotten how eager the American people were at this time to bring their soldiers, sailors, and airmen back home. The American military organization was dissolving fast under the clamor. Marshall had remarked on the meaning of this shortly before he knew he was going to be sent to China. "We are currently engaged in the demobilization of our war-time forces at the fastest possible rate. . . . It is certain, however, that the military establishment cannot hope to insure the safety of the United States very much longer at the present rate of demobilization unless some permanent peace-time program is established at an early date. For the moment, in a wide-spread emotional crisis of the American people, demobilization has become, in effect, disintegration, not only of the armed forces but apparently of all conception of world responsibility and what it demands of us."[19] In a meeting on October

[18] An interesting discussion of whether or not it was deemed essential, as one feature of this strategy, that the Kuomintang retain control and the Communists be subordinated, is to be found in the cross-examination of Vincent by the subcommittee, *Hearings: Institute of Pacific Relations*, pages 1722-1724.

[19] Extract from speech of General Marshall to the *New York Herald-Tribune* Forum, October 29, 1945.

16th Forrestal had tersely pointed out the conclusion which other countries, particularly the Soviet, were likely to draw, remarking that ". . .
our rapid demobilization . . . amounted to notification to the world that
we are through with the war and its problems." The other decision-
makers agreed.[20] But they could do little about it.

It was hard to find and keep even the small number of ships and men
needed to carry out the program with which Marshall was entrusted.
Shortly after V-J Day the War Department had told Congress that it
expected to reduce its forces in the Pacific within a year to eight hundred
and thirty thousand. By the end of 1945 its estimate of the authorized
strength in that area (as of July 1, 1946) had been reduced to less than
half that number. Of these, six thousand were designated for service
in China, and General Wedemeyer was expressing fear that in fact this
number would be reduced by discharges to barely three thousand men.
Even the future existence of the Marine divisions in China was in doubt.

In this ebb tide of our military effort it seemed unreal to consider any
course of action in China which might require the active employment
of substantial American forces for an indefinite period of time. There
were few then who would have spoken up for a prolongation of military
service in order to affect the outcome of the struggle in China, or even
to prevent the extension of Soviet control over Manchuria. We had
realized that it was essential to create a powerful military force to win
the war. But we had not learned that it was no less essential to maintain
an adequate military force in order to secure a satisfactory peace.

The United States was entering into another period, a brief one,
when it sought to achieve its purposes by incantation. Blithely we thought
that the world—even the Communist part of it—would be responsive
to our pleas and our dollars.

The President on the 15th issued his Statement on United States
Policy Toward China. The studious reader could gather from this a
roughly correct idea of our opinions and aims. But the careful array
of sentences did not tell everything about how we intended to try to
achieve them; of the pressures and rewards which we might exercise
upon both sides. It seemed best, no doubt, that each of the Chinese factions should be left in some degree of doubt as to how we would treat
it. It seemed essential also that Marshall should retain substantial freedom of decision in regard to what to offer to each and to demand of
each. It seemed wise to leave open all routes toward a truce and unifica-

[20] Memo, meeting Byrnes, Patterson, Forrestal, October 16, 1945.

tion. But the imprecision of this public statement was not altogether helpful to him. Soon after his arrival in China, Marshall discovered that "Each side found in the President's Statement of United States Policy Toward China justification for its attitude."

While Marshall was starting on his task Secretary Byrnes was trying to fit our China policy into the Allied pattern of peace-making. At a meeting of the Council of Foreign Ministers at Moscow he was seeking to ensure that the Soviet government would not frustrate Marshall's mission, particularly that it would not hinder the effectuation of Chinese government control of Manchuria. Byrnes's minimum purpose was to guard against the chances that the Soviet government, in violation of its agreements, would encourage the Chinese Communists not to compromise and enter a truce, and perhaps keep Soviet troops in Manchuria indefinitely. At best, he hoped that he might persuade the Soviet government to cooperate actively to bring about a truce, and facilitate the entry of the Chinese government administration in Manchuria. But he was not able to focus his efforts on those purposes as he wished. For the Soviet government diverted them.

On the agenda proposed by Byrnes, the transfer of the control of Manchuria to the Chinese National Government was listed. But the Soviet government refused to admit this item on the order paper. Molotov argued that it was not necessary since the Soviet government had a special agreement with China in regard to Manchuria and there was no difference between the two governments. He made much of the fact that Soviet troops had been evacuated from southern Manchuria and that they would have been out of northern Manchuria by this time if delay had not been arranged with the Chinese government. In its turn the Soviet government asked for an addition of an item to the agenda— the withdrawal of American troops from China. This the American government refused to place on the order paper. But need to discuss these subjects overflowed the formal ban. Byrnes candidly explained American policy, as written in Marshall's orders, not only at the regular sessions of the conference but also privately to Stalin and Molotov. His presentation turned into one of those stationary games of toss and catch and toss back again so usual with the Soviet rulers.

Byrnes justified the continued presence of the Marines in China by the need to complete the disarmament and evacuation of the Japanese. There were, he estimated, still some three hundred and twenty-five thousand armed Japanese in North China. The Chinese government did not yet have the necessary troops in position to complete this task; it needed more time to bring them up. Further, it faced the fact that there was in that region a great force of "revolutionaries," a force that he believed numbered about four hundred thousand. The Secretary commented on his use of the term "revolutionaries" by reference to Stalin's statement to President Truman in Potsdam that they were not Communists. The American plan, he explained, was to try its utmost to bring about a truce. If it succeeded, then the Chinese government forces could peacefully proceed to complete disarmament in North China; and the Marines would be able to go inland to hurry the job along without risk of getting involved in fighting between the Chinese factions. This was the way in which he was trying to work the situation out. As soon as that task was done—which he sincerely hoped would be soon—the Marines would be returned to the United States. If, he went on—presumably in order to make clear that Communist resistance would not by itself be enough to cause the American government to quit the scene —our efforts to obtain a truce failed, then we might be compelled to fly Chinese troops into North China much against our will. Or if it turned out that this could not be done, the United States might have to take on the task of completing the disarmament of the Japanese with its own forces.

The truce, Byrnes further explained, would be the prelude to our further effort to bring civil strife to a permanent end. As stated in the memo circulated by the American delegation at the first meeting (December 16th) of the conference, "We are very anxious that the differences which exist between the National Government and the dissident political factions be settled by methods of peaceful negotiation having as its objectives the broadening of the base of the present National Government of China to provide fair and effective representation to the principal political elements in China."

In sum, the Secretary of State tried to convince Stalin and Molotov that our program was truly intended to make it possible for us to get out of China without either deserting the friendly Chinese government or failing in our international duties; and that it was in pursuance of the policy which had been agreed on among the American, Soviet, and British governments not to interfere in the internal affairs of China. He reminded them that the Soviet government was obligated by treaty to cooperate with the Chinese government and to abstain from helping its opponents.

Molotov met Byrnes's presentation with cold skepticism. He denied that the Soviet Union was aiding the Chinese Communists. He said that he thought that the Chinese government was making the most of the difficulties of disarming the Japanese still in China and of Communist opposition in order to get others to do its work for it. With care to avoid language that would allow the accusation that the Soviet Union was not keeping its treaty promises, he carried his imputation on. The Chinese government, he implied, was not even eager to disarm and evacuate the Japanese, since it found them useful in battling its domestic opponents. For the same reason, he hinted, it wanted to retain the Americans in China. In short, Molotov argued that American forces were not needed to complete the disarmament of the Japanese if the Chinese government really set itself to do the job. And he insinuated that the real reason why they were kept in China was to protect the Chinese government, and hence that their presence was an interference in Chinese internal affairs.[21]

Molotov proposed that the American and Soviet governments should fix a date for the simultaneous withdrawal of American and Soviet troops—not later than January 15, 1946, just a few weeks off. Byrnes said he could not agree. For the American government, he explained once again, could not know when the disarmament of the Japanese would be complete and could not promise to withdraw its forces before then. Furthermore, he added, the American government could not do anything that would put the Chinese government in a worse position. Molotov so stubbornly persisted with his probe of American purposes that the soft-spoken Secretary of State remarked that he thought that the Foreign Minister was asking his questions merely because he liked to hear the sound of his, Byrnes's, voice. The southern drawl, perhaps.

This talk was in the forenoon of December 23rd. Late in the afternoon Byrnes went to see what Stalin had to say. While Molotov had been coldly resistant, the Marshal made himself appear almost benign. The Soviet government, he remarked, did not object to the United States leaving its troops in China but would merely like to be told about it. He remained, he continued, wholly in accord with the policy he had

---

[21] These judgments were advanced in a memo which the Soviet delegation presented on December 21st, title: Concerning American Armed Forces in China. They were more openly and bluntly expressed in the Soviet press. For example, in a special article in the December 19th issue of *Pravda*, the author, N. Sokolovski, stated that the presence of American forces in China "aroused alarm among democratic public opinion not only of China and the United States but of the entire world." He argued that their presence encouraged the "irreconcilable circles of Chinese reaction." He concluded that in any case there was more basis for having Soviet troops in Manchuria than American troops in North China.

agreed on with the American government that Chiang Kai-shek was to be supported as head of the Chinese government. But still the soft robe of his talk did not convey warm reassurance. He cast out the thought that Chiang Kai-shek would lose his influence if the Chinese people got the impression that he was depending on foreign troops. He also hinted that Chiang Kai-shek was intentionally exaggerating the size of the Communist forces which stood in his way. Fifty thousand government troops, he thought, ought to be enough to disarm the Japanese; had not two Japanese army corps surrendered to twenty-five Soviet aviators at Mukden? He asked how many Chinese Communists there were in the Tientsin area. Byrnes answered that Mao Tze Tung claimed to have six hundred thousand and undertook to picture the situation by arranging match sticks on the table. It is to be wondered whether the information received was new to the Soviet General Staff and Intelligence Service. Stalin laughed heartily and remarked that all Chinese were boasters. The talk ended with comments by Stalin that could almost be construed as leniency toward the American program. He said that he thought that General Marshall would settle the situation in China if any man could; further, that he would be strongly predisposed to agree with any recommendations regarding the Chinese situation which Marshall approved.[22]

Secretary Byrnes found the Soviet delegation better disposed after this talk with Stalin. They did not any longer insist that the American government promise to withdraw the Marines on any set date. Nor did they threaten to keep Soviet troops in Manchuria until we withdrew. By this time the Chinese and Soviet governments had agreed to a second prolongation of Soviet occupation of another month to February 3, 1946. All delegations recorded in the Final Protocol their agreement on ". . . the need for a unified and democratic China under the National Government, for broad participation by democratic elements in all branches of the National Government, and for a cessation of civil strife."

Byrnes left Moscow with the impression that Stalin intended to live up to his treaty with China, and would not intentionally do anything to destroy our efforts for a unified China. He so informed Marshall.[23] He had in fact managed to prevent open objections or measures against Marshall's mission without giving way on other disputed Far Eastern

---

[22] Telegram, December 29, 1945, Acheson to Marshall. Stalin had not always spoken so well of Marshall. He had apparently forgotten his complaint to Roosevelt about the intelligence which Marshall had given him regarding anticipated movements of the German armies on the eastern fronts. See Chapter 26.

[23] Telegram, Byrnes to Marshall, January 4, 1946.

issues—among them the direction of the control of Japan. But events proved that he had achieved nothing positive to make easier the task which Marshall faced.

As Marshall began his effort to arrange a quick truce, the reports that reached Washington did nothing to allay the fear that the Soviet Union was determined to make and keep an important place in Manchuria for itself, no matter how well Marshall got along. The Soviets continued to refuse to open the port of Dairen. They delayed evacuation of the three main towns of Mukden, Changchun, and Harbin, into which the Chinese government thought itself in a position to move enough troops to assure order.[24] They demanded that the Chinese government concede to them a controlling interest in the industrial properties in Manchuria formerly owned by the Japanese.[25] When the Chinese government refused they began to remove all the machinery and equipment into Siberia. As before, they continued to allow the Chinese Communists to move about Manchuria freely and establish themselves wherever they could. And all the while they remained undisturbed on their platform of maneuver—noninterference in Chinese internal affairs.

This is as far as my study of the China Tangle goes. It leaves Chiang Kai-shek striving to deal with a disintegrating situation within China, while seeking a way to gain control of Manchuria; and for all his many tasks needing American Marines, planes, ships, and supplies. It leaves the Communists standing in his way, gathering vigor and popular support, and getting arms from surrendering Japanese and puppet troops; and the Soviet forces so arranging their evacuation of Manchuria as to favor the Chinese Communists. The value of the agreement reached at Yalta and those signed between the Chinese and Soviet governments are in question. The chance of bringing about internal unity in China by peaceful, political means is poor; and the prospect that China could qualify as the great stabilizing power of the Pacific is misted with doubt. A somewhat dismayed American government is starting on a last determined attempt to bring about a truce in China, and then unity—but uncertain as to how firmly to support Chiang Kai-shek, and unwilling to risk the involvement of our fast-waning forces in the threatening civil war.

[24] Telegram, American Embassy, Chungking, February 26 (3:00 p.m.), 1946.

[25] Telegram, American Embassy, Chungking, February 26 (1:00 p.m.), 1946, printed in part in *United States Relations with China*, pages 597-598; and telegram, January 30, 1946, from Harriman (temporarily in Chungking) telling of talk with Chiang Kai-shek.

This unsettled scene hardly seems a satisfactory ending for a narrative of dramatic and portentous change. But for now it must be left there—to be read as a critical segment of the continuous and brisk flow that history is, revealing the meaning of previous events and forecasting later ones. The years since have forced us to realize how grave and hard was the mission on which Marshall set off; how bleak the outcome, how ominous the sequence.

It is essential that we should seek to understand the causes and reasons for the failure of our effort. It is natural that we should dispute among ourselves as we seek to locate the errors and place the blame. But we must not allow this examination of the past to distort the nature and meaning of what we tried to do.

In accord with the conceptions that then governed our idea of our interest and of the way in which relations between countries ought to be conducted, we made great exertions in behalf of China. Our friendship was firm, rejecting every chance to benefit by compromise with those who wanted to reduce or rule China. The call for help was made upon us while we were engaged in great battles elsewhere for freedom and justice in the Western world. These rival necessities caused us to limit the means and measures which we devoted to the struggle in China. In retrospect, we may have done less in and for China while the war for Europe was being fought out than we might safely and wisely have done. We thought we were only deferring the greater aid until that part of the worldwide struggle against tyranny was won. And then the unexpected happened: the war in the Pacific ended abruptly before our effort in behalf of China reached its planned fullness.

Well-wishing, that effort was bent to four connected ends: to uphold the Chinese people in the war against the common enemy; to restore China as a whole and independent country; to secure for China a place of great authority among the nations; and to bring to an end the grave social struggle among the Chinese people. The China we strove to create—a free, strong, democratic and friendly nation—would be, we conceived, a needed partner in assuring peace and security for all in the Far East. Such were our purposes and program.

Events have shown that there were flaws in them, as well as errors of decision in our attempt to make them effective. Then they were finally frustrated by the divisions within the Chinese people, by the revolutionary assault of Communism. In that civil war, American diplomacy and military planning got entangled, stumbled; and we failed in our attempt to shape the vast country of China into the image of our desires.

That being so, we still need not make excuses either to ourselves, the Chinese people, or the rest of the world for having pursued these purposes. Nor should we this soon conclude that a better appreciation of what we sought to do with and for China will not emerge out of the debris of hatred and regret which have silted over it.

Index